MW01027191

REPUBLICAN
CRACKHEAD

An addict's life in the FBI and DC's Hoods, while infiltrating HATERS

TODD A. BLODGETT

© Todd A. Blodgett, 2020

Print ISBN: 978-1-54398-602-0

eBook ISBN: 978-1-54398-603-7

All rights reserved. This book or any portion thereof may not be reproduced or used in any manner whatsoever without the express written permission of the publisher except for the use of brief quotations in a book review.

Dedicated to my parents

FORWARD

Thirty miles north of Manhattan, at a Hanukkah ceremony in December of 2019, a man whose face was covered barged into a rabbi's home as the celebration was ending. Unsheathing a sword nearly the length of a broomstick, he slashed his way through the house. As dozens of innocent worshippers – from small children to senior citizens – tried to flee, via a back door, five were stabbed. Weeks earlier, in a targeted attack on a kosher grocery store in New Jersey, four victims, one of them a Jersey City police officer, were shot and killed by yet another hateful, violent anti-Semite.

The day following the attack on the rabbi's guests, CNN reported that, during the previous week, "there was an attack on Jewish New Yorkers almost every day." On January 5, 2020, tens of thousands of concerned citizens marched in Manhattan to alert the public to these increasingly vile assaults on Jews. Horrifically, it appears that in some areas of the United States, it's open season on Jewish people. This unjust hatred is transpiring for nefarious reasons which many Americans, quite understandably, simply can't comprehend. However, its vile perpetrators didn't just suddenly decide that they hated Jews. This book explains why such awful crimes happen and what society must do to prevent their recurrence

Tragically, Nazism didn't end when Adolf Hitler shot himself dead in 1945. But the alarming success of organized, well-funded neo-Nazis, white supremacists and professional Holocaust deniers in keeping the Fuhrer's diabolical legacy alive has, until recently, largely escaped media scrutiny. Organized hatred is now frequently in the news and a topic of intense discussions throughout the world. But who truly understands why some people hold these despicable views and engage in such evil? How can society mitigate the violence that such thinking causes and prevent others from joining the odious activists who promote it, including on the worldwide web? Books by or about racists, anti-Semites and former bigots and violent skinheads have been published, and movies produced, about this sordid societal milieu. But the information in Republican Crackhead has never been featured elsewhere.

Concomitantly, the harm caused by drug addiction, including its adverse impact on innocent victims, has exploded. In these chapters you will learn how my addiction to crack cocaine nearly killed me, and came close to destroying my family - and how I kicked it, and got my life back together. What worked for me has worked for other junkies, and will work for those who want to beat addiction and remain drug-free.

In recent years, interest in the FBI has spiked; there's curiosity about how it operates and what it does. That's here, as well, taken from notes made during my 33 months as a paid, full-time FBI informant. In 2018 and 2019, anti-Semites in Pennsylvania and California shot up synagogues, exterminating innocent victims. Since the summer of 2016, when a young white supremacist shot and killed nine black members of a bible study group at a historic church, such awful tragedies have become ever more commonplace. In April of 2019, The New York Times featured a chilling article, headlined, 'Attacks by White Extremists are Growing. So are their Connections'. This story was published only weeks before the synagogue shooting in Poway, California.

Later in 2019, FBI informants helped to squelch planned attacks against Jewish people by veterans of the U.S. armed forces, in retaliation for shootings by white supremacists at two New Zealand mosques. To prevent such massacres, we must first understand why these ingrates commit such atrocities. That's because even the so-called 'Lone Wolves' who operate independently are nearly always heavily influenced by well-organized HATE organizations with deep pockets. Nowadays, haters don't need group leaders impelling them to commit violence; social media facilitates their radicalization and incents them to perpetrate violent crime. 'Republican Crackhead' fully exposes today's racist Far Right's modus operandi, from fundraising methods and organizational tactics to recruitment techniques to propaganda efforts and indoctrination procedures. After all, defeating an enemy requires knowing that enemy.

Deaths caused by illegal drugs, ranging from cocaine to opioids to crystal meth, to heroin, have affected, directly and indirectly, hundreds of millions of people worldwide. But if society will ever thwart drug addiction, people must realize why anyone would use drugs, and why it's so hard to stop, and how addicts can become – and remain – drug-free. That's all here, as well. As a recovering crackhead who has been clean since 2006, who worked – full-time, on a paid, professional basis – monitoring the racist far Right for the FBI, my experiences provided me with unique perspectives on these worlds.

For the nearly three years of my informant gig, I carefully observed the bureau's internal workings. Hundreds of times, I met with agents, analysts and administrators, while monitoring white supremacists, professional anti-Semites and money-laundering Holocaust deniers.

Detailed observations are provided here. I admire and respect the dedicated rank-and-file FBI agents I worked with, and their colleagues. However, the bureau has rightly come under fire since 2017 for partisan, wrongful, clandestine bias. This is tragic for and harmful to all Americans.

It would surprise many people to know that the Ku Klux Klan is, tragically, alive and well in the United States, and its leaders and rank-and-file members are, in some ways, now more influential – particularly with their internet presence – than ever. Had the late Charles Darwin met some of these rank-and-file racists, he might have reconsidered his theory of evolution. I've often said that the best way to refute the concept of White Supremacy is to attend meetings of the KKK and the Aryan Nations. That said, the vile leaders of these Hate organizations are highly intelligent and knowledgeable. That's our problem.

Recent polls reveal that shocking numbers of college students are ignorant of the Holocaust, with many even questioning its occurrence. How can this be? Largely, it's because the Holocaust denial movement – and it IS an organized, well-financed movement – has succeeded in spreading lies. Such dishonesty is particularly appealing to bigots who already dislike Jewish people. As the late novelist Saul Bellow said, "A great deal of intelligence can be invested in ignorance when the need for illusion is deep."

In August, 2019, a white supremacist gunned down 46 shoppers at a Wal-Mart in El Paso, Texas, killing 22. Prior to perpetrating this carnage, the 21-year-old shooter posted a 2,300-page 'manifesto', to a racist website and elsewhere online. Chillingly, he wrote, "if we can get rid of enough people, then our way of life can be more sustainable."

Within hours, another racist shooter – who was on cocaine and Xanax – shot and killed nine people, and wounded 27 others – at a gay bar in Dayton, Ohio. The El Paso shooter wore protective gear, including ear mufflers, a flak jacket, and body armor. Witnesses and police said that both of these killers operated with military-like efficacy. That same week, a 19-year veteran of the St. Louis (Missouri) Police Department, Sgt. Heather Taylor, revealed that there are numerous "white supremacists" serving on that city's police force. CBS News correspondent Jeffrey Pegues, who interviewed Sgt. Taylor, cited several racist FaceBook comments posted by police officers currently serving on the St. Louis force – some of whom were suspended.

Eleven weeks earlier, a retired U.S. Army Colonel, Jeff McCausland - who is a former member of the National Security Council, and served as the Dean of the U.S. Army War College - warned of the U.S. military's increasing problems with white supremacy and far right extremism among active duty soldiers and sailors. In his interview, McCausland cited a recent survey conducted by The Military TIMES, which revealed that "22 percent of service personnel had seen signs of white nationalism or racist ideology within the armed forces." 50 percent of the non-white personnel surveyed in 2018 said they knew service members who were involved with internal organizations based on "racist ideology", up from 42 percent in 2017. What will Americans do about it?

In June, 2019, the Governor of Oregon, with the support of that state's top lawmakers, shut down the state capitol after receiving threats from armed leaders of anti-government militia groups. The President of the Oregon state Senate informed his colleagues that the Oregon state Police had learned of "credible" physical "threats" against Democrats serving in the Oregon Legislature.

The March 20, 2019 issue of NEW YORK Magazine featured an article with this headline: 'Racism is good at hiding. Just ask this White Nationalist Police Officer.' Again, what will America do about this?

The Atlantic magazine published an article on May, 3, 2019 by Deborah Lipstadt, titled, 'Anti-Semitism is Thriving in America'. After reading it, a north Iowa friend of mine asked me to attend worship services at the Mason City synagogue he attends – and wanted me to be armed. Fearing violent, hateful anti-Semites, he wanted protection. I readily agreed to my friend's request. As it happened, some local law enforcement officers in north Iowa provided the protection. I told the head of the synagogue to contact me at any time, should a need ever arise. The kind of country America will be, now, and in the future, will depend, heavily, on how we deal with the issues, problems and people addressed in this memoir.

On June 6, 2019, Sacramento, California-based U.S. Attorney MacGregor Scott and other prosecutors confirmed, to the Associated Press, what I have known since 1999: White Supremacist gangs are partnering with the Mexican Mafia to smuggle cocaine, crystal meth, and heroin into the U.S.A. The Aryan Brotherhood prison gang is far more violent, influential, wealthy, and powerful, than any gangs comprised of black and brown inmates. For decades, U.S. authorities have tried, and failed, to bring down the Aryan Brotherhood – AKA 'The Brand'. Their efforts, and the harm The Brand does, are also covered in these pages.

A month later, authorities with the U.S. Customs and Border Protection agency seized 39,525 pounds of cocaine, with a street value of $1.3 billion, in Philadelphia. The 1,031-foot cargo foot ship on which it was stashed was owned by JP Morgan Asset Management, and operated by a Swiss corporation. The drug trade, like Holocaust denial and white supremacy, is fueled by enormous amounts of cash, much of it supplied by seemingly legitimate sources that would shock most people. In July of 2019, a white supremacist attempted to set a synagogue afire in the United Kingdom, near Devon. In the process of pouring the gasoline, he accidentally set himself aflame. He pleaded guilty to arson and was charged with two counts of terrorism. To me, this was poetic justice; this violent anti-Semite got exactly what he deserved. But all too often, such haters succeed in doing evil.

On June 30, 2019, CNN aired its documentary, 'The State of HATE', hosted by Fareed Zakaria. He stated, correctly, that "white militants" have become more violent, and "have attacked more often and with greater brutality." Mr. Zakaria also claimed, correctly, that "white militants want to do more than just protest. They make this clear in their internal communications. And they are planning for it every day.

Let's hope we can all recognize this danger before they succeed." Mr. Zakaria was, again, proven right: on August 17, 2019, FBI agents from the bureau's Violent Crimes Task Force arrested a 20-year-old anti-Semite in Ohio. This avowed white nationalist, James Reardon, Jr., possessed scores of rounds of ammunition, multiple semi-auto weaponry, bulletproof armor and gas masks. His plan was to shoot up a Jewish Community Center in New Middleton, Ohio. In 2017, Reardon had attended the obstreperous, deadly 'Unite the RIGHT' rally in Charlottesville, Virginia. The FBI agents also found large quantities of white supremacist, anti-Gay and anti-Jewish propaganda in Reardon's home.

Republican Crackhead isn't BASED on a true story; it IS one. I hope you'll enjoy this memoir and find it entertaining, useful and enlightening.

TODD BLODGETT

January, 2020

PROLOGUE: MAY, 2006. WASHINGTON, D.C.

From the White House to the crack house, to the BIG House
The District of Columbia: Superior Court

While entering the Washington, DC courtroom it didn't occur to me that within an hour, I'd be handcuffed, arrested, placed in the custody of U.S. Marshals and driven to the DC Jail aboard a crowded bus with violent felons. Superior Court judge Craig Iscoe had presided when, three months earlier, I was busted by some DC cops for possession of crack cocaine and placed on pre-trial status. He ordered me to submit to mandatory drug tests three times a week. This meant staying clean: no drugs. But the powerful allure of freebase coke was just too strong.

I used again and failed a drug test. As my lawyer addressed Judge Iscoe, my probation officer entered the courtroom and notified the Judge that I had tested positive for cocaine 90 minutes earlier. I didn't know it then, but being sentenced to jail by this Judge would turn out to be one of the best things to ever happen to me. That's because it put me on the road to the full recovery which I have maintained.

The D.C. Corrections authorities exchanged my seersucker suit for an orange jumpsuit. My watch, cash, cell phone, necktie, keys, money clip, belt, and shoes were confiscated. Across town, my father was attending meetings on Capitol Hill, in his capacity as an appointee of President George W. Bush. My mother was at the White House, where she served as a volunteer in the office of First Lady Laura Bush.

Luckily, I had removed my .380 Walther PPK, loaded with hollow-point rounds, and its ankle holster, before going to court. Had I been caught with it, I'd have been sentenced to federal prison.

The last time a Republican President was serving a second term, I was serving on his White House staff. I worked on the staffs of Ronald Reagan and the first President Bush, and for the Republican National Committee. During Bill Clinton's last years in office and for the first two years of George W. Bush's presidency, I worked for the FBI. The bureau had recruited me to surveil neo-Nazis, the KKK, Holocaust deniers, the Aryan Nations, violent, racist skinheads, and money-laundering professional white supremacists. For nearly 33 months, I monitored some of earth's nastiest people on a full-time, paid basis. The stress from this, and my drug addiction, led to my wife of nine years divorcing me in 2004.

It was my fault, and I didn't blame her. Who wants to be married to a junkie? Knowing that my stupidity had caused the loss of the lady I still loved only made things worse.

Now, I was charged with violating the laws of the same government that the FBI had granted me some high-level security clearances to serve. I decided that once the authorities released me, I'd plead guilty to illegal possession of narcotics and serve whatever sentence was imposed. After going from the White House to the crack house, it was now off to the Big House.

The District of Columbia's Central Detention facility is more like a prison than most jails. At any time, a substantial number of those in lock-up there have either been in prison or are headed to one, or both. Killers, rapists, and other violent offenders are there at nearly all times, and it had severe rat and roach infestations. "The DC joint ain't no club fed," is how a buddy who had done time there described it.

After my first arrest, I spent the night in the lower-security facility, in the basement of the DC courthouse. Those locked up there can wear the clothes they were wearing when arrested, and avoid the humiliation of wearing an orange jump suit. But what passed for edible food there could cause riots in some prisons, and some of the guards seemed as dubious and creepy as those behind bars.

While I was lost in such thoughts, a young black man sitting next to me said, "Ah knows who you is." I figured he'd seen me in the D.C. hoods, buying, using, or delivering drugs. I remained silent as he said, "y'all be goin' down, light skin." As he was also handcuffed and shackled, I didn't fear him. His eyes narrowed to a thin slit as he spoke.

He said I had pulled a gun on his "cuz" – cousin. "Y'all ain't gonna like what us niggas does to yo' white ass when we in lock-up. Dazz fo' real. My homeys be dere. Ah'm sayin'." If this mouthy punk was representative of the Welcoming Committee awaiting my arrival, I'd be about as pleased with being incarcerated as Hillary Clinton is with Jim Comey. "Yeah, 'dem niggas", he warned, "they gonna be helpin' me settles witt y'all. Umm-hmmm. Ah ain't playin', cracka." He then said that an already-incarcerated friend of his, a fellow named Qwanterrius, would "send yo' white ass straight to Hell."

I had pulled guns on some people who had tried to rob me or cause me or others physical harm, and squeezed off rounds to scare them off. I'm all for innocent citizens preventing being victimized by violent perps, and a loaded gun is highly persuasive. I looked him straight in the eye. "Be careful, punk,"

I warned. "Do dat be a threat?," he asked. "My buddies on the outside," I replied, "have friends on the inside. You're not the only dude on this bus with homeys. Mess with me, and my homeys will go on a little hunting trip. It'll be open season, no limit." He looked away, briefly, and said, "break off dat shit talk." I said, "I'm not shittin' you, ass-wipe. Keep threatening me, and you'll be what breaks. Like your jaw, teeth, your arms, legs and neck – just for starters." That shut him up.

I made a mental note to be wary of him and his violent posse upon my arrival. In just a few years, I had degenerated from lawful citizen to arrested junkie. In about thirty minutes, I'd enter the kind of Gated

Community which most people only know about from TV, movies, classrooms, or the internet. An armed corrections officer sat ten feet from me, suspiciously eyeing me and everyone else, as we rode to the jail in one of America's most violent cities. For some, being sentenced to jail in a major city is no big deal. They're actually relieved to go where they can't be evicted, and where they'll get regular, semi-nutritious meals, free health care, cable TV, a library and exercise equipment. This wasn't my view.

Being transported to jail while handcuffed focused me on what led to this dilemma, and how I might turn things around. Would I ever be able to recover from the self-inflicted, personal Hell I was going through? Could I ever kick my drug habit?

Would the threats I just received be followed up on upon my arrival? Would I be thrown into a cell with an inked-up, sociopathic, Aryan Nations knuckle-dragger, who'd view me as a race-traitor? Would my ex-wife ever take me back? If not, would ANY ladies go out with me, again? Would some violent black guy drop-kick me into a brick wall, or worse? Would the homeys in this hell hole try to make me their bitch? Why hadn't I listened better when Ronald Reagan said to "Just say NO to drugs"?

My work for the FBI and the crazy characters I dealt with has inspired reporters for years. Since 2009, five Holocaust deniers I knew have murdered innocent people. Articles about my involvement, even those detailing my FBI work, have made it hard to convince women to go out with me.

For the first few years after kicking my drug habit and leaving DC, I'd sometimes awaken in cold sweats. In my sleep, I'd relive my fights with drug dealers in the hoods, being chased by cops, and stabbed by a mugger who nearly killed me. A racist hillbilly also stomped, then drop-kicked me, out of a bar.

When one's existence alternates between neo-Nazis and KKK members and drug pushers and FBI agents and crack whores in the hoods and other junkies, nightmares like those happen. That's the reason for many of these articles, Op Ed columns, interviews and news reports citing my career as an FBI informant and years as an opportunistic profiteer.

Whenever journalists contact me, I'm reminded of a past that never lets go.

In August, 2017, The Huffington Post published my Open Letter to White Supremacists, in which I urged racists, neo-Nazis, and all bigoted haters to exit their putrid life. In October, 2017, my answers to a Huffington Post reporter's questions about Republican Roy Moore – the GOP nominee for an Alabama U.S. Senate seat – were consequential to Moore dropping five points in the polls against his Democratic opponent. Weeks later, Moore, the former Chief Justice of the Alabama Supreme Court, lost. On June 20, 2019, Roy Moore again announced his candidacy for the same U.S. Senate. My addiction caused more destruction in my life – and the lives of others – than the significant stress and worries associated with my working for the bureau. For the entire, nearly three years that the FBI retained me, I was addicted to crack cocaine; this was while my father served in the Bush administration in D.C., and before that, in elected public office, representing his Iowa constituents.

'Republican Crackhead' is essentially three stories in one: my life as a full-time, paid FBI informant, infiltrating White Supremacists, and as a drug addict in a crime-infested major urban area and all that went with it, while being a lifelong, conservative Republican in Washington, DC, whose father served in President Bush's administration. It's about the last eight years I lived in DC and the unique characters I encountered in the craziest, most unusual settings and circumstances.

Since the 9-11 attacks in 2001, hundreds of Americans have died in terrorist attacks and in shootings committed by white supremacists. During this same period, over 100,000 have lost their lives in our inner cities, due to urban violence. Most murders are due to this scourge, most of which is directly due to drugs. Sometimes, the killers – or, at least those involved in such murders – turned out to be police officers. This memoir is also about hope. I left the Hate movement, helped the FBI nail some bad guys and kicked my addiction. I've stayed clean, and I'm productive and live right. But I couldn't have survived, or get straightened out, without the dedicated efforts of people who cared enough to help me, and by the grace of our merciful God. The names of some people have been changed, but everyone is described precisely as they were. Conversations are reconstructed from memory and my detailed notes.

The hillbilly dialects of some of the white racists I encountered, as well as the ghetto slang of people I knew from the hoods, is left intact. Most of the places referenced in this book are where the events described actually occurred; but in a few cases, substitute locations are given, for valid reasons I'll not disclose. Nothing is sugar-coated here, and what you're about to read is precisely as it really was.

Our imperfect world is filled with flawed people, I among them. However, believing myself to be of fundamentally good character, my hope is that Heraclitus was right in saying that character is destiny.

Because if that's true, then I should be okay, and you will benefit from reading this memoir. In literature and in life, second acts are said to be uncommon. But my second act is going well. Since leaving drugs behind in May of 2006, I've tried to make up for my past transgressions. It's my desire to impart to you what I've learned in ways that will help readers and society.

Feel free to contact me, via my website:

www.ToddBlodgett.us.

TODD BLODGETT

Clear Lake, Iowa

January, 2020

INTRODUCTION

Clear Lake, Iowa: early August, 1972

A s my younger brother, Troy, and I carefully folded our main sail on the lawn facing the lake, our Dad told us to hurry up and get dressed for dinner. We had just finished racing our 16 foot sailboat, which we took turns skippering. Ten minutes after bagging the sail and jib, we were seated in the members dining room of the South Shore Outing club in Clear Lake, Iowa.

The brother of California's then-Governor and his wife were seated at the adjacent table. J. Neil 'Moon' Reagan was a born raconteur and a truly gregarious personality. He was a retired radio and TV producer who later was the vice president of the McCann-Erickson advertising agency. He and his wife, Bessie, were staying at the Outing club with friends. This historic, residential co-operative was founded in 1895, and has been open every summer since in its original location. I grew up in this unique, 19th century relic of communal living, with 20 summer cottages connected by a long, winding front Porch, spanning the entire length of the structure. My family still owns our cottage there, and members and their guests still eat in that same dining room.

While watching my father play tennis earlier that day on the club's court, Moon and I discussed the upcoming Olympics in Munich, and hoped that American Bobby Fischer would soon unseat Russia's Boris Spassky as the world Chess champion. Moon smiled readily, loved jokes and laughed often. His voice was raspy, resulting from the removal of some vocal cords. The next day, I watched the CBS Morning News with John Hart. President Richard Nixon was seeking re-election and California's governor was being interviewed. My 11-year-old mind noted this controversial celebrity, half a continent from Iowa, where he'd begun his career. Minutes later, when Neil and Bess walked in to the club's Dining Room for breakfast, I mentioned having seen his famous brother on TV.

"Meet me in an hour, Todd, on the swimming dock. We'll talk politics," Moon replied. He was sitting on a bench reading The Des Moines Register when I bounded onto the dock, and we spoke for over an hour. Moon and his wife had no children, but what a wonderful dad and grandfather he'd have made. That weekend, I spent more time with the Reagans in the cottage belonging their friends from Des Moines. The Reagans were there again, nearly each summer, through 1979. I corresponded with Moon, regularly spoke on the phone, and I received Christmas cards from him and Bess for the next two decades. Moon was afflicted with Alzheimers disease and died in 1996, aged 88. Bessie died in 2010 at the age of 102.

The Reagans spent two or three weeks each year with her sister, Pearl Lovejoy of Des Moines. In 1980, '81, '82, and '83, Neil visited me on the Drake campus. On two such visits, I took him to some sorority houses to impress the girls. Even the housemother of the Delta Gamma sorority was thrilled to meet him, as were about 30 DG's, who lined the staircase in the foyer to catch a glimpse of the popular President's brother.

Between 1976, when Ronald Reagan challenged President Ford for the Republican presidential nomination, and the fall of 1980, when he ousted Jimmy Carter, I had met with him over a dozen times. In 1981 President Reagan hosted me in the oval office. I also met with him in the White House rose garden that fall. I visited him at the White House again in 1983. After serving on his Inaugural Committee staff in 1984-85, I began serving on his White House staff and, later, on the staff of his Vice President, George H.W. Bush, before working for the Republican National Committee.

Years later, I associated with some people whom President Trump might call bad hombres.

These were professional white supremacists and Holocaust deniers, KKK members, drug dealers, violent drug addicts, hit men retained by members of the Aryan Nations, racist Skinheads, money-laundering neo-Nazis, and haters who murdered innocent victims. I wasn't raised to associate with such people or use illegal drugs. Becoming part of the realm of organized hatred and illicit drugs resulted from my own, stupid choices. But when the FBI recruited me to be a full-time, confidential informant, I saw an opportunity to atone for the consequences of my bad decisions. Having paid heavy prices for such bad decisions, I learned the hard way about danger and evil. My life is normal now, for which I'm glad.

'Republican Crackhead' is the true story of how it all happened.

CHATTING IT UP WITH RONALD REAGAN

Visiting the oval office to meet with any President is, for the few who ever get the opportunity, a truly unforgettable experience. My 1981 visit to Ronald Reagan's oval office was the first of several times I would be in that historic room with him between then and 1988. The receptionist who greeted me, Nell Yates, had worked for Presidents Nixon and Ford. She'd still be there when I joined Reagan's staff in 1985. A few months earlier, I had visited the President and chatted and joked in the Rose Garden.

I sat in one of the two matching chairs on both sides of the same massive, oval office desk that President Trump now uses. This desk was used by FDR, JFK, Jimmy Carter, and every President who followed Reagan, except George H.W. Bush. The 40th President greeted me like an old friend, putting me at immediate ease. "How are things at Drake?", he asked.

He said he wasn't much older than I then was when he hitch-hiked to Iowa, three weeks after graduating from Eureka college in 1932. "I loved my years in Des Moines," he told me. "My career got off to a great start in Davenport, at WOC Radio. They paid me five bucks a game, plus bus fare, to broadcast the Hawkeye's home games from what's now Kinnick stadium. After my first game, they doubled my salary. After covering the Drake Relays the following spring, I moved on to WHO."

[Author's note: Ronald Reagan later told me he was fired by WOC's owner, B.J. Palmer, despite his talent, solid work ethic, honesty and winning personality. But station manager Pete MacArthur, with Dave Palmer's imprimatur, helped Reagan to land the position at WHO radio in Des Moines.]

WHO was WOC's 50,000 Watt, clear-channel sister station, where 'Dutch' Reagan worked until leaving for Hollywood in 1937. "I dated a Drake gal who later married a fella from your hometown," Reagan said. "She was real fun," the President said. The lady, Jeanne Tesdell Burrington, was then still alive. She and her husband, Mason City attorney Don Burrington, were friends of my parents. Reagan told me about a bar in Des Moines called Cy's Moonlight Inn, where near-beer was served.

"It's long gone now," he said, wistfully. The President asked if I'd like some coffee, iced water, or a soft drink. Within 60 seconds, a Navy steward appeared; shortly thereafter, he brought me a glass of iced tea. "Neil says you're a Sig-Alph," he said, referencing my fraternity, Sigma Alpha Epsilon. "Do you live in the SAE house?" I replied I'd lived in the fraternity house as a sophomore, but was now sharing an apartment with another SAE. He was genuinely interested in hearing about my college experience, and confirmed what an elderly alum had once told me: Ronald Reagan had visited my fraternity house in the mid-1930s. "Moon said you had him over there last fall," the President said, "and he said it pretty much looks the same as it did back in our day."

Reagan looked me directly in the eye, nodding his head knowingly as I spoke. He said that were he to relive his college years, he'd have studied more. "Eureka awarded me an honorary degree about 15 years ago," he told me. Jokingly referencing his undistinguished grades, he said, "I told 'em I'd always figured that the first degree they gave me was honorary."

When I asked him how he got into politics, a sentimental expression swept over his face as he set his iced tea down on a presidential seal coaster.

"Well, my film career kinda took a nose dive after the war, and the early '50s weren't much better. So, Moon and Lew Wasserman got me to host the host the GE Theatre," he said, grinning. Wasserman had been Reagan's agent, and later headed MCA - Music Corporation of America. "Things were swell for several years. Walt Disney even invited me to help him open Disney-land to the public. But in the early '60s, I gave some speeches that took issue with the TVA. Are you familiar with the TVA?" I knew about the Tennessee Valley Authority. "Well," the President said, "General Electric had some hefty contracts with the TVA, and my views on big Government" – which Reagan always pronounced as "gub-mint" - "and in particular, the TVA, didn't go over too well with some of the higher-ups." Reagan said that expressing those views "was a no-no" with the corporate titans.

"Then there was Bobby Kennedy", he said, "who, as his brother's Attorney General, did me no favors." The President didn't elaborate on that, but 'Moon' later did. "So, inside of about two weeks," he said, "production stopped. No further episodes of the program were made, and I was out as the spokesman."

As the President recounted this, he pursed his lips, which signified skep-ticism or disapproval on his part. He stared, contemplatively, focusing on an oil portrait of Calvin Coolidge. Seconds later, his optimistic nature and humor returned. With a twinkle in his eye, he flashed his famous, crooked grin, cocked his head toward me, and said, "So I guess you could say GE kinda pulled the plug on me!" Reagan said, "but, you know, things worked out okay, just as they did after I lost in '76, to Jerry Ford."

Until that day, I hadn't known that Reagan had also sought the presidency in 1968. He lost to Richard Nixon at the Republican National convention in Miami. "Ya know", he said, "I arrived at that convention in Miami Beach with more votes than anyone," he said, shaking his head, smiling in a sentimental way. "But our mother, Nelle, always told us boys that everything happens for a reason. Now, we always can't see these reasons, Todd, at least not as things occur. But you can bet that God does. He knows."

It was fascinating to hear these behind-the-scenes perspectives, his rock-solid, unshakable belief in the Almighty. Ronald Reagan's religious beliefs were genuine and he was the real deal.

AUTHOR'S NOTE: Years later, while I served on his White House staff, President Reagan again spoke of his faith and its role in his extraordinary life. "I figure that whatever time I've left on this earth is up to Him," he said, referring to God. "I owe my life to the Lord, and I'm determined to use this remaining time to serve Him as best I can."

Ronald Reagan sought the presidency in three different decades, and ran against the three Presidents who served before him and the one who succeeded him, which no other American has ever done. Persistence, determination and optimism were lifelong attributes of America's 40th President. "Neil had been involved in Barry's campaign," Reagan said, referring to Senator Barry Goldwater, the 1964 GOP presidential nominee. "I'd just wrapped – finished filming – my last picture. I played a bad guy; had to slap Angie Dickinson full across her face."

The President's face actually tightened a bit as he described that scene. "Then I was shot and killed. You might say my film career went out with a bang," said Reagan, the born storyteller. "Well, Nancy's folks were neighbors in Scottsdale with Barry and Peggy," he said, referring to Dr. and Mrs. Loyal Davis, originally of Chicago, and the Goldwaters. "Neil had produced some TV and radio spots for Barry. Near the campaign's end, I gave that speech. Nationwide audience. That started the talk of me running for Governor. I won all but three counties in '66. So, there ya go. That's how it all began." The President then stood up to his full height of six feet, one inch.

"I'd love to chat more, Todd," he said, "but we'll do it another time. Secretary Regan will be here in ten minutes, and I've gotta read some reports for our meeting."

"Thanks, Mr. President," I said, as we shook hands. Reagan reached into a drawer in the historic oak desk and handed me a fancy box, embossed with the presidential seal. Inside was a set of cobalt blue, gold presidential cufflinks with Ronald Reagan's etched name on the back side. "These are for my ambassadors, Republican Governors, and my top contributors," he said. "You're not in that crowd – yet. But you've earned 'em. So enjoy 'em!" A White House photographer popped in and took a photo, which Reagan signed and mailed to me, at the Sigma Alpha Epsilon fraternity house in Des Moines.

"Great to see you again. I'm grateful for your support. Thanks, Todd, for dropping by." As our eyes met, he patted me on the shoulder and said, "Now, you go have a wonderful year back at Drake." Later that year, at the Euchre and Cycle club in Mason City, Iowa, I ran into the lady who'd dated Reagan in the 1930s, Jeanne Burrington. She fondly remembered him. She called him 'Dutch' and said, "He's a born politician," she said, smiling. "What a personality," she said. With her husband present, she added, "even then, he was preparing for what he's now doing. I'm not surprised he remembers me, because his mind is like a steel trap."

CHAPTER ONE

N eil and Bessie Reagan would frequently visit her sister at her home on Grand avenue in Des Moines throughout my years at Drake. Neil and I met for lunch in Des Moines twice in 1981, and in the spring, summer and fall of 1982, 1983 and 1984. At a restaurant called Jesse's Embers on Ingersoll avenue, Moon and his good friend Bob Dillon and I discussed my future in 1983.

Mr. Dillon was a veteran of Des Moines radio and TV, and knew that journalism was my major. He asked if I wanted to get into what he called "the communications field." I told him I'd keep that in mind, and he offered to open doors to a career in advertising. Neil then said, "Todd enjoys advertising, but I think he'd like to go into politics." Turning to me, he said he'd get me "hired on to Ron's re-election committee, if that's the path you want to take." Ronald Reagan hadn't yet announced his intentions at this point, and I was thrilled to learn he'd be running again. In the summer of 1984, we met again. "So, what's the plan, fella?", Neil asked. I told him I may be calling him that fall.

My boss was Iowa's senior U.S. Senator, Roger W. Jepsen; I worked on his re-election staff. Jepsen, a longtime GOP powerhouse in Iowa, had served as Lieutenant Governor in the 1960s and '70s. I wanted campaign experience and had no interest in working in government. As Neil drove me back to the campaign headquarters, he wished me luck and reminded me to call him if Jepsen lost. That happened. Congressman Tom Harkin defeated Senator Jepsen while Ronald Reagan won a 49-state landslide over Walter Mondale. Mondale carried only Minnesota, barely. The next day, while suffering from a bad hangover, I called Neil at his home in Rancho Santa Fe. "I've been expecting your call", he said, chuckling, "and I've lined up work for you."

My first paid job in Washington, DC was at the Presidential Inaugural Committee. A few months later, with help from Neil's good buddy Lyn Nofziger, I was serving on the White House staff at the age of 24. When I turned 25 on September 10, 1985, the President had just finished welcoming the Prime Minister of Denmark to the White House. As I was delivering the White House News Summary to the west wing, Reagan wished me a Happy Birthday. His brother had told him. The White House Chief of staff, Don Regan, noticed this, which made me feel kind of important. Over the next two years, I met James A. Baker, Lee Atwater, Haley Barbour, Roger Ailes, Ed Rollins, Mitch Daniels, Roger Stone, Andy Card, Ed Rogers, Ralph Reed, Debbie Steelman and other rising Republicans, who later played major roles in the GOP. Some still do. I also met Pat Buchanan and Richard Viguerie, and other GOP luminaries.

In 1987, I got a chance to triple my salary. Three leading Republican direct mail professionals, Steve Winchell, Wayne Johnson and John Whitehead, offered me a position with what was called the Hay-Adams Joint Venture. They were creating the largest GOP direct mail donor file ever assembled. This position required me to travel to the state capitals of most of America's lower 48 states over the following 18 months. Today, donor name acquisition is largely done via the internet. But back then, purchasing – from the offices of each state's Secretary of State – such records required in-person visits.

After researching campaign finance reports of candidates for statewide public office, and contributor records of candidates for state Senate and state Representative, and donor reports filed by each states political parties, I'd write a check to cover the cost of making copies. Payments ranged from under $500 for files from small states, to over $15,000 for copying and shipping, for records from larger states like New York, California, Texas, Pennsylvania, Ohio, Florida and Michigan.

It was then illegal to use donor information from Illinois for fundraising purposes, so we never bought records from that state. Once the copies arrived, I supervised the editing process, whereby Political Action Committees (PACs) donations were deleted and donor information was categorized by age, occupation, contribution amount and frequency. From there, the reports were sent to data entry specialists. The names were keyed into a database and then sent to a list management company. It was also my responsibility to come up with catchy names for these donor files, to attract the attention of list brokers who suggested to their clients which files to use for direct marketing. My direct marketing skills were later helpful in my father's campaigns for the Iowa Legislature. To this day, I assist candidates with their direct mail efforts.

I met with Lee Atwater at the Capitol Hill club just after Vice President Bush had won the 1988 New Hampshire presidential Primary. Of all the political operatives I've known, regardless of political party, Lee was the most unique. He was brilliant at what he did and loved doing it. He seemed to think about politics during every waking hour, and found ways to make politics resonate with average Americans so they'd vote Republican. Along with Ronald Reagan, Atwater seemed to innately understand the thoughts of rank-and-file citizens. Years later, when some really jacked-up crack heads moved about with abnormal energy levels, I'd think of Lee – who required no drugs to be hyperactive.

Whenever we spoke, I realized I was in the presence of a true genius. In the club's downstairs grill, he asked if I'd like to "go to work for the next President of the yew-nited states." Lee had been named as the campaign manager by Vice President Bush. By April, I was working, part-time, for the Bush for President campaign committee. Within six weeks, Lee asked me to devote full time to the campaign. I agreed, and took a leave of absence from my job with Hay-Adams with the option to return after the 1988 general election.

In June of 1988, Lee introduced me to Debbie Steelman, who was the Bush campaign's Domestic Policy director. A few weeks earlier, over dinner at an Italian restaurant called AV's, Lee told me he was transferring me to Debbie's department. He wanted me to work in domestic policy. Lee said that Bush – who'd face the Governor of Massachusetts, Michael Dukakis – would make big plays for blue collar votes. "Issues drive campaigns, Todd," Atwater said, "and this campaign will be VERY issue-oriented. No new taxes, tough on crime; pro-American military, law an' order, pro-Second amendment; support your local police, anti-ACLU, pro-Capital Punishment, support the Reagan agenda, be proud of the American flag, the whole nine yards. Full-stop, all the way. You'll be analyzin' what Dukakis says, and helpin' us devise ways to strip the bark off the little liberal bastard."

Stuffing garlic bread in his mouth, Lee – who knew I loved guns – said, "man, you'll be makin' AMMO! Now, what could be more excitin'?" Before I could answer, he thanked me. He then segued into his theory about what he termed as "the two breeds of presidential nominees", by which he compared candidates to hounds. "See," he said, "there's two kinds of political dogs in campaigns. There's what Ah call huntin' dogs. Now, Reagan, he's one. Nixon, too, as was ol' LBJ - and Ike, and even Abe Lincoln. Those kind usually win, see, 'cause they understand how most folks live, and what they're thinkin'. They can relate. Everything they got, they scratched for, and fight hard to keep it." Breaking off more garlic bread, Lee – a superb raconteur – said, "then there's what Ah call kennel-fed dogs. Now, George Bush is a great guy; don't get me wrong. But he's kennel-fed. Jerry Ford, Barry Goldwater, and ol' Nelson Rockefeller – they were all kennel-feds, as well."

Lee observed that Republicans like Ford, Rockefeller, Goldwater and Bush had either gone to Ivy League universities or came from well-to-do families, or both. "Now, JFK, he was kennel-fed," Atwater told me. "But, y'see, he only won by stealin' Illinois and Texas, so he's an anomaly."

"Didn't Nixon go to Duke?," I interjected. "Yeah," Atwater replied, "but Duke's only borderline Ivy League, and he only went there for law school. 'Ol Nixon was on a scholarship and he resented the silver spoon crowd by the time he arrived on that campus." Lee's objective was to present the

Yale-educated Vice President as being more in tune with Americans than the Harvard-educated Dukakis – which he was. Arching an eyebrow, Atwater stuffed some ravioli in his mouth. Before he'd fully swallowed it, he looked me in the eyes. "Y'all get what Ah'm sayin'?"

"Yeah. Candidates who grew up poor can better connect with average Americans, blue collar voters, veterans, retirees and union members. They make better candidates than those who – "

"Yew got it," he interrupted, "that's it. Exactly." Lee knew that being from a rural state with lots of blue collar voters made my perspectives valuable. He also knew that despite being the son of Greek immigrants, Michael Dukakis – with his Harvard connections, urbane, yoga instructor wife, and East coast lifestyle and demeanor – would have trouble connecting with most Americans. Lee then said, "ever hear of a guy named Willie Horton?"

"Didn't he play for the Detroit Tigers?"

Shaking his head from side to side, Lee replied, "Not THAT Willie Horton. Ahh mean the Willie Horton that's gonna help me elect George Bush as the forty-first President." The usage of the convicted killer Willie Horton was my introduction to the power of race in political campaigns. Not that Atwater was personally a bigot; he wasn't. Neither was George H.W. Bush. But Willie Horton was serving a life sentence for killing a Massachusetts teen when he was made eligible for weekend furloughs, under an existing law which was modified with the support of Dukakis. Conservative Legislators, fearing the worst, strongly opposed allowing weekend furloughs for such dangerous felons. While out on a furlough, Horton had raped a woman and brutally assaulted her boyfriend. He was presented by the Republicans in the '88 presidential campaign as symbolic of Liberals being soft on crime. It was a valid issue and represented legitimate concerns – and it worked brilliantly. My work on the Bush campaign required weekly, sometimes daily, contact with the Opposition Research division at the Republican National Committee.

Even as Dukakis held a 13-point lead over Bush, as was the case in late July of 1988, Lee said that Bush would win at least 35 states, and he ended up with 40.

In late August, Indiana Senator J. Danforth 'Dan' Quayle became Bush's running mate. The campaign Committee sent me to New Orleans in early August, to work at the Republican National Convention. Not ranking high enough to stay at the Marriott by the Convention Center, the campaign put me up for three weeks at the Olivier House on Toulouse street. Upon returning to DC, my job with the presidential campaign kept me busy six days a week, twelve hours a day. This pace continued through November. A few weeks later, at the Presidential Transition team offices in downtown Washington, Lee asked if I'd meet him for a drink that afternoon at the Old Ebbitt Grille. Lee had once been a pack-a-day smoker, but when I knew him, he only smoked a few cigars on Fridays only.

Looking back, it's hard to fathom that 16 months later, Lee would be diagnosed with inoperable brain cancer. On that day, though, he was as he'd always been: fit, energetic, mind racing, alert to everything and everyone around – and as energized as a team of six young, freshly-awakened mules.

"Drinks are on me," he said, as we sat at a corner table. "Todd, you wield the English language like a switchblade. That makes ya valuable. So, I'm sendin' you to see 'ol Don Todd. He's one of the sharpest political pros on our side. He runs the Opposition Research department at the RNC, and he can use your talents." Lee had recently been named by President-elect Bush as the new chairman of the Republican National Committee. "Andy Card and I think somebody who thinks and writes like you belongs in 'ole Don's shop. You're strategic, and y'all see what gets past most operatives. You'll write it up in ways that gets our guys the votes." Lee handed me his card, with the name Don Todd and Don's direct phone number written on the back. I began working at the RNC right after Thanksgiving of 1988.

My parents were in DC for the inauguration, the first of three inaugurals they'd attend in which Presidents named George Bush was sworn into office. One of the first projects I worked on as a political analyst in the RNC's 'Oppo' division was devising ways to defeat a former Ku Klux Klansman named David Duke. This was ironic, considering what was to come. Duke was running for the Louisiana House of Representatives in a special election, to represent a district north of New Orleans. He had finished first in a multi-candidate Primary election, and now was in the run-off, against the brother of the state's former Republican Governor, Dave Treen. My research and related efforts to help John Treen get his message across were doomed from the start.

I, and Don Todd, and the entire staff knew that Duke was a charlatan who hadn't changed his views. But Louisianans didn't take kindly to what they considered to be outside influence. Duke won the special election in February and took office the following day.

Later that year, I assisted the campaign staffs of Republicans running for governorships in New Jersey and Virginia. In early 1990, the NRCC (National Republican National Congressional Committee, which has offices at the RNC headquarters on Capitol Hill) assigned me to work a Congressional race in Fort Worth, Texas. I was paid by RNC and NRCC funds, and was provided with an apartment and a car in Fort Worth. I kept my apartment at the Kennedy-Warren while I worked that race, and flew back to DC about every five or six weeks.

In early March, I was in D.C. Eddie Chiles, the Texas oilman who sold the Texas Rangers to George W. Bush, had befriended me. He and his wife, Fran – who was the RNC's national committeewoman for Texas - arranged for me to meet some Texas donors, at an event for Senator Phil Gramm. As I left the NRCC, I knew I'd miss the breakfast at the Washington Hilton. Lee, who was speaking that morning to Gramm's supporters, was to introduce me to the Texans who were prospective contributors to the candidate for whom I worked. I arrived at the Hilton just as Bob Dole left. Phil and Sarah Guarino, an elderly couple who were full-time RNC volunteers, were there. "Did you hear about Lee?", Phil asked.

7

Atwater had collapsed while speaking to Gramm's patrons. "An ambulance took him to a hospital, probably George Washington University's," Phil told me. "It was terrible," Sarah said. "He was in horrible pain, screaming," she said, while clutching her rosary. Lee had suffered a seizure caused by an undiagnosed malignant tumor on his brain. That night, I had dinner with Linda, the oncology nurse I'd marry five years later. When I told her of Lee's diagnosis – which hadn't yet been made public – Linda said he probably had about a year to live. She was correct, as Lee died on March 29, 1991. He was 40 years old and had a lovely wife, Sally, and three little girls.

Along with the President and Mrs. Bush and 2,000 others, I attended Lee's memorial service at the Washington National Cathedral on April 4, 1991. Lee's death compounded my frustration with politics. I had sensed early on that George Bush might be a one-term President. The November, 1990 elections had been a disaster for the GOP. The candidate I worked for, and hundreds of Republicans running for the U.S. Congress, governorships and state legislative seats, lost. The Opposition Research department was unfairly blamed by some. Knowing that Lee was doomed, and that things didn't look good for the GOP in 1992, I wanted out of politics, at least for awhile.

While serving on Reagan's White House staff, I became friends with a DC businessman was a member of the Eagles – the high-level donors to the RNC. He owned several businesses, all based in DC, New York city, Maryland and Virginia. He was also a major benefactor to Jewish and Libertarian and causes, and lived in a beautiful penthouse co-op apartment at the Watergate. He hired me to work as a sales rep for one of his companies. I worked for this company for 18 months, but missed politics. In early 1993, I was offered, and accepted, the position of advertising manager for a start-up monthly publication called 'Slick Times'. This humor magazine was owned by Michael Dalton Johnson, a marketing and distribution wizard with a dry, rapier sense of humor. In late 1993, Mike promoted me to Associate Publisher.

My work with Slick Times was fun, profitable, and a real education in print advertising. I remained with SLICK TIMES through early 1995, after

Willis Carto made me an offer I felt would be stupid to turn down. Michael Johnson also made it clear that his Associate Publisher/ad director couldn't be affiliated with Liberty Lobby. Later that month, I began working as an advertising and marketing consultant to Carto's Liberty Lobby. From the outset, it was a most lucrative gig. My contract with Liberty Lobby also provided tremendous autonomy and professional independence.

Linda and I were married in June, 1995, in Mason city. Her father was a lawyer there, where my dad had been an orthodontist for 30 years. At the time of our wedding, my father's legislative district in the Iowa House of Representatives included Mason City and Clear Lake. Around 350 guests attended our wedding and the reception, and we honeymooned in Barbados. We bought a six bedroom, 4,500 square foot house in a beautiful, tree-lined neighborhood in Annandale, Virginia, hoping to fill it with children. At least, that was the plan. But we weren't rushing to start a family. Linda was 30 when we got married, and our jobs were demanding. But for the first three and a half years of our marriage, we were very happy.

A month after we returned from our honeymoon in Barbados, Willis called me into his private office and said he was sending me to Galveston, Texas. "You'll be the house guest of an eccentric multi-millionaire, whose family has long been among the richest in Texas," he informed me. This man, Shearn Moody, Jr., had been a client of the late, famed lawyer Roy Cohn. Shearn Moody had been in Carto's sphere for decades, and had once served time in federal prison for misappropriating millions of dollars from his family's foundation and the Moody Trust - which owned, collectively, assets worth over three billion dollars. A week later, I flew to Houston, rented a car, and drove to Galveston island.

While driving onto the grounds of the decrepit Moody estate, the place reminded me of the neglected mansion of Norma Desmond, the fading movie star immortalized in 'Sunset Boulevard'. Moody lived in the main house, which was staffed by a young man and his girlfriend. Another employee also lived on the grounds in a guest house. The twenty-something young lady told me I would stay in a suite on the second floor, with its own bathroom and sitting room. As her boyfriend carried my briefcase and luggage up the stairs, I noticed that his bicep was tattooed with a Swastika. As he sat down my luggage, I noticed that his gold ring featured a Confederate flag emblem. More than once, the two dudes and the girl, and another staffer, greeted one another by saying, '88' – neo-Nazi code for Heil, Hitler.

An hour later, I was shown into Mr. Moody's musty, book-lined study just before dinner was served. This room, like the entire house, reeked of cigarette and cigar smoke; ashtrays were in nearly every room. Rising from his desk, my host said, "welcome to Galveston. My family either owns, or has owned, nearly everything worth owning here for over a hundred years. I'll show you a good time." Over dinner, Moody told me that he had been convicted, years earlier, of wire fraud, mail fraud, and for "attempting to steer tens millions of dollars worth of grants" from his family foundation to himself. "I had to pay the IRS fourteen million bucks, and that was after I retained over one hundred attorneys to prove my innocence." He served just a few months in prison on a five-year sentence, he said, and his 1987 conviction was "over-turned on appeal." That same year, Moody told me, his face was featured on the cover of a magazine – Texas Monthly – under the heading, 'The Sleaziest Man in Texas'. I later learned that what he told me was all true.

After a few drinks, he reminisced about his old lawyer, Roy Cohn. "Roy was Jewish, but he hated nearly every Jew he knew," Moody said. This man was obsessed with Adolf Hitler and owned an impressive collection of Third Reich memorabilia. He showed me several items, including a bronze razor he said had belonged to the Fuhrer. As he cradled a fancy military cap that Hitler allegedly had worn, he gazed upon it like an adoring mother holding her newborn baby. The Texas Monthly article described Moody as having "an affinity for lowlife", and "a long-running pattern of attaching himself to crooks … and con men who do his bidding." The article also identified Moody as a homosexual, which I had surmised upon meeting him. I later found out that over the years, Willis and Elisabeth Carto, William Pierce, and other celebrated neo-Nazis had attended lavish cocktail parties and dinners hosted by Shearn Moody, atthis same mansion. Moody, himself, admitted that many of his frequent guests were either felons or under criminal prosecution. Laughing, he said that "the word about my parties is: If you're indicted, you're invited." The following day, his driver chauffeured us all around Galveston. Moody said that a former Attorney General of Texas had stripped him of his seat on the Board of Directors of the Moody Foundation, and that the trustees of another family Trust were "Jewing" him out of money that was his.

He then said he wanted to deed to Liberty Lobby "a very substantial parcel" of land, and required the services of a petroleum landman. "I don't suppose you know an honest petroleum landman?", he asked. As it turned out, I did. An old roommate of mine from boarding school, Tom Senft, was a Landman who lived near Houston, Texas. "Call him," Moody told me. I did. The next day, Tom drove to Moody's estate, along with a lawyer named Keith McCarty. An agreement had nearly been reached between them and Moody when a Carto-retained Texas-based attorney appeared on the scene.

This lawyer, Howard Singleton, seemed to fear that Senft and McCarty would take business from him. A Moody crony and Carto informant, a shadowy, pro-Confederate crony named Vance Beaudreau, had called Willis about my having arranged for Senft to meet with Moody. Nazis must like to keep money in the family, I surmised. I never learned what became of that land, or whether or not oil was under it, because Shearn Moody died less than a year later, in 1996. In 1997, I invited Singleton to join me on a hunting trip to Iowa, along with my good friend Simon Jacobsen. Singleton was no neo-Nazi, and his relationship to Carto and with Liberty Lobby was strictly professional.

The four days I spent with Shearn Moody at his Galveston mansion proved that major money, and substantial, high-level influences, provide backing to organized neo-Nazis and Holocaust deniers. In mid-1996, some very suspicious-looking people filtered in and out of Carto's office in Liberty Lobby's Capitol Hill headquarters. They ranged in age from college students to senior citizens in their late eighties and represented all walks of life. They were neo-Nazis. I first learned this when I stayed late, after most of the employees and consultants had left. As I quietly worked at my desk in the office directly across from Carto's, he was on the phone. Apparently, he'd forgotten I was still there. But his responses to the caller were vitriolically anti-Semitic and racist.

"There's not a day that goes by I don't feel AWFUL that those fuckin' Jews won World War Two," he said. Referencing how he had scammed some conservative Republicans, Carto said, "we pulled off a good one, with our kike lawyer and his jigaboo assistant." Willis also told the caller, referencing story ideas for the SPOTLIGHT newspaper: "I don't care how you do it, or what you have to make up. We're gonna prove that the defeat of German National Socialism was a DISASTER for white people, worldwide." Decades before the term, 'fake news' became part of the lexicon, Willis Carto created it. Carto also told his caller, "let the Hebes sue us. We'll raise a bundle from our readers." Willis then said to "transfer that other three mill to my Costa Rican account." Right before hanging up, he told the caller, "heil Hitler." I quickly covered the notes I'd taken while overhearing Carto and stayed quiet. He got up from his desk and walk down the hall. The next sound I heard was the restroom door near the stairwell being closed. I quickly, quietly tip-toed down the hall and stairs. Once I was outside the Liberty building, facing Independence avenue, S.E., I realized that there was no doubt: my lucrative client was a pro-Nazi hate profiteer, whose professed paleo-conservatism was merely a veneer for an unapologetic, aggressive, Hitlerarian agenda. My worst fears were now confirmed.

In mid-November, 1996, a California court ruled in a case which might be called Nazi vs. Nazi. Carto was ordered to pay nearly $9 million to the Institute for Historical Review, a Holocaust denying organization he'd founded in 1978. Judge Runston Maino then signed arrest warrants for Willis Carto and his crony Henry Fischer, who'd helped him to secure, embezzle and hide, about $8 million in the 1990s. The IHR was the world's premier Holocaust Denial organization. The dispute arose over a $17.5 Million bequest from inventor Thomas Edison's grandniece, Jean Edison Farrel. A few days later Willis was back in D.C., and we had dinner at the Jefferson hotel. "You need to accompany me to New York city on Thursday," he said. "We'll be gone for about twenty-four hours, total. I'll be armed, and you'll need to pack heat, too." Willis had stashed away umpteen millions of dollars in cash over many decades, some of which was in the hands of trusted fellow Holocaust deniers. One such supporter, whom I'll call Vince, owned some valuable real estate in the Bayside section of the Queens borough of New York. The purpose of this trip was to pick up over $2.5 million worth of uncirculated Double Eagles – U.S. $20 gold coins – South African Krugerrands, and Canadian Maple Leafs - all gold coins.

At the time, each coin was worth about $750. We were to bring back around thirty-three hundred coins, all rolled in plastic tubes. Each tube contained 20 coins, which meant that there were nearly 170 tubes, weighing over 200 pounds. It wasn't hard to see why he wanted to handle this privately, and for us to be strapped. The wealthy anti-Semite had kept this cache for him for years, Carto told me. "But now," he said, "with this pro-Jew Judge's ruling, I want it stashed elsewhere." We couldn't fly without disclosing the contents of the five locked, heavy strong boxes we ended up bringing back, and Carto was too cheap to charter private aircraft. Two days later, I was at Liberty Lobby's headquarters at five a.m. We arrived in Manhattan about five hours later. Willis and I checked into the Downtown Athletic club, courtesy of an IHR donor who was a member; the Holocaust denier paid for everything. Carto and I met with a prominent, highly successful tax lawyer named Harry Weyher, Jr. Mr. Weyher, a former editor of the Harvard Law Review and chief counsel to the New York State Crime Commission, was virulently anti-minority. He had served as the Deputy Attorney General of the state of New York under three of its Governors: Nelson Rockefeller, Malcolm Wilson and Hugh Carey.

Lunch was at the New York Racquet & Tennis club, where Weyher, a longtime member, was well-known. Weyher practiced law in New York city and his home state of North Carolina, and was of-counsel to a law firm in Manhattan. He, Roger Pearson, and Mark Cotterill were as thick as thieves. Harry Weyher's colleague, John B. Trevor, Jr., was an accomplished sailor who in the 1980s served as the Commodore of the St. Regis Yacht club in New York. He and Mr. Weyher operated a multi-million dollar foundation which Adolf Hitler had admired and endorsed: the Pioneer Fund.

Mr. Trevor also authored a classic book on sailing, titled, 'Wind and Tide in Yacht Racing', which I had read, as a teenager, when I raced my X boat. He was in his eighties when Carto and I were in New York with Weyher. But he – like Harry - hadn't slowed down.

Weyher told Carto he needed "to get back in touch with" Trevor, regarding a large bequest that Trevor was arranging for a Carto shell corporation. Willis later told me that a friend of Trevor's had wired $750,000 to an account controlled by Carto, to Bank Leu in Grand Cayman. Willis and I returned to our rooms at the Downtown Athletic club a few hours later. Two weeks later, Danny Wuerffel would be awarded the Heisman trophy there. The trophy is named for the club's first squash coach and athletic director. Carto said he was going to take a nap. "Meet me in the lobby at 8:30," Willis told me. "We'll check out and eat dinner in Queens," he said. "That's where we'll pick up the coins. We'll drive straight back to DC, so rest up, if you need to. It'll be around midnight when we hit the road. Be strapped."

He meant for me to not leave my gun in my suitcase. It was to be in my pocket. Illegally carrying a loaded gun in New York city was risky, but we did it.

His buddy ran a high-stakes poker club in Queens, in an old warehouse, on the second floor. When we were about five minutes away, Willis called him. Turning to me, Carto said the garage door would open as we got close. As I drove inside, a huge, mustachioed man who looked to be Italian pointed to where he wanted me to park. This industrial garage had once been a loading dock. Another big, tough-looking, no-nonsense kind of guy was patting down a man in a business suit. They were beside a door, inside of which were stairs. Carto and I were exempted from the pat-down, obviously on his friend's orders.

Vince greeted us warmly, motioning us toward a table covered by a red, checkered tablecloth. White cloth napkins were at three places, each encased in a bronze napkin holder with a silver swastika at its center. An old Italian-looking dude was cooking pasta in the open kitchen, which was served by two of the most voluptuous young gals I'd ever laid eyes on. I suspect the purpose of those gorgeous ladies may have been to distract poker players who had more money than brains. Vince was about 65, maybe 70, of Italian descent, and a rich neo-Nazi. He had slicked back white hair, a thin moustache, and wore thick, wire-rimmed spectacles with bifocal lenses. He wore a red smoking jacket, smoked Dunhill menthols the entire time, and immediately made it abundantly clear that he hated all Jews.

A life-sized, black-and-white photo of Benito Mussolini adorned a wall. Vince opened his illegal club to carefully selected players three nights a week. We ate with Vince in the ante room adjacent to the larger room where about 20 players sat at four of the six gaming tables. While a bartender mixed drinks for us, I looked into the gaming room. Each octagonal, mahogany table was covered with green felt, with ox blood leather cushioning along its edges. Four pedestal-style claw legs supported these tables. Players sat in overstuffed swivel chairs covered in tan leather, with rollers. The white ashtrays at each table were originally made for members of Hitler's Luftwaffe, with a black Swastika emblazoned in their center, Vince told us. "We're a smaller club", Vince said, "but it's not uncommon for six, or seven hundred grand to change hands here a coupla times a week." I asked Vince if he played. Stubbing out a Dunhill in an ancient ashtray, he smiled, replying, "Did Adolf Hitler have a huge gas bill?"

As Carto howled in laugher, Vince answered, "yeah. I play blackjack and Texas Hold 'em."

As the drinks were served, Vince said, "Willis always wants spaghetti with marinara meat sauce, with sautéed morel mushrooms. If you'd like something else, we've also got manicotti tonight, and some great New York strip steaks." I told Vince I'd have the spaghetti, which turned out to be delicious.

About 90 minutes later, Vince led Willis and I to the third floor. He led us through two locked, heavy metal doors, relocking each as we walked through. Toward the back side of the warehouse was a brick wall with two floor-to-ceiling windows. Every pane in each was about 18 inches tall and maybe 12 inches wide, tinted black. These were doors, disguised as windows. Vince stepped about two feet before the base of the wall, and dropped to his knees. He removed an old, thick, oval rope rug, about six feet long and four feet wide at the center, which was affixed to the floor by Velcro.

About six inches down was an iron lever. "Okay, guys," Vince said, "stand on each side of the frame." I heard a click as he applied his weight to the lever. He told us to push forward. The lower seven or eight feet of the window was rigged up to a sort of track, embedded in the floor behind the wall. As Willis and I pushed, the window/door propelled itself about eight feet into a vault-like room. Then it stopped. Motioning us inside, our host flipped on a light switch.

The cavernous room took my breath away, but not Carto's. He'd been here before. A life-sized mural of Adolf Hitler addressing a huge crowd covered an entire wall. This wall was 60 or 70 feet long, and at least fifteen feet high. On the opposite wall was a Confederate battle flag and a Third Reich flag, separated by a gigantic Swastika. On the side walls were murals featuring images of Charles Lindbergh, and the Nazi-funded American priest Charles Coughlin, George Lincoln Rockwell, and what appeared to be SS soldiers and members of the Hitler Youth, surrounded by shapely, blonde, blue-eyed Nordic girls.

The artwork was a gift from Carto's friend Francois Genoud, who'd been a close friend of Adolf Hitler. Mr. Genoud, whom historians refer to as the Swiss financier of the Third Reich, was a noted European banker and investor. He also raised money for the Palestine Liberation Organization and other anti-Israel terror groups until shortly before he died. Swiss authorities were investigating him for his murky ties and nefarious financial activities on Hitler's (and, Carto's) behalf when he committed suicide in 1996. These activities included acting as a 'fence' for those who illegally possessed stolen art work which rightfully belonged to the heirs of Jewish Holocaust victims. Two walnut display cases enshrined photos signed by Hitler, and books bearing his autograph. Taking up an entire, built-in bookshelf were old, pro-Nazi books, and tomes about eugenics. A first edition copy of 'The Protocols of the Learned Elders of Zion', signed by the inventor Henry Ford, was prominently displayed in the other case. Two first edition copies of Mein Kampf – in German - signed by Adolf Hitler, were also displayed.

Behind a thick, purple and gold velvet emblem of what looked something Masonic was a full-sized metal door with a combination and an indented lever. Once Vince opened it, he touched his fingers to another door. This one was fitted with a biometric lock. Seconds later, we were inside the vault. I noticed that each door was about three and a half inches thick. The vault measured about 20 by 20 feet, and on the floor were five locking strong boxes, with handles. Each loaded box weighed about 50 pounds, and they were already on an industrial-strength cart. "Willis, here's your gold," Vince said.

We rolled the cart out of the sealed area, and Vince shut the doors. He directed us to an old freight elevator that was manually operated, with a hydraulic mechanism.

"Why didn't we take this lift up," Willis asked, "instead of the stairs?" Vince, lighting another Dunhill, replied, "Because this elevator bypasses the first two floors. There's just brick walls." Once the boxes were securely in the back of my Range Rover, the three of us shook hands. "You've got close to three million in gold here, Willis," Vince said. "But if you buy Resistance Records, you'll own a gold mine."

We left Queens via the Verrazanno bridge, which is the longest suspension bridge in the Americas. This historic edifice marks the gateway to New York harbor, and was the world's longest suspension bridge until 1981. Every ship that arrives at the Port of New York and the Port of New Jersey must pass under it. Carto, who loved puns, said, "let's talk about the bridge I want to build to the next generation of racists." To white supremacists the term

17

racist isn't shameful; they speak it with pride. All the way back to Washington, Willis described his plan to broaden his appeal to this next generation of anti-Semites, white supremacists and Holocaust deniers. His vehicle for accomplishing this would be a two-year-old company called Resistance Records.

The managing partner was a Canadian skinhead named George Burdi. He and two other Holocaust deniers, Jason Snow and Joe Talic, had struck a profitable, highly responsive chord among 15-to-35-year-olds. But, Carto said, "these kids don't know how to maximize what they've got. Or maybe they do, but they're undercapitalized." Whichever the case, Carto wanted the company, and tasked me to represent him in dealing with the young Canadian haters. "Burdi will soon be in prison," Carto said. He had been convicted of assaulting a Jewish protester. "Too bad he didn't kill that kike bitch," Willis added.

"So, fly to Detroit next week, Todd. The accounting department will make your travel arrangements. Wine and dine those kids and spare no expense," Carto told me. "Hell, take 'em to strip clubs, rent 'em some hookers, and let 'em splurge at the best steakhouses in that nigger-infested dump. We'll make 'em an offer they can't refuse," he said. It was nearly 5:30 in the morning when we arrived at Liberty Lobby. Willis and I and the live-in custodian unloaded the five boxes and hauled them up to the third floor. Once they were securely stashed in the hidden safe inside Carto's apartment, Willis invited me to have coffee. "Todd," he said, "in many cases, ideology doesn't drive these young'uns to our side. They like violence, living on the edge, and proving that they're tough. They also seek a sense of belonging, which many of 'em don't have."

Stirring sugar into his mug, Carto added, "for those who aren't yet racists, Resistance Records is the device we'll use to snag 'em. From there, we'll convince 'em that our world view is correct."

Before I left, he opened one of the boxes, and took out a tube of Krugerrands. He handed me one, and said, "good work, Todd. We'll discuss your trip to Detroit when I get back from California." I flew to Detroit in early April, 1997. I stayed at the Detroit Athletic club, and visited the Resistance Records offices there and in Windsor, Ontario. I conveyed Carto's interest in buying the company, or at least a controlling interest. Upon my return a few days later, Willis, I and Mark Lane met for two hours in Carto's office, reviewing his offer and the counteroffer made by Jason Snow.

Lane, who always had an eye for manufacturing controversy for profit, said that once Willis owned the company, boycotts could be clandestinely organized by Liberty Lobby against record store chains like Tower Records who wouldn't stock Resistance Records products. Carto loved Lane's idea. "It'll be like when Hitler burned down the Reichstag!", he laughed. He told Lane he was "the world's smartest Jew." These boycotts and their organizers can be profiled in the SPOTLIGHT, Lane said. There would be lists of supporters throughout the USA, Lane told us, which can then receive complimentary subscriptions to the SPOTLIGHT, The Barnes Review, and other Liberty Lobby-funded publications. They could also receive, via email and regular mail, Resistance Records catalogues, and circulars promoting Carto's Liberty Library. Carto loved the idea. He said, "Blodgett, that's why this bearded, nigger-loving, brilliant Jew is on my payroll." Mark Lane smiled.

The next day, the Resistance Records offices in Detroit and in Windsor, Ontario, were raided, simultaneously, by U.S. and Canadian authorities. Strike forces from the state of Michigan and the U.S. government hit the Detroit location, while Canadian police and Provincial authorities raided the office in that country. George Burdi's house was also raided, but he wasn't home. He was in prison. But the Canadians didn't raid four storage units near Jason Snow's residence, where massive quantities of items were stored. For months, the staff members and offices had been under surveillance by a team of six investigators. I learned of these details once I began working as an informant for the bureau.

Authorities noticed that the company hadn't secured a license or paid sales tax, which legally justified the raids. At least a dozen officers spent nearly seven hours loading a semi-truck with computers and over 100 bankers boxes of company records and information on customers, bands, and promotional materials. Also confiscated was one of the three Resistance Records mailing lists, containing the names and addresses, and email addresses, of some 5,000 subscribers to Resistance magazine, and detailed information about distributors of the products. Carto's plans to buy the company were then on hold.

Six weeks after the raid, the authorities returned the material and no charges were filed. The company relocated to another Detroit location, became properly licensed, and was back in business. Resistance magazine, however, was placed on hold, and didn't resume publication until after Carto bought in. The next day, Lane called my office, and asked me to stop by his townhouse on Capitol Hill. He wanted to discuss marketing, and told me to replace Liberty Lobby's direct mail consultant, Tony Murray, with what he called a "more aggressive" fundraising firm. I balked, and told him that most top direct mail finance firms would probably rather try to raise money for a monument honoring Charles Manson.

"Utilize my being Jewish to positive effect," Lane told me. At the time, Liberty Lobby's subscriber lists netted approximately $60,000 in annual rental income from what are called end-users. Brokers of these files rented these names to clients for approximately $125 per thousand records. Direct mail marketers know that active subscribers to publications, and contributors to causes, and donors to political campaigns, are the best prospects for solicitation for other products, publications, political candidates, and charities. In 1995-97, Liberty Lobby had an active subscriber file of 165,000 records (names), and over 350,000 names of expired (former) subscribers to its three publications. These lists were cleaned every 90 days; names of deceased people were removed, addresses updated, and records of subscribers whose last name had changed due to marriage, divorce, or whatever, were made current.

Liberty Lobby also owned separate files consisting of about 220,000 names, of buyers of gold, silver, and books. The files comprising those 750,000 records were an asset to Carto's empire, just as any direct mail file is a revenue-producer to any corporate or political or non-profit entity. Carto later had Mark Lane create a separate corporation called AAA names and assigned ownership of these files to this entity. The owner of AAA names was Willis Carto.

"There's an enormous market out there," Lane said. "Let's tap it." There was, and we did.

Publications specializing in guns, coins, hunting, antiques, health foods and natural remedies, hunting suppliers like Cabela's, gun catalogues, and investment real estate ventures and high-end watercraft manufacturers, had been renting these files for decades when I came aboard Liberty Lobby in early 1995. After meeting with Lane, I visited the offices of Phillip Zodhiates, in Waynesboro, Virginia. Mr. Zodhiates owned Response Unlimited, a direct marketing firm which specialized in raising money for right-wing, conservative, and religious clients. He was no racist. Phil and his wife were Republicans who had adopted several children of color. He said a prayer over our food at lunch and eschewed profanity. As Lane had predicted, Zodhiates was concerned about his firm being associated with Willis Carto, SPOTLIGHT, the IHR, and Liberty Lobby. As Mark suggested, I told him that Liberty Lobby's lawyer was Jewish, and that FDR's son-in-law had been its chairman. That did the trick.

Zodhiates, surprised and relieved, presented a contract, as Lane had foreseen. Within three months of Response Unlimited taking over list promotion and rental, the net income – after commissions to brokers, and management fees paid to Zodhiates, and commissions paid to me – from such deals increased to twenty thousand dollars per month. By the time Carto fired me in late September, 1998, Liberty Lobby's net list rental income for the first eight months had already exceeded $385,000.

Willis Carto understood money laundering and profited from it, for many years. After he had embezzled over seven million dollars, while he had nine million more parked in secret accounts he feared would be found,

Willis went into over-drive on cleaning up dirty cash. This wasn't hard to do in the mid-1990s, and after Carto lost a nearly ten-million-dollar judgement to some rival neo-Nazis who had sued him, he wasn't taking any chances. Between 1991 and 1998, Willis Carto hid at least $15 million that I – as one of his facilitators – either knew about indirectly, or was involved with directly. This included some $7.5 million from the estate of Thomas Edison's grand-niece, Jean Edison Farrell. Willis wanted that cash out of the US, or converted to gold and hidden, or into accounts that he or Mark Lane controlled.

But first, all traces of it to Carto had to be severed. He also knew that he might be required to justify to courts in California and DC where all those millions went. Willis later was nailed for that, but he and Lane backdated corporate records, lied under oath, misled donors, created fake 'minutes' of Board meetings and intimidated outsiders and insiders, to salvage most of his personal fortune. To a greater extent than most observers ever realized, he succeeded. Carto paid $650,000 to the aging Nazi, Francois Genoud – who had been Adolf Hitler's personal banker – for his assistance in securing, and advice on how to hide, those funds. "Herr Genoud", as Willis called him, assisted in 1991 in securing about $7.5 million of Jean Farrell's $17 million bequest. In early 1996, Genoud - sensing that Liberty Lobby and the Cartos would soon lose in court – told Willis that casinos in Las Vegas, Atlantic City, and Reno, Nevada, were ideal for laundering money. My first trip to Atlantic City for Carto earned me $30,000. Had Carto ever learned that some of that money later ended up in the hands of black drug dealers, he'd have probably had a stroke. "The IHR lawyers are looking for my money," Willis told me, referencing the Institute for Historical Review. Carto had founded this Holo-caust-denying organization, but lost control of it sixteen years later, in 1993. Referencing his accounts, he said, "I'll empty 'em out, and then we'll clean up the cash." Checks made payable to dummy corporations, phony vendors, consulting services by so-called experts who did nothing, and to the Carto-owned SUN Radio Network, and to 'CASH' constituted phase one.

Carto kept millions of dollars in gold coins – Double Eagles – in two safes in his private apartment at Liberty Lobby's headquarters on Capitol

Hill. But he had much, much more money hidden in DC, New York city, and elsewhere. Approximately 40,000 crisp, 100-Dollar bills were cached in two large safes in Mike Piper's Capitol Hill apartment. Even more dirty dough was being stored in the basement of a Georgetown residence owned by a rabid anti-Semite who was associated with retired CIA officer Fletcher Prouty. Colonel Prouty, whom I met many times, is buried in Arlington national cemetery, and he was the inspiration for 'Mr. X' – played by Donald Sutherland – in Oliver Stone's movie, JFK. After Genoud committed suicide on May 30, 1996, Carto's money-shifting went into overdrive. At this time, he was trying to create paper trails which ostensibly extricated him, and his wife, from any connection to any of these funds. The goal was to then stash most of it in foreign accounts. But before he could deposit the money, it had to appear to have belonged to others, which was where the trail would stop.

Since 1996, many legal safeguards have been implemented to expose and prevent money-laundering, which then didn't exist. Willis Carto capitalized on that.

To comply with the Bank Secrecy act and other federal regulations, casino workers – even pit bosses, cage cashiers, and gaming floor personnel – are required to be on the lookout. This wasn't the case in 1996 and 1997, when Willis Carto and I cleaned up his dirty dollars. After 9-11, 2001, and again in 2011, the U.S. government really clamped down, hard, on money laundering. To prevent self-incrimination by me, Willis told me that these funds weren't illicit. Of course, I knew that this was nonsense, but it citing his statement helped, when I was subpoenaed in July of 1999 to testify in federal court in Washington, D.C., regarding Carto's theft of money, embezzlements, money laundering, clandestine deals, offshore accounts, and other financial crimes he committed.

My first, Carto-sponsored, clandestine trip to Atlantic city involved washing in excess of $1.3 million of C-notes, neatly packed in two suitcases. It transpired on short notice. A dapper older gentleman who was associated with longtime Carto insider named Henry Fischer was seated outside of

Willis's private office at Liberty Lobby when I arrived. He wore sunglasses, black brogues buffed to a high gloss, a snap-brim felt hat, and a 1940s-style Zoot suit. Minutes later, Carto – whose office was next to mine – asked me to join them in his office. I've since forgotten the dude's last name, but it was something along the lines of Scarpelli or Scandroli, or maybe Scarfenelli. The guy looked about 60 and was fit. He had a thin moustache and never removed his spectacles, his suit jacket, or his snap-brim.

During that 20-minute meeting, Willis asked me to drive to Atlantic City for a long weekend.

An hour later, I was in the large production area where The SPOTLIGHT was produced each week. Editor Fred Blahut signaled me to stop by his desk, in the newsroom. As I approached Fred's desk, he pointed to a handwritten note: 'Meet me at Sherrill's. 12 Noon.' Sherrill's was an old Capitol Hill restaurant, popular with Congressional staffers and Supreme Court employees. I nodded. Blahut was at a back booth when I arrived. "Todd, do you know who you met with this morning, in Carto's office?" Without awaiting my answer, Fred said, "he paints houses." Before I could respond, Blahut said, "he kills people. 'Paints' the walls and ceilings of wherever he shoots his victims with their blood."

"How do you know this, Fred?"

"Don't ask. But it's true. And this conversation never happened." Fred, whom I trusted and never knew to be wrong about Carto, was in very poor health, and only worked for Liberty Lobby because he needed the money. He suddenly stopped speaking as the waitress approached our booth. Setting down soup and a BLT sandwich that Blahut had ordered prior to my arrival, she asked, "are you eating, sir?" But I felt like I was underwater, trying to hear what was said. "Sir?" My neck jerked toward the server, and as I looked up at her, she again said, "sir?"

"Yeah, uh – well, I mean, no. No, thanks. I – I'm not hungry," I replied. "Water's fine, thanks." She eyed me, oddly, before handing me the tab. I placed a fifty dollar bill on the table and got up to leave. "Thanks, Fred. Keep the change," I told Blahut. As I rose to leave, he quietly said, "be careful, Todd." Years later, while working for the FBI and JTTF agents, I again heard the term, "paints houses" in that precise context. The phrase originated with the mob, and it meant exactly what Fred Blahut said.

Carto's longtime accountant, Blayne Hutzel, and Mark Lane handled the advance arrangements for that first weekend in Atlantic City. It always amazed me that, with the exception of Mike Piper, none of the Liberty Lobby staff knew, or cared to know, about Carto's clandestine, illegal activities.

On this trip, I was accompanied by an armed Nazi. Willis Carto never fully trusted anyone but his wife, Elisabeth, who was every bit as cynical, greedy, shadowy, as her husband. The cash I helped him to launder was all in hundred-dollar bills, and I was never told of its source. The total came to just over $1,300,000, not including the thirty grand Carto paid me, or the Ten Grand that each participant got. Three nights in hotels for the four suites, and restaurant and bar tabs, weren't cheap, either. The money was parceled out to the three scammers, but not in equal amounts.

As court documents and sworn depositions later revealed, some of this cash came from Carto's Kayla corporation. More was from Carto's tax-exempt Foundation to Defend the First Amendment, and from Carto's SUN Radio network. Another source was his Government Educational Foundation, and a non-profit entity called the Foundation for Economic Liberty. In the fall of 2016, it was reported by The Huffington Post that Carto had given Republican Roy Moore, then the GOP nominee for a U.S. Senate seat from Alabama, $1,000 from an FEL account. The Judges in Washington, DC and California, and the IHR's lawyers, were astonished by Carto's and Lane's illegal cash maneuvers.

Between about 1982 and 1990, at the urging of FDR's son-in-law, Curtis Dall, Carto began structuring his corporate entities so he could shift assets of any and all of them around on a moment's notice. This made them less attractive targets for lawyers and lawsuits, and enabled Carto to buy time and evade later court rulings. On the books of each nonprofit, such funds – including payments – were always listed as loans. This enabled Carto, once the money was removed, to claim that those monies didn't actually belong to the entities. But those tainted funds didn't stay parked with Carto's cronies for long.

Carto's trusted lackey, Mike Piper, stored several million dollars of Carto's C-notes at his apartment on Capitol Hill. He also kept a large quantity of gold coins there, after the Carto's Escondido, California home was raided by a SWAT Team comprised of county, municipal, and state law enforcement officers. Helicopters, police dogs and over 25 heavily-armed officers converged on the grounds of the estate. Carto's extensive gun collection, computers, filing cabinets, and over 30,000 pages of documents were confiscated, and returned six months later. This was in the mid-1990s. In Carto's guest house lived a Nazi named Michael Brown, who had been a bodyguard for the American Nazi Party leader George Lincoln Rockwell, who was assassinated in 1967.

On the morning of my first Carto-sponsored trip to Atlantic City, I met Willis and an illegally armed, neo-Nazi thug at Sherrill's cafe. Carto told me to walk over to Piper's apartment, which was a block away. Willis said he and his pistol-packing Nazi would be there in about 20 minutes. "We'll get the cash and bring it back here," Carto said. "Are you alone, Blodgett?", Mike Piper asked, from his side of his door.

"Yeah, open up." He unlocked the door and stood in the entryway in his boxer shorts. Once inside, I asked Piper if he was alone. He nodded no, placing his finger to his lips. "Shhh," he whispered, pointing to a closed door. "Blodgett, you guys are supposed to be here at nine, but it's only 7:40," he said, softly. When I told him that Carto would arrive in under 20 minutes, he panicked. Racing down the narrow hallway to a bedroom, cursing, he awakened someone. Back in his foyer, Piper warned: "Breathe one word to Willis about my guest, Todd, and The Des Moines Register gets a juicy story about how the son of a top Iowa Republican lawmaker raises major money for Jew haters."

Something was up. Piper, a cigar smoker, had ashtrays throughout his place. I lit a Marlboro. Seconds later, a barefoot, 30-ish, effeminate black dude wearing a ladies' negligee, a cheap necklace and bracelets, emerged. Slipping on a Washington Redskins T-shirt, he bitched about being abruptly put out. Piper handed him three one-hundred dollar bills. The tranny wore earrings and his eyelids were lined with green eye shadow. My jaw dropped upon seeing this spectacle. In the guy's unzipped duffel bag were a blonde wig, padded bra and high-heeled, red shoes. He had on bright red lipstick and his fingernails were painted yellow and blue. "Hey, howya doin', honey?", he asked. "Fine, sir," I replied, pointing to the door. Offended, he said, "Firth of all, thweetie, thith gorgeouth girl ith not no thirr."

Pointing to himself, he continued, "thecond – and pleath lithen to what Ahh ith thayin' – thith thweet girlth name ith Thabrina. Doeth thweetie underthand?" As he struggled to squeeze into a dark green, tight-fitting skirt, I cracked up. "Okay, Sabrina." Still laughing, I shut the door and said, "Piper, does Willis know you're gay? Or would he and David Duke and your SPOTLIGHT fans approve of you sleeping with a black, homosexual trans-vestite?" I got no response.

I never ratted him out, and his sexual preference didn't matter to me. Later, I learned that Elisabeth and Willis knew that Piper was gay.

But because Mike hated Jews and authored Holocaust-denying books, articles, Op-Eds and other anti-Semitic propaganda, he was employed by Liberty Lobby for over 33 years. Willis and I carried the cash-filled Samsonite luggage to Lib-Lob, escorted by the armed Nazi. Carto, with the smile of a jackal, was ecstatic that his ill-gotten gains were about to be cleaned up, and made invisible to the authorities. His method was inefficient, redundant, and unnecessary. But I followed orders.

At his office, Willis gave me a list of the participants and the names of the hotels they'd be staying at in Atlantic City. Using my cell phone, I called them and asked them the password. A different one was used for each participant. Carto chose these passwords: among them were Eva, Klara, and Blondie:

respectively, Adolf Hitler's wife, mother and dog. Samsonite suitcases were filled with packets of hundred-dollar bills, and each fraudster laundered approximately $350,000. Once in Atlantic City, I met each partner in crime, separately, in their hotel rooms. I'd have enjoyed having Linda join me for this trip, but for obvious reasons, she stayed home. Carto's cronies bought high-dollar chips at several casinos, and cashed out some of them a few hours later.

Each fraudster turned over to me about $250,000 worth of uncashed chips and cashiers checks which represented the balance on the Saturday evening before the mission was completed. During this time, Carto's thug disappeared.

In the 1990s, casino staffers didn't routinely check gaming tables to verify that gamblers cashing chips in had actually won at Baccarat, Black Jack, Five Card Stud, Texas Hold 'em, Seven Card Draw, and other games. That's no longer the case. Once Carto's facilitators bought the high-dollar chips, some of which were worth five, or ten thousand dollars, the placement phase of the gig was done. When they cashed out their chips and filled out the required paperwork, which included providing their Social Security number, they began the layering step. When cashiers checks were issued, that further insulated the funds from being tied to Willis. In the 1990s, casino cashiers were all human. That's not the case now. But dealing with people instead of machines made facilitating this fraud easier.

Upon being issued either cashiers checks or money orders, the layering was accomplished. Parking this money, and turning over some of those chips to Willis, removed Carto from the mix. It also commenced the integration stage. Once these monies were deposited in, and subsequently withdrawn via wire transfer or check, they were then back with Willis Carto. The funds were then fully integrated, and out of reach of the authorities and Carto's creditors. Over several months, Carto also kept well over $2 million worth of the casino chips, for later cash-outs.

Via third parties, Carto bought gold coins and bullion. Not all casinos then automatically deducted taxes from winnings, but Carto's scammers paid income tax on their pay-outs. Willis kicked back cash to them for such taxes and Blayne Hutzel issued receipts, falsely indicating they donated money to Liberty Lobby and other tax-exempt nonprofits under Carto's control. In so doing, they forced U.S. taxpayers to subsidize Holocaust Denial. The IRS, as far as I know, never caught on to any of these scams.

This included Piper's, Lane's, and Hutzel's lies, which they later told under oath in court, that they hadn't helped Willis launder, embezzle or hide money, or evade taxes.

One reason this could take place was that the participants each filled out the required paper work, that included forms which casinos must report to the IRS naming gamblers who cashed out $10,000 or more. Another reason it worked: the scammers reported their purported winnings as income to the Internal Revenue Service and paid taxes on them. With these cronies being given money for taxes and the faked donation receipts mitigating their tax bill, and their returns being properly and timely filed, risk was minimal, and no one was the wiser. Even after all of the costs were taken into account, these trips enabled Willis Carto to retain most of the eight or nine million bucks he sent to Atlantic City and Reno.

I collected the checks and chips from the participants and turned them over to Carto. Some of the money later ended up in numbered accounts in banks in Costa Rica, Grand Cayman, Switzerland, Liechtenstein, and other, far-off locales. Some went to gold. Participants on other trips to Atlantic City included an associate of Holocaust denier Carl Hottelet, and a David Duke campaign aide named Travis McCoy. Years later, an IRS agent I worked with told me that the laundering technique Carto used is called "smurfing". Smurfing means that a large chunk of dirty bills are parsed out to multiple fraudsters who take part in cleaning up dirty cash via separate, organized transactions. In banking circles, it also can include making structured deposits with laundered dough, to avoid triggering banks and other financial institutions to file legally mandated documents which are supposed to alert the authorities to money laundering. Effectively, smurfing is a structuring technique.

An article in the SPOTLIGHT by Marty Mann was published shortly thereafter. Its headline: 'Congress Ignores dirty Money-laundering'. Shamelessness and hypocrisy were endemic to Willis Carto's world.

Several Atlantic City casinos have paid hefty fines for failing to report information relating to customers who walked away with checks and/or cash which exceeded $10,000 in the 1990s. The IRS learned that on 106 occasions between 1993 and 1998, patrons who cashed out $10,000 or more in claimed winnings weren't reported, as required by law. Whether they were actual winners or money launderers, they weren't ever charged, or caught. Weeks before Liberty Lobby and Carto were slapped with that $10 million judgment by the California court, I asked Willis how he planned to account for his ill-gotten, illegally hidden and laundered gains. This conversation took place in the back dining room of Billy Martin's tavern in Georgetown. Reaching into his suit jacket pocket, Carto pulled out a single, handwritten sheet of notebook paper and handed it to me. Upon reading it, I said, "Willis, this accounts for only seven million bucks, and half your claims here are pure lies. No judge will accept this."

Snatching it back, he snapped, "That's all he's gettin'. No Jew Judge will screw me outta my money. Period." Incidentally, the Judge that Willis referenced wasn't Jewish. Carto's ruse failed in court. Just before Labor Day of 1998, Carto asked me to accompany him to visit the widow of Curtis Dall, Mrs. Katherine Dall. His goal was to snag a half million dollars from her. As I was ousted later that month, I never learned if Willis got that money. An IRS agent from Pittsburgh who was with the JTTF asked me about these shenanigans within six months of my signing on with the FBI. This was at Washington, DC's Buca di Beppo Italian restaurant on Connecticut avenue. Knowing I couldn't be charged for any crimes I committed prior to becoming a paid, full-time federal informant, I told him about those trips to Atlantic city. The FBI and IRS agents who oversaw my activities already knew all about those them, and my role. This knowledge was a big factor in the FBI and JTTF recruiting me. But as my agreement with the FBI covered immunity for any past illegalities I may have committed in service to Carto and Pierce, it was safe to disclose such. Over cigars in my office at the Kennedy Warren, this agent – who is now an esteemed Professor of Criminology – said, "hey, when a movie's made about this, maybe Brian Dennehy should play me!" Now, Mr. Dennehy is a fine actor, but now, he's too old to play my old buddy the IRS agent, who retired as a Fed in 2015.

Over the years, my mind has revisited the night I became a drug addict. The junkie who introduced me to crack cocaine was a highly paid, DC-based, WASPy Republican with ties to GOP Presidents from Nixon to George W. Bush. My involvement in the drug realm didn't begin at a crack house in the hoods of America's Capital city. It began after a boozy evening at an iconic, red brick, old-line establishment bastion of power called the University club of Washington, DC - not at some crack house in any hood.

But I was no stranger to DC's crack houses, and I witnessed the violence and craziness for which they're well known. That was because too many times, it involved me.

CHAPTER TWO

The enormous junkie's knife that was up against my throat could ruin my lunch plans, the new shirt my wife bought me, and wreck my whole day. Having my larynx pierced wasn't appealing, and involuntary tracheotomies performed without anesthetics aren't my thing. This was in late October of 2001 – about seven weeks after the 9/11 attacks. While I and my FBI handlers were intensely focused on domestic terrorism and violence, my drug addiction had led me directly into some potentially serious violence. As the angry doper's eyes bored into mine, I realized this situation was far scarier than getting punched out by the racist hillbilly who, two years earlier, had knocked me around in a West Virginia bar.

My confrontation with this crazed addict took place in one of the worst sections of Washington, D.C., inside a crack house. The switchblade-wielding, oversized crackhead had the home field advantage. He was from the hoods of Baltimore; I'm from Iowa. He stepped back, waving the blade around in a fury, slicing air. I was to meet with the FBI in just under seven hours. He'd have been as shocked to know I was a full-time, paid informant as the agents I reported to would've been to know they'd hired a doper. This huge ex-con was determined to keep me in that crack house until a dealer delivered the cocaine He had ordered - which was two hours late. I hadn't slept, showered, or shaved in over 24 hours. It was eight a.m., and I needed to get the hell out of there.

As I'd not see the FBI agents until 3 p.m., there was time to get myself together. I was no longer high, which would help in convincing this unpredictable, irate brute to let me leave his chick's apartment in one piece. "C'mon, dude," I said, "I've gotta go."

"Check ya self, whitey, befo' I breaks my foot off in yo' butt! What I say? Y'all ain't goin' nowhere. Least not till my boy get here. Ya feel me?" In ghetto jargon, "feel me" is slang for understanding what's been said. Three years as a junkie in the Hoods enabled my fluency in Ebonics. The crackhead was Jonesing, which is when a drug abuser's body wants more drugs but doesn't have any. That's a 'Jones' state. "Dude," I asked, "what makes your Jones my problem?"

"Dis here switchblade."

"Tyree, it's been two hours since your guy said he'd be here. Dealers need sleep, too. He's off duty; back with his chick. Turned off his phone." The giant backhanded a cheap table lamp, breaking it.

"It don't make no different. We waitin' fo' da nigga, 'cause him comin'. Chill. We be kickin' it fo' a minute. 'Dat homey comin'." In ghetto parlance, a 'minute' means anywhere from 60 seconds to about five years, depending on the judge. Time was of as little concern to Tyree as it was significant to me. He had no money, no cell phone, no job, no home of his own, no car and no self-worth. He was down to his last five cigarettes and his girl had left to appear in court, and wouldn't return for hours. Tyree, whom I'd met only hours before, had been out of prison for about a month. He said he'd served time for aggravated assault, which didn't surprise me. Hours earlier, he'd traded away his girlfriend's Food Stamp card for crack, at fifty cents on the dollar. He was becoming increasingly irate over the delay in getting his 8-ball – an eighth of an ounce – of crack cocaine. "What part don't you understand, Tyree?"

"I'm sayin' you stayin'. I ain't wants no drama. 'Dat nigga comin'."

"Maybe," I replied, pointing to an unframed poster of a black Jesus on the kitchen wall. "He's coming, too. Someday. But even if your guy gets here before ten, I don't have that kind of time."

"YO! What I care about yo' time? "What it is", he yelled, as I stepped back to avoid being sliced.

"Excuse me?," I asked. "Ain't doin' dat. Ain't healthy to disresseck a nigga in he crib." In the Hoods, a crib isn't only something a baby sleeps in – it's also a home. "'Dis here ain't no negotiation. When a cracka roll up in my nigga hood, he do shit my way. Stop triflin'. Soon's him leave outta here, y'all can get yo' white, rich, Republican ass back to Mayberry." The first person to jokingly ask if I was from Mayberry was Lee Atwater. President Reagan's adviser Lyn Nofziger and his chief of staff, Don Regan, had also cracked wise about my small town roots.

Even while professionally infiltrating the Aryan Nations and the Ku Klux Klan, and hanging out with the world's most violent, racist skinheads, I had never heard black neighborhoods described as "nigga hoods" until then. Having been raised as a churchgoing, conservative Presbyterian in a traditional home where the n-word wasn't spoken hadn't prepared me for the frequency with which I was hearing the term. It was a close call between which of my acquaintances used it more: the racists that the FBI paid me to spy on, or the gang-bangers with whom I got high. The guys in the hood probably had the edge. It was said more by blacks I knew than when Chris Rock played to a packed auditorium. Tyree then said, "dis here nigga hood ain't no country club, where you spoiled, light skin suckas always gets they way."

"No kidding?"

"Don't get smart-assy. Hear?," he replied. "Y'all ain't in no position. Nigga-hatin', bitch ass honkeys thinks they cool. 'Dem crackas always be messin' with us black folk."

"For someone who supposedly dislikes blacks, I sure spend lots of time with them."

"I ain't sayin' YOU hatin' on us. Y'all's okay. I mean, fo' a white dude."

"I'm okay, for a white guy?"

"Just sayin'. My cuz, and my bitch, and da homeys 'round here says y'all cool, so you is."

"Well, that's nice to know. I'd hate to see what you might do if you didn't like me."

"I knows you be knowin' some nigga-hatin' white peoples."

"I know some bigots. In my work, they're sort of an occupational hazard."

"Say, what?" He sliced the air again, trying to intimidate me. The knife-play was all part of his one-man, ghetto power show. But accidents happen, and becoming a bloody statistic wasn't on my 'to do' list. "Damn it, Tyree," I said, as I sidestepped again to avoid being cut, "That was CLOSE. You're twice my size. You don't need a weapon to make your point."

"If y'all ain't watch ya mouth, and stop yo bitchin', you gonna get my point." Suddenly, he sliced the air, this time missing my throat by about two inches. He was being reckless, and creeping me out. "You was talkin' about Jesus. Maybe next time y'all say he name, you be wiff dat Jew. Don't gets me no madder than I already is! Don't gimme no mouth; you dig?" I wasn't digging it, but I got it. Spinning around, the behemoth threw the knife directly into the Jesus poster, nailing Christ in the forehead. "That's an interesting way to show respect for the son of God," I said.

"Shut up and chill. Back in da day, yo dumb, white ass musta rode to school on da short bus. Zip it."

He was coming down from his high. He lit a KOOL, exhaled and said, "keep it real, Light skin."

"Keep WHAT real? Who likes the kind of reality that requires dodging a knife?"

"Dawg," he said, "my bitch done tell me y'all's daddy done gots his self a fancy job wiff da President.

She say him some kinda judge, or sumpin' like dat. Do 'dat be true?"

"My father is with the Bush administration."

"Whazz him do?"

"He adjudicates legal cases - issues rulings on administrative law relating to health care."

"I hears 'dat y'all knowed Ronnie Reagan, done worked fo' him."

"I met Reagan when I was 15, five years before he became President. I was on his White House staff, as was my sister. What of it?"

"So, knowin' Prezz-i-dints done run in y'all family." Ahh ain't never met me no Republican crackhead befo'. What would Ronnie say if him knowed you smokin' crack in 'dis hood, gettin' high wiff niggas?"

"He'd probably say I should've just said no."

"Y'all here 'cause after all dem years hangin' wiff low-life, Republican riff-raff, you wants to hang wiff a better class of losers." That was one way of describing how my life had changed. "Y'all is lucky, havin' all 'dem classy connections. Rich, powerful peoples in they high places."

He was implying that this was why he didn't harm me as he performed his Zorro-in-the-ghetto routine. But I played along. "What?"

"Dat's the onlyest reason I ain't takes yo money." There was another reason he wasn't taking my money. But I wasn't going to introduce him to my loaded .380 Walther PPK unless I had to. "I done did me some time fo' agg-uhh-vay-tidd assault."

"Somehow, I knew you weren't busted for insider trading."

It was a safe bet he hadn't qualified for reduced prison time for good behavior. He lit another KOOL, took a long drag, and exhaled smoke through his nose. He peered through the door's peephole, sensing no risk in turning his back to me. He couldn't imagine a smaller white man whom he believed to be unarmed fighting him on his turf. I'm 5'9", but he was about 6'5", and at least 320 pounds. Turning around, he said, "Y'all gots money, and Ahh needs me my fix! After you pays, y'all can leave. Ahh ain't 'zackly lookin' to play no front nine at yo' country club." When the 'high' wears off, junkies become more reasonable, sociable, and amenable to logic. It's all relative, of course. I reached into my pocket, pulled out my money clip, and peeled off two C-Notes.

"Here," I said, as I stuffed the bills into the addict's hand. "These Benjamins are yours. They'll cover an 8-ball, with enough left over for smokes, and then some." Glancing at the cracked, filthy, chipped, charred glass tubes we'd nearly destroyed with overuse, I said, "uhh, you also might want to buy some new crack pipes. Just sayin'." The big man smiled, exposing two chrome teeth, and returned his knife to his back pocket. "Ain't nothin' like a crackhead dat gots a fat wallet, even if him white! Ahh thanks ya fo' havin' my back." He high-fived me, and slapped me with a tighter bear hug than I thought was humanly possible. It cracked the joints in my back and hurt my spine as he lifted me six inches off of the floor. "My man!," he said, as I was temporarily unable to breathe, and felt my disks slightly compress. "Thanks fo' helpin' a nigga in need!" No problem, I said, as I caught my breath, straightened my posture, and rubbed my sore back. "Is y'all okay? I ain't mean to hurt ya."

"I'll be all right. I hope. But I've gotta go." With superhuman, strength like that, I thought, this giant needed no switchblade. "You be one cool cracka!," he said, as he unlocked the door and removed the chain latch. "hey, where's ya'll from?"

"We live in northern Virginia, but my wife and I are from Iowa."

"Ahh gots me a cuz in Cleveland."

"That's Ohio. I'm from IOWA. It's in the middle of the Midwest."

"I-o-wa? Iowa ... lotta corn, and shit dere, right?"

"Lots of both. It's primarily an agricultural state."

"I betcha dat 'fore y'all done come to DC, da closest thing you seen to a gang were watchin' 'Cops.'"

"Pretty much, yeah." As I left, Tyree said, "Come back any time, white boy. Is y'all meetin' a dealer?"

"Not this time."

After 30 months as a junkie, and 18 months infiltrating the KKK, neo-Nazis, and racist skinheads, I was accustomed to seeing and sometimes experiencing violence. Not only threats of it, but also the real deal. I learned that the key is to always remain calm and not be provocative. To be safe, I always was prepared to flick off the safety of the loaded .380 in my front pants pocket.

I always kept a round chambered, which saved my white butt from getting kicked more than once. To survive in the hood, white junkies can't leave much to chance. But packing heat didn't keep my back from hurting like hell.

I was the only white person on the crowded elevator, and the most unkempt. Everyone else was black or Hispanic. The aroma of a spray disinfectant was evident, probably to mitigate the odor of urine. A little black girl who was about three years old held her mother's hand as she stared at me like I was from Mars. I smiled at her, but she hid behind her mom. Her mother disdainfully eyed me in a suspicious manner. "Your daughter's pretty," I said. The lady looked me over, focusing on my wrinkled clothes, unshaven face, bloodshot eyes, and uncombed hair. After an uncomfortable silence, I said, "she's shy?"

"She ain't shy," the woman said, as the doors opened and they exited. "She just don't like crackheads."

My car was parked on a side street about two hundred yards east of the apartment building where I'd spent the last 12 hours. I'd been a junkie since late 1998, and had signed up as a paid FBI informant in March of 2000. I'd kept my addiction a secret from my wife, my parents, siblings, grandparents, friends, and the FBI agents who directed my work infiltrating neo-Nazis, racist skinheads, Holocaust deniers, members of the Ku Klux Klan and the Aryan Nations. I was discreet about carrying guns in DC, where doing so is illegal. I'm what some would call a gun nut, and have been since the age of eight. My father's fellow orthodontist and business partner gave me a .410 bore, bolt-action shotgun that year – 1969. Since then, I've bought, sold, hunted with, carried, shot, and traded hundreds of them. Rifles, revolvers, shotguns, handguns – you name it, and I either own it, have owned it, or fired or traded or carried it. In 2012, carrying a Ruger .380 prevented my being robbed of $500 cash, and my wallet.

An editorial was published about the incident in an Iowa publication, where the columnist referenced me as "Todd Blodgett, Gunslinger". In a news article, the sub-headline was: "Some Locals say Todd Blodgett is Trigger-Happy". I'm a member of the U.S. Concealed Carry Association and an NRA Life member. I can legally carry in over 40 states, but not in Washington, D.C.

However, technicalities have never stopped me from doing what I think is right, even when the price is heavy. Herman Melville wrote that "truth uncompromisingly told will always have its jagged edges." I like that because it's true. Being truthful, living honestly, and speaking with frankness is my credo. But pushing the envelope has at times been problematic. In 1989, while serving on the staff of the Republican National Committee, I brought a 9 mm Sig-Sauer model P-226, double-action, with two loaded, 15-round clips, to the RNC headquarters on Capitol Hill. Within hours, Don Todd – the director of Opposition Research - admonished me, and ordered me to "take that damn thing home, and don't bring it back!" Atwater also chewed me out for that one.

That incident earned me a reputation as an uncompromising Conservative – jagged edges and all.By this point in my drug addiction, in 2001, I was a familiar sight in several DC hoods. As I approached my car, my cell phone rang. A small child's voice said, "Mister Todd!" The caller was the young son of one of my crackhead friends. Corey was about six, and a very smart, good kid. He was from a broken home, and lived in the building next to the one I'd just left. I'd smoked crack with his mom, Tamika.

Corey had a little sister named Shaveeka. Corey and I were buddies, and I'd take him to McDonalds on occasion. "What's up, Corey?" The boy said, nearly out of breath, said, "I can't finds me no PO-leece. My momma need yo' help!" I asked him to slow down and be more specific. "My momma let a bad dude in our crib. They be in she bedroom. Him gonna hurt her."

"Who is he?"

"I ain't know he name, but him maked me leave. I'm in da hall outside our crib. Gots me a key. Dude tryin' to have he way wiff my momma." Realizing that a first grader knew what was happening made me feel sorry for kids who grow up so fast. "Momma say him ain't s'posed to be in they, 'cause a Judge done slap him wiff a restrainin' order. Shaveeka in she playpen. She cryin'. I be scared, Mister Todd."

"I'll be there, Corey. But why would he ignore a Judge's restraining order?"

"Mama say it be 'cause dat's how he why. Da dude just be why 'dat way."

"What?"

"Him ain't why right." Corey was referencing how the dude was wired. Anyone who disobeys a court-issued restraining order isn't someone wired to respect the law. His fear, and concern for his infant sister, while their mom was being attacked, did it for me. "Corey," I said, "I'll be there in three minutes."

Their apartment building lacked a staffed front desk or security personnel. Racing up the stairs to the second floor, I met Corey in the hall. He carefully unlocked the door. I told him to shut it behind me, and stay put. The TV volume was turned up, and two chipped, half-eaten bowls of oatmeal were on a card table, along with a knocked-over coffee cup. The threadbare, wall-to-wall carpet, and the walls in dire need of a paint job, matched the cheap décor.

Corey's sister was in her playpen, crying, needing a diaper change. Muffled groans emanating from the back bedroom indicated Corey was right about his mother being in trouble. I pulled my .380, flicked off the safety, and inched over to the bedroom. The door was cracked open about two inches, enabling me to see Corey's fears. I've never killed or injured anyone with a firearm, and hope I never have to. But perception is power, especially when it's in a barrel attached to a trigger. The gang banger was atop his victim on

40

a twin bed. Placing my left index finger on my lips as Tamika saw me was a good move, as she stayed quiet. Her unwelcome guest was too preoccupied with forcing himself on her to notice me.

Side-stepping to the right of the broken down bed, I was prepared to fire, if necessary. About three seconds later, the creep averted his eyes toward me. Slowly, and fearfully, the miscreant turned his head in my direction. As he saw the gun, his eyes widened and his jaw dropped. He said nothing. "I don't miss much at this range," I warned. My .380 was two feet from his temple. He froze with fear, staring at the gun. "Put your clothes on, loser, or I'll paint the ceiling with your brains."

I wasn't going to shoot him, but he didn't know that, and fear influences behavior. Tamika rolled off the bed, and donned a robe. The fool was in shock, didn't move, or blink an eye. "You'll decide how this ends, asshole," I warned. "But the offer", I said, while chambering a round, "expires in five seconds."

I asked Tamika if she was OK. "I am NOW, Mister Todd," she replied. "Y'all is my friend. I thank ya." With my gun still aimed at the thug's head, I backed up about two feet. He placed his hands atop his head and kept staring at me, with his mouth wide open. "Tamika, does Rollo still live in this building?"

"Him sure do. He be right upstairs. Him probably ain't up yet, though, 'cause it's only ten fo-tee five."

"Your son's outside your front door. He's worried. Have Corey bring Rollo down." As she made for the door I turned to the gang banger, who was pulling on his socks. "Stay where you are, shit head. This is loaded with hollow point rounds. They'll blast your thick skull wide open and explode on impact."

"Y'all gonna shoots me?" I told him I'd call it taking out the trash. "Don't shoots my ass!"

"No worries there, dude. If I squeeze off a round, it'll be a head shot. Less noise."

"Rounds is loud when they fired."

"I wasn't referring to the sound the gun makes. You know," I told him, "creeps like you sicken me. You violate a judge's order and assault an innocent lady. It's bad enough what you did to Tamika. But putting her son through this, trying to rape his mother while his little sister's in her playpen, crying? I'm mad enough to just - "

Interrupting me, he yelled, "don't play God."

"God will decide your fate, in the afterlife. But I may hasten your exit from this one. Tamika's my friend, dirt bag. And I've got two nephews Corey's age and the wife and I are trying to make a baby. You ticked off the wrong guy."

"Lemme off 'dis time. I be goin' some place."

"You're not calling the shots, homey, and I know where you're going."

"Where I'm goin'?"

"Eventually, to Hell. But today, to an Emergency Room, if you're lucky." He kept his eyes on the gun. "Make one move and you've got lunch with the devil." The stricken look in his eyes indicated he feared being blown away. This citizen of the hood had likely never encountered a white man with a loaded gun. He was probably questioning my sanity. That's another advantage, incidentally - when your adversaries fear you may be crazy. "Y'all be callin' da cops?"

"Why? So you can rat me out for packing heat, and threatening your life? No way. Some liberal judge would blame society for what you did. Besides, I like being the judge and jury."

"So, I ain't goin' down fo' diss?"

"Oh, you're definitely going down. But not at the hands of the law."

"SHII-EET", the thug replied. "Yeah, that's right. Because you stepped into a steaming pile of it."

As I slipped a Marlboro into my mouth and lit it, I said, "you should've stayed in bed today. Instead, you acted like the loser you are. Now, you'll pay." The man's life was never in danger, but he didn't know that. "If this thing had a silencer", I said, "your next stop would be a dumpster. So, you'll deal with a different type of silencer."

"What kind?"

"His name's Rollo, and he'll be here in a minute. A short minute," I replied, blowing smoke in his face. He lowered his head, gulping, his fate clearly registering. "Rollo won't need a gun to silence you." That threat was real, and this thug's appointment for a semi-professional ass-kicking would soon begin. As he reached for his boots, I said, "leave 'em there. I sometimes keep extra heat in my boots, so I'm thinking you might, as well. Nice try, though. I've got a buddy who needs some boots, so they'll leave with me. Besides, it'll be awhile before you'll need any boots."

"Why?"

"Because it's hard to walk with broken legs, knees, and ankles. Touch those boots, and I'll blow your fuckin' hands off." Rollo then burst into the room, with Tamika and Corey. "Hey, Mistuh Todd," Rollo said, as he and I bumped fists. "Ah gots 'dis." With my .380 still aimed at the gang banger, I replied,

"I'm sure you do. But check this loser for weapons. He's probably packing." Sure enough, the creep had a mini switchblade in his boot and a box cutter in his pocket. "I'd love to stay for the show, Rollo, but I'm out of here. Have fun doing your thing."

"I show will," Rollo said, while yanking his heavy belt out of its loops. Not that he needed it. "WAIT!", the creep screeched. "It weren't like you thinkin'! Bitch done AXED fo' it!" I never heard the rest of that loser's BS, because Rollo's kick to his head knocked him off the bed and out cold. "You surprised me, Rollo. You didn't use your belt or your fists," I said, walking toward the door. "Dem gettin' used, soon's dis nigga come 'round, him gettin' 'em BOTH. After dat, I'm-a drop kick his ass out into da hall," Rollo announced, as he pocketed the thug's knife and box cutter. "I don't doubt that, Rollo, but please be careful. Don't catch a murder charge and make me an accessory."

"I ain't killin' da MoFo. But when Ahh finishes, him gonna wish I did." I high-fived Corey, who told me I was his "hero". But I'm no hero, never have been. I've done things that aren't cool. But I'll never pass up an opportunity to punish anyone who is so cruel to innocent, helpless victims, especially those who harm women, children, or animals. We only pass through life once, and I believe we should make this old world a better place than we found it. My view on firearms is that when good people have them, it's good for good people. If that makes me a vigilante, so be it. I'm not saying everyone should carry a gun and threaten violence to resolve differences with troublemakers. But it's worked well for me.

As I drove out of the hood, my mind drifted back to a day in the late fall of 1998. That's when I received a strange phone from a very strange man. It was election night, November, 1998, at the University club of Washington, D.C. I was shooting pool in the upstairs bar of the University club of Washington, D.C., with some buddies when my cell phone began vibrating. The bar was then called the men's grille. As we were watching the midterm elections returns, I let the call go to voice mail. It was marked PRIVATE, and I'm uneasy not knowing who calls me. The Democrats did better than expected that year, but a bright spot for me was my father's re-election. He was seeking his fourth term in the Iowa Legislature, where he was the Deputy Majority Leader. He was first elected in 1992 and this term would be his last. As my parents were also University club members, several of them congratulated me on Dad's victory. Whoever called me left no message. The next night, while drinking at the corner table with my regular group, my cell phone again vibrated.

Club rules prohibited cell phones unless the ring was silent. The screen again read 'PRIVATE'. I excused myself and took the call in the cloak room. "Todd Blodgett?", the caller asked. "Yes."

"I'll pay you two hundred-fifty thousand dollars for your Resistance Records stock. Interested?"

"Who's this?" The caller identified himself as Dr. William Pierce, and asked if we could meet. I'd heard of Pierce, whose bestselling novel, 'The Turner Diaries', was like a bible for the racist Far Right in the U.S. and elsewhere. His organization, The National Alliance, was headquartered on a compound comprised of several hundred acres in West Virginia. His publications and radio broadcasts were believed by federal investigators to have inspired the 1995 Oklahoma City bombings and other hate-motivated violence in the USA, and Europe. "How'd you find out I own the shares?"

"We'll discuss that in person. How's tomorrow? One o'clock?"

"Okay. Do you want to come to my office? I've got a feeling you know the address."

"I do. Maybe we'll go there afterwards. How about we meet at Martin's tavern?"

The stock certificates Pierce wanted were class 'A' shares which represented the controlling interest in a corporation called Resistance Records. I owned them due to a convoluted payment of funds owed to my ad agency by Liberty Lobby and its subsidiaries. It was a mistake for me to have ever affiliated with Carto, and for my advertising agency to represent The SPOTLIGHT and The Barnes Review. But this offer was too tempting; I got greedy and have paid for it ever since.

From day one, this client and his numerous, well-funded, tax-exempt subsidiaries were extraordinarily lucrative. Carto provided me with office space, a secretary, an assistant, and two other, part-time employees. During the nearly four years I was affiliated with the Liberty Lobby, my direct, indirect, and deferred compensation, commissions and payments to my advertising agency amounted to an average of approximately of $350,000 a year, net. I also earned another approximately $125,000, personally, from my retainer fees and commissions on money I raised for Liberty Lobby and direct mail list rental income. That was good money for an Iowan in his thirties in the 1990s.

As earlier referenced, when he was convicted of embezzling most of a $17 Million bequest from Thomas Edison's anti-Jewish grandniece, Liberty Lobby and Carto declared bankruptcy. As owner of the class 'A' shares, I effectively controlled Resistance Records and the assets of the world's largest, most profitable racist music company. YouTube didn't exist until 2005, so these CDs and DVDs were big money makers.

Today, many of the bands whose music was produced and distributed by Resistance Records are on YouTube. The valuable assets the corporation owned included nearly one million produced CDs and DVDs, and a monthly revenue stream of over $50,000. The combined balances of the company's two bank accounts exceeded $150,000. It also owned two vehicles, high-end computers in offices in Detroit, Michigan and southern California, carried on its books several outstanding loans and advanced payments to bands, a high-end internet server and other expensive, up-to-date electronic equipment, and a state-of-the-art recording studio. An enormous warehouse was loaded with T-shirts and other promotional clothing, books, and over 150,000 color, back issues of the company's monthly magazine – titled 'RESISTANCE'. The corporation also owned the exclusive distribution rights to the work of around 80 heavy-metal signed bands and 30 affiliated independent bands. 12,500 racists subscribed to its magazine, and another 15,000 issues were sold each month at Gun Shows, KKK meetings, Holocaust Denial conferences, and even at some VFWs and American Legion lodges.

Its list of purchasers of Resistance products going back for three years contained over 100,000 records. Each edition of the publication generated between $20,000 and $30,000 worth of paid advertisements. The company's assets also included instruments used by bands, scheduled royalty payments, liens on income from band members' day jobs, recording distribution contracts, and other revenue-generating property. Pierce wanted my shares as badly as I wanted to rid myself of them. The game was on, and I decided to profitably play my hand out.

Billy Martin's Tavern is one of the best-known, 'must-see' spots in DC's historic Georgetown district. The first Billy Martin established it in 1930, when Herbert Hoover was President. His great-grandson, my friend Billy Martin, IV, has owned and operated the legendary establishment since the late 1980s. In the 1940s, Congressman Jack Kennedy was a Martin's regular. JFK's Congressmen, Richard Nixon and Gerald Ford, were frequent patrons. As a Senator, JFK often was often there; legend has it that he proposed to Jackie while seated in a booth at Martin's.

I had been a Martin's regular since 1984, after arriving in D. C. to work on the Reagan-Bush Inaugural Committee. Pierce and I sat in a wooden booth in the back of the main dining room. America's most notorious, prolific neo-Nazi was right on time, and headed straight to my booth. Pierce was about 6'4, trim, and wore thick glasses. He dressed casually, and looked every inch the university Physics professor he'd been prior to getting in the business of Hatred. He got right down to business. "Resistance Records can expand our outreach. Some rival organizations within The Movement are attracting younger, racially conscious, committed Caucasians who spend money and time online," he said. Pierce, like other professional racists and Holocaust deniers, referenced their ideological allies and customers as "The Movement".

After we ordered, Pierce gushed about his cause and using Resistance Records as a recruitment tool and for profits. "In our 24/7 war against the Jews and all minorities," Pierce said, "an established, proven success like Resistance Records will also help us to attract new members and major money." I told him my goal was to unload my shares. He said, "it's my understanding you're not in synch with our views, or supportive of The Movement." He glared at me as I admitted to that. "I'm not into denying that the

Holocaust happened, sir, and I don't hate anyone, or judge them because of their race, faith, gender, or sexual preference. I admire nothing about Adolf Hitler and David Duke, and have contempt for their views and followers."

Pierce looked away for a moment and then replied, "The deal I'm offering is for $250,000, gross."

Knowing how badly he wanted the shares, I told him the deal I'd accept is two-fifty, net." Smirking, he told me I was "talking like a damned Jew." Pierce asked about my life, my wife, parents, and career. He talked about himself, the five women he'd married, and how he'd left a promising career as a nuclear physicist to switch to hatred for profit. My car was parked on a side street just off Wisconsin avenue.

As I drove to my office on Connecticut avenue, Pierce rattled off information about me. He'd done his research, which creeped me out. My goal was to seal the deal and end my brief association with this vile record label. And to pick up a quick and easy quarter of a million bucks.

Pierce's Hate empire included the National Alliance, Vanguard Books, and several other corporate entities. His donor base numbered over thirty thousand supporters, many of whom also subscribed to his monthly magazines, catalogs, and newsletters. One of his publications was called 'ATTACK'; another was titled The National Vanguard.

"We've got some new products in the works," he said. One of them was a poster of Hillary Clinton wearing a yarmulke with a shooter's target superimposed on her face. They also offered clay pigeons – used by skeet shooters – which featured the faces of Mrs. Clinton, Jesse Jackson, U.S. Senators Chuck Schumer and Diane Feinstein, and the Rev. Al Sharpton, Bill Clinton, actor Rob Reiner, singer Barbra Streisand, and the-then Israeli Prime Minister, Ben 'Bibi' Netanyahu. "I'm sure you'll sell lots of those," I told him. Pierce grinned, and said, "Let's discuss you helping us make inroads with these college Republican organizations. I know you were a college Republican, and you knew Ronald Reagan for years before he was President and served on his White House staff." When I didn't reply, he said, "you'll earn some substantial consulting fees for your efforts." I ignored that, too. He later tied the consulting fees and other payments to the sale of my shares. We arrived at my office in the historic Kennedy-Warren building, which is a cool, art deco landmark built in 1931.

In my office, Pierce studied the framed photos – all of them autographed – of me with Ronald Reagan, Gerald Ford, Lee Atwater, George Bush, Bob Dole, Senators Chuck Grassley, John McCain, Roger W.Jepsen, and Governors Terry Branstad, George W. Bush, Jeb Bush, and Bob Ray, Congressmen Fred Grandy and Tom Latham, and other well-known Republicans.

He said, "Now I know why you won't help us fight the Jews." His slurs were offensive, but I wasn't going to jeopardize this transaction – even when he called me "a whore of the GOP Establishment." My wife called while we were talking. I told my secretary to tell her I'd not be home for dinner. The agreement we reached would enrich me by north of $350,000. I disliked the requirement that I serve as a consultant to the corporation for all of 1999 and through 2000. "You'll get five grand a month for that," he said, "and we'll pay your office rent." Those provisions meant another $125,000. What I agreed to was morally wrong, and William Pierce was a bad man. He promoted racism, hatred, anti-Semitism and violence. His fans were bad people, as well. I rationalized by telling myself I was like a lawyer who was representing a low-life client. A low-life who was about to dump $475,000 into my lap. I convinced myself that being a party to this didn't make me a bad guy. After all, it's only business, right?

I wouldn't be running the company. Harry Truman once said that "three things can ruin a man: money, power and women." By the time I dealt with William Pierce, power was no longer my goal. I was happily married to a wife whom I loved. I was fairly financially successful. But greed kicked in, and the consequences of my decisions that fateful day would haunt me for years.

Pierce liked dealing in cash. He said he'd deliver the first $250,000, in cash, to my office in a few days. Three days later he walked in with a briefcase containing 2,500 hundred-dollar bills. One of his lawyers had already sent documents for me to sign, and the transaction went smoothly. The C-notes were bundled in packets of fifty 100 bills each, all fifty of them. I removed 10 'Benjamins' from the mix and locked the rest in my safe. It was almost 12 noon, and I figured that under the circumstances, I could buy him lunch. "If you're hungry, I'll take you down the street for lunch." But Pierce had another idea.

"Your biography in 'Who's Who in America' indicates you're a member of the University club. Let's eat there." Looking back, taking Pierce to the University club was like accompanying David Duke to Barack Obama's inauguration. But that's how crazy my life was rapidly becoming.

For many years, I'd been a member of the University club of D.C. The impressive, seven story structure on 16th Street, N. W., is nine blocks from the White House. Established in 1904, the red brick clubhouse was, and is, a gathering spot for DC's power brokers, lawyers, political consultants, Senators, Supreme Court Justices and federal judges, bankers, lobbyists, and other influential players. Over the years, guests I hosted there included members of Congress, U.S. Senators, a former IRS Commissioner, and a former U.S. Secretary of Transportation and future White House chief of staff, my old friend Andy Card.

As Pierce and I pulled into the semi-circular driveway, the then-Chief Justice of the United States, William Rehnquist, emerged from his shiny, black, chauffeured Lincoln Town Car, arriving for his daily swim. We entered the lobby where a friend of mine, Paul 'Red' Fay, had just arrived. 'Red' Fay was a California businessman who had been a close friend of President Kennedy. They served in the Navy together in World War II; later, he was JFK's Secretary of the Navy. We exchanged greetings, and the front desk clerk asked him to sign in – which enabled me to avoid introducing him to William Pierce. I didn't want the gregarious Red Fay to engage Pierce in a conversation in which my guest might say that 'Red' and JFK had fought on the wrong side in World War II.

The hostess seated us in the Taft Dining room, named for President William H. Taft, who'd also been the President of the University club. Associate Justices Antonin Scalia and Clarence Thomas were seated two tables from us, and U. S. Senators Chuck Hagel and Howard Metzenbaum sat at tables on the same side of the room. A fellow Iowan, Chuck Manatt, beckoned me over to his table. Excusing myself, I told my guest I'd soon return. "Todd, this is Congressman Leonard Boswell," Manatt said. "He's friends with your dad. They served together in the Iowa Legislature." Chuck Manatt had been the chairman of the Democratic National Committee in the Reagan years, and was an ambassador under Bill Clinton.

Our political differences never negatively affected our friendship. Chuck was a lifelong hunter who loved guns. Returning to my table, Pierce quietly looked around the room, and said, "it's a shame the Jews forced their way into this club. Kikes, niggers, spicks, queers and women shouldn't be here." I stared at my plate and placed the cloth napkin on my lap. Making a football referee's time-out signal with my hands, I asked him to not speak that way. He then took a different tack.

"You're a card-carrying Republican and you work with the GOP Establishment," he said. "But do you know that Thomas Edison, Henry Ford, Ben Franklin, and John F. Kennedy's father, hated Jews?" I'd read that. "Charles Lindbergh also detested them," the neo-Nazi said, "and Walt Disney and John Wayne weren't fond of them." I pointed out that Disney was then run by Mike Eisner, who is Jewish. He ignored that, and claimed Walt Disney also disliked blacks. "That's news to me," I told him. "Isn't Mickey Mouse black?" We left the club an hour later and I drove Pierce to Union Station.

He invited me to his compound in West Virginia. He owned 346 acres near a town called Hillsboro, where his Hate Empire was based. He lived there with his fifth wife and about two dozen staffers. "When you visit our headquarters, Todd, I'll introduce you to the top staff and our volunteers." 20-plus full-time staffers worked there, and even more volunteers. Everyone worked 14-hour days, every day, spreading hatred, raking in cash, and promoting William Pierce and his books and other publications.

"Okay, see you soon," I replied. Driving back to my office, I instantly regretted the deal I'd signed. Over the next few months, my work with my clients kept me busy. My wife, who was a registered nurse, had a Masters' degree in Bone Marrow transplantation procedure. Linda worked long hours at the INOVA Fairfax hospital in northern Virginia. We were married in Iowa in 1995, and were happy. We wanted children, but weren't having any luck in trying. But our life was good.

We spent Christmas, enjoying our time with my parents and hers, and our siblings. In early January, 1999, crack cocaine entered my life. Linda and I had entertained another couple at the U club. After dinner, I wanted to go up to the second floor bar. As she had to be at the hospital early the next morning, she drove home to our Fairfax county house. I told her not to wait up.

By 11 p.m., I was too drunk to drive. I went down to the lobby and told the attendant I wanted to stay in one of the club's guest rooms. "Sorry, Mr.

Blodgett," I was told. "All our rooms are occupied." This staffer added that the Jefferson hotel across the street also had no vacancies. I walked to the club's library and stumbled, landing on a thick, plush Persian rug, directly in front of a man sitting in large, overstuffed leather chair. He tossed aside his magazine, and asked, "aren't you Todd Blodgett?"

He was waiting for the lobby clerk to notify him when the valet brought his car to the club's front drive. As I thanked him for his assistance, he introduced himself as Republican strategist named Greg Stevens. He worked with my friend Haley Barbour, with whom I'd served on Reagan's White House staff. Haley later was the chairman of the Republican National Committee, and – from 2004 to 2012 – Governor of Mississippi. Stevens said he'd seen some campaign finance DVDs I'd made for GOPAC, a Republican organization. He'd heard my father speak at a conference of ALEC - the American Legislative Exchange Council, and was a fan of his. "What're you doing for Haley?"

He said he was a registered lobbyist and ran political campaigns in various countries.

I shouldn't even think about trying to drive, he said. I said I'd hail a taxi and try to get a hotel room downtown. "Don't," he said. "My condo's a three-minute drive from here. Stay in one of my guest rooms. Sleep it off." Senators, ambassadors, lobbyists, pricey lawyers, Congressmen and other power players lived in Greg's building. His neighbor was the former Senate Majority Leader Howard Baker and his wife, Nancy, who was a former Senator from Kansas. Greg's condo was a swanky, uber-modern bachelor pad, expensively furnished and filled with Euro-style fixtures. Prominently displayed was a huge campaign poster from President Nixon's 1972 re-election campaign, signed by the former President to Greg Stevens. "I'm from San Clemente, California," he said. "That's where Nixon's western White House was. Sit down, make yourself at home."

Stevens brought out a cigarette lighter, a razor blade, two small glass cylinders, a small ball of shiny copper wire, and a bag of what looked like white rock, which was about the size of a marble. "This'll help you sober up," he said. "It's a wonderful high."

"What is it?" It was crack cocaine, but my host didn't inform me of that – not immediately. He chopped off a small bit of rock – about half the size of a standard pearl in a lady's necklace – which he packed into the front end of one of the glass tubes. I asked again what it was. "Freebase coke," he said. "Best stuff around. Here, try it," he said, handing it to me. "I'll help you." Stevens held the lighter to the pipe. The crack was packed tight against the copper wire filter at one end. I took the other end into my mouth and looked his way, for directions. "Inhale, now. C'mon, inhale, inhale, real deep!", he said, as I drew in the white smoke. "Keep going, and twirl the pipe. Take in all your lungs can hold," he instructed, as my lungs kept filling. "Jesus, you've got powerful lungs," he said, as I continued drawing on the pipe. Ten or 12 seconds later, I was still inhaling, which amazed him.

"You ran track in high school, didn't you?" I nodded yes and kept on inhaling. After another ten seconds, he asked if I had been on my college track team. I nodded no. Finally, I signaled with my free hand for him to take away the lighter. "Okay, now hold it in for as long as possible," he advised. "You're about to experience the best, most relaxing high of your life." He was right. Until then, I hadn't tried drugs since college, in my fraternity house, where I'd smoked pot, twice.

But this feeling was unlike any 'high' I'd ever experienced.

Suddenly, I felt as though I was weightless, and floating. Worries, fears and frustrations, all disappeared into plumes of thick, white smoke. The room appeared to spin, and I didn't feel tired. I was exhilarated. Totally relaxed. There was no headache, no hangover. I felt vibrantly alive, bereft of any stress. A superb, tingling, gorgeous feeling permeated my entire body; nothing before had ever felt so pleasant. I opened my mouth to speak, but all that emanated was a mellow, contented, low "aaahhhhh." A smile formed on my face, and all seemed right with me and the world. After about 90 seconds, I came down from being high. But it still felt wonderful. Stevens grinned, and asked me if I'd like another hit. Hell, yes, I did. After that hit, I took another, and another, and then another.

Within about 45 minutes, the crack was gone. Stevens said more was available, and he'd call a dealer. I told him I'd gladly cover my share of any cost. He called a pusher who said he'd be at his door with an 8-ball in 20 minutes. An 8-ball is an eighth of an ounce. While we waited, I told him Stevens had a nice place. As we chatted, I asked if he was married. He said no, and then said he was gay.

"Does that bother you?," he asked. I told him I was okay with it. But it concerned me somewhat, considering I was in a compromised, vulnerable situation. I said, "hey, dude - you live your way, and I'll live mine. That's my view." He replied, "I figured you're straight."

"Yeah, that's why my wife's a chick."

As we awaited his dealer, I realized I had just been initiated into the world of crack cocaine by a gay Republican junkie who worked for the former chairman of the Republican National Committee, and who would soon be elected Governor of Mississippi. When the dealer arrived, Stevens told me to stay put while he went to the door. They quietly talked before he brought the dealer into the den. Greg's drug dealer was a tall black guy who seemed about 35 years old. "My name's Kenny," he said, as we shook hands. "Greg just bought an 8-ball. I've got me six dime bags left. You wanna buy 'em?"

I asked how much. "Six dimes be sixty bucks." Greg's rock was wrapped in foil, while mine were in plastic bags. Greg told him I was "cool", meaning I wasn't a cop, my money was good, and I'd not rat him out. Kenny handed me a small piece of paper with his name and cell phone number. "If you need more, just call. I'm available from about 5 p.m. until about 4 a.m., nearly every day."

He also said he could usually deliver orders in northwest DC with a half hours' notice. "Do you provide discounts if you're late, like Domino's?" Kenny said no. Taking Kenny up on his offer, I called him two weeks later. Over the next three years, I bought over seventy grand worth of drugs from him. Our dealings ended abruptly when he was busted by the D.C. cops and went back to prison.

It was five in the morning when Greg and I finished smoking crack. Being no longer tired, I straightened myself up and walked to the U club. As I arrived, I remembered that I had schedules a squash game with my friend Greg Brake, for six thirty a.m. Heading into the library, my friend Terry Scanlon was reading newspapers and drinking coffee in the same chair that Stevens had sat in, just six hours earlier. "Well, good morning, Todd, m'boy", Terry said, "grab a cup of coffee and join me!" After about a half hour, I took the elevator to the locker room in the basement. I lost, badly, to my buddy on the squash court, but it wasn't due to lack of energy. I then shaved, showered, dressed, and drove to my office. I worked the entire day, and felt as though I'd slept like a baby the previous night. I never used drugs with Stevens again, although he invited me over to smoke crack several times.

I saw him only twice after that night. The next time was at a reception at the Capitol Hill club, the old-line, white brick GOP club on Capitol hill. The last time was right before Christmas of 2004. By then, I was a hard-core crackhead, and Stevens and I were among some junkies inside a rancid drug den in N.E. Washington. He looked unwell, and said he'd recently been busted by the D. C. police while buying cocaine. He was charged with possession of narcotics and drug paraphernalia, and was no longer working for Haley Barbour, Lanny Griffith and Ed Rogers.

A few months later, on the night before the 2005 Academy awards, the late actress Carrie Fisher found Stevens, who was a guest in her house, dead of a drug overdose. They actually were sharing a bed when she awakened to find him dead, next to her. Greg's death was a tragic end to a brilliant career. But for some reason, I believed myself to be immune to any negative consequences of drug usage. Beginning in March, 1999, I was obligated to be in West Virginia every other month on business for Dr. Pierce. He thought that by seeing his operation in action, I might change my thinking and become an enthusiastic ally, which didn't happen. But he never gave up on trying to interest me in taking a leading role in the realm of white supremacy, anti-Semitism, and organized hatred.

It never occurred to me then that I'd someday write about my experiences, but I filled several notebooks with my observations of the man, his thoughts, noxious ideology and associates. My first assignment was to function as the middleman between Pierce and a Canadian who owned the other 66 shares – all Class B stock – in Resistance Records. Because these shares weren't class 'A' issues, their value was lower. Pierce bought them for $130,000, with me brokering the transaction. The Canadian, Jason Snowe, was one of the company's founders, and had originally sold his shares to a Liberty Lobby subsidiary called the Government Educational Foundation. This organization later made a substantial contribution to Judge Roy Moore's 2017 U.S. Senate campaign.

After Willis Carto and I had an acrimonious dispute over $87,000 worth of advertising commissions my ad agency was owed, Carto fired me. The Canadian bought his shares back from Carto for $1,000 each – which was substantially less than Carto's GEF had paid for them - before reselling them to Pierce for approximately $1,975 each.

That transaction took place in my office in D.C's Cleveland Park. As had been done when Pierce brought 2,500 $100 bills to my office, each C-note was counted, twice, before the agreement was inked. In both meetings, I noticed that every hundred-dollar bill was of the series of 1981. The U.S. Treasury Secretary whose signature was affixed was Donald T. Regan, who later was President Reagan's Chief of Staff when I served on the White House staff. But within a three-week period, 4,975 Benjamins of this vintage passed through my hands.

Seeing those C-notes, I thought: besides coin dealers and currency collectors, who had nearly 5,000 crisp, uncirculated $100 bills that were printed nearly 20 years ago? William Pierce did. They came them from a violent white supremacist named Bob Matthews, who in 1984 robbed a Brinks armored vehicle in California. The heist yielded over $3.6 million, nearly all in hundreds. The funds were then disbursed to neo-Nazis, Holocaust Deniers, and their organizations. Mark Lane – the well-known lawyer who was Liberty Lobby's legal counsel – said that Pierce's National Alliance received nearly $3 million of the ill-gotten gains from Matthews before Matthews was incinerated in a fiery shoot-out with FBI agents and U.S. Marshals in December, 1984.

After Pierce confessed to the cash having been given to him by two Matthews subordinates, I shared this information with the FBI. To protect his new toy, Pierce had one of his lawyers reincorporate the company. The old shares were retired and new stock issued. The new corporation was called Resistance Records, L.L.C., incorporated in Delaware. Of the 50 states, only Rhode Island is smaller than Delaware in size, but nearly 60 percent of all FORTUNE 500 companies are incorporated there, and over 50 percent of all U.S. publicly traded corporations. Aside from tax advantages, Delaware is the only state with a separate court system that specializes in corporate law. Pierce also retained a registered agent, whose name and company would be the recorded face of Resistance Records. This made it very difficult for anyone to learn the identity of its owners.

My first working trip to Pierce's 346-acre headquarters near Hillsboro, West Virginia was in February of 1999. While I made it clear to Pierce that I wasn't interested in joining his cause or running this record company, he never gave up hope. He provided me a desk in his main building, and kept saying how much I "could do for white people, worldwide", if only I became more "racially aware". During these trips, I often met band members who wanted to sign with the Resistance label. I felt like a lawyer whose clients were bottom feeders. A weird, racist Skinhead named Wade Michael Page was annoyingly persistent. He sent letters, emailed, made phone calls, and even drove to West Virginia, hoping to be signed by Resistance. The guy was a loser among losers, and I basically told him to go away. He did, but in 2012, Wade Page gunned down 10 innocent members of a Sikh temple in Wisconsin, killing six.

Eric 'The Butcher' Fairburn was also wicked. Working for Resistance when it was based in Michigan, he later worked for Willis Carto at Liberty Lobby. He detested my distaste for anti-Semitism and racial bigotry, and posted online attacks on me, calling me 'Fraud' Blodgett. Fairburn threatened to beat me to a pulp, behead me, and dump my remains at what he called a "Kike cemetery" located in "Jew York City." Fairburn is currently serving a Life Sentence for killing two men he shot in cold blood.

But the scariest racist I encountered via my connection to Pierce was a young German murderer named Hendrik Mobus. At age 17, Mobus and some friends had stabbed and strangled a teenager in Germany. While he was imprisoned for five years, he wrote, recorded, and promoted racist, anti-Semitic music called NSBM: National Socialist Black Metal. In 1999, he fled to the U.S., to meet Dr. Pierce, who was his hero. Pierce and Mobus facilitated ways to bring Euro White Power music to America. He overstayed his 90-day Visa waiver by over six months; INTERPOL authorities notified the FBI and the U.S. Marshals that there was an outstanding warrant for his arrest in Germany, for other hate-related crimes. While this neo-Nazi was on the lam, I encountered him at Pierce's compound.

Nearly everything he said centered on his profound hatred of Jews. "Vee chusst gotta keel off awl da chews, yah", he repeatedly chirped. To this Hitler-adoring creep, Pierce was his modern Fuehrer. FBI agents and U.S. Marshals apprehended Mobus in 2000 near Pierce's compound and extra-dited him to Germany. As far as I know, he's still there, hating.

While this was going on, I also represented other clients, including a Texas-based nonprofit organization called the Association of Finance and Insurance Professionals. I spoke on a regular basis to groups of politically active college students who attended seminars sponsored by a conservative organization called The Leadership Institute. I also provided strategic and campaign finance consulting services for candidates running for the U.S. Congress, state Legislature, and county and municipal offices. Unlike my prior work with Willis Carto, I kept my dealings with Pierce a secret from my wife and family. At the outset, neither Linda or my parents knew I was affiliated with America's OTHER most notorious neo-Nazi. Each visit to Pierce's compound reinforced my abhorrence of his ideas. Yet, as a coldly opportunistic profiteer, I was part of this. I wasn't running Resistance Records, but my hands weren't clean and my conscience wasn't clear. By arranging deals which involved the swapping of mailing lists, and facilitating advertising trades with other publications serving a similar readership, and applying my marketing skills to such projects, I earned my retainer fees. And while I despised what Dr. Pierce represented, I chose to take part in these endeavors.

I was as addicted to making money as I was to smoking crack cocaine.

My marriage began to suffer, as did my relationships with several friends. My wife, my parents, and her parents all were worried. At this point, my drug addiction hadn't yet reached the point where I couldn't work. I kept it hidden, as most junkies can do, at least at the outset. Over the course of the next few months, the word circulated among white supremacists that a non-sympathizer (me) was involved with these projects. In September, 1999, I had to make a report to over 250 of Pierce's top donors and organizers. The three-day conclave was held at his mountainside retreat. I was booed by the hostile audience. It got even worse on the next day, and into the evening. While with some knuckle draggers at a redneck bar near Hillsboro, a hillbilly woman who must've been in around 30 began aggressively hitting on me. I tried to be polite, and showed her my wedding ring. "Sorry, honey," I said, "but I'm married. Find another dude."

But she wouldn't let up. She ran her fingers through my hair and tried to kiss me. I was raised to never hit ladies, and tried to get away, but the Bitch latched on me and groped me. Moments later, a hillbilly brute tapped my shoulder. This angry mountain of a man stood a good 6'4", weighed at least 300 lbs., and made Larry the Cable Guy look like George Clooney. His face was red and full of hatred. This would not end well for me.

"Y'all's a-hittin' on muh woman," he roared, and took a swing at me. I ducked that swing, and the next. On his third attempt, he connected, clocking me in the temple. I felt woozy and tried staggering away, but my legs felt like warm rubber. The other patrons either laughed, or kept on drinking, ignoring my plight. They'd seen such skirmishes before, and found them to be entertaining. I fell against the bar, and he picked me up and carried me toward the front door. I then weighed about 160 and I stand 5'9, but he strained not a bit. Another hillbilly who looked and spoke like a character straight out of 'Deliverance' held the door open. The brute held me in a vise-like grip. Grabbing my neck, he jerked me upwards, faced me toward the front wall, and drop-kicked me like a football. His boot landed flat on my kiester, causing me to fly toward – and, through – the entrance. My head cleared the doorway by two inches. I landed hard in the parking lot and rolled in the gravel.

Someone who saw it called a reporter, because within weeks, an article with the headline, 'Money, Music, and the Doctor' was published in a monthly magazine called The Intelligence Report. This periodical, published by the Southern Poverty Law Center, reached subscribers in every state and outside the U.S. It truthfully claimed that "Blodgett is mistrusted by veteran Skinheads." It also stated that I wasn't "well received" by Pierce and his supporters, and that "Blodgett was flogged by white Nationalists via the internet." The article also referenced a " 'Movement Warning' flyer" … in which "Blodgett is described as a 'parasite' …" This article also described my getting roughed up: "To cap off his weekend humiliation at the hands of Dr. Pierce, Blodgett managed to get himself punched out in a bar near Hillsboro by an irate West Virginian who took offense at his attentions toward a local young lady." This lie didn't please my wife or my parents, or hers. I'd been exposed, and now, it was online. My father still held public office in Iowa, which made matters worse. Several Legislators and a top aide to the then-Governor of Iowa, Tom Vilsack, asked him about it.

Journalists representing The New York Times, The Washington Post, The Des Moines Register, and the Associated Press called me. One reporter from The Washington Post, David Segal, was particularly adept and resourceful. He asked me if William Pierce had ever been my guest at the club. Yes, I told him. Pierce phoned me in advance of Segal's call, and told me that in his interview with Segal, he was evasive when asked about being my guest at the club. But dishonesty isn't cool, and any protection it may provide is always undeserved, in my view. A page one story appeared in the Post's Style section on Jan. 12, 2000. It rocked my world and everyone in it. The article stated that our deal was sealed at "the University club, an oak-paneled gathering point for the city's elite, where control of Resistance was haggled over" between "Todd Blodgett and William Pierce." It described me as "a protégé of the late GOP strategist Lee Atwater" and caused an uproar at the University club.

CHAPTER THREE: ENTER THE FBI

Late January, 2001 – Washington, D.C.

About a week after The Washington Post story appeared, I walked into the Kennedy-Warren lobby to go to my office. The front desk receptionist called me over, and said two men in suits wanted to see me. "They're in the restaurant," she said. They had asked her to notify them when I arrived. I asked her to wait five minutes before telling them I was available. It was about 7 p.m., and in my pocket was an 8-ball of crack cocaine I'd bought 40 minutes earlier.

Upon entering my office, I stuffed the drugs in a drawer. Two minutes later, the agents were there. Both were from Pittsburgh. One agent was with the FBI; the other with the IRS. They were affiliated with the JTTF: the Joint Terrorism Task Force. The JTTF is a law enforcement consortium, a partnership, between U.S. law enforcement agencies and bureaus. Its purpose is to investigate, and take action against, terrorism. Among the agencies which comprise it are the FBI, the U.S. Secret Service, the U.S. Department of Homeland Security, ICE, U.S. Customs & Border Protection, U.S. Customs & Immigration Enforcement, and the TSA (Transportation Security Administration). They showed me their badges and IDs, and handed me business cards, and were professional, polite, and respectful.

"Do I need to call my lawyer?" No, the IRS agent replied, "not unless you're doing something illegal." Otherwise, the FBI agent said, "this is a friendly visit". I'd been on their radar for "quite awhile", they said. They assured me I wasn't under formal surveillance, but several people I had associated with were being targeted, and under investigation, by the bureau and JTTF. Prior to coming, the agents and their supervisors reviewed FBI documents pertaining to the security clearances that the bureau had granted me in the 1980s, including for my position on President Reagan's White House staff. The agents had seen phone records, tax returns, bank statements, credit card charges, and other information relating to me and my business activities. They knew where I had been and for whom, and specific places I had travelled to, and when. They knew who I knew, and even knew about some secondary parties to transactions I'd helped facilitate. For purposes here, I'll refer to these agents as Smith and Jones.

"We represent the FBI director," agent Smith said. "And we know you're on a first-name basis with every major neo-Nazi in America and several in Europe. You know more people in the hierarchy of the violent, organized, racist far right than any other American, and you're well-connected to many rank-and-file members, and the major financial backers of these organizations."

They also knew that Carto and Pierce and their associates were laundering money, scamming their supporters, evading taxes, and hiding illicit funds. They knew Carto embezzled $7.5 million and that he had suborned me to falsely book ad revenue as tax-deductible donations. Were they also on to me?

Agent Smith was about 45; Jones around 30. Smith did most of the talking, and they tag-teamed me.

"Your involvement in the commercial enterprises and the tax-exempt entities of our country's two best-funded professional racists is incredibly extensive. We've read your FBI files, and we don't believe you're a hater. But you and your advertising agency have profited handsomely from what these groups publish and distribute. You've assisted Willis Carto in laundering money, and even traveled overseas to do it. Then there's the very substantial mailing list rental income, and donations of cash, farm land, and investment real estate you helped Carto to snag, from major donors. You've made a good living, doing all this, and with William Pierce, you're still at it."

They're on to me.

The agents also told me they knew I was on a first-name basis with several major white supremacists and professional haters operating overseas. Jones said, "you're an opportunistic profiteer." After glancing at each other, agent Smith pointed to the bookshelf on the side wall. He picked out a book on offshore banking and glared at me. "I see you like to read. This one looks interesting." As he thumbed through it, he asked, "Mr. Blodgett, did the information in this book come in handy when you were in Switzerland, Grand Cayman, Austria, and Liechtenstein, representing Willis Carto? I didn't respond. Agent Jones asked me, "Do you know where David Duke is now?"

"I've heard he's in Russia, on a speaking tour."

"That's correct," Jones answered. "Federal agents raided his residence a few weeks ago, and carted off tons of incriminating evidence. This includes hundreds of documents which Justice Department lawyers believe will prove he's bilked his contributors, committed mail fraud, and fraudulently spent campaign funds. Illegally, he spent that money on rental properties and gambled away hundreds of thousands of dollars. He even spent some of it on hookers. But you know all that, don't you, Mr. Blodgett?"

Gulping, I said, "yeah."

Agent Jones then followed up, and said, "documents show that as part of your work for Carto, you assisted Duke in marketing his book and with his direct mail fundraising. You also authorized Mr. Duke to use several direct mail contributor lists that you and Mr. Carto owned, correct?"

"Yes." These guys were REALLY on to me.

"Made a lot of money on those deals?"

"We did okay."

"Yeah, you did. Well, the FBI would like you to work, full-time, as a paid confidential informant. You can help the country and do what's right. For a change. Consider our offer, and we'll call you in ten days." Before I could respond, Smith winked as we shook hands. Then he added, "you've got time to extricate yourself from anything that might present a problem for the FBI, or for you, should you come aboard." As he walked to the door Jones said, "something tells me that you'll soon be working with us." Agent Smith added, "It'll be good for the country, the bureau, and good for Todd Blodgett."

Oh, fuck.

After they left my office, I sat for a long time at my desk. Linda called twice, asking what was wrong. Before I drove home, a drug pusher who regularly supplied me called, wanting to know if I needed anything. Around midnight, as I slipped into bed, Linda asked what was bothering me. Unlike the first several years of our marriage, I was no longer very open with her. When I awoke at six a.m., she had already left for work. While shaving I wondered what those federal agents would think if they knew that their prospective, full-time, paid informant has a serious drug addiction.

At dinner that night, Linda again asked what was bothering me. I brushed her off, because I didn't even know how to begin to tell her about all that was swirling around me.

The UK professional racist Mark Cotterill, who worked in DC, was being scrutinized by the JTTF. Cotterill was later banned from the U.S., for illegally financing British political campaigns for racist candidates. No one at the FBI knew I was a junkie because, unlike FBI agents, informants aren't required to submit to mandatory, random drug-testing. So I used drugs for the entire time I worked for them.

There are major differences between informants and FBI undercover agents. Informants are civilians and sometimes, criminals; they work for the bureau in hopes of getting reduced charges, money, or a pending indictment dismissed. Some informants only uncover and supply information. The bureau uses others to infiltrate criminal operations, and/or to ingratiate themselves with subjects under surveillance, and explain how to use such information. The FBI had me perform all of these functions.

Within a few months of buying fixes from the dealer that Greg Stevens introduced me to, I began buying from other pushers. Over nearly eight years,

I bought drugs from about 200 different dealers. Two were recommended by Kenny – the first dealer I bought from – when I wanted crack, and he'd either gone in for the night, or was out of inventory, or locked up. In both cases, Kenny assigned a password which the other dealers asked of me when we made contact. I also learned how drug buys go down in DC and other major cities. I met the dealers Kenny had recommended over the phone, after Kenny set it up. The first pusher told me his name was 'Q' – that was the name he provided. 'Q' instructed me to go to an old church at the corner of 15th Street, N.W., and 'V' Street. The church - St. Augustine's – was known as the "Crack-thee-drall".

He said to pull up to the 15th Street side of the church and park and turn my lights off. He told me to be alone. The password Greg assigned was Homer Simpson. Within about 40 seconds of parking my Range Rover and turning the lights off, a black man knocked on my front passenger door. The window scrolled down and he said, "password?" I said, "Homer Simpson", and asked my name. "Todd," I replied.

"Unlock your door, Todd. Drive straight up Fifteenth street, and keep yo' eyes on da road. I've got what you want." As he entered my vehicle, he said, "put the three hundred in y'all right hand and close it into a fist. Keep 'dem hands below window level. Den hand me da money." I complied while keeping my eyes on the road. "Okay," he said, "now, I'm leavin' yo' stuff under dis here seat." He then said to drop him off in the next block, which was Taylor Street. "Pull over here, just past the stop sign. Once I leave out, don't say nothin', and don't look at me." Before he got out, he said, "Nice doin' bidness with y'all."

"Later, dude."

Other dealers I bought from often employed 'runners'. A drug runner is usually a teenager who doesn't want to work at McDonalds. But some are adults. Runners can make several hundred dollars a night delivering drugs to a pusher's customers. Because they're under 18, they won't be charged as adults if they're busted, or ensnared in a police sting operation.

The more successful dealers also will often pay court costs and lawyer's fees for their runners, as part of the bargain. I actually got to know several of my drug dealers quite well, became friends with some. Not long after meeting the drug pusher at the crack-thee-dral, I was stopped at a red light near D.C's Union Station. A young drug runner I knew named Jamal ran up to my car and rapped on the passenger door window, needing a ride. Jamal liked my Range Rover. "I be diggin' dis wheel, lightskin – 'wheel' being ghetto-speak for a vehicle.

"What up, Mistuh Tawd?" Before I could reply, Jamal made his sales pitch. "Listen, dude, I can get y'all da BOMB! I means, this shit be da Master Blaster! I'm sayin, dem rocks be BUTTERS!" Jamal was working me, as drug peddlers do when they're with a junkie who has money. He was describing what I knew to be some really potent crack cocaine. "Forget it. Not this time. I'm taking Connecticut avenue to Cleveland Park. I can take you as far as National Zoo. No stuff for me, at least until tomorrow."

"Dat's cool, dude. Just drop me at Adams Morgan, by the Taft bridge. I'll walk the rest the way to my baby momma crib." In ghetto jargon, this meant he was going to the home of his kid's mother.

"I thought the mother of your child lived on Capitol Hill."

"Dat one do. She my son baby mama. 'Dis'n over here be my daughter baby mama." I asked Jamal the name of his daughter. He said, "she name be Ribidria".

"Ribidria?"

"Yeah, she be named fo' my favit food, barbequed ribs." As Jamal shut the passenger door, my cellphone rang. It was the FBI agent who had visited me in my office, wanting to know if I'd reached a decision. "I've got a call in to my lawyer, Jack Fornaciari," I told him. "If Jack thinks it's a good idea, I'll discuss it with my wife. If Linda is thumbs up on it, I'll get back to you, and we'll take it from there." A week later, two FBI agents, an IRS agent and an agent from the JTTF joined me for a meeting with Jack at his law firm in downtown D.C.

My attorney was also a member of the University club. I had hired him to represent me in the fight to remain a member there. Under pressure from some of the members, a majority of the club's Board of Governors had suspended me, and were threatening to expel me. So Jack was already my lawyer when the Feds came calling. "I'll need your business cards, cell phone numbers, ID numbers on your badges, email addresses, and office contact information," Fornaciari told the agents. As I wasn't under any investigation, or being prosecuted, I held the cards in this meeting. Fornaciari did most of the talking.

"We're all agreed my client has done nothing for which he'll be prosecuted, and that he's here on his own volition," he told the agents. "Right, guys?", Jack asked. All agreed.

"There'll be a record of this meeting, and if at any time I decide I want Mr. Blodgett to extricate himself from this arrangement, he will be done, right then and there. Understood?" Again, the agents complied with Jack's terms. Two hours later, we hammered out my deal. The bureau would pay me $6,000 a month, plus all out-of-pocket expenses, in return for me working for them as a full-time confidential informant. The agents left the law office ahead of me so that no one would see us together.

This was a clandestine operation, they emphasized, and either party could call it quits on a moment's notice. As I left Jack's office that day, I had no idea that I'd be working for the bureau and the Joint Terrorism Task Force for the next 33 months. It was agreed that whenever the agents needed to see me, we'd meet at a remote location they'd determined. The code name the bureau assigned to me was 'Rommel' – Hitler's WW II general, Irwin Rommel.

A few days after I'd signed on as an asset, one of my controlling agents called my cell phone. He wanted to meet, as did a top JTTF administrator who had flown in from Pittsburgh. "Rommel?," the agent said. "Let's meet at two o'clock tomorrow, at the national building museum, at the Smithsonian." The famed Smithsonian Institute is a top DC tourist attraction, filled with millions of artifacts from American history. The 46-carat Hope diamond is there, along with President Harry Truman's White House bowling alley and Dorothy's ruby red slippers from The Wizard of OZ. Archie Bunker's chair form All in the Family and Star Trek's Captain James T. Kirk's Phaser guns are also housed at this world-renowned museum.

"Sure thing. See you then." One of JFK's inaugural balls was held at this historical building, which was formerly known as the Pension Building. It dates back to 1887. Years later, as I watched President and Mrs. Donald Trump dancing at the inaugural ball in that beautiful structure, my mind took me back to my meetings there with the FBI agents. As I made my way up the two flights of stairs to the reserved room where the agents and I always met, my thoughts focused on the risky, multi-faceted, potentially dangerous life I was leading. Being a junkie isn't easy, especially when the addict is married, has a stressful, demanding job, and hides his habit from his wife, friends, parents, and family members. Being a full-time, paid, DC-based FBI informant further complicates matters, particularly when the gig requires dealing with the KKK, the Aryan Nations, and money-laundering Holocaust deniers.

Then there was the constant fear of being busted by the cops, generating unfavorable publicity, and harming my father's governmental career. But I somehow managed to pull it off. For a while.

The agents briefed me on several new developments taking place in what they called The Movement, which consisted of various racist, hate-oriented groups, violent, well-financed Holocaust Deniers, and leaders of America's militant, racist Far Right, some of which I'd already heard about. They showed me some documents and photos, which were clandestinely taken of activists in citizen militias by cameras hidden on other informants.

I knew most of the individuals in these photos and identified them for the agents, including some that they hadn't heretofore known about. Paramilitary, anti-government militias were proliferating in the far west, the deep south and Midwest. We discussed the tax-evading activities of Ku Klux Klan honcho and professional anti-Semite David Duke, and how he'd scammed his own supporters. We also talked about the methods that William Pierce was using step up recruitment for his National Alliance.

We also discussed Willis Carto's illegal tactics, which included bankruptcy fraud, RICO violations, embezzlement, money-laundering and mail fraud, among other serious charges. "We'll be sending you to New York, Reno, Nevada, Atlanta, Georgia, and Grand Cayman in the next three to five months," an agent told me. "We'll also fly you to California, and to South Carolina, Alabama, Louisiana, and some other locales. We'll get memoranda, photos, and documents to you prior to these trips," his partner said. "That's fine," I replied. "I'll have on-the-ground agent back-up at every point, right?"

"Yes. In the case of Cayman, we'll alert the bureau's Cayman field office ahead of your arrival that you'll be working the island." Back-up was important to me, as it is to any informant. I learned from my years working political campaigns to leave as little to chance as possible. Not only that, but I wanted to avoid getting punched out and drop-kicked again, as I was while down at Pierce's Nazi Nest three months earlier. After about an hour, we got to the best part of the meeting.

" … Fifty-six, Fifty-seven, fifty-eight, fifty-nine, sixty," the agent said, as he finished counting out the 60 one hundred-dollar bills comprising my monthly retainer fee. "Okay, there's your six grand. We're expecting great work from you. You know all the right people and what they're doing. Thanks, Rommel. You're free to go"

Free to go buy crack.

I squared the 60 Benjamins, stuffed them into my suit coat pocket, and walked out. The agents waited until I'd left the room before leaving. From then on, they did this after every meeting. The agents didn't leave the room until after I'd left the building. The FBI protects confidential informants and the secrecy of their association. Before I could hook up with one of my crack dealers, I had to keep an appointment with Mark Cotterill, the nefarious British white supremacist who was illegally in the United States.

70

His employer was an old-line, wealthy, aristocratic British racist named Roger Pearson, Ph. D. American authorities were highly suspicious of Cotterill: they believed he was laundering money, evading taxes, and illegally channeling it into a UK-based, pro-white, racist organization called the 'American Friends of the British National Party'. In November, 2002, Cotterill was given, on short notice, 90 days to vacate the USA. Under an Exclusion Order, he and his wife were ordered to not return for ten years.

In later meetings with Cotterill, and many others, I would be wired with a recording device, to capture on silicone what was discussed. On this occasion, I wasn't wired. While later conducting surveillance for the bureau, I'd literally wear a wire; that is, wires were taped to my chest, and connected to a small recording device. But by November, 2000, the agents furnished me with a pager look-alike apparatus which could record up to eight hours of conversation. No one I surveilled ever suspected that the inconspicuous device was recording them. It could be activated, paused, and turned on and off with the casual flip of a switch. Stenographers at FBI headquarters would then listen to what was on the cartridge, and transcribe what was said. In cases where conversations involved multiple participants, I'd sometimes identify the voices and names for the agents, in advance of the transcribing process.

The offices of Roger Pearson, Ph.D. were located on 13th Street, N.W. Pearson was out of the country, and Cotterill was taking an inventory of book titles. The books lining the shelves wouldn't be selected for a Pulitzer prize, or Oprah's Book Club.

Among them were 'The Myth of the Six Million', 'Holocaust or Holo-HOAX?', 'The Holocaust Industry', 'Slavery and the Negro', 'The South Was RIGHT!', 'Manage Your Money like a JEW', 'Civil War II', 'The Protocols of the Learned Elders of Zion', 'Gestapo Chief' and 'Hitler: Hero for the Ages', and hundreds of other nefarious, offbeat, racist and anti-Semitic books and periodicals. Thousands of copies of The Barnes Review, a monthly anti-Semitic magazine published by Willis Carto, were stacked on other shelves. I grabbed one and flipped to an article suggesting that Adolf Hitler should've been awarded the Nobel Peace prize for his alleged "humanitarian" efforts.

Such insanity was common among those I surveilled. Cotterill and I had lunch at a place called the Post Pub, which was a favorite of many DC-based reporters. He had something up his sleeve, and it was clandestine. "Please sign these forms," he asked. The forms pertained to three accounts at a northern Virginia bank, all in the name of his organization. "Signing these will make you the signatory, as the Treasurer, of one of my political committees." I asked him why he needed me to do this. "Because I'm an illegal alien. And as a non- citizen, I can't legally be the Treasurer of the American Friends of the British National party."

"Mark, is there any way I can get in legal trouble over this?" No, he said, adding that I "needn't worry about keeping track of monthly bank statements, or anything like that."

"How so?" Because, he said, the statements would go to a P.O. box rented under the name of another professional Anti-Semite. The account would cause me no worries. I knew that signing the forms would provide me with access to those accounts, and online information, which the bureau could use.

"Okay," I told Cotterill. As we ate, it dawned on me that all of Cotterill's racist American friends and supporters would demand his instant deportation if he'd been Mexican, and not an English-speaking Caucasian. In 2009, one of Cotterill's neo-Nazi buddies, Jamie Von Brunn, walked into the Holocaust Museum in DC and shot it up. Von Brunn wanted to kill Jewish people, but he ended up killing a black guard, who had held the door open for him as he walked in. Federal officers returned fire, nailing the old Nazi before he could squeeze off more rounds. Ensuing news stories tied me to Cotterill and Von Brunn, and mentioned my work as a paid FBI informant. London newspaper articles, and TV and radio broadcasts throughout Europe also exposed my having been the AFBNP's treasurer, as well as having co-owned Resistance Records with William Pierce. After nearly two hours with Cotterill, I dropped him back off at his office, and later wrote a brief synopsis of our meeting for the agents.

Then I pulled over to a nearby gas station and called a cocaine dealer I knew who lived nearby, in the district's historic Adams Morgan neighborhood. The pusher was from Trinidad. He was called 'Dreds, because of his dreadlocks, which passed for a hairstyle. The dude's real name was Bryan and he lived in a pre-World War II large apartment building called Harvard Hall. Dreds was actually a nice guy, bright. I never felt the need to carry a gun when I bought and used crack there. When Dreds answered his phone, I said I wanted to "play pool." That's junkie slang for an 8-ball of cocaine.

One of the first things I learned as an addict was to speak in code. "Hard or soft", he asked, wanting to know if I wanted rock, or powder. "Hard", I said. "Where you at, Fancy Pants?"

"I'm in my car, heading up 15th street," I replied. "Okay, white boy, come on. I'm home." I drove up 15th street, passing the hotel where, in 1990, the-then mayor of DC, Marion Barry, was busted by the feds for smoking crack. Barry went to prison, got out, and reclaimed his office in 1994. He served as Mayor until 1999. Barry died in 2014, broke and still addicted to crack - his drug habit having wiped him out financially. About 15 blocks further, I turned off of 15th street, and onto Harvard street, N.W. As I rolled down the hill, a 'DRUG FREE ZONE' sign was to my right, which was a joke. In DC back then, such signs were sure clues that you were in a junkie 'hood' with readily available drugs of all kinds.

In 2001, Harvard Hall apartments was an ornate, vintage structure that had seen better days. It was a good address in a hip neighborhood, but crack cocaine usage was rampant, and all which went with it. Harvard Hall has since been renovated, and is now a condo, or a co-op, filled with yuppies. How times change. At the double doors to the building's main entrance, I dialed the code number corresponding to the pusher's' fourth floor unit. He picked up, saying, "Hell-O, who is dere?" Dreds lived with his wife, who was at work. "It's me," I replied. When the entry device made its BUZZZ, BUZZZ, BUZZZ, sound, I entered the lobby, walked past the front desk and took the elevator to the fourth floor. At Bryans' door, I knocked twice. The door's peephole cover moved, and as his eye darted from side to side, Dreds quietly asked, "you be alone, Fancy Pants?"

"No," I replied, sarcastically. "Marion Barry's with me, and he wants you to front him a dime bag. Of course I'm alone! Let me in!" Dreds removed the chain from the door, threw the bolt lock and admitted me to his drug den. He said nothing as I entered the dingy place, with the blinds drawn. Dim light bulbs were in every lamp that worked - both of them. He locked the doorknob and re-bolted the heavy lock and re-latched the chain on the door. "You bein' stupid, talkin' dat sheet. Don't go speakin' dat way 'round here no more. You feel me?" I nodded, and he asked, "how much you want diss time?"

Pulling out four one hundred-dollar bills, I told him that while we'd discussed an 8-ball, I'd buy three 8-balls if $400 would cover it. "Normal price for three 8-balls be four hundred feefty. You know dat, Lightskin." I knew the price, but wanted a deal. "Dreds, I was just –"

"You was just bein' Republican, is what you doin'. I know you, Todd. All you rich, white dope fiends be da same. Tryin' to save feefty bucks on crack, while you wearin' a suit dat cost three grand, and drivin' a wheel worth twenty times dat. I know how dat go. Umm-hmmm. You preppy junkies always tryin' to Jew us poor, black immigrants outta money." Obviously, misusing the pronoun, "Jew" as a verb of derogation wasn't an abuse of the English language committed only by white supremacists, or members of the Aryan Nations and Holocaust deniers.

Around this time, the then-Texas Governor, George W. Bush, nailed down the Republican nomination. Since late 1998, my parents had been extensively involved in his presidential campaign.

Between the summer of 1999 and June, 2000, my parents hosted George and Laura Bush in north Iowa on several occasions.

In March, 2000, the Board of Governors of the University club of Washington, DC voted to ask me to resign my membership. This request was precipitated by The Washington Post article detailing my ownership of Resistance Records and hosting William Pierce as my guest at the club. This demand was immensely unfair, unjustified, and just plain wrong. I refused to submit to their demands, and warned them that if the club expelled me, I'd sue. No small number of club members – including some who were Jewish, black, and female - supported me, and I had support on the Board. However, the winds of PC – political correctness - blew hard, and my arrogant detractors were determined and intolerant.

Meanwhile, my mother was elected as a Bush delegate to the Republican National Convention, which would be in Philadelphia. The manager of the University club, Albert Armstrong, met with me in his office. When I arrived, Armstrong and the club's president, Scott Beck, awaited me. "Mr. Blodgett," Armstrong said, "the publicity you've received has embarrassed this club. If you don't resign, you'll be expelled." On his desk was a copy of The Washington Post that featured the article that precipitated all this. "Forget it," I said. "That's unfair. I'll fight you, and this club, in court. I won't be railroaded."

Despite knowing that club members who were, themselves, minorities and Democrats supported me, they didn't care. "Very well," Armstrong said. "Your membership is immediately suspended. The Board of Governors will start internal proceedings which won't go well for you." He said no information would be released, including the names of the members pushing for my ouster. "It will be after it gets subpoenaed," I warned him. He said that neither he or any Board members would ever discuss this case at any time. The entire time, Scott Beck sat there like a dim-witted client whose attorney had to do the heavy lifting he'd directed. "You will when a Judge orders you guys to sit for a deposition," I replied, while resisting the urge to administer a beatdown that would have resulted in their hospitalization.

Meeting in the manager's office at the club that day was eerily reminiscent of when I was kicked out of boarding school at age 16. The private office of the school's headmaster wasn't unlike Armstrong's: plush carpet, matching thick draperies, an ornate, hand-carved, highly polished walnut desk, expensive

Ox blood leather chairs, solid brass lamps, and other fancy décor. I've been in the offices of many honorable people. And genuinely successful individuals merit such offices, because they've EARNED them. But overpaid, self-important, bureaucratic bullies merit nice offices about as much as Bill Cosby should be commended for showing respect to women. I detest pretension and phonies, and the late Albert Armstrong was a phony, insecure, sleazy, manipulative, pretentious bully. His sidekick, Beck, was a better-tailored, less conniving version of Armstrong, but without the brains.

Being expelled from my club was fundamentally different from being kicked out of Shattuck-St. Mary's. In the case of being booted from boarding school, I wanted out. Not so this private club, where I'd been a member for many years, all of them in good standing.

I was true to my word, and followed up on my threat. I filed suit against the club, its manager, and every member of the club's Board of Governors who had voted to expel me. This precedent-setting legal battle lasted seven years, costing me over $450,000. The club's legal fees exceeded $1 million, according to documents obtained in the discovery process.

The case of 'Blodgett vs. The University club of Washington, D.C.' has inspired articles, debates, and legal analyses in numerous publications. These include the Journal of the American Bar Association, the Legal Times, and the National Law Journal, as well as books, newspapers, and other periodicals. The case took on a life of its own. It has been referenced in state and federal courts in numerous states. It's been cited in law schools by professors, written about by legal scholars, judges, lawmakers, and attorneys throughout the United States as THE definitive constitutional law case concerning the powers of private organizations, and private clubs, in particular, to discriminate, balanced against the individual rights of members. The article in The ABA Journal was headlined with: 'BLODGETT GETS THE BOOT' – and other stories were even more damning. In retrospect, I'd rather have back my 450 grand.

After The Washington Post ran its article, 'The Pied Piper of Racism' on January 12, 2000, the story was big news in D.C. and elsewhere. The news of the Resistance Records deal's connection to the club was on all the local DC TV news broadcasts, and Billy Bush mentioned it on his radio program. In 2016, when Billy became embroiled in the video controversy during the presidential race, I felt sorry for him. Bush learned, the hard way, how it feels to be subjected to intense, unfavorable scrutiny over past actions.

Bush, with whom I'd chatted, played pool and knocked back drinks at the club, told his listeners he was ashamed to belong to a club that would have someone such as I as a member. He was much more cordial only months earlier, when – at the University club - he commended Linda and I for each having contributed $1,000 to the presidential campaign of his first cousin, George W. Bush.

But the media wasn't through with me. After I refused to resign, the club's Board of Governors voted to expel me. Someone leaked this to the Journal of the American Bar association, and to The Washington Post, and other media, both print and electronic. The April 12, 2000 edition of The Washington Post ran yet another article. The headline read: 'Creating a Furor – Or, is it, Fuehrer? – at the University Club?' Once again, the phones at my office rang all day long, and into the next day. The ABA Journal, again, got in on it, and a reporter from that magazine called me for a quote. I hung up on her, as I did on dozens of other journalists. In Washington, DC, such controversy sells newspapers and generates TV and radio coverage - especially when it involves conservative Republicans.

My wife was out of town on the day this made the news, at an Oncology conference in Atlanta. I was so upset over this negative publicity that I drove into the hoods to get high. By this point in my drug usage, I'd gotten to know several fellow junkies. Many of them lived in the hoods, and most were black. I was on good terms with them, some of whom invited me into their homes, where we smoked crack. Many were good friends with cops who were assigned to their neighborhoods. For forty or fifty bucks a month, these police officers looked the other way when drug buys went down, or when dealers came to their cribs, and drugs were being used, bought, and sold, inside.

After drugging all night long, by daybreak I crashed on a sofa in the rundown apartment of the crack whore with whom I'd gotten high. Drug addicts rarely buy newspapers; they've got other priorities for their limited funds. But back then, on any given day, thousands of newspapers were left in DC's subway stations, on buses, and on the METRO trains, by METRO riders.

One of the passengers who picked up the Style section of The Washington Post featuring my photo and the article on Resistance Records was a crack whore whose nickname was 'Koolaidria' – with whom I had smoked crack the previous night. Koolaidria, incidentally, had a young son named Mohammed Shaquan, whom she called Moshaq, and a little girl whose real name was Crackeetra. Koolaidria saw the story and brought it back to the crack house after meeting with her welfare case worker. I was abruptly shaken awake by a big, very irate addict who'd just read the article. This giant was surrounded by seven or eight other junkies. None were pleased, all wanted answers, and they all were black.

Holding the Style section with my photo in it, a junkie named Leon said, "Hey, white boy! What 'DIS be? See here? What y'all doin', ownin' some motha-fuckin' RACIST record company?" I had to think very, very fast. My teeth and everything above and below depended on it. "Oh, THAT?," I asked.

"Yeah, 'DIS," he replied, holding it like a weapon over me.

"It's no big deal, Leon." My interrogator felt otherwise.

"Yeah? Well, we say it IS. And in 'dis here hood, what WE thinks be what matters. 'Cause when it's sumpin' racist, us niggas be whatcha call a party of interest." He had me there.

"What y'all gots to say fo' y'self, Mista White Boy Republican?" The furor in his face was real as he added, "and don't start out wiff no fuckin' fo' sco' and seven years ago."

All the years I'd spent spinning for GOP candidates wouldn't be of use in this situation. The only thing that might work was the truth, so, I laid out the facts. I wasn't calm, but pretended to be. "I never wanted anything to do with this," I told them. "I'm not a racist, or hateful. Never have been. If I was, you wouldn't see me driving into the hood to get high with you." So far, so good. "Would a racist feel comfortable enough around black people," I asked, "to crash on their couches?" Another crackhead, sitting over by the TV, said, "it ain't too late to get outta 'dis wiff yo' nuts still in they sack. But we serious. So skip da dance, and jump to da song."

I felt like a tennis player who'd broken my opponent's serve. Now it was up to me to hold serve and score some points, quickly. "My business was owed money by a client," I said. "This guy also owed me, personally. But he went bankrupt, and paid me with shares of stock in a racist music corporation."

"That'd be Resistance Records?," one asked. "Right," I said. "My shares were Class A issues. That meant they had more voting power than the others. That's how I came into the controlling interest in that company. I was glad to unload my shares." The mood of everyone there was palpably improving.

They were coming around, so I poured it on. There's nothing quite like facing a Jury of one's peers when your peers are junkies. "If I didn't enjoy your company, and didn't consider you my friends, I'd just buy my stuff and go smoke it in a hotel, or at some other place. But I don't do that, do I?" That resonated.

"I thinks him be tellin' da troof," a female addict named Kaleesha said. "Dis crazy white boy been here a whole lotta times. But when him gets high in my crib, he always share his shit. Dat's fo' real." Her sentiments were echoed by Koolaidria, which helped. Another crackhead, Devronte, endorsed Kaleesha's words. "Dis dude DO share. I knows, 'cause he done share witt me. Juzz lazz week, Todd done gimme two dime bags. And him ain't even axed me to pay him back!" Another junkie said, "Nigga, go easy on whitey. But if y'all stomps him out, don't axe me to help cleans it up, or get rid of his bloody, dead, white ass. I'm here to get high."

Finally, the gal who lived in the crack house said, "Mister Todd here, he ain't no racist. Besides, if y'all ain't lets him live, him ain't bring no mo' crack over here. Just sayin'." Hearing a conversation about whether I lived or died was way creepy, but par for the course in the hood. Luther, a perpetually drunken addict, said, "Yeah, dog, dis here white dude can't brings us no mo' shit if him dead. Don't just think only about y'seff, nigga. 'Dat be selfish. Dey's other peoples to consider."

Everyone in DC is pragmatic, even dopers in the hood.

LaTrinka offered perhaps the best insight. "It look like Mister Todd just throwed in wiff da wrong peoples," she observed. "But him doin' good now; he hangin' wiff us. When somebody swim in da sewer, dem getting' some turds in they pockets. Fo' real." Koolaidria again reinforced her view. The big addict holding the newspaper asked, "so, where all dat MONEY be?"

"The money? That's what I've been using to buy all this crack I've been sharing with you people."

"Whatcha mean when y'all say, you peoples?"

Damn, I thought. Here I'd been doing so well, and now, just a little slip of the tongue might derail it. I said, "I'm talking about peoples – PEOPLE - like US! You and me. All of us. We're ALL junkies, and crack is our drug. THAT'S what I mean. People like US!" A big smile creased every face. I was home free.

"So, y'all sayin' dat da dough you be spendin' on all dem drugs done come from a bunch of racist, honkey motha fuckas?"

"Yeah" I replied. Tossing the paper away, the big dude said, "I'll be DAMNED! 'Dazz cool as shit! You be buyin' crack you shares wiff us niggas, payin' fo' it from yo' stash done come from 'dem bitch-ass, Kloo Kluck Klan crackas!"

"Right on, dude. You got it." I'd survived. My life hadn't come to an abrupt, violent, end. In the hoods, and within the drug realm, weird things happen nearly every day.

As the summer of 2000 ended, the Bush campaign was in full swing. Vice President Al Gore was Bush'sopponent, and my parents were busy with the Iowa campaign. For the first time since 1992, my dad wasn't on the ballot. He had promised voters that after four terms, he'd retire from elective office. Laura and George W. Bush campaigned in Iowa, and on nearly each visit, Gary and Sandy Blodgett accompanied them. But I had other things on my mind. The FBI was pleased with my work, and the tabs I kept on the targets I was assigned to monitor.

The bureau's honchos knew I was acquainted with every major ringleader of the violent, racist Far Right, and was more aware of what went on in the top echelons of America's Far Right than anyone. Like the agents I worked with, these administrators knew I wasn't a racist, but had profited handsomely from that racket. The agents told me to notify them whenever anyone under surveillance contacted me.

When William Pierce called, the agents wanted to know all about the conversation. Pierce had said he would be soon in Washington he and invited me to meet him for dinner.

The only people who knew I was working for the bureau besides my wife and my lawyer were my parents, and hers. My then-father-in-law was a lawyer, as well, and had concerns. "Todd," he told me, "if Bush becomes President, he'll probably name your dad to a position in his administration," Linda's dad said. "You need to make sure that your being a paid informant won't cause trouble for him." I assured John Reuber that "all of my undercover work will be kept completely confidential" And it was. I met the agents at Buca di Bepo, an Italian restaurant on Connecticut avenue. The restaurant featured a private booth and table just off the kitchen area. We sat there, where no diners could see us.

"Todd, we're going to have you look into some white Nationalists who operate in London, England. They've got ties to some racists you've worked with, and you'll have cover from the bureau while overseas, as well as from MI-5." I thanked them, and ordered a drink and pasta, and wondered what

81

the hell I'd gotten myself into. The agents left the place a few minutes ahead of me, to be inconspicuous. I left the restaurant, and called a drug dealer from my cell phone.

I was self-medicating with illicit drugs to help deal with my stress. At least, that's how I convinced myself that my addiction wasn't all that bad. The dealer, a black guy named Latrell knew my number, just as most drug dealers know the numbers of their regular customers. "Wazzup, PC?" PC was Latrell's nickname for me: Preppy Crackhead. "I'd like ten slices of pizza," I said, using drug slang. "You done call da right nigga. Where's you at, white boy?" I was parked just down the street from where he lived.

"I'm driving, Latrell. I can meet you anywhere in the city. Are you holding?," I asked, wanting to know if he had some crack for sale. "Course I'm holdin', Lightskin. I'se da next buildin', at my baby mama house. Tell da bitch at the front dexx 'dat y'all be's a friend of mines and give she yo name. I be callin' her now. I'm a-tell her to let yo honky ass in." Baby Mama's house, here comes Lightskin.

I laughed as I thought of what William Pierce would think of his business partner being deep into the hood, about to visit a black drug dealer in a public housing project, buy crack cocaine from him and get high with people he hated.

There's something incongruent about a former member of the White House staff, who was a Boy Scout in Iowa, who regularly attended church, played Little League baseball and had a newspaper route while growing up, and earned a degree from a well-regarded private university, who, now – as a married man in his early forties – now being on the streets surrounding a public housing project in a high-crime, DC 'hood', buying crack cocaine.

Or, is there?

It may amaze some people to learn that crack cocaine isn't only a "ghetto drug". They'd be surprised to learn that many frequent users are white, and that their professional backgrounds and educational and socioeconomic status, are high – no pun intended. But it's true. Illegal drugs are the great equalizer: once hooked, everyone is down on the same level. By the time I was addicted, I learned that the shared misery caused by drugs enveloped many people, from all races, religions, and social milieu. Addiction invades the lives of people from all walks of life, all socioeconomic backgrounds, and every type of family. When smoking crack, the only thing that junkies care or think about is their next hit, and how they'll get it, and when. One hit – meaning, one deep drag on the crack pipe – was all it took to get me hooked. Over the years I used, and in the years since getting clean, I've heard thousands of junkies say they were hooked on crack, or crystal meth, upon finishing their first hit.

Narcotics Anonymous members are taught that addicts "didn't become addicted in one day." I dispute that premise, based on my experience and that of others.

After parking my car about a block from 'Baby mama' house, I walked to the housing project. On the street was a crackhead I knew. She was a young black lady in her late twenties who went by the nick-name of Teeny Weeny. "Hey, Fancy pants!," she said, "How's y'all doin'?" Teeny Weeny always called me Fancy Pants, even when I was wearing jeans. She was a single mom on welfare, who turned tricks to finance her drug habit. She also supported her addiction by working as a runner, delivering crack for dealers who were too busy – or, cautious - to cover all of their clients themselves. Sometimes she would hide drugs on her baby, when delivering them. A dependable, cautious, resourceful drug runner can earn several hundred dollars a night. Teeny Weeny often was paid in crack, a common arrangement.

I did as Latrell instructed, and the security lady at the front desk waved me through. The elevator, one of three, was slow and crowded. Single mothers, many in their late teens, with their babies and toddlers, comprised most of my fellow passengers. Latrell was waiting in the hallway as I exited the elevator, and he silently motioned me to follow him down the hall to the appropriate apartment. Like nearly all successful drug dealers, he never used the drugs he sold.

83

Latrell was bright and highly perceptive. Had he not been born to a single mother on welfare and then dropped out of school at 16, or if he'd had some positive male role models while growing up, he might have become a successful businessman, lawyer, or lobbyist. He may have become a Congressman. Latrell had a quirky, almost rapier, sense of humor. As we walked down the hall, he said, "This here ain't exactly da Watergate, is it, Lightskin?" A month earlier, he'd delivered $1,500 worth of crack to the apartment of an addict who smoked it at that famous address. "No, it's not the Watergate, Latrell."

He then said, "small-time thieves live here, but thieves livin' at the Watergate steal from stockholders." As we entered baby mama's unit, no one was home. The place was a disaster: unwashed dishes and jelly jars in the sink, boxes of diapers on the floor, half-eaten fried chicken on dirty paper plates, stained carpet, and a pile of laundry four feet high in the front room. "Guess who live here, Light skin?"

"Not Martha Stewart."

"My baby mama and my son. And for a minute, I do." When a black pusher I knew finished three years in prison, the outgoing voicemail announcement said he'd "been away fo' a minute." When I asked him about his minute, he said he was referring to "C-P time": colored people's time. I paid for the crack, left Baby Mama's crib and drove to what addicts call a safe house to get high. A safe house is a home – usually a separate-standing building, a townhouse, or a brownstone – where it's safe to buy, use and sell drugs. They're considered safe from being hassled by the police. The owners, tenants, or both, work a deal with the cop, or cops, assigned to the street where it's located.

For a price, police won't bother with such places. The only time any cops show up at safe houses is either with a search warrant or if a murder took place and was reported. Such arrangements make safe houses ideal for addicts and dealers. It's also not unusual for hookers to crash – reside, temporarily – and ply their trade in safe houses, for the same reason. I knew some gals who paid crooked cops with sex, to get safe house status assigned to their place of residence. Such arrangements are common in D.C, Baltimore, New

York, and other major U.S. cities. Safe houses also enable crooked cops to earn tax-free money on the side. The cash is paid directly by those, including known drug dealers, with a stake in assuring the house is "safe".

For decades, DC's police force has been the "most policed city" in America. GOVERNING magazine reported in 2015 that "even with declining membership, the District was still the most policed city in the U.S.", with "nearly 57 cops for every 10,000 Washingtonians – almost twice the average for big cities and about four times the national average." So with all these cops, why is violent crime rampant in DC?

CHAPTER FOUR

P olice corruption is a major problem in large American cities, with much of it tied directly to drugs, and crooked cops cause much misery for lots of innocent citizens. I saw this while using and buying crack in DC and Baltimore, New York City and Philadelphia. A DC police officer once stopped me for speeding as a young drug pusher - was part of a drug ring – was my passenger. The cop issued no ticket, no warning, and didn't ask to see the ID of the dealer sitting next to me, with warrants out on him. The policeman let us slide because he knew that the dealer in my car could implicate him for operating his own, highly profitable drug-dealing sideline. This incident occurred in the fall of either 2004, or 2005. A few years following my departure from D.C., that same crooked cop was busted.

His name was Reginald Jones, and he was known to my drug dealer buddy as "officer Reggie". This crooked cop's shadowy, lucrative sideline involved protecting, and facilitating crack and heroin rings in which he actively participated. After many years at it, in 2011, officer Jones was finally busted. He was sentenced to 15 years in prison for his role in this drug ring, in which a member shot and killed a rival.

Officer Reggie had served as a lookout in his police cruiser while five gang members tried to rob their competitor. Prior to the robbery going down, Jones raced his police cruiser up and down the street, in an effort to "sweep the area", and scare people, who might otherwise witness the impending crime, into leaving the crime scene. This greedy, sociopathic cop was on duty at the time of the botched robbery and murder. When a female witness to the shooting ran up to the police car asking for assistance, Jones sped away.

It was only a matter of time before Reggie would underwrite his own demise. That was obvious on the very night he pulled me over. I hadn't turned on my headlights until I'd driven about half a block, which Jones noticed. He clocked me for doing 35 mph in a 25 zone and issued a verbal warning.

I drove off, as the pusher in my front seat said we were lucky that officer Reggie had stopped us. "Why? I asked. "Because, that crooked cop know my cuz work wiff him, sellin' dat PCP, crack and heroin. Other homeys from my hood in on it, too," he said. "Dat's why officer Reggie ain't axed to see my ID. Nigga know me and my boys knows what up wiff him." I asked the drug dealer how a police officer could be involved in drug running. He replied, "Dis be D.C. Everything corrupt. Bein' a cop make it easier to line they pockets. 'Specially if y'all do like Reggie, and throws in wiff da right crowd."

Former DC cop Jared Weinberg in 2013 was charged with, and pleaded guilty to, operating a multi-state, drug-trafficking scheme. This former police officer allegedly also laundered drug money by opening multiple bank accounts at 29 banks in New York, Baltimore, and Chicago. More than 300 deposits to those accounts were made in under a year, totaling over one million dollars. Over a dozen other DC Metro police officers allegedly were involved with Weinberg, who supplied drug dealers with product and assisted them in money-laundering.

Another crooked DC cop is officer Richmond Phillips, who worked undercover operations. In 2013, he was sentenced to life in prison for murdering the mother of his daughter and their little girl, whose bodies were found in a park. Then there's DC officer Aisha Hackley, who in 2011 was charged with scamming over $43,000 from an 85-year-old lady whom she claimed to care for. In 2012, DC police officer William Anderson, III was arrested in Pittsburgh, after he threatened a bus driver with his expandable baton. Also in 2012, a DC police captain, Lamar West, was arrested on charges of choking his wife. DC officer Kenny Furr was charged with soliciting a prostitute and firing a dangerous weapon.

After officer Furr was refused by the hooker, the crooked cop jumped up and down on the hood of her car. He then fired five shots into the vehicle, injuring three passengers. At his trial, Furr was fined $150, given 100 hours of Community Service, and three years of probation. DC residents were stunned by the light sentence. Speculation ensued that the judge went easy on Furr because the victims were black, transgendered women.

In 2018, nine Baltimore city crooked cops were convicted of robbery, fraud, and racketeering. Several were members of an elite law enforcement squad known as the Gun Trace Task Force. This unit was supposed to reduce the number of illegal firearms in Baltimore. Detectives Marcus Taylor and Danny Hersl had previously for years denied that they stole tens of thousands of dollars of drugs, guns, cash and luxury items while they went through the motions of seizing the valuables as police evidence. The detectives fabricated reasons to justify chasing down and searching suspects, and invaded private homes absent any warrants to hunt for these goods. These crooked cops' former Sergeant, Wayne Jenkins, was sentenced to 25 years in federal prison for his role in the scam. His accomplices each received between seven and 25 years.

In September, 2012, a District newspaper, The Washington Examiner, reported that since 2009, over 90 DC cops had been arrested for crimes ranging from extortion to drug dealing to murder. Much of the problem with DC's police force resulted from Marion Barry's four terms as Mayor. His race-based hiring policies resulted in unqualified minorities being hired, instead of qualified applicants. Barry even demoted white detectives and replaced them with blacks, many of whom were objectively deemed by even other black cops to be professionally unsuitable.

In Baltimore, where I also bought, used, and delivered crack cocaine, police corruption is also a major concern. In 2010, Baltimore city cop Keith Nowlin was fired he accessed a protected police computer for department information on a drug dealer friend of his. The pusher was being monitored by federal agents, and the crooked cop shared that information with his buddy, the drug dealer who supplemented this crooked officer's salary. In 2011, Baltimore officer Gahiji Tshamba was convicted of manslaughter in the 2010 shooting death of Tyrone Brown, a nightclub patron who got into a scuffle with the officer.

Then there's the Baltimore police officer charged with stealing from a grocery store. His daughter, who worked there as a cashier, routinely rang up his food bills at reduced prices. In July of 2019, a crooked cop in Jackson county, Florida – Deputy Zach Webster – was charged with planting drugs, including cocaine, on people he arrested. Nearly 120 cases involving people he had arrested had to be dropped, and over a dozen lawsuits were filed against the Jackson county Sheriff's department. Also in July, 2019, a former cop from Mexico - who was illegally residing in the USA - was charged with trafficking enough fentanyl that, according to experts at the Drug Enforcement Administration (DEA), could easily kill over ten million people. Crooked Mexican cop Assmir Conteras-Martinez told Texas authorities he was paid $6,000 each time he smuggled loads of fentanyl from California to Florida. Conterras-Martinez acknowledged having illegally crossed into America from Mexico in December of 2018, and was busted by a Texas trooper employed by the Texas Department of Public Safety.

A crooked Baltimore cop, Danny Redd, was arrested in 2011 for running a heroin ring that pulled in several other officers. Redd had been a city cop since 1994, and was fired in 2002 for sleeping on the job. He returned to the force in 2003 and resumed his involvement with a profitable heroin ring. I had my own, indirect dealings with this crooked Baltimore cop with the memorable name. I recognized his photo and name from news reports, after his fellow officers busted him.

Around 2003-04, I was with some addicts in an Anacostia crack house. Anacostia is among DC's most crime-infested sections outside of Georgetown, where criminals tend to be white-collar, and white. Around 10 p.m., a flashy drug pusher wearing a long shiny, black leather coat and Stevie Wonder-style, tinted shades, arrived at a crack den where I'd lined up a buy.

After talking with the black dude who lived there, they entered the main room. My host pointed at me, saying, "Yeah, him cool." The flashy guy then asked if we could talk alone. We stepped into a bathroom where he said his "people around here say you're honest, and straight-up." He needed a ride to Baltimore's inner city, and back to D.C.

"I've gotta meet a dude, tonight, and pick up something," he said. "We can be there and back in three hours," he said, before asking if I'd chauffeur him. "Sorry," I replied. " I'm here to get high. I've already sent someone out with $350 to get some 8-balls. She'll be back any minute."

The dealer pulled out a wad of C-Notes and peeled off four Benjamins. He said, "That'll cover what you ordered." He peeled off five more, and shoved it on the counter towards me. "That's nine hundred bucks. All yours, if you take me now. I'll make sure your stuff is here when we get back." I asked him why this was so important. He hesitated, and said, "I'm picking up some packets of DT."

"What's DT?"

"Downtown. Heroin."

"Forget it," I said, shoving his money away. "Are you nuts? You realize what happens to people who get busted with that?" He knew, and replied, "it's never happened to me, and never will. My Baltimore boy is as safe as safe gets." I refused, again. "My man," he said, "this is your lucky day. I won't get my drivers license back until next week. Well, an hour ago, the dude who agreed to drive me to Baltimore and back was arrested. I've gotta hire some-one I can trust, now, and that's you." Pulling out his wad of hundreds again, he counted out another ten, and stuffed them in my front shirt pocket. "Now you're up to nineteen hundred. For three hours' work. How about it?" While not eager to make the trip, I was intrigued. "Listen," he said. "I've got a Ferrari and a Mercedes, but a suspended license. You know what cops think when they see a black man drivin' a Ferrari, or a Mercedes, in a bad part of any city, right?" I nodded.

"Okay, then", he said, "there's lots of black dudes who'd gladly take me there and back. But I don't take dumb chances. Those guys either have warrants out on 'em, or their cars might be stolen. Hell, their bitch-ass vehicles might not even make it to Baltimore. Besides," he said, "most blacks are shitty drivers. But you're white, sober, and you own a Range Rover. My homeys like you. Say yes in the next ten seconds, and there's another six hundred for you."

This guy was obviously a player, and he could, and perhaps, would, be in a position to do me some favors someday. "Okay," I said, "let's go." He handed me another five hundred, bringing my compensation to twenty-five hundred, for three hours of work. Over $800 an hour, net. "You are the man!," he said. On the way to Baltimore, he said I was smart. I replied, "yeah? I've killed lots of brain cells, smoking crack." He asked how long I'd been on drugs, and I said, "for too damn long."

"When you've had enough," he replied, "and totally wrecked your life, you'll hit bottom and quit."

"Think so?"

"You'll either see the light, and stop using, or you'll go to prison, or you'll die. And if you go to prison, you'll likely die there." About halfway down the Baltimore-Washington Parkway, his cell phone rang. "Green Range Rover, recent model," he told the caller, and said I was safe. "Yeah. He checks out. He's cool, and white. Makes it even better, doesn't it? See you in thirty minutes." As we approached the location where he was to meet this contact, I noticed we were uncomfortably close to the Northwest district police station. "You realize, don't you, that we're in cop country?"

"No worries," he said. "Seriously?," I asked. "Listen-I-know-what-I'm-doing," he replied. About eight blocks later, one block from the cop shop, he told me to pull over. He had been sending and receiving text messages for the previous 10 minutes. I pulled over and turned off the lights. "My man will be here in less than three minutes." Two minutes later, a black man approached the passenger side of the car.

91

The dealer pressed the window control, and I got a good look at the contact. He was a cop, in uniform. From the streetlight, I saw his badge. The hand-off was made in less than ten seconds.

The heroin – also known as "downtown" – was stuffed in a paper grocery bag. Inside, it was in an over-sized Zip-Loc bag, inside of a Tupperware container about half the size of a shoebox. As my passenger said, "thanks, Red," his window scrolled up. The dealer said, "let's go." Back on the Baltimore-Washington parkway, I asked what had just gone down. "That's my contact; he's one of the finest of Baltimore's finest!"

"He's hardly among Baltimore's finest, but as cops go, he's probably among Baltimore's richest."

"Yeah, Redd does all right, for sure."

"How does a black guy get the nickname, 'Red'?"

"It's not a nickname. That's his real name. Officer Redd. As in, R-E-D-D. Danny Redd. And I'm only telling you that because I know you saw his badge."

"I read it." He smirked at the pun. I asked if his cop friend was on duty. "Yeah," he told me. "He's working. That's the best time to make these transactions."

"A crook, hiding in the open, in uniform. Breaking the law while being paid to uphold it."

"Something like that. Based on a concept originated by Richard Nixon. One of your heroes, I'm sure. Red's just a frustrated, third-rate cop that's tired of the bad guys makin' all the jack. So he became one. Sort of like some Republicans you've worked for."

"How do you know?"

"Charles and Antwan told me about you. So did Miss Kitty. Then I Googled you. I've known about you for months. You're the Republican Crackhead. When I first heard your story, I said, DAMN! This guy should write a book, if he ever gets clean. And, of course, after his daddy retires from the Bush administration." I found his suggestion amusing, because he didn't even know the half of it. "Maybe I will, someday. If you don't mind my asking," I said, "how much is that stuff worth?"

"I do mind. But I'll tell you. What I've got here will net me about four hundred fifty grand on the street, when all's said and done. The dealers I'll sell it to will cut it, and they'll make some good dough, as well. Now you see how I can pay you your exorbitant compensation."

"That's amazing."

"What's amazing? My profit, or are you amazed that a black drug dealer can accurately estimate his net profit against his costs?" An hour later, we arrived back in D.C. It was past midnight. He asked me to drop him off on upper Wisconsin avenue, at a place called Alban Towers. He told me that Frank Sinatra stayed in this swanky building during JFK's inaugural week, where he literally ran the show, at Kennedy's request. We shook hands, and as he got out of my car, he said, "You're a good man, Blodgett, and whip smart. But I've seen lots of good, smart junkies bite the dust. Do whatever you gotta do to get clean. It can be done. I know, from personal experience." I thanked him, and as the window rolled up, he said,

"Oh, one more thing." I stopped the window rolling, and he said, "If you ever write that book, you don't have my permission to use my name. We good on that?"

"We're good." Then he was gone. I kept my word.

Later, I learned he was right: Frank Sinatra DID stay at the Alban Towers when he came to DC to emcee President Kennedy's inaugural festivities. But as the lyrics to one his best-known songs - 'I get a kick out of you' - indicate, 'old Blue Eyes' got "no kick from cocaine." I sure did, though, before coke kicked me.

My brief encounter with Baltimore's infamous ex-cop, Danny Redd, ultimately proved that Baltimore is as plagued with corrupt police officers as Washington, D.C. In July and September of 2017, several Baltimore police officers were arrested for, and charged with, illegally planting evidence to make people into suspects, and make suspects in other crimes appear to be guilty. In one case, crooked cop Richard Pinheiro was caught by his own body camera as he planted drugs in a garbage-strewn alley. Unknown to the dishonest officer, his body camera featured a mechanism which saved the 30 seconds of footage taken prior to its activation. Automatically recorded footage captured 30 seconds before the crooked cop activated his body-cam shows him placing a bag of drugs in a soup can, and setting the soup can in a trash bin. Once Pinheiro activates his body-cam, the ethically and intellectually challenged policeman can be heard saying, "I'm gonna check here."

Fellow officers Jamal Brunson and Hovhannes Simonyan are shown in the same video observing Pinheiro as he perpetrated his illegality. Melba Saunders, a spokesperson for the Baltimore state's Attorney's Office, called the video "troubling", and the guilty cop had no comment when asked about his role in the attempted corruption. Two weeks later, defense attorney Josh Insley got all of the charges dropped against his client, Shamere Collins, after video revealed that multiple Baltimore policemen, working as a team, planted marijuana and other illicit drugs in her vehicle.

Weeks earlier, seven officers of an elite Police Gun Squad unit came under federal indictment. Those crooked Baltimore cops were accused of robbing citizens, filing false court paperwork and receiving overtime pay for work and hours that they hadn't performed. Prosecutors in Baltimore county were forced to drop scores of strong cases due to the illicit actions of those crooked cops. In the first eight months of 2017, Baltimore was the scene of 205 homicides: an average of nearly one murder per day.

If anything, Baltimore has more problems with dirty cops than Washington, D.C. This was true when I was using, buying, and delivering illegal drugs, and it's still true today. In 2011, 23 DC cops were charged with crimes ranging from sexual assault to murder. That same year, 17 Baltimore police officers were charged in an extortion scheme, involving illegal kickbacks paid to cops who illicitly steered accident victims to an auto repair shop. These enterprising, crooked cops, responding to 911 calls involving auto accidents, violated a department directive and diverted accident victims from calling a city-owned towing service. Then they convinced the drivers of damaged cars to call a repair shop whose owner paid them the kickbacks.

One bad cop made $14,000 – all cash, and unreported - in the scheme, and each participating officer was paid $300 per vehicle. Crooked cops wanting to illegally pad their salary know that drugs are the easiest, quickest, best way to increase their take-home pay – tax-free. Also in 2011, a sting operation netted three more crooked cops in Washington, D.C.

Those uniformed lawbreakers were nailed for attempting to receive stolen property – expensive electronic equipment that they knew was stolen. From iPads, to flat screen TVs and computer monitors, to iPhones, and other merchandise, these cops paid cash for the contraband.

But it was videotaped. One officer bought a flat screen TV and iPads worth $5,000, and two others blew over $3,500 on other electronic goods. That same month, DC police officer Jenni Green was charged with accepting cash she believed was stolen during a home burglary. Green planned a burglary with an acquaintance who, unknown to the crooked cop, was actually a police informant. She drove the man to a house that she knew contained a large amount of cash. Using a crowbar from the back seat of Green's car, the informant broke into the house, and stole $1,050 in cash. The crooked cop took $600 of it, and was arrested in front of her house as she returned home.

The sting operation was conducted by the Internal Affairs Unit, in response to citizen complaints about police corruption. In 2013, ten current and former law enforcement officers were among fifteen co-conspirators indicted in Atlanta, Georgia, for selling protective services to drug traffickers. It didn't surprise me; I knew some DC cops who also did that.

In the Atlanta case, an FBI informant provided inside information which busted the greedy lawmen, as was the case with the DC jail guard, Jonny Womble. Mr. Womble was indicted in 2013 for smuggling marijuana, cocaine, heroin, and other drugs, into the DC jail. Officer Womble delivered the drugs to a prisoner, who sold them to addicted inmates.

From 1998 and until the early 2000s, a racist crooked cop in Texas named Tom Coleman began arresting blacks – basically, any blacks whom he decided to charge with drug dealing – even though, in nearly every case, their innocence was as clear as day. Officer Coleman, who subscribed to The SPOT-LIGHT and contributed to Pierce's National Alliance, literally manufactured the charges, and arrested 48 citizens under flagrantly false charges.

They were all locked up and nearly all convicted. This, despite evidence, in some cases, that time cards from the victims' employers provided ironclad alibis and disproved Coleman's claims that they'd offered to sell drugs to him, and others who purportedly worked undercover. This crooked, racist police officer was convicted of his crimes in 2005. In December, 2018, a concerned, honest DC police officer told FOX News that the higher-ups in the District of Columbia Police Department were routinely downgrading crime reports in an organized scheme to reclassify violent felonies as non-violent misdemeanors. This veteran officer revealed that such falsified filings have been going on for many years, to convince the public that violent crime is declining in the District.

"If it's a burglary and someone enters the home," he disclosed, "they'll have us re-classify it as Unlawful Entry which brings the crime down from a felony to a misdemeanor. Felonies, but not misdemeanors, are reported to the FBI, which compiles the statistics. In cases of physical assault, the honest cop said, "if the victim doesn't want to give up any information, then they change it to "Injured Person to Hospital." Reclassifying it that way turns the shooting into a mere "incident", not a crime. DC police reports for the 19-month period ending in April of 2018 revealed that nearly 3,000 reports were taken for 'Injured Person to Hospital'. But of those, only 61 were for gunshot wounds, only 11 of which had been self-inflicted. However, due to the reclassification, those reports implied that no crimes were committed. In some cases, shell casings covered the street and sidewalk; in other instances, victims told the cops that they'd been shot by someone else. But with these shootings now categorized as incidents and not crimes, investigations, according to this concerned officer, often end there and then. This honest cop said he's actually been on crime scenes where he was ordered to reclassify such felonies.

The DC police brass, known as "white shirts", say, "no, we're not going to make it this," the officer told reporter Marina Marraco. "We're looking at each other like WOW, and we're like, 'okay'. There's no need to get disciplined over that, so we just go ahead and reclassify," he said. According to FOX, several 'white shirt' sources refused requests to be interviewed, on-camera, out of fear of retaliation. The officer who spoke on condition of anonymity to FOX News, said the 'white shirts' are being pressured "to cook the numbers." Another DC police officer described the sordid practice as "embarrassing, because ... we're reclassifying these crimes and [creating] the falsehood that the District of Columbia is safer than it actually is." A spokesman for the DCPD said that, "The Metropolitan Police Department has not been made aware of any allegations of "illegitimate crime re-classification to "lower crime statistics." We would consider such an allegation to be extremely serious."

Their motto is 'Serve and Protect', and for honest officers, it fits. But for crooked cops, instead of serve and protect, it's more like serve with disrespect. My dealings with the police didn't end with my brief dealings with officers like Reggie Jones and Danny Redd. In fact, as my addiction worsened, my experiences with cops – good and bad – took a sharp turn for the worse. But at least when I was finally busted, I was guilty. The DC police officers who arrested me on possession of illegal substances charges were honorable, dedicated and honest, and I fully deserved what I got. It can be incredibly difficult to convict dirty police officers on corruption charges.

However, crooked cops who try to hire hit men to commit murder are easier to charge, prosecute, and convict. In May of 2019, a New York City police officer, Valerie Cincinelli, was charged with two counts of murder-for-hire, along with one count of obstructing justice, after she allegedly retained the services of a hired assassin to kill her estranged husband and the teenaged daughter of her boyfriend. The hit man's fee in this case was $7,000 up front, with $3,000 more to be paid after the two targets were dead.

Officer Cincinelli, a twelve-year veteran of the NYPD, is claimed to have insisted that the killings take place in "the hood", or "the ghetto" – her words - so that "it would not look too suspicious", court papers indicated. According to her boyfriend, who exposed Cincinelli's murder scheme to the police and subsequently worked with them to snag her, she wanted the hit man to "run" her boyfriend's 14-year-old daughter "the fuck over" in order to make her murder to appear to be a hit-and-run. Officer Cincinelli has proclaimed her innocence, and for her sake, she'd better be correct. That's because if she's convicted, she will face up to forty years behind bars.

Lack of evidence and problems with witness credibility can kill prosecutor's cases from the get-go. Dirty cops aren't usually stealing diamonds from Tiffany's, Corum wristwatches, or new Cobalt motor boats. They don't often car-jack a wealthy lawyer's Bentley, Rolls-Royce, or Mercedes Benz. Their victims tend to be hookers, drug pushers, thieves, gang members and drug addicts – often with criminal records. Most law enforcement officers in America are ethical, professional, competent, honest, and honorable. But many are not.

The FBI flew me from Washington, DC to Huntsville, Alabama, where the space center is located. There, I spent three nights and four days at a racist conclave. Several white supremacist organizations had sponsored the event, which drew over 500 attendees. The confab featured lectures, seminars, power point presentations and panel discussions, all of which included extensive audience participation. Many attendees brought their children and even grandchildren, to the function, which made it even more bizarre. After renting a car at the Huntsville airport, I drove to the motel just outside of Huntsville where the event was already underway. I paid my $50 registration fee, checked into my room, and headed for the motel's main convention hall. Inside, a couple of hundred racists busied themselves with hatred. Not long before this conference, the killers of a 49-year-old black man named James Byrd, Jr., were sentenced for his murder. Three white supremacists had roughed him up before chaining him to a pickup truck. Then they took off, dragging the poor man at high speed for two miles to his death. When Byrd's body was found, his head was a couple of miles away.

Two of his killers, John William King and Lawrence Brewer, got the death penalty; the third got life. One of Mr. Byrd's killers, 23-year-old John William King, was a fan of William Pierce and 'The Turner Diaries'. King's tattoos included an image of a black man hanging from a tree, a Confederate Knights of America insignia, and the words Aryan Pride. In April, 2019, John William King was executed.

Months after Byrd's murder, a DC radio host who disliked a song performed by a black artist said, "no wonder people drag them behind trucks." James Byrd's brutal death and the trials of his killers were still in the news in the summer of 2000, when the FBI sent me to a three-day gathering near New Orleans, Louisiana. Of course, these three were heroes among white supremacists. But knowing that Mr. Byrd's murderers were worshipped by this crowd didn't prepare me for what was in the corner of the cavernous main exhibit hall, next to the convention room.

Under the banner of, BYE, BYE, BLACK BYRD, a slick-talking, oily bigot was selling, for $25 a pop, tickets to enter a contest. 'Bye, Bye, Black Byrd' was developed by a racist computer whiz and was being market-tested at the event. Twelve or fifteen contestants were playing it on laptop computers. I asked a young lady wearing a white cowgirl hat about this game. She said, "use the curser to aim the truck to where ya want it to go. Don't go too fast, though, or you'll lose the nigger's head. Whoever goes the fastest and keeps the coon on the chain in one piece for the longest time wins. The object," she explained, "is to keep the Jigboo's head from a-separatin' from his body fer as long as possible."

First prize was a new, .12 gauge Browning Citori over-and-under shotgun with invector chokes. Second prize was a pre-owned, .30/30 Mossberg rifle with a scope. Third prize was a blued steel Smith & Wesson .38 revolver. The guns had been donated to a white supremacist tax-exempt entity which allowed the original owner a tax deduction for his generosity. The promoter bought a booth at the conclave, and by the time I arrived, over 50 tickets had already been sold to enter the contest. I bought one and walked over to the laptop computers. All were loaded with software for 'Bye, Bye, Black Byrd'.

On each computer screen was an image of a pickup truck, and a chain pulling the image of a black man. Simulated scenes of various terrain imagery cropped up during the duration of the game, which lasted either six minutes or until the contestant lost control, and the black man's head separated itself from the body image. A heavyset guy with a scruffy beard told me, "be careful to not wipe out, or hit a tree, or go off the road," he said. "Just keep the porch monkey's head from a-comin' off, and don't hit no telephone poles, or dogs, or parked vee-hick-ills."

At the end of the game, the head would automatically disconnect from the image of the body, for those who skillfully navigated their vehicle. A North Carolina college student told me, "If more than one contestant keeps the jungle bunny's head on throughout the course, the contestant who went the fastest wins." At the end of each game, the players' speed was clocked. Two young men and lady who appeared to be about 75 were the top three finishers. First prize was awarded to a young painting contractor from South Carolina. Finishing second was a college student from Louisiana. Third place was claimed by the Florida grandmother whose blouse was emblazoned with the Confederate battle flag, and a campaign-style button which read: 'Proud Grandma'. "I just wish my husband was alive to see me win this," she drawled, in a thick twang. "His old grandpappy used to go a-coon huntin' every other weekend." Somehow, I knew she wasn't referring to raccoons.

"In just one year, back in the '30s," she said, "him and his buddies done killed 'em thirteen niggers. Either shot 'em or hung 'em from trees. Then they'd feed 'em to the hogs." This old gal spoke these words with the type of enthusiasm and pride that normal grandmothers gush about their grandchildren making the honor roll or the Dean's list, of joining the U.S. military, or getting engaged. Ingratiating myself with those I surveilled meant engaging them in conversation, so I asked how, even in the 1930s Deep South, her husband's grandfather had managed to hunt down and kill thirteen people without getting caught. "Oh, it wasn't hard," she replied. Winking at me, she said, "See, he was a deputy Sheriff in Mississippi, and one of his huntin' buddies was the Mayor, so that helped."

With the racist right, it's not only okay to kill minorities, it's even better when cops allow it, or do it, themselves. This morbid computer video game was developed by racist, college-age computer geeks, and it inspired William Pierce to commission some software engineers to create his DVD game called 'Ethnic Cleansing'. "Why create a DVD game in which players can kill only one nigger?," he asked. "With Ethnic Cleansing, players can kill hundreds of niggers, Jews, spicks and fags." 'Ethnic Cleansing' hit the market in January, 2002. Just as William Pierce had said, his racist DVD game was far more violent than 'Bye, Bye, Black Byrd'. A dispute arose over the ownership and distribution rights to 'Bye, Bye, Black Byrd', which prevented it from ever being marketed. But it didn't fail due to any lack of enthusiasm or interest on the part of its fans.

The setting for 'Ethnic Cleansing' was New York City ghettoes and underground subway stations. Players could be either a Skinhead or a Klansman. The object was to shoot as many blacks, Jews, Hispanics, and homosexuals as possible. To win, players had to kill enough people to reach the 'Jewish Control Center'. Once there, they had to kill Israeli Prime Minister Ben Netanyahu, who yells, "oy vey" when hit. Pierce didn't attend this gathering, but later said that based on the popularity of 'Bye, Bye, Black Byrd', he anticipated that 'Ethnic Cleansing' would be an economic and recruitment success.

Pierce was interviewed in early 2002 by 'Wired' magazine about 'Ethnic Cleansing'. He said that, "from the very beginning we've been a multimedia organization … using every medium that we can to reach the public effectively." Pierce later told 'Wired.com' that after only a couple of weeks after the game's debut, Resistance Records had already sold a "couple thousand" copies of it. He added that "about 90 percent" of the 'Ethnic Cleansing' buyers were white, teenaged boys.

If you feel nauseous reading this, I apologize. But if you didn't, I'd question your humanity. The level of inhumanity I saw and heard at such gatherings was horrific, evil, and sick. But that's how it was, and is.

Organized hatred can be as addictive and dangerous as crack cocaine or any other illegal drugs. It's weird to listen to an old man in a black robe with title of "Reverend" deliver a church sermon from behind a pulpit emblazoned with a swastika. It's even stranger when his congregation looks just like parishioners in a conventional church, of the type I grew up attending in north Iowa. The worst part was when this neo-Nazi preacher called the kids down to the front for what he called the "children's sermon". About halfway through the 60-minute service, just before the collection plates were passed around, about a dozen little kids went up to the front of the makeshift sanctuary.

There, the grandfatherly minister sat in an overstuffed chair, with the youngsters sitting cross-legged in front of him. Smiling sweetly, the old bigot told these children how "only us white folks are the true Israelites", and that "Jews are the devil's spawn." These impressionable children were indoctrinated with the idea that as the "killers of Christ, Jews have been doing Satan's work forever."

For his main sermon to the congregants, this so-called man of God castigated Jews, homosexuals, blacks and Hispanics, the last of whom he called "mud people". Urging the crowd to take "decisive action", the faux preacher said it was God's desire that the USA never becomes what he called a "majority-minority nation." As he spewed his vitriol, a lady with closed eyes sitting next to me silently prayed. She raised both of her hands to the ceiling, in the preacher's direction. Tears streamed from her eyes, which she wiped with a tissue. A heavyset, bearded man in a cheap, ill-fitting suit would occasionally whisper, "Yay, Yaweh", and "Power to Wotan", in response to the so-called minister's words. "Wotan" is the acronym for "Will Of The Aryan Nation", and mentioning this term sends holocaust deniers into near delirium. A parishioner told me that Butler's sermon had made her "pandalirious" with joy.

The fervor of this throng exceeded, anything I'd ever seen – including crowds at a Donald Trump rally, or at any fundamentalist church of the sort I'd been in while working on GOP political races. "The good Lord ordained that blacks and browns cannot reach OUR levels of attainment! God clearly INTENDED for these LOWER species to serve the interests of WHITE, Christian PATRIOTS!" He said Adolf Hitler was "chosen by God to set things right, but then the Jews ruined his glorious plans."

The demagogue whipped the crowd into a frenzy, proclaiming that, "sometimes, in order to maintain and promote OUR culture, we must battle and defeat those who'd destroy it!" The fired-up crowd left the place with even more hate in their hearts than they'd brought into the place. A little boy, no more than eight years old, asked his father, "daddy, are niggers people?" With a paternalistic hand on his son's shoulder, his father said, "Well, son, some folks think niggers is humans, 'cause they can talk. The reverend, he was just remindin' us that they ain't OUR kinda humans. That's why we gotta do what we're a-gonna do. We owe it to our race, our heritage, and to the good Lord. It's God's will."

I wondered what evil that this little boy might grow up to someday do, in the name of God. Firebomb a synagogue? Shoot up an NAACP meeting? "Weren't them there words just about the most inspirational thing y'all ever done heard?," asked a pretty teenager, whose white dress and blouse matched her shoes, stockings, belt, head band, and purse. "Oh, my GOD - Hell, yes," her young friend replied. "I'm a-gonna get me a CD of that there sermon, so's I can send it off to my granny in Florida. She's been a-warnin' about Jews, niggers, spicks and queers since I was knee high to a grasshopper." None of these fervent worshippers, I suspect, ever applied to Harvard's Divinity school. After the so-called sermon, I joined about 50 congregants for coffee and rolls in an adjacent room, for "fellowship time".

This fellowship consisted mostly of ranting and raving about how minorities – mainly Jews - were ruining America, and how there will "be Hell to pay when Jesus returns." These buffoons made Hulk Hogan look like Alan

Dershowitz, and some of the women weighed half as much as a Harley Davidson Road King bike with all the extras. These reprobates even had their own, oddball way of pronouncing "Jesus". They spoke his name as if it contained three syllables: 'Juhh-EEE-zuzz'. If anything is worse than some violent, crazy people, it's evil, racist, violent crazies who indoctrinate these innocent, impressionable youngsters into racial bigotry and religious hatred.

These True Believers were, and are, convinced that Caucasian gentiles should be exempt from having to atone for anything, even racist hate crimes. To the extent that the old saying about children living as they learn holds true, I'm not optimistic about the futures of these brainwashed kids. As I left the pseudo sanctuary, a little blond girl, no more than six years old, looked earnestly at her mother and asked, "Mommy, why does God let Jews live?" The lady bent down, looked her daughter straight in the eye, smiled, and said, "Darlin', the Lord lets snakes and mosquitoes live, too. And we know how nasty they are, right?" As the child nodded, her mother told her that "lots of bad things get to live, and it's up to us to stay away from evil. But some day, all those evil Jews will be gone. We'll stop 'em. That there's what the pastor was a-sayin'."

Comparing human beings to annoying insects and deadly serpents is par for the course in the wacky world of hate. The little girl was intrigued, but still curious. "So, what'll we DO, Mommy?"

"Well, honey, remember when that pesky hornet landed on our kitchen sink last week?"

"Yes."

"What'd Daddy do?"

"He SMUSHED it with a newspaper, and flicked it off, and he washed it down the drain!"

"That's right, sweetie," her mother replied, with a wink and a smile. Her daughter got the message. She replied, "okay, now I understand." I walked away from there as fast as my legs could take me, only to find myself in the midst of even more hatred, disguised as compassion, by smiling, evil people.

Alan Berg was a popular Jewish radio talk show host based in Denver. For years, he entertained and outraged listeners, often challenging anti-Semites. Mr. Berg was shot dead by Bob Mathews and three others in 1984. Mathews was the professional racist whom Pierce acknowledged had given him millions of dollars in stolen U.S. currency. One of his accomplices was a virulent hater named David lane. Lane also drove the getaway car as Alan Berg lay dying. For his role in the killing, Lane was sentenced to 150 years in prison. He died in 2007.

Added to this sentence was another 40 years for his role in stealing the $4.1 Million, counterfeiting, and other RICO violations. For his part in Berg's murder, Lane became a bona fide celebrity among racialists.

They sent him money, bought him subscriptions to publications he enjoyed, and made him the recipient of much veneration throughout the white supremacy movement. Following the pro-Hitler church service I walked with several racists in the motel's large exhibit hall. An auction was being held. Its promoters said the proceeds would benefit imprisoned, violent bigots like David Lane.

Furnishing comfort to convicted racist murderers incarcerated for killing blacks, Hispanics, homosexuals, and Jews represented humanitarianism for these folks. Haters from all across America and Canada donated the items on the chopping block.

"SOLD!," the auctioneer yelled, as he banged his gavel down, "for four hundred dollars, to the little lady in the third row!" A Betty White lookalike in a polka dot dress had just bought an original copy of The Denver Post, which published a detailed account of Berg's murder. It was autographed by David Lane. Lane was still alive then, which made me wonder why his signature would go for four hundred bucks. But it did, because these people were True Believers who supported The Cause. The next item for sale was a letter from Byron de la Beckwith, the convicted assassin of the civil rights leader Medgar Evers. The de la Beckwith letter was written to an admirer, just after the killer went off to prison in 1997 – 34 years after he murdered Medgar

Evers in front of his wife and children. De la Beckwith had just died in prison a few months earlier, which raised interest in the document. It went for six hundred fifty bucks. Each item being auctioned came with its own story and a purported provenance.

"These patriots lost their FREEDOM, because of ZOG," the fat auctioneer barked to the crowd of about 175. 'ZOG' stood for Zionist Occupied Government, which is an oft-spoken, anti-Semitic phrase popular with white supremacists. They believe Jews have taken over the U. S. government, and that it primarily serves Israel's interests. So they call it ZOG.

"These dedicated, principled, REAL Americans will be incarcerated until they die, OR until the White Revolution, whichever comes first!," the auctioneer screeched. The seersucker-suited charlatan then picked up a blued-steel, Sig-Sauer 9 mm handgun, ostentatiously displaying it. He said that the weapon was about 20 years old, and "from the private collection of the late Bob Matthews." The crowd collectively gasped at the mere mention of this revered name. One bearded, overweight, middle-aged Aryan Nations member removed his NASCAR cap as soon as he heard the auctioneer mention the name Bob Mathews. The guy suddenly became solemn, and blinked back tears.

As the fat racist wiped his blue eyes with a Confederate flag-patterned handkerchief, the auctioneer barked, "This here beauty's in sue-perb workin' order." The focused crowd stood at reverent attention as the auctioneer announced, "biddin' starts at twelve hundred dollars. What am I bid?" Several hands went up at once, signifying the opening price. When all was said and done, the gun sold for $3,900, to three racists who had pooled their cash. One of the buyers told me he and his two buddies had "gone in together on a coupla huntin' dawgs. Thirteen hundred bucks apiece ain't a bad price to own a piece uh history." The firearm's provenance, which purportedly verified that the weaponhad actually once belonged to Mathews, was a notarized statement signed by the "Reverend" Richard Butler. Pastor Butler, as he was known, was another revered figure among white supremacists and Holocaust deniers.

An engineer, Richard Butler got into the Hate Movement after, he told me, he "decided" that "Jews must be eliminated." I met Butler a few times, and his views were even more extreme than the ersatz pastor who'd preached the sermon the previous day. Butler was as much of a legitimate minister as a 7-11 taco is authentic Mexican food. But that didn't matter to this flock; as far as they were concerned, if a great man like Pastor Butler said the gun had belonged to Bob Mathews, then it had. When it comes to auctions, the world of white supremacy isn't exactly Sotheby's.

The following day, Saturday, was the biggest of the conclave. Several seminars were being conducted simultaneously, and I sat in on them. One of the best-attended was titled, 'Manage and Invest Your Money Like a Hebe'. Like most scam artists, the promoter appealed to ignorance, hatred and greed. I chatted with Chris Temple, a self-styled financial advisor in the movement whom I'd met while working for Carto. Temple was later convicted of, and imprisoned for, scamming far-right clients on investment portfolios he managed for them. We discussed Willis Carto's dwindling empire. I then left the hotel in my rental car and drove to a backwoods bar ten miles away. The smoke-filled, West Virginia hillbilly tavern was packed with rough, mean-looking, loud-mouthed, tattooed bikers in leather jackets. Their brawny forearms, tobacco juice-infested beards, and putrid, greasy ponytails, were as menacing as they were hideous. And the crude guys in there were even worse than the skanky chicks I just described.

I pulled up a chair, and ordered a double Jack Daniels. Patsy Cline's song, 'Crazy' was playing on the jukebox. It was appropriate for that oldie to blare as I sat quietly and looked around. The noisy honky tonk was infested with crazy, wild-eyed lunatics. My entire world had become crazy. It became even crazier a few hours later, when a racist multimillionaire called, inviting me to a private party at a local hater's 'man cave' – at a large, converted barn on property he owned north of our hotel.

This wasn't a party to which most of the event's attendees were invited. The 40 or 50 invitees, all men, were professionals, business owners, bankers, wealthy farmers, and retired oilmen and ranchers. Most were on a first-name basis with Carto, Pierce, and other Movement honchos. Dirty money, laundered by a tax-evading, anti-Semitic, money-laundering racist funded the joint, which was largely infested with loud, cash-clashing, nouveau riche, heavy-drinking bigots. Some were old money types whose neckties featured fly-fishing lures, sailboats, elephants, and school insignias, attached to shirts with button down collars, and affixed with a gold or silver tie bar.

The blonde strippers on the shiny brass poles were high-end, with busty bosoms as fake as their bottle blonde hair. Their big, bare breasts were affixed with red Swastikas, and their tiny hats featured black and gold lightning bolts, symbolizing Hitler's infamous SS. Before they stripped down to their G-Strings, they wore short shorts emblazoned with the Confederate Battle Flag. Their nightclub act opened when a sultry, platinum blonde whose age I guessed was about 30 came onstage. Between puffs on her Virginia Slims cigarette, she belted out her rendition of Eddy Arnold's monster hit, 'Make the World go Away' – with lyrics customized for this affluent audience of well-connected haters.

"Make the Jews go away … Let us whites enjoy America –

Git 'em out, without delay … Just make them Jews all go away;

Do yew re-mem-ber how our country … did just fine without Jews –

That's why us Christians will change things … because all Jews are such bad news

Make the Jews go away … another Hitler's what we're hopin' for

It's what we pray for, night and day … just make them Jews all go away"

Her next number was a bastardized rendition of Tammy Wynette's signature song, 'Stand by your Man':

"These days, it's hard to be white man … ever since Jews destroyed our land

Jews love all wetbacks, niggers and fairies; dis-plac-in' whitey, that's their plan

But our brave white men will rise up – take back our nation – yes, they can

Christ killers hate Christians, they push fer race quotas – but, from our schools, it's God they ban

So … Love yore white man, and he'll love you back, and protect ya

Against the eeeeeviiillll Hebrews

And Spicks, and fags, and Jig-jig-a-boos

Love yore white man

And show the world he's a-worthy

He'll stomp out all … the … Jews … he … caaannnn -

Sooooo … Love … yore … white … man

Next was her rendition of Nancy Sinatra's number-one hit, 'These Boots are Made for Walkin' '. This lyrical modification was perhaps the nastiest of anything I'd ever heard, but the adoring crowd was absolutely transfixed, as the sexy singer belted out her bastardized, racist lyrics:

"These boots are made for stompin', and stompin' is what they'll do; One of these days, these boots are gon-na stomp our every JEW. Da-da-da … da-da-da … da-da-da … Ready, BOOTS? Start stompin' "

Her next song was set to the melody of 'Can't Get Used to Losin' You', a popular 1960s tune by crooner Andy Williams, a native Iowan. The title of this song was, 'Missin' Adolf Every Day'.

"If you're like me, you're sick of Jews; it's time we deport all Hebrews

Coons and Spicks, and fairies, they'll go, too – once we e-ject every evil Jew

I miss our Fuhrer every day, 'cuz he's the man who knew the way –

Gon-na make ev-ry Jew pay, despite what Liberals say

It's time us whites push back; we should – as Adolf Hitler said we could

We'll clean up every neighborhood, 'cause it's for the greater good

I miss the Fuhrer every day, 'cuz he's the man who knew the way ...

Missin' Adolf every day; love him more than I can say ...

As she sang, two equally attractive, gorgeously-busted blondes placed small envelopes in front of each man at every table. One of the guys seated at my table, a manufacturer from Kentucky, leaned over and whispered to me, "this is for any cash, or check, you may wanna contribute. The chicks keep ten percent of your donation; the rest goes to Dr. Pierce."

As a veteran drinker, I noticed the bottles behind the leather bar. Blanton's bourbon, Oban and other single-malt scotches, Tanqueray and Beefeater gin, Jameson whiskey, Ketal One and Absolut vodka, Gosling's rum, Cristal champagne, Bailey's Irish Crème, Hennessey cognac, Taylor Port, and just about every other top-shelf bottle of any and every liquor and liqueur available from all over the world. After another hour, I left the place. The FBI agents wouldn't be pleased to know that I exited early, but I was tired, and needed to rest for the following day's activities. Upon my return to the hotel, I went straight to my room to sleep. Spying on racist haters is as exhausting as it is exasperating.

The following week, William Pierce drove from his West Virginia Nazi Nest to Washington, D.C. After spending the night with some wealthy supporters in Georgetown, he called and told me to meet him at One p.m., at the Tombs. This subterranean landmark is on the edge of Georgetown university's campus, in the basement of a fancy restaurant called '1789', and was featured in the popular 1980s movie, 'St. Elmo's Fire'. On the way down the stairs to the bar area I hoped nobody would recognize the author of The Turner Diaries, or me. Beginning in 1981, when I was an intern on Capitol Hill, this classic tavern has been one of my favorites. It hadn't changed much over the years. Its hardwood floors, bare brick walls, and classic rowing décor – including the cool, old oars on the walls – set it apart from other college bars. Pierce was alone, in a booth beneath a mural of rowers.

"I figured you'd like a burger," he said, "so I ordered one for you, with fries." After two hours of discussing business, we were in Pierce's Ford pickup truck, on the way to Annapolis. "Our host and hostess live on the Severn river, about two miles from the U.S. Naval Academy," Pierce told me. This pro-Hitler couple, whom I'll call Dick and Barb, were "quite wealthy", according to Pierce.

"That's cool. How'd they get their dough?" Looking a bit peeved, he replied, "you get right to the point, don't you? They inherited substantial money, and they've invested heavily in real estate, mostly inAnnapolis and Chevy Chase. When I last saw them, Dick gave me two hundred grand."

"All in Benjamins?."

"No. Cashiers check." Their house was surrounded by large trees, hidden from the road. Pierce parked in their driveway, about forty feet from the house. On their front patio was a cast iron figure holding a lamp in his hand. As we walked closer, I noticed that the figure was that of a black slave. Pierce aimed his remote key at his vehicle and locked it. "Never trust a nigger," he said, "not even a statue of one." Dick and Barb were each about 70, and fit. Throughout the meal, they lavished praise on Pierce, and told me how lucky I was to be working "with this Aryan genius." It was all rather sickening.

Their two golden retrievers, both females scampered in and out of their living room for the hour we chatted, before being shown into their dining room. The dogs kept up their sporadic visits for the following two hours, as we ate crab cakes, lobster, and shrimp. After Barb brought in an after dinner liqueur, she excused herself. "Let's go into the den," Dick said, leading us down the hall. Pierce, who detested tobacco smoke, didn't complain when Dick lit up a Cuban cigar and offered me one. His humidor was filled with Cohibas, Macanudos, Habanas and other high-end, then-illegal smokes. As we finished our stogies, Pierce nodded, silently, to our host.

Dick said, "young man, you're a bright guy with a marvelous future. Come with me, and I'll show you something very special. I know I can trust you to never reveal what you're about to see." Motioning Pierce and I through a door behind the desk in his den, he led us downstairs to his cavernous basement. Behind a fake bookshelf was a steel door, which Dick said was fireproof, which opened to a narrow, paneled hallway. At the end of the hall and to the right was a door with a combination lock.

As Pierce and I stayed back, Dick worked the dial, pulled the lever below, and flung the door open. Once We were inside, he flipped a light switch. Pointing to what looked like a steel version of mini frisbees, he said, "enriched uranium, and high-grade plutonium. It was smuggled over here around 1991, after the USSR collapsed." Pierce, who had seen this before, said, "the Jews and their traitorous backers are in for a real surprise when the White Revolution begins. Most people don't know that there's lots of this stuff in the hands of patriots like Dick."

I'm no scientist, but I knew that this is used to make atomic bombs, and it's not easy for private citizens to own so much of it. "Each of these babies weighs about eight pounds," Dick said, proudly pointing to the hundreds of pellets, stacked behind inch-thick, crystal clear plexiglass. "But they can release as much energy as two hundred thousand gallons of natural gas. They're baked at 3,100 degrees Fahrenheit, to give 'em strength." The discs were approximately five or six inches in diameter, and perhaps a quarter inch thick. Pierce stepped into his physicist role while gazing at the deadly contraband. "A chunk of this highly enriched uranium that's the size of a standard bowling ball," he said, "and some of this high-grade plutonium the size of a billiard ball, could power a nuclear bomb with enough knock-down power to wipe out everyone and everything for ten square miles." As I contemplated that, he added, "There's enough enriched uranium and high-grade plutonium here to make at least twenty such devices." As Dick smiled, Pierce said, "that's enough to wipe out America's 25 largest cities, and then some." Back upstairs, Dick's wife reappeared. "Thanks, Bill, for joining us," Barb told Pierce, as they hugged. She took my hand in hers, and her husband shook my hand as we moved toward their front door. On the return trip to DC, Pierce handed me an envelope that Dick had given him while I washed up in their bathroom before dinner.

"Take a look," he said, as he switched on the interior dome light. Inside was a Money Order for $150,000, payable to cash. For the remainder of our time in Pierce's truck, I didn't think much about his well-heeled, influential Backers and how they enthusiastically financed racist hatred. Instead, I focused on how this evil genius and his wealthy, anti-Semitic supporters could so casually discuss the potential annihilation – via domestic nuclear terrorism – of the United States.

It was late when Pierce and I arrived back in Georgetown. I had parked my Range Rover in the under-ground garage at the Georgetown Park Mall, in the 3200 block of 'M' Street, N.W. After getting my car, I checked my voice mail messages, having turned my phone off earlier. A dealer who always sold high-end crack invited me to her apartment near RFK stadium. What with Linda being at an Oncology Nursing conference in Houston, I had the opportunity to get high without her knowing. So, twenty minutes later I arrived at this gal's building, and found parking on the street, about 100 yards from her apartment. To be buzzed inside, I dialed the number to her unit from the internal telephone to the right of the front entrance. As she buzzed me inside, a young black man, who seemed to appear spontaneously, grabbed my left wrist with both hands. "Fuck off, dude", I said, while replacing the receiver.

The guy said nothing as he tried to pry my watch off of my wrist. Instinctively, I pulled my .380 from my right pocket and shoved it directly into his face. I'm certain I broke some teeth as my gun crashed through his lips. Even the dim light near the door enabled this thieving fool to see what had caused his pain. By this time, he had backed away and brought his hands to his mouth. At this moment, the dealer, arriving at the entrance, saw what had gone down. "Cap 'dis nigga, Todd," she said. "Dis ain't da first time him done try robbin' peoples 'round 'dis hood." The young man looked at me with the fearful expression of someone who thought he'd die, right then and there. "Not tonight, sweetie", I replied, keeping my eyes on the would-be thief. "He's learned his lesson. And he's leaving right now."

Within five seconds, he was out of sight. Once inside the chick's apartment, I wanted to get high immediately. Her stuff WAS great. After about two hours of smoking, the two of us drank Jack Daniels on the rocks. Once I felt okay to drive, I left, but not before having to fend off her unwanted advances. Being a junkie was bad enough, I told myself; I wasn't going to violate my marriage vows.

Years later, my mind drifted back to that night with William L. Pierce and his pro-Nazi backers. In 2014, at The Hague, President Barack Obama said he was less worried about the threat posed by Russia than over "the prospect of a nuclear weapon going off in Manhattan." TIME Magazine reported that such a nuclear "threat itself remains all too real" to America's major cities. Reporter Michael Crowley wrote in the March 26, 2014 issue of TIME magazine that "experts have estimated the probability of such an attack in the near future at between 30% and 50 percent."

Referencing nuclear-savvy terrorists, TIME stated that, "a small group with modest scientific knowledge and a low budget … probably could make a Hiroshima-grade bomb from highly enriched uranium." This article also mentioned that terrorists could buy highly enriched uranium and high-grade plutonium "from smugglers, who continue to be caught peddling uranium stolen from the old Soviet nuclear complex." Two years after that article was published, enriched uranium that the United States had sold to Russia became an issue in the 2016 presidential campaign. Depleting the former USSR's enriched uranium supply motivated the Russians to replenish their reserves. The April 10, 2017 issue of TIME magazine reported that "a device no bigger than a suitcase could contaminate several city blocks – and potentially much more if the wind helps the fallout to spread." This article quoted President Donald Trump as saying that the risk of "some maniac" getting a nuclear weapon is "the single biggest problem" Americans face. "Entire neighborhoods, airports or subway stations" could be affected "for months after such an attack," according to TIME's 2017 report.

U.S. officials at the Pentagon, the FBI, CIA, and JTTF, know that private citizens own enriched uranium and high-grade plutonium, and that it's stored on American soil. Hopefully, the nuclearized, destructive 'White Revolution' envisioned by Dr. William L. Pierce and his evil backers will never come to pass.

But who knows?

CHAPTER FIVE

Balancing my association with the ghetto junkies and drug pushers I hung out with in DC and the haters I monitored, and the FBI agents I reported to, and my parents and their political friends, and those with whom Linda and I regularly socialized made my life a multi-faceted fiasco. By the late Spring of 2000, I had settled into the routine of operating professionally as a full-time federal informant while addicted to crack. Being a junkie isn't only counterproductive. It can be as demanding as a full-time job.

My parents were full-time volunteers with George W. Bush's presidential Campaign. They hosted the then-Governor and Laura in north Iowa on several campaign visits, and my mother was elected as a delegate to the Republican National Convention. Gov. Bush had won the Iowa Presidential caucuses in January. Upon nailing down the nomination, he returned to Iowa in June, to thank his early supporters. My father introduced Bush to a crowd of about 3,500 cheering supporters in downtown Clear Lake. The town square features a 1930s era band shell from which my dad and Bush spoke. This was dad's last full year holding elective office. Linda and I watched the broadcast of this event from our home in Virginia. Following that event, my parents, the Bushes, Senator Grassley, and former (and future) Governor Terry Branstad and U.S. Rep. Tom Latham met privately. Bush's closest political adviser Karl Rove suggested that if Bush was elected, my father would be "a great fit" for a position in his administration.

In December, 2000, Gov. Bush was declared the winner by the United States Supreme Court. My father was in his office in the state Capitol in Des Moines when a Des Moines-based reporter called him. This reporter had covered my father's career, and he was a good, ethical journalist. He had recently seen The Washington Post articles – from January and April – regarding my involvement with Resistance Records. This was six weeks before Bush would take office.

A story about any neo-Nazi connections to the son of one of Bush's top Iowa supporters, particularly The Deputy Majority in the state Legislature, who was being considered for a position in the incoming administration, would've caused turmoil for the President-elect, the Republican party, and my family. It also would have been picked up by the Associated Press and become a national story, embarrassing George W. Bush. The reporter knew that, as did my father. "My son is not, and never has been, a neo-Nazi," my dad told him. "He regrets having been associated with that nonsense. It has nothing to do with me, or the President-elect, or his campaign, or the Republican party. I have no further comment."

Luckily for me, the reporter left the matter alone, and never wrote an article about it.

"Todd," my dad said, "Dave Yepsen" – the reporter – "is a good, fair-minded man. Tom Vilsack is also a decent man." Mr. Vilsack was then Iowa's Governor, a Democrat with whom my father had served when Vilsack was a state Senator. Vilsack, who was later President Obama's Secretary of Agriculture, also had seen the article. "The Governor and I discussed it," my dad told me. "He has two sons, and he knows families can have problems. He feels sorry for your mother and I, and for your wife."

I'm eternally grateful to Dave Yepsen and former Secretary Vilsack.

When America's founders wrote, "All men are created equal", they clearly didn't intend equality for blacks. Slavery didn't end until nearly 30 years after the death of the last founder, James Madison. Being untrue to their own words nearly 250 years ago still haunts America, and in some ways, race relations are worse now than they've been in decades. In 2016, the burial of a man who described himself as Adolf Hitler's "number one fan" made international news. Willis Carto, whose World War II combat service entitled him to burial at Arlington National cemetery. Carto often said he had "fought on the wrong side" of that war. He and his followers believed that their racist, anti-Semitic views were fundamentally in line with those of America's founders.

So how does someone who fought against the Nazis become one, and how did Willis Carto create a multi-million-dollar empire of Hate? How was he able to count among his supporters members of both houses of the U.S. Congress, major film stars, and a prominent member of a President's family?

Carto believed that Jewish people – whom he always referred to as 'the Jews" – were causal to most of America's problems. He believed that blacks, Hispanics, Asians, and other non-whites, were detrimental to American culture, heritage, and success., and that they were all controlled by "the Jews." Carto also disliked homosexuals, despite employing some over the years. He was also resourceful. For decades, a top supporter of Carto's Liberty Lobby was FDR's son-in-law, Curtis Dall. "Colonel Dall", as he was known, died at age 95 in 1991. Dall and FDR's daughter Anna divorced while her father was President, and Dall believed FDR was in the grip of, and manipulated by, what he called "sinister forces." By this he meant Jews, whom he claimed controlled blacks and all minorities. I had met the genteel Mr. Dall while serving on Ronald Reagan's White House staff, at a reception at the Cosmos club of Washington, DC, in 1986. Not long after, we met again, at the National Press Club, where he and Carto were guests of longtime member Jim Tucker, an editor who was on Liberty Lobby's payroll.

I had no idea then of what Dall called "an evil global conspiracy." In attracting supporters like Mr. Dall, Carto avoided – for awhile – being labeled a hate monger. Actors John Wayne and Eddie Albert had subscribed to the SPOTLIGHT, which was Liberty Lobby's flagship publication.

Recruiting the famous lawyer, Civil Rights activist, and author Mark Lane as Liberty Lobby's legal counsel also aided Carto in his quest for pseudo respectability. Lane's best-selling books on the assassinations of JFK and Dr. Martin Luther King, Jr., and the 1978 Jonestown, Guyana massacre are still in print. Lane helped Carto embezzle enormous sums, scam elderly, wealthy anti-Semites out of fortunes, and hide, illegally divert, and launder multiple millions of dollars. Some of these efforts involved me. Previously, Lane had represented Reverend Jim Jones of Jonestown infamy, and he was Carto's personal lawyer.

Among his other clients were James Earl Ray, who assassinated Dr. Martin Luther King, Jr. He also represented actress Jane Fonda. Lee Harvey Oswald's mother appointed Lane as her son's defense attorney after JFK's murder, even though the assassin died two days after killing President Kennedy. Prior to working for Jim Jones, Lane worked with the Vietnam Veterans against the War. This group's more radical members called for the assassination of pro-Vietnam War members of the U.S. House and Senate. Lane also coached non-soldiers to masquerade as combatants, who then attested to alleged atrocities, which they blamed on American servicemen.

To give credence to the positions taken by Liberty Lobby, Carto appointed to his Board of Directors some retired, former high-ranking CIA and U. S. Army officers like Fletcher Prouty and Victor Marchetti. He even retained the services of some members of the Yale University faculty. From the time he founded Liberty Lobby in 1955 until the late 1990s, no small number of wealthy anti-Semites collectively donated scores of millions of dollars to Carto's empire. The grand-niece of inventor Thomas Edison, Jean Edison Farrel, bequeathed $17 million to a Holocaust-denying, Carto-controlled entity called The Institute for Historical Review. Willis fought off other claimants to Farrel's money on three continents when they challenged her will. Upon settlement in 1991, Carto netted about $8.5 million after paying legal fees and other costs. His weekly newspaper, the SPOTLIGHT, had a paid subscriber base of over 300,000 at its peak. 60,000 additional copies were printed each week and sold on newsstands and by distributors at gun shows, senior citizen centers, Bingo games, VFW posts, shooting clubs, American Legion lodges, Masonic Lodges, assisted-care homes, hunting lodges and other gathering points for fans of Carto's propaganda. Thousands of Carto supporters left substantial assets, including tens of thousands of acres of tillable farmland, gold bullion, and valuable residential and commercial properties, to Liberty Lobby and other Carto-controlled entities between 1955 and 1998.

In some cases, Willis took personal possession of such real estate, after transferring it to a revocable trust, and then sold it before any capital gains taxes were due. Willis also owned the Sun Radio network, which promoted his numerous publications. These periodicals ranged from a newsletter called Zionist Watch to The National Investor, the New American View, The Journal of Historical Review, the Liberty Letter, a newsletter called, Rights and Property, The Barnes Review and a bi-monthly spreadsheet newspaper called Firearms & Personal Protection. Gross revenues from all sources of Liberty Lobby income over those 44 years exceeded $95 million, according to Carto, Mark Lane and their associates Andrew Gray, Michael Piper, and the Liberty Lobby's longtime Chief Financial Officer, Blayne Hutzel. People have asked why I stayed on with Carto after learning about his true agenda. Partly, it was greed. Another reason is I was grossly insensitive, and felt impervious to any consequences of being associated with racism. Then there was the autonomy and authority that Carto delegated to me.

But there was also another, yet equally important reason. Throughout my career, nearly every job I'd ever had – until Willis Carto hired me – had been obtained via my family's connections. Absent those contacts, I'd not have worked for Senator Jepsen, or interned for him in DC while I was in college. My father arranged it and funded me. The same was true for the Presidential Inaugural Committee and serving on President Reagan's White House staff, and my positions with the first President Bush. Absent my family's influence and resources, those jobs would've never materialized. My dad subsidized me while I worked at the Republican National Committee and at the White House. I've never lacked for self-confidence, but this perception bothered me.

I was capable, resourceful, and always worked very hard. But over the years, knowing that I and others knew how these positions had transpired bugged me. I was qualified, honest, intelligent, hardworking, loyal and conscientious. But so are tens of millions of deserving people who lacked my opportunities, which by then included working for two Presidents, two U.S. Senators and the RNC chairman. Carto offered me opportunities for professional autonomy and an arrangement that enabled me to earn more money than ever before in my life. Yes, Willis Carto often operated like a crooked Sheriff in a 1950s, low-budget Western. At the time, I thought I'd never look back, which turned out not to be the case. In addition to selling advertising space in the SPOTLIGHT, I also managed Liberty Lobby's mailing lists.

I rented the names and addresses, which included former subscribers, to thousands of marketers who knew that those records could yield substantial sales of their products and services. Charitable entities, political parties, and candidates and like causes also rented those names. Most of those mailers weren't racist or bigoted. Their goal was the same as those who bought ad space in the SPOTLIGHT: making money. From the time Carto got started, until into the early 1970s, he received support from U.S. Senators, southern Governors and U.S. Representatives. But after a cover story in William F. Buckley's National Review (Sept. 10, 1971 issue: 'The strange story of Willis Carto', and his 'Lobby for Patriotism'), Carto and his hate network became marginalized. From then on, Carto operated chiefly on the fringes of Far Right, militant, racist, anti-Semitic politics. But not always.

In 1981, President Reagan nominated Liberty Lobby's former legal counsel, Warren Richardson, to serve as the Assistant Secretary of the U.S. Department of Health and Human Services. Mr. Richardson, whom I knew, was on Willis Carto's payroll from 1969 to 1973. In the end, Richardson's connection to Liberty Lobby and the SPOTLIGHT derailed his nomination, and he withdrew from consideration in April of 1981. Around this time, Carto's rival neo-Nazi, Dr. William Luther Pierce, launched the National Alliance.

Pierce was a brilliant Ph. D., and far more publicly obstreperous in his views than Carto. Whereas Willis played varied roles and modified his rhetoric depending on his audience, Pierce didn't pretend to be anything but a virulent, professional anti-Semite who openly called for a race revolution which would "cleanse" the U.S.A. of all but conservative, heterosexual whites. Like most hateful bigots, Pierce and Carto reserved their most vicious enmity for the Jews, whom they considered to be a separate, vile race, which warranted outright extermination. Pierce and Carto told me they considered Adolf Hitler to be "the greatest man of the twentieth century."

Despite their shared views and mutual friends and supporters, William Pierce and Willis Carto were bitter rivals, fierce competitors, and personal enemies. But once Pierce got millions of dollars from the 1984 Brinks armored car robbery, courtesy of Bob Matthews, he ramped up his operations. From his 346-acre compound in West Virginia, Pierce recorded his weekly radio broadcasts, which were played on radio stations in several states. Pierce's radio broadcasts were funded by wealthy anti-Semites from Florida, New York, Ohio, California, Texas, Illinois, Georgia, Michigan, Iowa, Nebraska, Tennessee, Kansas, Louisiana, Kentucky, the Carolinas and other states. In many cases, these supporters paid the radio stations and networks directly, and then deducted what, in reality, amounted to political contributions as a business expense on their taxes.

In other instances, checks were written to churches whose preachers clandestinely kicked the money back to William Pierce. Like Carto, Pierce also owned a highly lucrative book club. Among hundreds of other titles, Pierce's best-selling novels, 'The Turner Diaries', and 'Hunter', other published works provided steady, significant revenue. From Carto, Pierce learned how to advise wealthy supporters to leave money to his organizations in their wills. Dr. Pierce told me in 2001 that over the three years ending in 2000, some 300 valuable guns and nearly $5 million in gold coins, bars, and ingots, were either bequeathed to or received by the National Alliance, along with cash, jewelry, Treasury bills and other tangible assets. National Alliance member Robert McCorkill was a Canadian to whom Pierce introduced me in 2000. He was living on Pierce's West Virginia property when Pierce died in July, 2002. When McCorkill died, his will left 350 gold coins valued at approximately $550,000 to the National Alliance. When his estate was finally settled in 2016, the only reason those assets didn't go to what remained of Pierce's organization was that Canadian law prohibited the transfer of property to individuals or entities that promote hatred.

When Timothy McVeigh bombed the Murrah building in Oklahoma City, Oklahoma, in 1995, items found in his car included copies of the SPOTLIGHT, a Long Distance calling card he purchased from a Liberty Lobby-connected card issuer, and a copy of The Turner Diaries. Pierce publicly condemned the evil done by his follower, but privately he gloated over it. News reports connecting the neo-Nazi bomber to The Turner Diaries not only sparked a huge rise in sales of Pierce's books, but also resulted in more than 500 new, dues-paying members joining the National Alliance. Humanity's tragedy meant profits for Hate.

Willis Carto shunned publicity, but Pierce welcomed it. When reporter Mike Wallace asked Pierce if he would agree to be interviewed for the CBS program '60 Minutes', the former physics professor readily agreed. Several times, I was with Pierce as he spoke on the phone to journalists who called him from the four corners of the globe. I was also with Carto several times when he'd slam the phone down on reporters, often using profanity. He accused journalists of being "tools" of what he derided as "the Jew's media", sometimes to their faces. But Pierce craved media coverage, skillfully using it to spread his message, recruit new members, and raise even more money.

As much as they hated blacks, Pierce and Carto would clandestinely align with them when it served their purposes, especially with Nation of Islam black nationalists who shared their hatred of Jewish people. Willis funded black nationalist Robert Brock via an entity called the Foundation to Defend the First Amendment and other organizations under his jurisdiction. He would order his underling Mike Piper to pay pro-Louis Farrakhan blacks recruited by Brock to protest outside of the Israeli embassy in D.C., and to harass visitors lining up to tour the U.S. Holocaust museum in D.C. William Pierce denied having taken part in such efforts, but I was present when Brock paid – with funds provided by the National Alliance - black Muslims to harass Jewish tourists.

Pierce even formed a religion of sorts, called Cosmotheism, which he created to receive tax-exempt status. Quite unlike his crude followers, Skinhead fans, and knuckle-dragging, hateful bigots, William Pierce was erudite, and very much the intellectual heavyweight he'd been when he became a full professor of Physics before he was 30 years old. As such, he wasn't in synch, in terms of taste, culture and lifestyle, with his most ardent admirers.

But they were all on the same, hateful page regarding their shared goal of eradicating non-whites, Jews and homosexuals. A notorious ideological ally of these two architects of 20th and 21st century hatred is David Duke. Of all the professional racists and anti-Semites I encountered, Duke was the only one who managed to get elected to U.S. public office, as referenced earlier in this book. In so doing, he provided credibility to the Racist far Right and its agenda.

David Duke first attained significant public notice in the early 1970s while he was a student at Louisiana State University in Baton Rouge, Louisiana. Duke had joined the Ku Klux Klan in 1967, while still in high school, and built his college organization with help from the National Socialist White People's Party. While at LSU, Duke frequently appeared on campus wearing a Nazi uniform, and held annual parties to celebrate the April 20 birthday of his idol, Adolf Hitler. After graduating from LSU in 1974, Duke spent the next year organizing and recruiting for the Ku Klux Klan. During this time, he worked with William Pierce, whose office was then still in Washington, D.C., and also for Willis Carto.

Pierce and Carto later told me that after Duke stole mailing lists from them, they ended their professional association with him. With Carto, though, Duke had an on-again/off-again relationship, as the two men used one another. In 1975 and 1979, Duke ran for the state Senate in Louisiana. But in losing, he attracted the attention of the news media, which led to paid speaking gigs on the campuses of the University of Southern California, Vanderbilt, Tulane, Indiana University, and Stanford. In the process, he became well-known as the KKK's youthful, modern face.

Throughout the 1980s, Duke busied himself with various racist organizations, got married, and started a family. In 1988, Duke enhanced his notoriety by entering and winning the New Hampshire Primary for the Democratic party nomination for Vice President of the United States. He was the only candidate. Parlaying his success in the Granite state, Duke turned his sights to another campaign for the Louisiana legislature. Switching party affiliation from Democrat to Republican, Duke defeated two GOP opponents for the nomination for the Louisiana House of Representatives. In advance of his campaign, Duke dyed his hair, underwent plastic surgery, and began wearing contact lenses. He upgraded his wardrobe.

This campaign attracted financial support from contributors in all 50 states. Duke then parlayed this minor public office into national and international, prominence. With bigger plans in mind, he tried to reconfigure his image by repudiating the Klan. He achieved a new level of political viability. The "new" David Duke spoke not of race or about Jews, but instead described his concern for the "growing underclass" – by which he meant poor, uneducated whites and fear of "greedy, international bankers" – code for Jews. In 1990, while still in office, Duke founded the NAAWP – the National Association for the Advancement of White People. The media attention and fundraising success of this organization provided a stepping stone to Duke's U.S. Senate candidacy.

His opponent was a three-term incumbent, the highly respected J. Bennett Johnston. This campaign turned out to be the closest re-election of Johnston's long career. Duke dubbed the senior Senator as "J. Benedict Johnston", and convinced white voters that their Senator didn't have their back and was part of the liberal "mess in Washington, D.C." Senator Johnston had no idea he was in the political fight of his life until it was almost too late. Polls showed a very close race, and Johnston prevailed only after another candidate, state Legislator Ben Bagert, dropped out. Johnston then got nearly all of Bagert's votes and won a fourth term with just over 53 percent. In 1990, 4.2 million people lived in Louisiana. If only 75,000 voters had switched their votes that year, Duke would've been elected.

Undaunted by this defeat, which he ascribed to "Jewish-directed agitation", Duke next set his sights on the Governor's office. His new target was the elected incumbent governor, a skillful politician named Buddy Roemer. Roemer was a graduate of Harvard University and Harvard Business school. He had founded two successful banks and owned a computer business. Elected to the U.S. House of Representatives in 1980, he was re-elected three times without opposition. Roemer's chief opponent in the 1987 governor's race was the popular, three-term incumbent, Edwin Edwards. He handily beat Edwards, who until then had never lost. Edwards won only 28 percent of the vote. In his gubernatorial campaign, Duke used many of the same issues he'd used in his Senate race. In 1991, they worked; Roemer got 27 percent of the vote in the Primary. Like Bennett Johnston, he never knew what hit him.

Duke's defeat of the elected incumbent Louisiana governor produced political shock waves worldwide. His sizable national fan base came through with money, and volunteers poured into the state from all across the country to help him. Proclaiming himself as the spokesman for "the white majority", the ex-Klansman appeared to be on his way to becoming governor. Duke's opponent in the general election was none other than Edwin Edwards, who resurrected his political career to seek a fourth gubernatorial term. After his 1987 defeat, a reporter for the Shreveport Journal observed that the only way Edwards could ever be elected to any office again would be for him run against Adolf Hitler. That journalist came close to being exactly right. Edwards, who was known for his philandering, deftly used sly humor against Duke. "The only thing we have in common", the former Governor said, "is that we've both been wizards beneath the sheets." But it took more than rogue charm for Edwards to beat Duke.

Unprecedented amounts of cash found its way in to the Edwards campaign, and it was good for Louisiana that it did. These funds included significant sums from Wall Street executives and investors, Hollywood actors, and major donors to the RNC and the Democratic National Committee. President Bush again got involved, denouncing Duke for the third time since taking office. Major professional sports teams threatened to not play in Louisiana if Duke won. Duke's foes made it clear that they weren't fans of Edwards. But they convinced a majority of Louisiana voters that their state would become a pariah if Duke won. Bumper stickers were distributed featuring the slogan, 'Vote for the Crook, not the Nazi'. A decisive moment came a few weeks before the election, when Tim Russert, the moderator of NBC's Meet the Press, asked Duke questions about issues which any candidate for governor of any state ought to know.

But Duke didn't know who the state's three largest employers were, and lacked correct answers to other relevant inquiries. Undecided voters suddenly realized that while Duke was articulate and smart, he lacked the knowledge, experience and skill set that a Governor must have. By election day, it all came together for Edwards. But as Duke correctly pointed out, he won 55 percent of the white vote overall, and got over 65 percent of the white male vote, while being outspent by 10-to-One. Things went downhill for David Duke after that. He ran for President and wrote his autobiography, and occasionally popped up on the news. But as a potent political force, David Duke was spent. By 1999, his gambling habit, fondness for hookers, living large, and chronic difficulties managing money finally caught up to him.

He served nearly two years in federal prison for misappropriating cash raised in support of racist, anti-Semitic causes, using it to pay for structural improvements to his houses and for slot machines and other forms of gambling. Prior to sentencing, Duke had spent the previous two years abroad, fearing arrest. He cut a deal with the U.S. government to return to America, where he plead guilty to felony mail and tax fraud charges. He served his time in a federal prison in Texas, and was fined $10,000. During the 2016 U.S. presidential race, Duke briefly made news by endorsing Republican Donald Trump. Trump's campaign seemed about as pleased with that endorsement as Bill Clinton was with Monica Lewinsky.

A longtime David Duke ally is a former Grand Dragon of the Ku Klux Klan named Don Black. Now married to Duke's first wife, Chloe, Don Black is a highly intelligent, resourceful white supremacist and online entrepreneur. Since 1995, he has owned and operated STORMFRONT, which, until its domain was dropped by its server, was one of the most popular – and profitable – sources of racist propaganda and content on the worldwide web.

As a student in Alabama's public schools, Black distributed racist publications. This caused the school board to ban the distribution of all political literature. But that didn't stop Black, who obtained the home addresses of his classmates from student handbooks, and mailed racist materials to them directly. Black began working on political campaigns in 1970 in Georgia. That year, he served as an aide to a gubernatorial candidate whose name was on the same ballot with future President Jimmy Carter.

During that campaign, a man named Jerry Ray shot Black in the chest with a .38-caliber hollow-point bullet, when he caught Black stealing mailing lists from the campaign offices of candidate J. B. Stoner. Luckily for Don Black, Jerry Ray wasn't as skillful with guns as his brother, James Earl Ray, who shot Dr. Martin Luther King, Jr. After high school in Alabama, Black graduated from the University of Alabama. In 1978, Black became the national director of the Ku Klux Klan, and was subsequently elected Grand Wizard of the organization, which he'd helped revive. Along with Duke, he opened up the organization to women, Catholics, and others who had previously been excluded. This resulted in a substantial rise in membership, and stabilized the group financially. Black was imprisoned for three years after being sentenced in 1981. He and a group of well-armed white supremacists chartered a yacht headed for Dominica, a primarily black nation then governed by a black head of state.

Black and his comrades had planned to overthrow the government by force, in violation of the U. S. Neutrality Act. A key figure in this ludicrous fiasco was a Canadian racist (and alcoholic, and cocaine user) named Wolfgang Droege, whom I met in the late 1990s. According to testimony at Droeg's trial, their plan was to return to power the deposed former Prime Minister Patrick Power. In return for so doing, Droege was to have been allowed to use the island for the purpose of a drug processing and distribution operation. Droege was sentenced to three years in a Canadian prison for his role in this scheme, and was later arrested for drug dealing and auto theft. Wolfgang Droege was shot to death in 2005 in Scarborough, Ontario. While in prison, Black studied computer technology. He became highly proficient at programming, writing code, and all aspects of the field. Upon his release, in 1984, Black put his expertise to profitable use, and has done so ever since.

Black rejuvenated his racist and Holocaust-denying activities, picking up where he had left off. In 1995, he launched STORMFRONT, which was the worldwide web's first major White Nationalist website. Articles and Op-Ed columns by David Duke, William Pierce, Willis Carto, Dr. Ed Fields, Tom Metzger, Richard Butler, Chris Temple, and other self-proclaimed "racialists" were, and still are regularly posted on STORMFRONT, along with racist and anti-Jewish articles and editorials. In 1999, Black created the website titled 'martinlutherking.org', which is operated by STORMFRONT.

Its purpose, besides raising money and recruiting racists for the movement, is to vilify the late Civil Rights leader. A STORMFRONT 'Forum' was, for years, one of the largest online gathering points of Holocaust deniers. It features links to other websites and radio programs featuring anti-minority and Holocaust denial themes. Black was the first professional white supremacist to successfully monetize, in a major way, the internet. Others in the Movement, including the Canadian Resistance Records founders, succeeded only after STORMFRONT paved the way, showing that money can be made online from hatred. Until early 2017, Black also earned substantial fees by designing online ads, including for clients who placed such advertisements on STORMFRONT and buy ad space on other websites.

Black asked visitors to STORMFRONT help him raise – via donations - $7,500 per month, which he claimed were the monthly costs to operate the site. STORMFRONT also offered premium memberships at a higher cost. According to the Southern Poverty Law Center, in January of 1992, STORMFRONT had 5,000 members. "Members" are defined as those who are allowed to post messages, and can view personal information posted by and about other members. By 2004, membership had reached 23,000; by 2008, it reached nearly 133,000 registered users. As of May, 2015, the number of registered users had climbed to over 300,000. These numbers are even more impressive when taking into account that they didn't include the even larger numbers of visitors who read STORMFRONT without actually joining, or signing up as registered users. Less impressive is the proven revelation by the Southern Poverty Law Center that STORMFRONT readers have been implicated in, or involved directly in, nearly 100 murders.

The motto atop the STORMFRONT masthead is 'WHITE PRIDE, WORLDWIDE'.

However, since early 2017, Stormfront has been rocked, chiefly by competitors like The Daily Stormer, which were inspired by Don Black's creation. Black in early 2019 said that Stormfront was going broke, partly because of competition from these newer, more obstreperous, hatred-promoting sites.

However, The Daily Stormer also has problems. In June of 2019, an American muslim from New Jersey, Dean Obediallah, was awarded $4.1 million in a judgment against TDS and its publisher, Andrew Anglin. Mr. Anglin went into hiding shortly after the defamation lawsuit was filed, failing to even contest it. But such victories against organized hatred are rare.

A major reason for hate's online success is that members of such communities, and even non-members, engage in discussions via vitriolic public forums with like-minded individuals. In 2012, it was revealed that a racist who had visited Black's site and posted there at least seven times was Wade Michael Page. I had met Page several times while representing Resistance Records, before he shot up a Sikh temple near Milwaukee, Wisconsin. He killed six people and injured four others before the cops took him out.

Another fan of online hate was Jamie Von Brunn. Mr. Von Brunn was over the age of 75 when I first met him, which was at Liberty Lobby's headquarters on Capitol Hill. Von Brunn was then working as a full-time distributor for the SPOTLIGHT, and The Barnes Review, which was Carto's Holocaust-denying monthly magazine. In 1981, an armed Von Brunn attempted to take hostage the members of the Board of Governors of the Federal Reserve as they met in Washington, D.C. Charged with attempted kid-napping, assault, weapons possession, and hostage taking, he said he was trying to make a citizens arrest the of Federal Reserve Board members for treason. Von Brunn was convicted in 1983 and completed his prison sentence in 1989. This is the same Jamie Von Brunn – referenced earlier – who in 2009, shot a and killed a black guard in DC's U. S. Holocaust museum.

Having worked with and spoke to him on numerous occasions, I know that Don Black is preparing for a race war. Should one ever materialize, Mr. Black and STORMFRONT will have played a key role in coalescing keyboard warriors into admirers of Adolf Hitler and the evil he perpetrated. If they could, these people would readily replicate it and install a Fourth Reich in the U.S. The work of Willis Carto, William Pierce, David Duke and Don Black has been indispensable to creating and maintaining Holocaust Denial, and enabling bigots worldwide to monetize racial hatred, indoctrinate and recruit new members, and effectuate violence.

Black indoctrinated his son, Derek, into hatred from the time the boy could talk. Before Derek Black was ten years old, he was creating racist, anti-Jewish websites which targeted elementary school aged kids. As a teenager, he created and operated one of the internet's first 24-hour racist radio networks. As a 22-year-old College Junior, Derek conducted seminars to teach racists and Holocaust deniers to optimize messaging code and memes, to infiltrate the worldwide web. Some of those memes were written by a former Reagan administration appointee, Bob Whitaker.

Around 2013, Derek began reconsidering anti-Semitism, racial prejudice, and all forms of bigotry and hatred. The irony of the son of a founding father of online hate-for-profit breaking with his racist dad sat not well with haters, who continue to support Don Black and his agenda. I got to know Derek during my years with Carto, Pierce, and the FBI. I felt sorry for him, as he was being involuntarily pushed into the ranks of HATE. On one occasion, at a weekend confab in D.C., he seemed particularly withdrawn.

We chatted awhile, and he said he wanted to see a movie called, 'Sleepy Hollow'. After his Dad gave me permission, I took Derek to the movie and, later, to dinner. From then on, at other Holocaust Denial and racist confabs, I made it a point to talk with Derek and take him to nearby restaurants. Eli Saslow's superb 2018 book about Derek's 2016 transformation from racist to open-minded collegian, 'Rising out of Hatred', describes some of my efforts to help Derek. Saslow writes that Derek "went to see the movie Sleepy Hollow at a theater in Washington with an undercover FBI informant named Todd Blodgett, who had infiltrated the higher ranks of the white supremacy movement and then taking a liking to Derek. 'An exceptionally bright kid being brainwashed into the realm of racist hatred,' Blodgett said of Derek then, so Blodgett made it a part of his job to occasionally take Derek away from conferences for short outings, hoping to give the boy's mind a break." Obviously, back then I couldn't reveal to Derek that I was working for the FBI. But his transformation into a fair-minded young man is wonderful. Hopefully, other young people who are flirting with, or involved in, organized HATE will read this book, and change their ways, and hearts, as well.

What makes anyone hate minorities, Jews, and others, because of their race, faith or sexual preference? Whether its the Aryan Nations, the KKK, or bigoted Skinheads, the more thuggish members of the New Black Panthers, or some of the violent leaders of the Black Lives Matter crowd, hatred is on the rise in America. Violence perpetrated by some activists is sometimes fatal, always destructive, and frequently costly. Leaders and rank-and-file members of most Hate organizations believe black and brown people are innately inferior to whites. But hating Jewish people is based on their own feelings of inferiority.

Most anti-Semites seemed to fear that, deep down, Jews are superior. But sometimes, governmental action drives Americans into the evil arms of White Supremacy and anti-Semitism. The tragic case of Randy Weaver is a classic example of this. Mr. Weaver was a factory worker who was originally from Iowa. He was also a veteran, having served as a combat engineer in the U.S. Army. In the early 1980s, he moved his family to northern Idaho to escape what he and his wife, Vicky, considered to be a corrupted society. While Weaver's views were militant, he simply wished to be left alone, and had no arrest record. In 1983, the Weavers bought 20 acres in a place called Ruby Ridge and built a home.

They were poor, and began attending meetings at Richard Butler's Hayden Lakes compound around 1984. A neighbor who had lost a lawsuit over a land deal with Weaver claimed Weaver was an active Aryan nations member who had threatened to kill then-President Reagan, Pope John Paul II, and John Evans, who was then Idaho's Governor. FBI agents interviewed Mr. Weaver over these claims, but no charges were ever filed against him based on those allegations.

Weaver came under the radar of the BATF in 1986, after an informant met him at a neo-Nazi meeting and finagled an invitation to Weaver's home. Weaver, an accomplished gunsmith, agreed to illegally modify two 12 gauge shotguns by shortening the barrels. Once he was paid, the informant tried to use this act to get Weaver to become an informant for the U.S. government. Weaver's refusal led to the ATF filing gun charges against him in June, 1990. These filed charges falsely alleged that Weaver was a bank robber with criminal convictions, despite the fact that Weaver had no criminal record and was never even a suspect in any bank robberies. After Weaver was indicted in December, 1990 by a federal grand jury for making and possessing illegal weapons, ATF agents posed as motorists with car trouble.

When Randy and Vicki Weaver stopped to help them, he was arrested. Later, Weaver received a letter from his temporary probation officer indicating that his trial date was for March 20, 1991, when the actual date was February 20. Weaver's failure to appear on February 20, 1991 resulted in the issuance of a bench warrant. The DOJ later said that had he shown up, the charges would've been dropped. But instead of waiting until March 20 to see if he would appear in court, the U.S. Attorney's office convened a grand jury on March 14. However, this grand jury wasn't provided with the letter stating that the trial date was March 20. The case then passed from the ATF to the U.S. Marshalls Service, with no one informing them of the ATF's attempt to enlist Weaver as an informant.

This all culminated in the infamous siege of August, 1992, now known as Ruby Ridge.

Vicki Weaver suffered a fatal shot to her head while she was holding her 10-month-old baby. After their dog was shot, Weaver's son, Sammy, confronted the agents. Yelling, "you shot my dog, you son of a bitch," Sammy Weaver fired a shot at an agent. Another agent, armed with an M16, then emerged from the woods surrounding the house and shot Sammy in the arm. As Sammy Weaver retreated, yet another agent fired the kill shot, hitting the teenager in the back.

The siege at Ruby Ridge made international news, and enraged millions of Americans. The racist Far Right, especially, was livid, with operatives like Willis Carto, William Pierce, Ed Fields, Paul Hall, Jr., Jim Thomas, Richard Butler, Clay Douglas, David Duke, Tom Metzger, Don Black, Gregory Douglas, Mark Cotterill and Chris Temple, publishing stories about it. Carto's SPOTLIGHT newspaper published a Page One article with this headline and these sub-headlines:

While Criminals run loose ...

UNDECLARED WAR AGAINST CHRISTIAN AMERICANS

Weaver set up by Feds; Mother, son MURDERED

Then there was this, from SOLDIER of FORTUNE: 'Randy Weaver IDAHO Shoot-Out: The REAL Story!'

Weaver was taken into custody and incarcerated for several months. After he and his surviving family members filed a $200 million wrongful death lawsuit, the federal government awarded Randy Weaver $100,000, and each of his three daughters received $1 million. The U.S. government admitted no wrongdoing, and a high-ranking DOJ official told The Washington Post that he believed that had the case gone to trial, the Weavers would have won the full amount sought. While I never met Randy Weaver in person, I spoke – via telephone – with him, twice, in 1997-98, about ads in The SPOTLIGHT for his book. He soft-spoken, pleasant, and cooperative. His book sold well and generated substantial revenue for him, Liberty Lobby, and my ad agency.

Ultimately, the Ruby Ridge siege became the chief motive for Timothy McVeigh and Terry Nichols, who perpetrated the Oklahoma City bombing in 1995, which killed 168 people and injured hundreds more. McVeigh claimed his action was "retaliation" for what the feds did to the Weaver family. When, in 1993, the Branch Davidians of Waco, Texas, were burned out of existence by federal agents, it reinforced the thinking among Far Right racists that the U.S. government was out to get them, due to their beliefs and their possession of firearms. McVeigh also cited Waco as evidence that the federal government was evil. As a U.S. Army veteran, McVeigh was adept with firearms and explosives. Having been bullied as a kid, he transferred this hatred to the U.S. government. He was the top gun at Fort Riley, and his supervisors said that he showed leadership potential.

His service as a sniper in the first Iraqi war made him question what the USA was doing over there; he viewed the U.S. as a bully. The Army selected McVeigh to attend Ranger School, but he washed out. He felt like a failure. He also was an avid reader of SPOTLIGHT and a huge fan of William Pierce's bestselling novel, 'The Turner Diaries', and began frequently attending gun shows in multiple states.

He met numerous White Supremacists at such events and sold them copies of 'The Turner Diaries' and Pierce's other book, 'Hunter'. When the Brady Bill – named for Ronald Reagan's former White House press secretary, Jim Brady – was signed into law by Bill Clinton, McVeigh was livid.

Incidentally, while the Brady Bill was being debated in Congress, Jim's wife, Sarah, called my office. She asked me if she could add my name to a list of former Reagan White House staff members who supported this legislation. Because of the onerous restrictions the legislation imposed, I politely and respectfully told her no. Sarah wasn't pleased. Coincidentally, the Brady's assistant at the time, Mrs. Shirley Sandage, was from my hometown of Mason City, Iowa. When President Clinton signed the Brady Bill into law, Tim McVeigh decided to make his mark as a terrorist. He was later executed, but his beliefs – and the underlying reasons for them – still attract a strong and active following.

Most white supremacists and anti-Semites believe that government policies since the mid-1960s have favored minorities at their expense. In this thinking, they're not alone. Affirmative action, racial set-asides and race-based quotas for jobs, college admissions, loans, scholarships, government contracts, etc., have reinforced such resentments, exacerbating existing tensions. In 1972, LBJ said, "if a candidate can make the lowest white man feel superior to the highest black man, then that politician can pick his pocket while he's not lookin.'" Comedian Chris Rock says, "there's nothin' a white dude with a penny hates more than a nigga with a nickel." But prejudice can't be overcome with more prejudice.

Disregarding the legitimate concerns over such policies ignores the damage they cause. No small number of white supremacists I knew contrasted how things operate in professional sports, and, particularly, in the National Basketball Association (NBA), with the everyday situations they encounter in their workaday lives. It would be ludicrous to require professional athletic teams to hire players based on their race, needs, or any factor other than ability. Performance is what counts.

Professional basketball, football, and baseball teams exist to make money. It would be foolish to require such enterprises to hire applicants who are wheelchair-bound, grossly out of shape, or past their physical or mental prime. Team owners also shouldn't be mandated to take into consideration any obstacles which prospective players have had to overcome in order to be in contention for positions. If such owners wish to do this of their own volition, fine. But should government force employers to implement such policies? Were the NBA to require team owners to recruit and hire basketball players based on race, owners would rebel, and rightly so. Coming from the same, flawed perspective, should an overweight 45-year-old who wants to be a professional boxer get extra points per round to compensate for his age, flab, and slower reflexes? Such logic forms the basis for affirmative action.

Then there's the other side. Lack of opportunity among many minorities has had a corrosive impact on their lives and their chances for advancement. I saw, while using drugs in the 'hoods' of D.C., Baltimore, and New York City, the real-life consequences of this tragic reality. I lost count of all the clever blacks I knew who, but for lack of a sound education, positive male role models in their lives, and some decent opportunities, could have enjoyed tremendous personal, professional, social, and financial success. It's not a child's fault to be born to poor, ignorant, lazy parents who live in an inferior school district.

Growing up in a substandard home in a marginal neighborhood that's headed by a drug-addicted single-parent on welfare isn't exactly conducive to present or future success. At the root of this dilemma is a failure to differentiate between liberty and license.

Most Americans today also don't understand or care about this difference and the harsh consequences thereof. Being able to produce babies while lacking the ability to support oneself doesn't mean it's okay to do so, and causes trouble for law-abiding taxpayers. Conflating liberty with license is sinful. This isn't about race; out-of-wedlock, taxpayer-supported children born to indigent parents who lack the skills to raise them is a huge problem, and not uncommon, among folks of all races. Anyone who doubts this need only visit a Wal-Mart in cities all across America. On any given day, hundreds of welfare-supported Caucasians are there, whose messed-up lives are testament to the unwise consequences caused by conflating liberty with license. Although I've never been on welfare, as a former drug user, I know about such conflation. Until America's leaders face these truths and implement policies that will effectuate genuine and positive change, people of all races who comprise this underclass will continue to aimlessly drift, like leaky boats on choppy waters, without a rudder or a compass.

My fear is that white bigots and contentious black activists will continue exploiting such frustrations, circumventing a more productive, politically cohesive, and peaceful United States. Chaos can, and likely will, ensue. In June and May of 2017, these headlines graced the pages of two of America's oldest, most respected newspapers: Drug Deaths in America are Rising faster than Ever – The New York Times; More American workers Test Positive for Drugs – The Wall Street Journal. Approximately 59,000 Americans died of drug overdoses in 2016, which represented a 19 percent increase over the 52,404 such deaths recorded in 2015. Coroner's offices throughout the United States are being overwhelmed; refrigerated trailers are now requested to store corpses due to lack of space in morgues.

For addicts, the appeal of cocaine, crystal meth, heroin, opioids, and other illicit drugs mean a constant supply of substances that enriches manufacturers, distributors, street pushers, and others who supply them, directly or indirectly, to users. The damage caused by addiction destroys lives, relationships, careers, cultures, and nations. Americans comprise only four percent of the world's population, but we consume 66 percent of the world's illegal drugs.

Then there's the violence, which has been described at length in this memoir. Former HHS Secretary Joe Califano found that 80 percent of America's adult inmates and minors who get arrested committed their crimes while they were either high, stealing to obtain money to feed their habit, have a history of drug addiction or substance abuse, or were violating laws prohibiting drug usage, or raised in homes by parents with substance abuse issues. It's not hard to see where this is leading, and will continue to go, if addiction wins the War on Drugs.

Federal policies haven't only failed to solve this increasingly ominous problem, but based on my experiences, such warped ideas and resulting government programs have exacerbated it. Compassion seems to be the catch-all term for Liberals who oppose proposals by Conservatives to help people become accountable. Liberal friends have told me that mandatory, random drug-testing of welfare recipients is lacking in compassion. But is it compassionate to fail to instill in society's most vulnerable members a modicum of self-discipline, responsibility, and respect for the law, work, and themselves? Perhaps the most difficult challenges involve addicts who are of low intelligence. These unfortunate junkies realize that landing a good job, and becoming successful – by society's standards - probably isn't in their future. But under the present set-up, they have no incentive to get clean. However, they can break the bondage of addiction once they understand that having the security of a warm place to live, food, medical care, freedom, and other necessities - which will keep coming their way only if they abstain from using illegal drugs, and get jobs, if they're able-bodied.

Tough Love? Maybe. It's also common sense. For those who consider this proposal draconian, I'd ask: What about the taxpayers, many of whom are, as a condition of employment, themselves subject to such testing? They foot the bills. Shouldn't they be allowed to set the terms and conditions for those who want their money? As the saying goes: Those who pay the piper should get to call the tune.

Even people of limited intellectual ability can perform valuable tasks as a condition of receiving welfare. Such wards of the state can clean up parks, pick up trash in cities, and along highways. They can wash police vehicles, or assist maintenance workers and custodians. I associated with Welfare-supported junkies who knew nothing about economics, financial reality, or even basic common sense. Keeping them busy will build self-esteem. Physical exertion will help to ensure they'll need rest at night, instead of sleeping until noon, smoking crack – often bought with EBT cards - until two a.m., and stealing to support their habit. Their children will respect them, and the intergenerational cycle of poverty can cease. Those who may believe that such self-limiting people and counterproductive lifestyles aren't a problem haven't seen what I have.

During my years as an addict, among the worst people I encountered were dirty cops. Crooks wearing badges who protect drug pushers, help to facilitate drug transactions, blackmail junkies and drug runners, or steal cash, and/or drugs from dealers they bust, are bereft of a conscience. Robbing drug dealers is nearly the perfect crime, because pushers and runners know that accusing police officers of the theft of drugs and cash can result in even more severe sentencing. This is especially true if the charges are proven. Knowing that some crooked cops may do prison time won't offset the fears their accusers harbor of their own sentences being increased.

A recovering junkie I knew worked as a remitter for a successful, DC-based supplier of coke and heroin who was originally from a central or South American nation. Three or four times a week, she'd drive residents of public housing to some of the hundreds of small businesses in Washington, D.C., Maryland, and Virginia, which were licensed to wire funds. Employees of check-cashing businesses, Pay Day loan enterprises, pawn shops, even some travel agencies and other establishments, bail bonding operations, and beauty salons, wired money for her, to whomever and wherever her employer directed.

By using real people with valid IDs and a District of Columbia address, questions weren't asked. Some of the employees of such businesses may have been suspicious, but it mattered not. They always accommodated this remitter and her decoys. These decoys were paid $40 for each wired transaction. In some cases, funds were wired out of the U.S., and each such transaction always involved amounts of slightly under $10,000 - to comply with federal reporting requirements.

A DC police officer figured the ruse out and blackmailed her. He received $400 a week for years. An extra, tax-free, under-the-table, annual windfall exceeding $20,000 was the price of that crooked cop's silence.

In 2016, NEWSWEEK magazine reported that a crooked New York City detective, Rafael Astacio, had for years been the key player in a professional burglary ring that stole over $8 million in cash and valuable items from homes, stores, a warehouse and a medical practice between 2009 and 2012. So thorough was this greedy detective that he even illicitly logged onto the FBI's database to obtain criminal history reports pertaining to felons whom his partners in crime wanted to recruit for their theft ring.

In January of 2016, Astacio was sentenced by a federal Judge to six years in prison. A 2018 episode of AMERICAN GREED featured his story. Also that year (2010), three NYPD officers, one of whom was a former undercover cop who worked for years in the department's Intelligence Division, stole over $500,000 worth of high-end, exotic perfume from a New Jersey warehouse. The former member of the elite investigative unit masterminded the scheme, which was predicated on intimidating employees with their police department badges. These crooked cops then tied up twelve workers before filling three rental trucks with the pricey, designer perfume. Soon after their getaway, the NYPD collared them, and all were convicted on federal interstate robbery charges.

Among the customers of Resistance Records CDs, DVDs, and other items were law enforcement officers, military reservists, and active duty service personnel. On several occasions, off-duty cops from various states provided security services at gatherings of organized white supremacists, Holocaust deniers and at Resistance Records concerts and other racist events.

As stated, Resistance Records was created by three young, ambitious, well-educated Canadians from Windsor, Ontario. George Burdi, Jason Snowe, and Joe Talic had been impressed by the success of Don Black's STORMFRONT. They recognized the potential for the internet to spread their message and help them to make some big money.

These guys were fans of what came to be known as 'Hate Metal' music and the bands that produced it. In 1993, George Burdi formed his own band, called RAHOWA – for Racial Holy War. Later that year, the three buddies pooled their funds, attracted some investors, incorporated the business, and launched the company. By late 1994, business was booming; over 35,000 satisfied customers had purchased CDs. Plans were announced for a monthly magazine. Before its first issue was published in 1995, over 13,000 prepaid subscriptions had already been sold, and nearly 300 distributors signed up to disseminate it.

The initial press run was for 25,000 issues. After subscribers received their copies, the additional 12,000 issues of RESISTANCE magazine were sold within weeks, at Hate Rock concerts, gun shows, gatherings of organized racists, and even at some VFWs and American Legion posts. The press run for all subsequent monthly editions of RESISTANCE magazine increased to 40,000 copies.

The initial investors, who were chiefly white supremacists and affluent anti-Semites in America and Canada, were fully repaid with 10 percent interest. By 1996, over 50,000 customers had bought nearly 300,000 CDs and DVDs from Resistance Records.

Many of these CDs were recorded at Resistance Records' in-house studio. The company also booked performances for bands which had signed with Resistance, and hired a full-time office staff, including an employee who dealt directly with bands who wanted their already-produced content promoted, sold, and distributed by Resistance Records. Another staffer arranged for venues for Hate Metal concerts and served as the liaison to vendors who sold products, including food, at the events. By early 1997, employees were drawing substantial salaries from the enterprise, which were paid off-the-books, to facilitate tax evasion. The Resistance Records offices featured the latest, state-of-the-art computers and CD pressing equipment. The company owned its own cyberspace server, had no debt, nearly $90,000 in two bank accounts, and owned $85,000 in Certificates of Deposit. Resistance began selling T-shirts, cheap custom jewelry, wallets, Gift Cards, belt buckles and caps emblazoned with the label's logo.

These young racists were succeeding. In late 1995, George Burdi – whose Cyber World name became George Eric Hawthorne – was charged with vicious assault. While attending anti-Jewish street rally in mid-1993, he was accused of kicking a lady in the face. He was convicted in 1996 of intentionally causing bodily harm and sentenced to twelve months in a Canadian prison. When he began serving his time, in 1997, Joe Talic and Jason Snow took control of RESISTANCE. Fearing Canadian Hate Speech laws, the company rented a four-bedroom house in Milford, Michigan, a Detroit suburb. Most of the operations were run out of that location until April of 1997.

But on April 19, 1997, U.S. Marshalls and the Michigan Tax authorities raided the company's U.S. headquarters. The federal Marshalls were acting under the authority of the IRS, which had ordered the seizure of the inventory, most of the computers, business records, mailing lists and some electronic equipment. Removing and loading everything required several employees, who sweated for ten straight hours. The confiscated items filled four of the largest-sized U-Haul trucks and two vans. Two employees later told me that most of the company's funds were kept on deposit in two Canadian banks in accounts which were under the names of the two owners. Had U.S. authorities accessed those records, they'd have learned the names of some heavy hitters on the racist Far Right who had invested and lent the business its early seed money. Resistance Records then briefly ceased operations.

The day after the Resistance Records offices in Detroit were raided, U.S. and Canadian authorities raided the company's offices in Windsor, Ontario. Strike forces from the state of Michigan and the federal government had hit the Detroit headquarters; Canadian police and Provincial law enforcement officers raided Burdi's house in that country. George Burdi wasn't home; he was in prison. However, the Canadian officers never raided the storage facility near the Burdi residence, where a massive quantity of items were maintained – including most of the lists of customers, contracts with bands, and information relating to the distribution channels for the company's products.

For months, the staff members and two known locations of the company had been under surveillance by a team of six investigators. Resistance Records hadn't paid sales taxes and lacked a business license, which legally justified the raids. At least a dozen officers spent nearly seven hours loading computers on the Canadian side, and over 100 large cardboard boxes and plastic tubs containing receipts, information on customers, bands members, and other important records. Also from that branch was confiscated one of the three mailing lists which featured names, addresses, and email and other contact information for over 5,000 subscribers to Resistance magazine.

But the items locked in the storage unit north of Windsor, Ontario escaped detection and confiscation. Six weeks later, the authorities returned the material and no charges were filed. The company relocated to another Detroit location, got properly licensed, and was back in business. Shortly thereafter, Willis Carto stepped into the picture, and bought the company. During this time I met with Mark Lane, Carto's self-promoting lawyer. He'd written about 15 books, all of which were sold by Carto-controlled entities, including his Liberty Library and the Noontide Press.

"Todd, Willis wants you to replace our direct mail firm with a more aggressive agency," Lane said. The firm, Tony Murray & associates, had done a good job of list rental and management. My work in GOP political campaigns and in direct marketing was why Carto named me as Liberty Lobby's in-house liaison to the Murray operation. I was reluctant to effectuate this change, and I told Lane so. "Utilize my being Jewish to our advantage," Lane told me. He knew that most top direct marketing firms wouldn't consider representing Liberty Lobby, regardless of how much money they could earn renting out the files owned by the Carto-controlled entities.

At the time, Liberty Lobby's lists consisted of SPOTLIGHT subscribers and former subscribers, and subscribers to The Barnes Review, former subscribers to The IHR Journal, buyers of books from the Liberty Library, and a list of donors to David Duke's 1991 campaign for Governor of Louisiana. Carto also owned lists of buyers of silver bars, commemorative gold and silver coins, and collectors of Third Reich memorabilia. Collectively, his files contained over 600,000 unique records (names and addresses), and were generating – after commissions, management and brokerage fees, and computer costs – approximately $175,000 per year. These revenues more than doubled in the following 18 months.

Direct mail marketers know that active and former subscribers to publications, donors to political candidates and causes, and known buyers of products via mail, are great prospects for solicitation for like-minded appeals. There's also tremendous crossover: donors to David Duke are likely to be responsive to offers to subscribe to, say, Soldier of Fortune magazine, or The SPOTLIGHT. These lists were updated every 90 days. Names of the deceased were removed, new addresses replaced old ones, and people whose last name had changed were corrected. Thousands of list brokers paid $125 per thousand records to rent Carto's direct mail files, most of which included phone numbers. By mid-1998, some of these records also included email addresses. Gun and hunting publications, investment news letters, coin and antiques magazines, Book clubs, marketers of health products, conservative Republican candidates and PACs, and other marketers, learned that Liberty Lobby's subscriber and donor files generated high response rates for their clients.

This was especially true of entities like Cabelas and manufacturers of products used by senior citizens. Many of the actual end users of these files never even realized that Carto, or Liberty Lobby, actually owned the mailing lists brokers were renting on behalf of their marketing efforts. That's because many such files weren't specifically identified as having been generated by Willis Carto and his entities.

The following week I drove to Waynesboro, Virginia, to visit the offices of Response Unlimited, a direct marketing firm whose clients were very conservative, Republican-oriented, religious, and right-wing.Mr. Zodhiates was very nice, and no racist; he and his wife had adopted several children of color, and they were pro-Zionist. He even said a prayer before we ate lunch. He then told me that he had sincere reservations about representing Carto's lists.

As Mark Lane had suggested, I told him that Liberty Lobby's lawyer was Jewish, which did the trick. By the time I left his office, I had a contract ready for Carto's signature. Within a few months of Response Unlimited handling list promotions and rentals, the net monthly income from Liberty Lobby's seven direct mail files had tripled, to about $12,500. By the end of 1997, net list rental income had climbed to over $20,000 per month. By the time Willis Carto fired me in late September of 1998, the net list rental income – after commissions were paid to brokers and fees paid to managers, and service costs paid for computer operations – for the first nine months of that year had already exceeded $350,000.

Once Resistance Records paid a fine for its failure to pay state sales tax, everything was returned by the authorities and a brisk business resumed. After that occurred, and after his Nazi buddy Vince urged Willis Carto to purchase the company, he designated me to facilitate the transaction.

He offered substantial cash to Jason Snow, along with a job. Collectively, several Carto-controlled entities, including a tax-exempt foundation and another corporation, paid, over time, about $350,000 for the company's assets. This included nearly $80,000 up-front for Snow's Class B shares. Monies in the company checking accounts weren't part of the transaction; the sellers split that. This was when I entered the picture the reluctant co-owner. I flew to Detroit three times to hammer out the purchase agreement. Shortly there-after, in late September, 1998, Carto and I parted ways. It was acrimonious, and nearly became violent. But beating up a 72-year-old man isn't my thing, and besides, Willis Carto was always armed, even while in D.C. Liberty Lobby and its subsidiaries owed my advertising agency $87,000 in commissions and I was owed over $15,000 in retainer fees and other commissions.

Carto claimed he didn't have the money to pay me, which I knew was a lie. I called him out on this, which led to more acrimony. Our association abruptly ended but we still co-owned the corporation.

Between then and when William Pierce first contacted me in early November of that year, I drank too much and was angry, made me highly vulnerable to experimenting with illegal drugs. Months later, my attitude worsened, as my FBI surveillance work messed with my mind for the entire 33 months I worked for the bureau. There were some close calls, and a few times, my carelessness almost resulted in my cover being blown. In the summer and fall of 2000, Pierce visited my DC office on four occasions. He'd also be there twice in 2001, and once in early 2002. Pierce had relocated the corporate offices of Resistance records from Etiwanda, California, where it had been headquartered since Carto and I bought it. However, bad weather and other complications delayed construction on the cavernous warehouse Pierce was building on his West Virginia compound.

He came to DC to meet with four supporters who were to fly to California and rent two 18-wheel semis. They were to load and then drive the trucks from Etiwanda, California to Pierce's West Virginia compound. I didn't want Pierce coming to my office, but had no choice in the matter.

After the University club's Board of Governors had expelled me when I refused their offer to resign my membership, I hired lawyers from two law firms to file a $6 million discrimination lawsuit against the club, and every board member who had voted to boot me. I also sued the club manager and three other members who had pressured the Board to kick me out. The last thing I needed was for William Pierce to be seen in my office. But I risked it, and no one learned he'd been there. The FBI agents wired my office for sound so they could hear, in real time, what Pierce and I discussed. Prior to his arrival, they planted four mini-microphones around my desk and near where Pierce would sit.

Two were hidden behind books on a shelf. One was attached to the base of the chair where he would sit, and another was under the knee well of my desk. Another was affixed to the cord of a lamp, which sat on an end table next to the chairs facing my desk. Shortly before Pierce arrived, the agents left. While the meeting took place, they were inside an FBI van which was parked less than a half block from the Kennedy-Warren. An advantage of being an FBI agent is that they can park basically wherever they want. They parked in a 'no parking' space near the National Zoo, on Connecticut avenue.

After they left my office, and with only about 20 or so minutes before Pierce was to arrive, the receptionist at the front desk in the Kennedy-Warren lobby called me.

"There's someone here to see you, Mr. Blodgett," she said. It was a drug dealer who had, in recent months, delivered crack cocaine to my office. He had just delivered drugs there only a week earlier, in fact. The receptionist asked if I wanted her to send the man to my office. I went to the lobby to meet him. Luckily, Latrelle was a presentable, well-dressed, fairly soft-spoken pusher with a pleasant disposition. But he still stood out at the Kennedy-Warren. As we shook hands, he said he "was in the hood" and wanted to say hi. Lowering his voice, he also said he had on him "some really good shit" – meaning, high-grade crack cocaine.

I motioned toward the stairs, which led toward the public restroom. Once we were far away enough from the doorman, I said, "Latrelle, it's nice of you to stop by, but we can't talk right now."

"Zupp, dude?", he asked. "I can't meet with you now," I said. "An important man is coming to my office. He'll be here any minute." At that moment, my cell phone rang. It was William Pierce.

"Hold on a second," I told the pusher. "Hey, doctor", I said to Pierce, who said he was fifteen minutes away. He said he'd park in the Kennedy-Warren garage. "No problem, doctor. See you soon." No sooner had I hung up than Latrelle asked if I was sick. After all, I'd addressed the caller as "doctor".

"A doctor be comin' to yo' office? If y'all sick, den 'dis here shit in my pocket be just what you needs. Just smoke two rocks and call me in da mornin'," he said, grinning.

"He's not that kind of doctor, Latrelle. He's a Ph. D., not an M.D."

"Well, what kinda doctorin' him do?" The minutes were ticking away, but I had to be diplomatic. "Well, you see, uh, he sort of, uh, he kind of promotes ideas on how he thinks society could be, uh, improved."

"Well, den I need to meet 'dis dude. Him sound smart, and we need lotsa help in da black community."

"He's probably not the right guy for that, Latrelle. Can we talk later?"

Motioning toward the men's restroom, he whispered he needed to sell his two 8-balls of crack cocaine. In my dire need to get him out, and with my appetite whetted for this great stuff, I followed him. After ascertaining no one was present, I handed the dealer three C-notes. He stuffed the two 8-balls into my hand and was out the door five seconds later. I stuffed them into my pocket, and rushed back to my office. Minutes later, America's most notorious neo-Nazi arrived. As he greeted me, Pierce complained about "all the damn niggers" he always saw every time he visited the District of Columbia. We met for about 30 minutes. Every word spoken was heard by FBI agents, recorded, and later transcribed by stenographers at the J. Edgar Hoover building in downtown D.C.

By the end of my first year (2000) of working as a confidential informant, I lived my disparate lives in ways which were fairly manageable. But it was never easy. I also found intriguing that some innate similarities exist between the realms of White Supremacy and illegal drugs. In each milieu, reprobates call the shots while lower-echelon grunts do the heavy lifting. Theft, even grand larceny, and murder, and other violent crimes figure prominently in both worlds. Tax evasion, fraud, scams and money laundering are commonplace in each domain. White Supremacists and drug suppliers and their minions are frequently targeted by law enforcement, often successfully. Governments employ the clandestine services of professional infiltrators to monitor, and bring down, participants in both environments. Gang activity permeates drug trafficking and drug usage, as it does organized Hate.

Both societal sub-sets feature many individuals who don't want their associations known to outsiders. The sheer inhumanity, creepy people, and unusually gross physical brutality, which can involve weapons, both illegal and legal, are part and parcel to both sectors. Being part of these worlds can and does destroy lives, including those of innocent, unsuspecting victims and those directly affiliated with these realms. Killing people fits with these dangerous territories, and leaders suborn underlings to murder. Finally, the milieus of White Supremacy and illegal drugs are infested with almost as many sociopaths and degenerates as serve in the United States Congress.

The U.S. Congress, and, particularly the Senate, were very much on my father's mind as he and my mother were in D.C. for the inauguration of George H. W. Bush, in January of 2001. Some close family friends joined my parents at the Inaugural festivities. A prominent north Iowa lawyer, Harold 'Hal' Winston and his wife, Carol – now both deceased - flew to Washington to participate in the hoopla generated by the return of GOP rule. On the night before the inauguration, Linda and I, my parents and the Winstons, had drinks and dinner at Nancy Reagan's favorite D.C. restaurant, the Jockey club. The hotel where this legendary, now-vanished Washington landmark was located is where former Vice President Al Gore grew up while his dad was a Senator.

Briefly joining us at our table was Dan Rather, the then-anchorman of the CBS Evening news. We also met Jerry Jones, the owner of the Dallas Cowboys.

A few days later, my father met with Senator Chuck Grassley, and U.S. Representatives Tom Latham, Jim Nussle, and Steve King. These Iowans were all on board supporting my dad for the position that Karl Rove had discussed with the President-elect. President Bush later said that my Dad's decades as a practicing orthodontist, followed by four terms as Deputy majority Leader of the Iowa Legislature, and his 35 years of active involvement in Republican campaigns, and his record of winning every race in which he was a candidate, made him ideal for a substantial presidential appointment.

In April, 2001, my dad began his duties at the U. S. Department of Health and Human Services. A little-known, yet highly influential HHS division called the Provider Reimbursement Review Board was where he served. He held the title of Federal Administrative Judge. He adjudicated, along with four other presidential appointees, disputes involving what collectively amounted to billions of dollars. These legal cases ranged from hospital corporations and Health Maintenance Organizations fighting the details over mergers and hostile takeovers, to state governments demanding more Medicare and Medicaid funds, to pharmaceutical manufacturers and medical device distributors claiming that rivals weren't entitled to funds they regarded as theirs.

By the time my parents moved to Washington, my drug addiction was in its 30th month. At that point, neither my parents or Linda knew of it. But my secret wouldn't remain secret for much longer. My parents and wife worried about my informant work and were concerned for my safety. Their concerns weren't unwarranted, as bad things have happened to bureau informants whose cover is blown, and to undercover FBI agents who are exposed. The agents I worked with were first-rate pros, whose concern for my safety was always paramount. Always, they undertook every precaution to ensure that all of my assignments went off without a hitch, and I completed each mission safely.

Most people have no concept of just how difficult it is to become an FBI agent, or an agent with the Joint Terrorism Task Force. Those who make the cut are among the world's most elite law enforcement specialists, to whom Americans and the citizens of the world owe a tremendous debt of gratitude.

CHAPTER SIX

Situated on nearly 550 acres in Quantico, Virginia, within the Marine Corps Base of the same name, is the FBI Academy. It was first opened in 1972, when Richard Nixon was President, and no public tours of this secretive facility are allowed. Being just an hour's drive from downtown D.C., it was convenient for me to meet with agents, their supervisors, and various higher-ups at 'Quantico' – as FBI agents, analysts, administrators, trainees, and basically everyone affiliated with the bureau calls the place. On my first visit there, the purpose was to brief my controlling agents, meet their boss and the deputy director of the Joint Terrorism Task Force, who had flown in from Pittsburgh.

Once there, I noticed a sign: "Be kinder than necessary, for everyone you meet is fighting some battle". When I saw that, I thought: these guys have no idea of the battles I'm fighting. Because if they did, they'd have never retained my services!

Working as a full-time, professional informant was stressful. According to my handlers, I was among the highest-paid of the bureau's confidential informants. I was assigned to surveil and infiltrate the nastiest racists anywhere, and some of their foreign counterparts. The $6 million lawsuit I'd hired lawyers to file against the University club of DC only added to the daily pressures I felt. By this point in my drug usage, I was fighting a losing battle. How I managed to even stay in the game for so long I'll never understand. The bureau employs about 35,000 people and each year, approximately 70,000 Americans apply to become FBI agents. Of these, fewer than two-hundredths of one percent make it. For every newly-graduated FBI agent, over 69,000 highly qualified candidates didn't, and don't, reach their goal.

In the past, the efficacy of the FBI and CIA was compromised by turf battles between the intelligence-gathering entities. But when I signed on, major strides had been made among those agencies in this regard, which improved further after 9/11. As of 2011, over 100 FBI agents were detailed to the CIA, and CIA officers and agents have been assigned to every FBI field office and to the JTTF – the Joint Terrorism Task Force. I learned this from some counterterrorism analysts and FBI agents.

As an informant, I had the best of all possible worlds. I made more money than most beginning agents, but my work – while not without risk – was easier than theirs. I wasn't subjected to any drug testing, random or otherwise, and didn't have to put my life on the line to save anyone else's. About a year after I began working for the FBI, President Bush replaced director Louie Freeh with Robert 'Bob' Mueller. An ex-Marine who had been awarded the Purple Heart in Vietnam, Mueller was a tough, determined federal prosecutor who rapidly earned the respect, admiration, and support of the agents.

Mueller didn't view agents as subordinates. To him, everyone at the bureau was united in the fight against crime and terror, and the perpetrators. He also was a major supporter of the bureau's technology and constantly pushed for upgrades. These attributes and his highly regarded, consistent professionalism undoubtedly played major roles in his being selected in 2017, to head the special investigation into the Trump administration.

Mueller ordered technological innovations, increased efficiency, and eradicated duplication of efforts, Which enabled even the least technologically adept agents and other bureau staffers to improve their skills to research, flush out, and assist in identifying, and apprehending, people who may pose threats to U.S. society and to national security.

One such innovation which directly made my job easier was the hidden microphone that accompanied me to about half of the scheduled encounters I had with the targets I was assigned to surveil. When I began working for the FBI, I had to be wired, with the hidden recording device's thin wires literally taped to my chest, just like on TV. But shortly after Mr. Mueller took charge, I was provided with a faux pager (which also actually functioned as a pager) that was a recorder. It could store up to eight hours of conversation and was turned on and off by pressing a disguised switch.

Other cool gadgetry, electronic surveillance equipment, and sophisticated techie stuff was also used, but describing it might result in legal trouble for this author. Suffice to say, the FBI possesses some amazing capabilities – especially since the Patriot Act became law - which would blow the minds of most people. Unbeknownst to most Americans, the FBI's powers, including surveillance authority, were tremendously enhanced in the wake of the 9/11 attacks of September of 2001. In some cases, the bureau can countermand, or obviate, regulations and rules for the purposes of planting undercover agents, and/or informants, into businesses, private clubs, religious and political organizations, and even schools.

The bureau would've preferred the public not knowing about what intelligence analysts and security experts call infiltration loopholes. Due to lawsuits in which the findings were made public in redacted form, the FBI's Domestic Investigations and Operations Guide, is publicly available. The DIOG, as the manual is known internally, features information regarding investigative procedures and how obtained information is to be used.

The FBI's website, www.fbi.gov, states that "combatting terrorism is the FBI's top investigative priority", with its National Security branch in the forefront of efforts to "detect, deter, and disrupt terrorist threats to the United States and its interests." Among these threats identified by the bureau are "homegrown terrorists who may aspire to attack the United States from within." As referenced earlier in this memoir, more than 100 Joint Terrorism Task Forces are under the jurisdiction and management of the JTTF's leadership, which is based in Pittsburgh, Pennsylvania, and Washington, D.C. Over 500 state and local agencies and 55 federal agencies assist the JTTF in its efforts to uncover terrorist activity.

An FBI spokesman referred to the JTTF as America's "front line on terrorism". Counterintelligence, cybercrime, Weapons of Mass Destruction (WMDs), public corruption, organized crime, Civil Rights, and white-collar crime and violent crime, all fall within the FBI's and JTTF's purview. Unlike the CIA, the FBI possesses full law enforcement powers; indeed, it is one of the chief U.S. law enforcement agencies. Well over 200 categories of federal laws fall under the bureau's jurisdiction. Regarding domestic Hate Groups and affiliated individuals, the FBI – consistent with guidelines issued by the Attorney General – initiates and administers investigations.

Information obtained by FBI agents and informants assists in establishing a basis for an eventual prosecution, and helps to prevent planned, or future, terrorist attacks. Information collected also is used to build files on those deemed to be potential threats to national security, or to U. S. citizens and others. The first step to establishing an FBI investigation is the assessment process, which any agent can effectuate for up to 30 days without approval from a Supervisor. That's helpful, as many high-yield investigations commence based on an agent's suspicions, or hunches. If, after 30 days, the agent – or agents working together – wish to continue, then supervisory approval is required. Permission to continue must be granted every 30 days until an investigation is officially opened.

Some assessments die on the vine for various reasons. Others lead to preliminary investigations, while still others are determined to warrant a full investigation. My FBI work was facilitated as a complete investigative project from the outset. The agents I worked with told me, however, that most full investigations originally began as preliminary investigations. Informants can be recruited during the assessment process to monitor the subject, or subjects, including physical surveillance of their public activity. If the assessment leads to a preliminary investigation, additional techniques may be used.

These can include tracing phone numbers of incoming and outgoing calls, acquiring records of internet activity, including emails, Facebook communications, and text messaging, and obtaining records held by internet service providers, banks, phone companies, credit unions, and utilizing hidden, high-powered microphones to eavesdrop on conversations spoken in public places.

When full investigations are effectuated, judge-approved actions like wiretaps, the opening of mail, interception of all emails and text messages, monitoring all private Facebook conversations, and all cell phone texting, and the attachment of electronic tracking devices to vehicles used by targets. Covert searches of private residences and homes and offices, can, and often does, commence.

Some of these actions may require a separate issuance of judicial approval each time they're under- taken. In full investigations, a team of agents is usually used, which is also true in certain preliminary investigations. Most FBI investigations aren't one-agent or two-agent operations, and limited resources requires choosing targets carefully. This can mean declining to investigate certain organizations and individuals. It can, at times, cause universal regret. One such case was the 2015 murders of nine black church members in a South Carolina bible study meeting. FBI spokesperson Jillian Stickels said there is no record of any investigation into the Council of Conservative Citizens.

But the C of CC's website was frequently viewed by Dylann Roof, the young racist who murdered those people in that church. The bureau likely considered the C of CC to be too mainstream – relative to other such orga- nizations - to warrant investigation. This was wrong, because members of many so-called mainstream groups are as dangerous as members of the most obstreperous organizations, which equate blacks with apes and denigrate Jewish people as greedy Christ-killers. FBI officials have publicly acknowl- edged that some of their undercover operations have been "intrusive" and can pose "a greater risk to civil liberties" than others. Requiring internal approval and/or legal review for investigations depends on the level of involvement that agents, or informants, will be tasked by the bureau to have with targets under surveillance, and the type of organizations being monitored.

In my case, the FBI already knew of my years with the so-called Hate Movement. They knew, before any agents ever recruited me, that I had associated with dangerous individuals. The agents knew I wouldn't need to go through the usual motions of what they call the "set-up" phase, which FBI agents, and even some informants, must first undergo at the outset of an investigation. As someone who was already well-known within the Hate Movement, and knew more about its top players than anyone else, this step was, in my case, deemed unnecessary. Two different standards are employed typically regarding FBI involvement when targets and groups are monitored. These two categories are: "Sensitive, undisclosed participation", and "non-sensitive, undisclosed participation".

To authorize infiltration of non-sensitive groups, a supervising agent has to approve if plans call for an FBI agent to do the infiltrating for the purpose of obtaining information, or as a component to an investigation. This rule, however, doesn't apply to confidential informants who do the same. When it is known, or believed, that an agent's or an FBI informant's participation could influence the activities of the target, targets, or group, or groups, then permission must be granted by the division chief, upon reviewing the plans with an FBI staff attorney. My work for the bureau was approved by lawyers in the FBI's Office of General Counsel and other senior officials, and signed off on a Deputy U.S. Attorney General. Things get even stickier when it comes to the requirements for monitoring, or infiltrating, an organization which is considered to be sensitive.

The FBI agent, or agents, who push for such investigations must secure permission from a supervisor and from the chief legal counsel of his or her division. Additionally, the requesting agent, or agents, must also apprise a special committee within the bureau which holds sway over such operations. If the honchos believe it's likely the infiltration might influence a sensitive organization's exercise of its first amendment rights or those of its members, the FBI director must personally sign off. In practice, such regulations result in multiple levels of oversight. Agents are provided with substantial discretion to determine whether infiltering these targets, and/or groups, may constitute what's called "undisclosed participation", and, tacitly, if the extra approvals are even needed.

For example, if a foreign government either operates or funds a group, or it's believed that foreigners may benefit from its activities, or the organization has foreigners as members, or leaders, then none of these rules apply. Such rules also don't apply to groups which the bureau considers illegitimate. For these purposes, the FBI defines as "legitimate" organizations those which are "formed for lawful purposes", and the "activities" of which "are primarily lawful". Informants are apprised of such rules and warned to never place themselves, or the bureau, in the position of potentially being accused of being an agent provocateur. Criminal networks, gangs, and other groups can also be excluded from such rules if an FBI agent claims he or she believes that the "primary purpose" of such organizations is to sponsor protests which may involve illegality.

Former FBI agent Mike German is now with New York University's Brennan Center for Justice. He claims this type of language provides leeway to FBI agents, which can protect them against any accusations of violating proper investigative procedures. "Do we want to have agents parsing the language of what's legitimate and what isn't legitimate, without that oversight?" To "investigate a legitimate organization", Mr. German says, "requires an additional level of oversight because of the history of abuse."

A loophole which concerns some observers – and I disagree with their concerns in this regard – allows agents to accept and use information about targets and regarding groups furnished by informants via undisclosed participation. When J. Edgar Hoover died in 1972, few rules governed the FBI. Every President Hoover served, especially LBJ and Richard Nixon, either tacitly gave him free rein or were afraid – as was JFK – that Mr. Hoover would disclose sensitive personal information about them which would prove to be disastrous, politically and personally. Professor of Law Emily Berman, who teaches at the University of Houston Law school, says, "in the1970s … there were no rules governing the FBI."

Informants are often cited in affidavits submitted to courts when the bureau requests permission from Judges to facilitate a more intrusive investigation. The mere assertion by an FBI agent, and/or lawyers employed by the bureau, of an ongoing investigation, can result in obtaining judicial sanction to trace phone calls, and – in certain cases, relating to national security – to wiretap the phones of targets. The agents I worked with told me that there was always a chance I could be called as a witness in a criminal trial. But because this would've caused me to lose my anonymity, every effort was made to prevent, or minimize, the inclusion of me being identified as a paid, full-time, confidential informant for the bureau. In some internal reports my name is redacted, to provide further protection of my identity.

In May of 2019, a professional informant helped the FBI to snare a pro-Muslim terrorist named Mark Domingo, according to The Army Times and the Associated Press. Domingo, a combat veteran who had served in Afghanistan before being booted by the U.S. Army, wanted revenge for the March, 2019 killings at two New Zealand mosques. The full-time confidential informant, who began work for the FBI in August of 2013, won the trust of the would-be terrorist and enabled the FBI to foil the planned bombing. The violent attack was to have taken place near Los Angeles.

Obviously, disclosing this informant's identity could place him or her in physical jeopardy. A few months after my parents arrived in Washington, I chatted briefly with George W. Bush, for the first time after he became President. This was after I had been working for the the FBI for about 18 months. The event was a reception on behalf of the Republican National Committee. He was the same fun, witty, genuine, sharp politico whose office had been two floors above mine, at the headquarters of his father's 1988 presidential campaign in D.C's Woodward building. Along with Ronald Reagan and Donald Trump, George W. Bush is the most politically gifted Republican President since Richard Nixon.

He's innately gregarious, has a wonderful way with people, and is a natural campaigner. Mr. Bush's phenomenal memory for names easily surpasses that of Reagan, Gerald Ford and Bush's father. Ronald Reagan, despite having a nearly photographic memory, never was great with names. Bush and I spoke of some mutual friends we'd worked with on the 1988 campaign, on which he served as an unpaid adviser. The name of former Iowa Congressman Tom Tauke came up in that conversation. President Bush instantly smiled, and said, "I really like Tom Tauke." Bush had met Tauke in 1978, when the two of them were running for Congress in their respective states. The 43rd President recounted how he and Tauke had attended a week-long seminar for GOP congressional candidates.

Bush called it "charm school", and remembered even the smallest details of the experience. Tauke won his race that year, while Bush lost. As President #43 wrapped up the recollection, he said, with a wink, "that charm school did Tauke a heckuva lot more good than it did me!" His self-deprecation was as genuine in 2001 as it was when our mutual friend, Kevin Moley, introduced us in 1986. Days after that reception, I met with two FBI agents at the old Pension Building on the grounds of the Smithsonian Institute. They had uncovered more proof of how Carto had defrauded his supporters who funded his entities. In this case, the agents wanted to know about a Carto D.B.A. – doing business as – organization which had raised substantial funds that, somehow, weren't being deposited into the organization's bank accounts. The entity was called Caucasians Actively Saving Humanity.

I knew about that ruse, which Willis Carto had pulled several times. The canny old scammer, after delivering a speech, told the faithful that donations to his new organization would be accepted on the spot. In an audience whose average is about 75, many will have problems with arthritis, rheumatism, and other maladies which make handwriting difficult. Carto knew this, and told his adoring admirers to "just abbreviate" the name of his new group on their checks. Nobody noticed the slick trick he'd pulled. "Use the acronym for this organization as you write out your checks, folks," the con man told the crowd. In his hotel room the next morning, he and I counted out over 200 checks, every ill-gotten one of them made out to CASH.

When the codgers got their cashed checks back in their bank statements, no one called Liberty Lobby or Willis Carto to complain. That was because the signature endorsing each check presented for payment was that of Willis A. Carto – whom they all trusted. The scam artist had screwed them again.

The value of one such haul to Carto was just over $130,000. Every cent was tax-exempt, and the full amount was deposited into Willis Carto's personal checking account. I know this because after he endorsed those drafts, I walked over to the National Capital Bank of Washington and deposited them. Carto's business manager at Liberty Lobby, Blayne Hutzel, mailed each donor an acknowledgement of their contribution, written on stationary with the name of a tax-exempt Carto-controlled corporation.

Doing so enabled the donors to claim an illicit deduction on their income tax returns. Carto enriched himself and obtained what amounted to an illegal subsidy from U.S. taxpayers. As required by my contract with William Pierce, I took AMTRAK to his West Virginia compound, which I referred to as the 'Nazi Nest'. My agreement required me to make semi-monthly trips there. There, I'd usually spend a three or four-day weekend, from a Thursday afternoon through a Monday morning. As I arrived, several young National Alliance staffers were in the recording studio, listening to live auditions of some Hate Metal bands. One such band, comprised of five amateur musicians from Philadelphia, had re-worked the lyrics to 'Hey, Jude', and other popular, mainstream hits for racist audiences.

Their lyrical alterations provided an entirely new meaning to abusing artistic license. This was particularly the case with their anti-Semitic variations of Christmas music. Listed here are some examples of their repulsive revisionism. To the melody and tune of 'Hey, Jude' – by the Beatles:

"Hey, Jew, bad news for you; We're gonna bake you, and every other Jew, too … "

"The Holocaust, again tonight will begin; you'll be gassed at ten – have fun in our oven."

Then, this stanza:

"Any time that you see me, you, Jew, should flee; or, you'll wish you lived in Hitler's Germany"

"We're gonna GAS you, YOU dirty Jewwwww"

Staffers, volunteers, and Pierce supporters who were present – which included some high-dollar donors to the National Alliance – all applauded and laughed. To say that they enjoyed the music is an understatement. These lyrics were from a song titled, 'If I could be a Nigger for a Day':

"If I could be a nigger for a day, I'd live my life the free and easy way ...

I'd take from Uncle Sam, and let the white man pay – If I could be a nigger, for a day"

"I'd get money a-workin' for the mob; I'd sell some dope, and find liquor stores to rob...

That'll make me self-employed, so I wouldn't need a job ... If I could be a nigger, for a day."

"Whenever I'd need somethin', I'd steal; wouldn't have to buy it; If the cops arrest me, I'd just deny it. I'd call Jesse, or Al Sharpton - and they'd start a riot - if I could be a nigger, for a day."

"A Jew Social Worker will get me Welfare; I'd get Food Stamps, a medical card, and free Child Care – for all the bastard kids I'd have scattered everywhere"

One particularly vile song auditioned by one band went this way:

"Burn a Jew, everybody wants to; Good white folks love hatin' a Hebrew...

Get rid of every Jew; they're trouble for us; stuff 'em in the ovens, turn 'em to dust."

"Burnin' Jews will make your day; when it's done, they're in an ashtray ..."

William Pierce, who generally disliked Hate Metal music, laughed uproariously at a song titled, 'Quit your bitchin', Nigger'. Here's a verse from that tune:

"Quit your bitchin', nigger; just let things be –

Shut up now, or you'll swing from a tree -

Quit your bitchin', nigger, or you'll get your due

'Cause the Ku Klux Klan'll come a-gunnin' for you"

The above song was one of Willis Carto's favorites.

The bastardized versions of Christmas carols were among the most offensive noise I've ever heard. The bigoted carolers sang this one, to the tune of 'Jingle Bells':

"Jingle bells, jingle bells, jingle all the way; Oh, what fun it is to gas some Hebes on Christmas Day-aayy ...

Dashin' through the snow, on the way to gas some Jews; ain't no better way - to cure them Christmas

blues ... Niggers pull our sleigh; spicks are shovelin' snow – what fun it is to burn some Yids, and see

'em all aglow ... Ohh, jingle bells, jingle bells, jingle all the way; hang some coons and burn some kikes,

and shoot some Queers today-aayy ... "

Incidentally, during the Christmas holidays, this same, bastardized version of 'Jingle Bells' was sung at a party in Fauquier county, Virginia, at the elegant home of a well-to-do retired lawyer who had once worked for the CIA under director Richard Helms. Video was filmed of this by a Pierce supporter who attended this function and sent it to William Pierce. Months later, Pierce delighted in showing me the appalling, videotaped proof which confirmed that those he called "high end, classy people" supported his efforts and agenda. The partiers on this video were dressed like they had arrived at the event right after attending a concert put on by a symphony orchestra at the John F. Kennedy center for the Performing Arts. Pierce's musicians left no stone untuned.

They even changed, 'Felice Navidad', to 'Illegals Should be Shot". Here's an excerpt:

"Illegals should be shot … Illegals should be shot … just line them up, and shoot the whole damn lot.

They trespass onto my yard; sixteen arrived in a stolen car… Illegals in my yard; Illegals in my yard –

when they're not workin', they get drunk in the bars… Illegals in my yard, illegals in my yard …

runnin' past the Border Guards… they're gonna invade us this Christmas … yeah, be on your guard."

Around 2008, a tune appeared on YouTube, titled, 'Illegals in my Yard' – which, basically, is a reworked version of 'Illegals Should be Shot'. In 1932, an anti-black song called 'That's why Darkies were born' hit #12 on the Popular Charts. It was sung by Kate Smith, among other popular entertainers. This tune was also performed that day. Among its blatantly racist lyrics:

"Someone had to pick the cotton; someone had to pick the corn – Someone had to slave, and sing, and teach white folks to dance; That's why Darkies were born … "

Kate Smith was famous for her beautiful rendition of 'God Bless America', but she – and black activist and entertainer Paul Robeson - also recorded this tune. In 2019, the New York Yankees baseball team and Philadelphia Flyers hockey team announced that Miss Smith's version of 'God Bless America' would no longer be played at their games, amid concerns over her song about blacks. Professional Baseball knows about racial discrimination, having banned blacks from playing pro ball for its first 50-plus years.

When I mentioned to William Pierce that as far as I knew, the only lyrically-altered song we'd just heard that was no longer protected by copyright was 'Jingle Bells', he wasn't worried. "I know," he replied. "Let Paul McCartney and José' Feliciano make a public outcry over these versions. The publicity will be worth it. It sells CDs," he said, as he picked up his cat, Hadley, and returned to his office. If you're offended by these lyrics, you should be. But when hearing them for the first time, I was basically indifferent to them and

164

the hatred it signified. While being indifferent toward hatred, and insensitive about it, aren't the same as supporting it, it's still pretty bad. That's because those who actually believe in such hatefulness benefit from those whose live-and-let-live attitude allows it to thrive, and permits environments for them to spread it. When I began this memoir, I met with some Jewish friends of mine.

They knew I wasn't anti-Semitic and hadn't ever been. I shared with them my concerns. They told me if readers of this book are to gain any worthwhile knowledge, and learn what actually happened, and still happens, then the best way to facilitate that would be to write the truth, with nothing sugar-coated.

As a junkie, I didn't restrict my drug use to crack houses in the hoods of DC, Baltimore, New York City, and Philadelphia. Few locations were off-limits when it came to blazing crack. I got high in the house my wife and I owned, in my office in northwest DC, in my parents' condo in Washington, and at the Watergate apartments and hotel, and even at my family's summer cottage in north Iowa. I used drugs in at probably 200 different crack houses and motel and hotel rooms. Drugs are as addictive as politics. For some people, racism can be even more addictive. There were some comical moments in my life as a junkie. Few things are ever totally serious, all good, or bad, all the time.

The unique characters I encountered during my addiction would boggle the minds of Hollywood's most imaginative, creative screenwriters. No fictional screenplay could come close to capturing these real-life, drug-addled junkies and their crazy lives. One of my favorites was a crackhead whom I'll call Myles Mandell. He was in his early forties when we met, around 2002. After losing his wife and teenaged son to drug overdoses, Myles lived alone in a spacious, elegant, older co-op unit he had inherited.

His place was in upper northwest DC at the intersection of 17th and 'R' streets. Myles had worked for years at the U.S. Department of Justice and retired early, upon inheriting substantial money. In his twenties, he had been an actor in New York, appearing in hundreds of off-Broadway productions, and worked as a stage director. He had lost all but one vocal cord after accidentally inhaling a crack pipe's hot wire filter, leaving him with little more than a whisper of a voice.

Myles was a freebase cocaine connoisseur extraordinaire, routinely blowing through ten grand a month of it. When he'd get real high, he'd dramatically quote lines from Shakespeare. These recitations were all from memory. His monologues ranged from excerpts from Romeo and Juliet, to Hamlet, to The Merchant of Venice, A Midsummer Night's Dream, Julius Caesar, and other Shakespearean dramas.

When he'd put on a solo mini-performance, he'd even affect the accents to differentiate the various characters portrayed in his one-man gigs. Of course, an audience comprised of crackheads wasn't that appreciative of these performances. Late one evening I sat with Myles in his book-lined den, its walls lined with framed oil portraits of his ancestors. It was monologue time. Myles set his crack pipe down on an ashtray and the bardolatry commenced, sweeping gestures, and all.

"To be, or not to be: That is the question," Myles intoned, in his raspy voice. "This is the very ecstasy of love. Though this be madness, there is method in it." DeShawn, a black crackhead in his mid-twenties, was about as interested in Shakespeare as Myles was in hip-hop. "What him SAY?", he asked. Erskine, who actually was paying attention, interpreted for DeShawn. "Him talkin' about ECSTASY and METH. If y'all want some later, den shut da fuck up." Myles then segued to 'The Merchant of Venice'. "A devil can cite scripture for his purpose."

"Him gonna recite some bible talk now?", asked Shaniqlia. "I done O'D on dat shit when I were growin' up!" Unfazed, Myles continued. "Mislike me not for his complexion."

"I likes me 'dat one," said Skillet. "Shakespeare weren't no racist." From the corner of his eye, Myles saw a druggie pick up a bong from the floor. As the addict fumbled for a hit of crack that was in his front shirt pocket, Myles was quoting a line from 'Romeo and Juliet'. He was in the midst of a line from 'Julius Caesar' when he took umbrage. "Fear him not, Caesar; for he is not dangerous." Then, suddenly, the old actor yelled, "touch that goddamned bong, or try blazing a rock while I'm onstage, and you're OUT!" The junkie put everything down on the coffee table. Max was still pissed off. "You shit heads don't appreciate culture! You're uncouth SWINE! I'm quoting from the best dramas by history's greatest playwright, a gifted writer who hailed from the land of my forefathers!"

"Say, whahh?", asked Earl. "Sumpin' about swine," said Juanita. "Don't dat mean pigs?" 'Pinball' had a different take on what Myles had just said. "Him sayin' he gots him FOUR fathers." Shavisa said, "He trippin' now. Ain't nobody gots fo' fathers." Ignoring their play- by-play commentary, Myles exclaimed, "Come, come, good wine is a good, familiar creature."

That line caught the interest of another junkie, who said, "Dat Shake-speare dude musta liked wine, but just think what he coulda wrote if he ever done smoked him some crack. Ahh'm sayin' "

"Parting is such sweet sorrow, that I shall say goodnight till tomorrow."

"Now, he talkin' like Jesse Jackson, all dat rhymin' and shit," observed Katrina. Seemingly impervious to this, Myles continued with his 'Caesar' interpretation. "Let me have men about me that are fat."

A young black replied, "ain't no such thing as a fat crackhead."

The performance continued unabated. "Tempt not a desperate man," Myles exclaimed.

"I'se be desperate fo' some hits," said another junkie who was sitting in the corner on the floor. "If dis here dude don't gimme one soon, I'm gonna knock me off a 7-Eleven ."

Myles continued his recital. "Cassius has a mean and hungry look."

"Now him talkin' boxin'," said Antwon. "Hear dat shit? He talkin' about Muhammad Ali, back in da day. See, Ali done call hisself Cassius Clay. Fo real. Dat were after whitey done take away him title, 'cause him ain't wanna fight in 'Nam, see, and – "

"AAAHHRRRGGHHH,!" Myles interrupted. "Goddamnit, you crack-head SHITS!," Myles erupted, his eyes bulging and cheeks a bright crimson. After screaming as best he could with his one vocal cord, the old trouper finally gave up. If he wanted an appreciative audience for his one-man rendition of history's greatest playwright, it wouldn't be here. As he dispensed rocks to us, I conveyed my appreciation of his culture-promoting efforts. "That was great, Myles! You're still a hell of an actor. You know – "

"Shut the fuck up, Todd. And don't tip the crack pipe down. You'll get spit in it!"

As I raised to pipe to a safe, 60 angle facing upward, I replied, "Spit happens."

"Shut up and take your fuckin' hit."

"Okay. As you like it."

"Not a bad pun, for a Republican," Myles said. I smiled and replied, "All's well that ends well."

No small number of drug pushers and ghetto homeys trusted me, and not only because my money was always good. When I gave my word, I kept it. That trust was such that when I had exhausted my ready cash and was out of drugs, and had already gotten the maximum daily amount from ATM's, pushers extended me credit. They knew I'd keep my promise to pay, and always did. With several dealers, I became very friendly. One of them even invited me to his 100-year-old grandmother's birthday party, at an AME church in N.E. Washington. When I complimented her on her youthful, unwrinkled complexion, the old gal said, "honey, black don't crack." Some of them even had me watch their kids, when they left their homes to re-up. That's when drug dealers replenish their inventory by suppliers, who act as wholesalers to their customers, the street dealers.

As confusing as it often was to communicate with crackheads from DC's hoods, trying to understand white racists was frequently even more perplexing. The bureau sent me to Georgia to attend the funeral of a local, well-connected Klansman. The decedent was laid out in his coffin, hands folded, supporting a small Confederate battle flag. The decedent's brass belt buckle was emblazoned with a the image of General Robert E. Lee, and the cap on his head featured the National Rifle Association logo. As I entered the funeral home, several dozen mourners had already gathered. I signed the guest book, greeted the man's wife and children, took a seat, and began reading the program. I was one of maybe a half dozen men wearing a suit, and probably the only man whose suit contained no polyester.

Elvis Presley's renditions of 'How Great Thou Art,' 'In the Garden' and 'You'll Never Walk Alone', and other gospel hymns by The King blared from hidden stereo speakers. Most of the men looked as though they'd just come from a NASCAR event and about half of the women needed to join Weight Watchers, or at least stop watching Paula Deen. Because I wore a suit, and wasn't known to anyone there, some suspicion was aroused as I sat down.

The gregarious dude seated next to me looked like he could be related to Larry the Cable Guy, and smelled like he'd just finished slopping some hogs. Extending his hand, he said, "Howdy, friend. Mah name's Buford. What's yore's, and where's y'all from?" I said, "I'm Todd, sir, from Virginia.

"You're from around here, Buford?," I asked. "Just up the road apiece," he replied, "been knowin' the dearly departed all muh life. Used to go a-coon huntin' together. Hunted both kinds of coons," Buford rambled. "Two-legged and four-legged, yessir." He then said, "Ah'm the deceased's urologist." Now, having grown up around doctors, and being married to a registered nurse, I knew how physicians speak, act, look, and dress. And smell. And this redneck was even less likely to be a urologist than he was to have completed the sixth grade. But I pretended to accept his word as the truth.

My job was to glean information, and ticking off my surveillance targets would be a deal-breaker. A moment later, an enormous woman, probably 350 pounds, waddled over and sat down next to my new acquaintance. Her muumuu was emblazoned with a Confederate flag. Her cheap, oversized earrings were in the shape of Swastikas. Both of her forearms were tattooed with Hell's Angels logos, and she was sweaty. "This here's muh wife. Wanda, this here's Tawd. Done come all the way from Virginny."

Nodding at me, the obese woman asked her bigoted husband if he'd written his "urology."

"Sure thang, sugar plum," he replied, patting the front pocket of his overalls. Sure enough, about 15 minutes into the service, Buford rose, went up to the podium, and delivered his "urology". Urologist, eulogist; eulogy; urology: in the realm of racist stupidity, it's all the same.

The following day, there was a very different, invitation-only, different kind of memorial ceremony. This service was held in a chapel in a private, members-only hunt club. Following the sermon, a neo-Nazi preacher announced to the assembled what he called "a special treat." Fifteen or 20 youngsters, the average age of which was probably about seven, gathered at the altar. One of the kids was the deceased's great nephew, and another was his granddaughter. On cue, the children all began to sing.

"Jee-zuss loves white lit-tle children, all white chil-dren of the world; Just as long as we are white, we are prec-ious in his sight; Je-zuss loves white lit-tle chil-dren of the world."

After this performance, another corpulent, dark-haired lady wearing a powder blue mumu took her place behind the lectern, and music began playing from up in the balcony. Her song was set to the melody of the 1960s hit, 'More' - by the late, Iowa-born singer Andy Williams. After dedicating the tune to the dearly departed, she began her contralto rendition of it.

"Pray that America becomes Jew-free; that's how our country is supposed to be –

Once Jews are out, the Spics and Queers go, too; then we will hunt down every Jigaboo

These evil parasites, despicable Israelites, they'll be in our rifle sights –

We'll bring 'em down, each day and night

America, then, will truly be free; as it was meant to be, for you, and me

Jews will be gone, for good; we'll win, as Hit-ler said we would

Life will be just wonderful, in every Jew-free neigh-bor-hood … "

And this took place in what these people considered to be a church.

Following these performances, a beautiful, well-groomed golden retriever, maybe three or four years old, was led out to the front of the sanctuary. The dog was introduced as 'Blondie' – which was the name of Adolf Hitler's dog, of the same breed. This Blondie was trained to raise her front right paw on command, Hitler-style. When she did this, she held the Nazi/SS salute in place for about ten seconds. The crowd went nuts at the sight of this well- trained, beautiful canine, saluting, Hitler-style.

At the reception following this second service, several attendees greeted one another by saying, "88". As previously noted, '88' stood for the letter 'H', the eighth letter of the alphabet. Doubling it up meant "Heil Hitler". I introduced myself to a clean-cut, blue-collar young man who was about 25 years old. He said his name was Jake, and he worked as a mechanic at a local service station. Jake's father worked at a Wal-Mart, and his mother cooked at a nursing home. I asked him if he'd known the decedent.

"Oh, yeah", he answered. "He was the patriot who hooked me up with the National Alliance. I owe lots to him." He then launched into a vicious tirade against Jews, blacks, Hispanics and others he called "mud people", or just "muds". He condemned Asians, whom he called "slope heads", or "slopes". Wanting to keep him talking, I said, "Our country sure has changed."

"Yeah, and it ain't fer the better, neither," he replied. "The damn JEWS have done wrecked America, 'specially with how they got all them there anti-white laws passed. Kikes always sides with niggers, spicks, and lazy-ass white trash, race-mixers, queers, and all that there." I asked Jake if his parents shared his views. "Hell, YES! My folks knows that them Jews hates on us REAL Americans"

"What do you think the future will bring, Jake?"

"It'll be total chaos. If we-all don't git to reinin' 'em in, and I'm a-talkin' real soon, then them there kikes and the muds is a-gonna do us ALL in. Yessir. Y'all just wait, see fer yore self. But I'm a-hopin' they's a-gonna git theirs, yessirree. Them there Christ killers ain't even a-gonna know what in tarnation ever done hit 'em, I'm tellin' ya. That there's a fact."

I guzzled a double Jack Daniels and Root Beer and then another drink as he kept rolling. "I'm serious as a heart attack, here, now. We're a-gittin' them there hebes, gonna string 'em all up!"

"Yeah?"

"Are the Kennedys gun shy?"

"Them Jews," he said, "is in fer a real sue-PRIZE. Day's a-comin' when a bunch of us good ole boys, we gonna get 'em good, do 'em in. Gonna put 'em ALL outta bidness, hear?" I had heard, all right, and so would the FBI agents to whom I'd turn over the taped conversation. I asked Jake what he thought such ambitious plans might entail. Laughing, as he lit another Camel, he said, "Let's just say that when we git done with 'em, if they's any LEFT, them Jews is gonna wish they'd a-never done come to OUR country."

"Why?"

"This here's the yew-ess of A, that's why. We got righteous anger goin' fer us. And we'll turn it agin' them Yids, Coons, Spicks, Queers, and Slopes. Ole Hitler was right. The only good hebe's a dead hebe. And we're gettin' the Jews first, 'cause them's the ones done started all this shit. Once the Jews is dead, everything else will just fall into place."

Jake, noticing a cute young gal across the room, then shook my hand. "Hey, sir, good talkin' with y'all. Maybe I'll catch ya later. But right now, I gotta go check out that there little filly," he said, pointing to the pretty blonde girl, smoking by herself. If I'd not been working undercover, I'd have enjoyed debating this kid. I could've dealt him a memorable verbal beat down, and perhaps gotten him to change his hateful ways. But the FBI was paying me to fit in, which meant at least appearing to agree with beliefs expressed by the targets. Still, keeping my mouth shut at such events was often a challenge.

Later, I was alarmed to learn that Jake had served four years in the Army, where he specialized in manufacturing and detonating high-powered explosives. As I walked past the punch bowl to leave, the fat lady wearing the powder blue mumu was talking with the urologist and his wife. The fabric of her muumuu featured one-inch by one-inch Swastikas.

I flew back to DC to a very worried wife, who still knew nothing of my drug addiction. But her concerns about my safety mounted by the week. Linda picked me up at Washington DC's Ronald Reagan national airport just before lunch time. "I'm very worried," she told me over lunch at the Have-a-Bite café in Fairfax, Virginia. "You're associating with some nasty, evil people. When you're out of town, or out late while you're here, I can't get it out of my mind that you could be threatened, hurt, or even killed. I don't want you involved with this, dealing with such horrible people. Even if it is for the FBI."

"It's my job, Linda."

"Well, it's affecting me, badly. It's impacting my sleep, and I've lost nine pounds since you started." I assured her that the bureau always knew where I was, and who I was with, and had my back. Most of the time, I told Linda, the agents provided on-site back-up protection, just in case anything went awry. "I'm safe, honey. Don't worry." Gently cupping her chin and cheek into my hand, I looked her in the eyes, and said, "Okay?" She nodded in ascent, but she wasn't convinced.

The next week, we had house guests at our Annandale home. Iowa's Former U.S. Senator Roger W. Jepsen, an old family friend, was in DC on business. Senator Jepsen, now living in Florida, represented some Chinese business interests and often stayed with us when he was in town. During this visit, the now-retired Senator got together with my parents and made the rounds on Capitol Hill. One evening, my parents, Senator Jepsen, and Linda and I had dinner at the Caucus Room, a steakhouse in downtown Washington that was owned by Haley Barbour and some other politicos. Roger Jepsen was one of the few people outside of my family who knew I was working for the FBI.

Jepsen, in his fatherly way, told me I had "always been a risk taker", which was true. "I know that no one works harder than you, Todd. But be discreet. If at any time you feel you should get out of this, then resign." I eventually came around to the Senator's way of thinking. But at that time, I was all in. Senator Jepsen left the following morning. With an entire day ahead of me and nothing scheduled, it felt like a good time to drive into DC, cop some crack, and get high. I convinced myself I'd be home in time for dinner with Linda. None of the three drug dealers I phoned picked up or returned my calls.

I stopped at the home of a junkie I'd gotten to know early in my addiction. This junkie dealt crack to support his own drug habit. He was on Social Security disability, collected Food Stamps and SSI benefits, Medicaid, and lived in subsidized housing. Meals on wheels were delivered daily to his apartment. We walked to a black church that served cheap, soul food lunches to the public. Over fried chicken, collard greens, and other soul food, he said he couldn't get high for awhile. "My baby mama be locked up, Todd. Bitch got busted turnin' tricks. I gots da kids livin' wiff me. Gotta pick 'em up from day care in a minute. They gonna be wiff me all damn weekend. So I ain't gettin' high."

As we walked the few blocks to where I'd parked near his building, my cell phone rang. It was one of the dealers I'd left messages with, calling to invite me to his place. "I gotta re-up, Lightskin. Get y'all white ass over here soon's ya'll can, and I takes care of ya." To re-up means a drug dealer obtains more product from a supplier. It's not a term addicts like to hear, as it means having to wait for a fix. But it was either wait for Tremaine to re-up, or go home without getting high. Tremaine lived in a dangerous DC public housing project called Sersum Corda. Locals referred to it as "Sursa Quarters", or, simply, "the Quarters". It's filled with junkies, hookers, killers, drug pushers and violent ex-cons.

When I arrived, Tremaine's buddy DeShawn was in his apartment, and they were discussing a fenced gift that Tremaine had given DeShawn two grand to buy, for 'T' to give to his mother. "Where dat mink coat fo' my mama be?"

"Dude bringin' it tomorrow, 'T'. It's real nice. Y'all mama be LOVIN' it," said DeShawn.

"Do dat joint be hot?" DeShawn said, "No, sir, I gots it on da up-and-up. Just chill. I done made sure it all legit, I'm sayin'."

"Fo' real?"

"Damn straight, nigga. I'm on it. But since when y'all ever give a damn if sumpin' be a little warm?"

"I don't care if it hot, dude, but my mama DO."

"Say, what?"

"She done tell me she don't want no mink stole." That observation reminded me of Buford's urology.

Because my money was always good, and I was a regular customer, and I was always respectful toward dealers and never condescending, pushers trusted me. That's important for a junkie, especially when the crackhead is temporarily low on cash and asks for credit, known as a "front". Fronting drugs is also called "buying on tick" – as in, time ticking away while dealers wait for the cash. After DeShawn left Tremaine's place, 'T' told me to await his return. "Help y'self to sumpin' to eat if y'all want. I be back in a minute." The wait took about an hour, which I spent channel surfing, and checking voice mail messages, which had backed up on my cell phone.

When 'T' returned, I bought two 8-balls, and was ready to leave when he asked me where I'd go to smoke it. "Probably the Braxton Hotel," I replied, referring to an old, decrepit establishment on Rhode Island avenue, N.W. "Tellya what, Todd. Instead of wastin' fifty bucks on that roach hotel, y'all should meet Shavonda. Share some crack with the bitch, and she gonna tell y'all about a bidness deal that means some big money. I been meanin' to call you about this, but it kept slippin' my mind."

"I'm not interested in illegal deals, Tremaine. Besides, I've got money for my habit.

"I know. But y'all still should meets dis chick, 'cause maybe someday you and her can do some good bidness. " Tremaine was entrepreneurial, always looking to make money, nearly always illegally. He bragged about how he'd filed no tax returns since he was in high school.

"She's safe?," I asked. "How well do you know her?"

"Shavonda cool, Todd."

"I'm married, you know. Not interested in getting into something along those lines."

"Don't worry about 'dat. She gots a boyfriend, him get high, too. Dat nigga be from Nigeria."

"Have you told these people about me?"

"Yeah, is you in?" Figuring it may prove interesting, I said okay. 'T' called Shavonda, who asked to speak with me. I got directions and drove to her place Shavonda and her Nigerian boyfriend were waiting for me. We briefly got acquainted, and then fired up our pipes, and got buzzed. As we came down from our first few hits, I asked them about the business proposition Tremaine had mentioned. That's when the Nigerian took over.

"Before we go into this, you must give us your word that this conversation remains completely confidential, regardless of what you decide. Okay?" I agreed. "Very well, then," he replied.

"You own an ad agency, and a record company," he said, with the certainty of someone who'd prepared for this meeting. Tremayne, assures me you're not a racist, so you're cool with me."

"Alright."

"We wish to purchase from you records of credit card information pertaining to your advertising clients, as well as customers of Resistance Records, and subscribers to Resistance magazine. I estimate you've got tens of thousands of such." He was correct about the numbers. The TAB agency had sold print ads and classifieds to thousands of clients for The SPOT-LIGHT. Since Resistance Record's founding, nearly 80,000 customers had purchased CD's and other racist products, and/or subscribed to its magazine. For such a brazen offer to be tendered by someone I'd just met was stunning. I was speechless. "We realize," he said, "that some records will be out of date, expired, and of no value to us. So we will compensate you for those which are still current. I'll pay the costs involved in sorting that out."

This guy was serious, and professional, and wasn't the veteran junkie Shavonda was.

The entire time, she smoked hit after hit, while the Nigerian smoked only weed, and took no drags from his chick's crack pipe. "We shall pay you, in cash, twenty dollars for information relating to each valid MasterCard and VISA card, twenty-five dollars for every valid DISCOVER card, and thirty for each valid American Express card you furnish." The guy was as much all business as his girl was gorgeous. As he wrapped up his sales pitch, Shavonda winked at me, smiled, and slowly ran the top of her tongue across the base of her upper teeth. This orthodontist's son couldn't help noticing that she was either born with perfect teeth, or someone had done a hell of a job of straightening them.

"So, Mister Todd, what say you? Have we a deal?"

"No. I don't go for that kind of thing. Sorry." The Nigerian briefly closed his eyes, opened them, and flashed a phony smile which made Jimmy Carter's grin look almost sincere. "Very well. But I want you to keep us in mind, if and when you find yourself needing cash. Which, if you continue smoking crack, you will, someday." I said there was no way that would ever happen. "That's what you believe at this time. But if you continue to smoke this shit, your circumstances may change. However, by that time, the percentage of valid credit card information in your possession will decline. But that's your business, and your decision. Regardless, this conversation, as you have agreed, remains completely confidential. We're clear on that, correct?"

"Yeah."

"Good. I deal only with honorable associates who keep their word." At that time, Shavonda excused herself, and returned about two minutes later, and handed me a DVD. "This is for you, Mr. Blodgett," she said, stating my last name for the only time since I'd arrived 90 minutes earlier. "What's this?" "It's a copy of a video that's just been made of part of our conversation," the Nigerian replied.

"What?"

"This DVD shows you entering our apartment with illegal drugs, placing the 8-balls on the table, and smoking crack." I noticed that the crack pipe they'd furnished me to use was no longer on the table.

"And you've got my fingerprints and DNA on the crack pipe," I said.

"Yes, Mister Todd - we've stored the pipe, in a Zip-Lock bag. You see, sir, we agree with what your former boss used to say."

"What?"

"Ronald Reagan said to say no to drugs."

"He also said that one should trust, but verify, didn't he, Mister Blodgett? We know from our mutual friend Tremaine that by all indications, you're honorable and your word is good. But if you're ever inclined to run your mouth about our activities, watching what's on this video should make you reconsider. The news media had a field day with the video of Marion Barry smoking crack. As a political aide to two Republican Presidents, who worked for the national Republican party, and whose father is an appointee of the current President, you know what public exposure of this will cause. This meeting is now concluded," he said.

"Thank you for your time, Mister Todd, and don't forget to take your drugs with you. Shavonda will show you out."

I was completely dumbfounded, especially as he said, "I still hope we can someday do business. Goodbye, Mr. Todd Blodgett. Drive carefully on your way to Annandale." Once back in my car, I called Tremaine. "I've gotta see you, 'T' – now," I told the dealer. "How much more y'all wants?," Tremaine asked. None, I told him. "But we've gotta talk."

"Okay, dude. But I ain't at my crib. I'm at the Black Cat, 14th Street."

"Be alone when I arrive. Get us a back table. See you in 10 minutes." For an hour, Tremaine and I discussed about what had just occurred. As we spoke, among the songs played on the jukebox was 'Harlem Nocturne' – the version by Randy Brooks. That jazzy old tune seemed appropriate for this Conversation. I was one of two white dudes in the bar. The Nigerian was part of an underground ID theft network. Fraudsters bought credit card information, mainly from servers – waiters, waitresses, and bartenders – working in mid-level and high-end restaurants and bars in D.C., Maryland, and Virginia.

"I ain't makin' no 'scuses fo' what they done, Todd. But you safe, long as y'all ain't rats 'em out." That's comforting to know, I replied. I asked how grifters get all this information. Tremaine said that Shavonda and the Nigerian furnished their partners in crime with hand-held electronic scanning devices called skimmers, which scan info contained in the magnetic strip on the back of the cards. "It only takes a coupla seconds," 'T' said. Each device, he told me, is about two-thirds the size of a pack of cigarettes, and can hold information for up to 150 credit cards. "How do these employees use their skimmers in full view of their customers, and their supervisors, and other employees?"

"Them don't," Tremaine explained. The crooks engaging in this activity, he told me, are very adept at avoiding detection. It's done, sometimes two or three at a time, during a restroom break, or in an isolated area of their workplace. Once they sell it to the Nigerian, it's processed for resale, to some New York-based professionals, who manufacture fake, duplicate credit cards. Most of these phony cards usually feature another name embossed on them. File-sharing computer applications, like LiveWire, easily facilitate issuance of the new, counterfeit credit cards. The middlemen who buy the info from suppliers were paying between $25 and $40 for Master Card and VISA records, 'T' explained.

They paid up to $60 for Discover cards, and $75-$80, for American Express card information. End users pay at least triple these amounts for each record. In some cases, exact replicas – with the real names of the cardholders intact - of stolen cards are manufactured, for use with a fake ID. Other illicit credit cards are under new names, but with the same, pertinent numerical information, so the cards are still honored. Well, at least they're accepted until the real owners wise up. The illicit end users typically max the cards out quickly, sometimes within two hours of getting them.

By the time the legitimate cardholders figure out what's happened, the crooks already have their ill-gotten gains. This type of theft costs U.S. and European consumers BILLIONS of dollars per year, and has become costlier since I learned of it. 'T' said that it's only a matter of a few days between the time that the card info is collected by a skimmer and its counterfeit counterparts are created and sold. "I s'pose Shavonda boyfriend must've figured dat anybody done worked in politics, and wiff Nazis, and smoke crack, probably won't have no problem doin' dat deal," Tremaine said.

He was right. I was being judged by the company I kept.

It was surreal to be working for the FBI while being unable to do anything about what I'd just learned regarding this financial crime. A retired U.S. Secret Service agent told me that this type of ID theft costs innocent Americans billions of dollars every year. As I left the Black Cat, 'T' said, "if y'all changes yo' mind about dealin' wiff Shavonda and she nigga, dey's money in it from me, Todd." How's that, I asked.

"Because that dark skin nigga done promised me five large if y'all throws in with him." In ghetto lingo, a "Large" means a thousand dollars. "If ya do," he said, "I'll give ya'll twelve hundid of it, for real. Hear?"

"Tremaine," I replied, "has anyone told you you'd make a good Republican? Except for being on welfare, you think like a Republican."

"Like they ain't no Republicans on welfare?", Tremaine replied. "What about all dem rich, Republican Farmers rakin' it in? Dem be on welfare. Dem Republicans must get a thousand times what I gets." He had me there.

Tremaine would've made a good trial lawyer. I never did business with Shavonda 'sboyfriend. I destroyed the DVD the following day and 'T' and I remained on good terms.

A week later, an FBI agent I reported to asked me to meet him and some others at the Marine base in Quantico, Virginia – at the FBI Training Academy. The deputy director of the Joint Terrorism Task Force was flying in from Pittsburgh, and wanted to meet with me. While driving to Quantico, it occurred to me that no one else in America would buy crack from felons – and smoke it, with criminals - directly after meeting with high-level honchos from the world's best-known investigative agency.

CHAPTER SEVEN

After meeting with the bureau bigwigs for over three hours, I had dinner with two agents, the deputy JTTF director, and an FBI analyst whose specialty was the clandestine activities of racist, far Right organizations. My work was valued, and it felt good to truly help my country and perhaps make people safer. The following year, I'd have more meetings at Quantico. When I got home, Linda was already asleep. Because our bedroom was directly above our garage, I parked my Range Rover on the street in front of our house, so as not awaken her with the garage door.

As I quietly opened the front door to our home, I received a text message. It was from Diablo, a DC drug pusher. "I got the bomb, TB. Master-blaster," the message read. It was a classic, junkie-style dilemma: do I go upstairs and join my wife in bed, or …? It didn't take long to decide. After getting seven C-notes from the safe in my den, I left the house as silently as I had entered five minutes earlier. I had already removed my sport coat and necktie, so upon arriving in the hood, I'd not be over-dressed. From my first weeks as a customer of multiple dealers, I learned that wearing clean, expensive clothing in 'Drug-Free' neighborhoods caused residents to suspect me of being an undercover cop.

Countless times, I was asked, "Is y'all a PO-leece?" by small-time dealers. What they didn't realize is that courts have ruled that law enforcement officers are allowed to lie about their line of work. Though I always denied being a cop, the truth wasn't always convincing; several times, the pushers and runners bolted. As I sped east up Route 66 to D.C., I didn't expect to learn that the dealer who sold me the crack relied heavily on Fed-Ex, and the U.

S. Postal Service, to float his business. You read that right. In 2016, The Wall Street Journal published an article, 'Why drug runners love the U.S. Postal Service'. Another expose': 'Fed-Ex is in court for allegedly being the World's most Efficient Drug Dealer', also ran in 2016, by National Security reporter J.D. Carroll, of The Daily Caller.

These articles confirmed what I learned that night at Diablo's apartment.

He counted out 12 'dub' bags of crack, and I gave him $240. A 'dub' is short for a $20 bag – as in, double dime. Several packages from the USPS and Fed-Ex stacked beside his desk. "What's that?" As he weighed cocaine on his electronic scale, he replied, "It's how I get some of my best stuff." He wasn't worried about getting snared by either the USPS, or Fed-Ex. "How can anyone ship cocaine, or other illegal drugs, through the Postal Service, or Fed-Ex?", I asked.

Because, he said, "them folks don't care. It's about money. And bein' lazy." Diablo was correct; drug suppliers today still do this, and Americans provide this life line to manufacturers and suppliers of illegal drugs, including crystal meth, cocaine, and heroin. The Universal Postal Union is a United Nations agency which coordinates international shipments. 192 nations are members. Effectively, the USA subsidizes most of them. As of 2019, the U.S. State Department, which has ultimate jurisdiction over such matters, hadn't made substantive efforts to stop this. That's despite the fact that in 2015, a consulting firm, LegitScript, conducted 29 test buys from illegal online pharmacies.

Once these 29 illicit packages, each shipped via a government-sponsored shipping service, reached the USA, they were delivered by the U.S. Postal Service.

In July, 2016, Fed-Ex was on trial for illegal drug shipments. But federal prosecutors requested that the charges be dropped, citing lack of sufficient evidence. These charges included conspiracy and money- laundering counts, and began after United Parcel Service decided to not battle allegations regarding illegal deliveries of illicit drugs. In nearly every room of Diablo's apartment, there were eight, maybe ten, heavy-duty microwave ovens. In some cases, they were stacked atop one another, all of them plugged into electrical outlets. "Dude, how many micro-waves are here?" Forty-one, as of last night, he replied. "They're all used every day," he added.

"C'mere," Diablo said, as he walked down the hall to a locked door. Behind the door was an another 3-bedroom apartment to which the only entrance was from Diablo's unit. The landlord had plastered over the hall entrance to this unit to ensure Diablo's privacy. During my years as a drug addict, I learned it was common for owners of buildings to accommodate drug dealers, manufacturers, and suppliers, in this manner. That's because money is the name of the game. The microwave ovens were used to melt down large candles. Once the wax was liquified, Diablo would drop packets of cocaine, crystal meth, and heroin, into each candle's glass container. After the wax re-solidified, the packets were invisible, and drug-sniffing dogs couldn't detect anything.

To ship the candles, Diablo enlisted a defrocked Catholic priest who was a professor at DC's American University. Father Christian Mendenhall, a native Iowan, was one of Diablo's three or four shippers of record. As far as anyone knew, 'Father Christian' sold candles to raise money for various charitable endeavors, including a tax-exempt theatrical production company. But the money went to Mendenhall. Corruption in the realm of illicit drugs was as rampant as it is among professional anti-Semites and money-laundering white supremacists.

As Diablo and I concluded our deal, his phone rang. It was the front desk of his building. "Okay, send him up," he said. The person Diablo allowed up was a drug dealer who introduced himself as 'Suspect'. Quite a nickname, I thought. 'Suspect' was a friendly competitor of Diablo's.

Dealers who work the same city, or even the same section of the same city, often will supply one another with product as long as it's not sold in their territory. 'Suspect' mainly worked Southeast and Southwest Washington, while Diablo chiefly worked northwest, and northeast. Such agreements kept things cool and obviated violence. 'Suspect' handed me an index card with his cell phone number on it. He told me to call him if I was ever in his territory and wanted "some buttuhs" – butters, as in great coke. I tucked his card in my shirt pocket, left Diablo's apartment, and drove to the Dupont Circle area, where lived some junkies who were always willing to party with anyone who had some "masta blasta".

A crackhead I met in Georgetown that night was a Yale graduate with a law degree from Tulane. He was a staff attorney for the SEC - the U.S. Securities and Exchange Commission. He later became the chief counsel for NASDAQ. Over the course of my drug addiction, I became friends with this brilliant, highly amusing, gregarious addict. His name was Traynham Mitchell, Jr., and he knew much about how the worlds of illegal drugs, banks, and commerce traverse, and collide. Tray died of cancer in 2012, after beating his crack addiction.

It was about four a.m. when I got home. I quietly entered the house and discreetly went upstairs to join my sleeping wife in our bed. When the alarm went off at 6 a.m., I got up, as did she. Cocaine keeps users awake, minimizing the need for sleep.

Long before President Bush appointed my dad to a position in his administration, my parents were in DC frequently. Since I arrived there in 1984, they had visited the Capital city about 30 times before President Bush appointed my father to his position. They were also very active on the D.C. social circuit, often attending as many as six receptions a week, plus dinner parties and other events. They took to life in Washington, DC like a pot smoker takes to a bag of weed. One evening, as my parents, Linda, and I were leaving the Palm steakhouse, the shoe shine dude working outside the restaurant was a small-time, five-block drug dealer I knew. He went by the name of 'Boo'. I never knew his real name, and he liked it that way. As we waited for the valet to bring my dad's car around, I walked over to him.

"Whazzup, my man?", he asked. "Just finished a great steak dinner," I replied. As the valet returned with my father's Cadillac, my mother walked over to Boo and I. "Mom," I said, "this is a friend of mine." Turning to Boo, I said, "this is my mother." My mom smiled, nodded, and held out her hand. "Hello, I'm Sandy Blodgett," she said. Boo smiled and said, "My name be Boo." My mother replied, "Nice to meet you, Mr. Beboo." Boo then met my Dad, just as the valet slowed his car and got out. After my father handed the man ten dollars, the valet said, "Thank you, Judge. Have a nice evening, your honor."

By the time Linda and I were in the car's back seat, Boo was gone – having learned of my father's job title. At our home later, Linda asked what was bothering me. "Why do you ask?" Because, she said, "you don't seem to be your usual self, Todd. What's wrong?"

"I guess it's just the demands of working for the feds," I replied. She looked at me for a long time, unsure of what to say. "Really?," she asked. "Yeah," I replied, before going outside for a smoke. As I enjoyed a late night cigar, I realized it's not easy for a smoker to be married to an oncology nurse who formerly smoked cigarettes. I also realized how shocked and hurt Linda would be if she knew I was regularly smoking something far worse than cigars, or the occasional cigarette.

For my first 18 months with the bureau, the September 11 attacks hadn't yet occurred. Sept. 11 was also William Pierce's birthday, and for a man in his late sixties, he was remarkably vigorous. His 24/7 efforts to expand his empire of hatred were as thorough as any well-organized political campaign in which I'd ever participated. His main organization, the National Alliance, had units called cells, in over 40 states. Its active membership numbered around 3,000, and of those, about 2,200 paid monthly dues on a sliding scale. By 2001, the paid subscribers to his three publications and his National Vanguard book entity, and Resistance records, over 150,000 reliable, revenue-producing supporters comprised his various mailing lists, including email addresses and cell phone numbers.

That year, I sold Pierce two lists with a combined 375,000 records that Carto and I had compiled over the years. He paid me $70,000 all in hundred dollar bills. From about January of 2000 until early 2002, William Pierce tried to get me to help him to expand his empire of Hate. This included meeting with wealthy supporters and other prospective benefactors. Among his goals was to refashion the National Alliance for college campuses. "That's where the big money is, and the built-in networks which can be most efficacious to us," Pierce told me. He was particularly interested in making inroads with College Republican organizations and fraternities and sororities.

In April, 2000, some of his rich backers hosted a stag party for him. Pierce asked me to be in Hillsboro on the Friday before, as the party was to be on Sunday. "That way," he said, "we can work all day on Saturday." Pierce and I worked Saturday in his office, while at least a dozen staffers were busy for the entire time. People who love their work don't mind working six or seven days a week, even if their job is to foment hatred. He wanted to crack the collegiate market, with the goal of hijacking College Republican chapters at U.S. universities to spread his message.

The estate where the West Virginia gathering was held was about a 90-minute drive west of Pierce's compound. It was, indeed, ritzy. Before dinner was served, the guests were invited out on the massive, sweeping stone patio to shoot clay pigeons. I was the youngest guest by at least 15 years. Some of these guys had extensive oil interests in Texas and Oklahoma, and opposed Israel because their interests were in Saudi Arabia and other Mideast countries. Dinner at the impressive, old estate, which followed the reception, was in the main house's cavernous dining room. This was quite a place. I've shot skeet many times, but the skeet shoot at that estate was unlike any other. The clay pigeons were embossed with color decals featuring the faces of people they hated.

Hillary and Bill Clinton, Oprah Winfrey, Jesse Jackson, Benjamin Netanyahu, Al Sharpton, U.S. Senator Chuck Schumer, singer Barbra Streisand, New York City mayor Michael Bloomberg, Vernon Jordan, actor Rob Reiner, Justice Ruth Ginsberg, talk show hostess Rosie O'Donnell, CBS newsman Mike Wallace, and Holocaust survivor Elie Wiesel, were among those I recall. I picked up one of the 'Mike Wallace' discs, and was about to ask if

I could keep it as a souvenir. Until that afternoon, I hadn't even known that Mike Wallace was Jewish.

As I held it in my hand, a nattily attired, WASPy codger said, "Gimme that, son, and watch me blow this Jew bastard to smithereens." The Netanyahu clay pigeons disappeared first, because he was Israel's Prime Minster. Oprah and Hillary's pigeons got blown to bits pretty quickly, too. As one anti-Semite picked up a clay pigeon with Rob Reiner's face on it, he said, "Okay, meathead, now I'll do to you what Archie should've!" He was referencing Mr. Reiner's role in the 'All in the family' TV program, and that character's conflicts with his anti-Jewish father-in-law, Archie Bunker. As a 70-ish man wearing a plaid jacket yelled, "pull", the guy standing next to me expressed his fear of Hillary being elected to the U. S. Senate that fall. "That commie dyke better not win," he said. "She won't," replied another. "Hell, we'll have a nigger President before Hillary ever makes Senator. And we all know that'll never happen."

Watching these guys shoot clay pigeons with Elie Wiesel's face painted on them was disgusting. Who does this, I thought, and mocks a Holocaust survivor who dedicated his life and career to humanitarian causes? Pierce seemed pleased with the rapport I was establishing with these major donors. "I hear you're an SAE," said one of the guests, referring to my college fraternity. I nodded, and he mentioned that Willis Carto, James Von Brunn, and several other prominent white supremacists had also been members of Sigma Alpha Epsilon in college. I thought about this years later, when some SAE pledges were filmed singing a racist tune at the University of Oklahoma.

Author's note: The Sigma Alpha Epsilon fraternity (S.A.E.) isn't racist. It just happened that Willis Carto and Jamie Von Brunn were members.

"Yes, sir," I told the guy. "Drake University chapter, in Des Moines, Iowa." The man slipped me our fraternity's secret handshake and beckoned me over to a cement bench at the edge of the patio. He pulled out a monogrammed gold cigarette case and withdrew a Benson & Hedges. He lit his smoke, took two puffs, and – catching the eye of a server – pointed to his empty glass. "Double Jameson, on the rocks," he told her. "America's going straight into the toilet," he told me. "Democrat, Republican; Clinton, Bush," he said, "it makes no difference. Our problems are Jews, coons, queers, and spicks. And Commies, like the Clintons, of course."

To these guys, the Bushes and Clintons were just different sides of the same coin, and detrimental to America. "My grandchildren are in college," he continued, "and one's in law school. This country had best turn the corner, especially about this subversive Jewish influence. We've got to wake up before it's too late. Dr. Pierce wants to try to spread the word to campuses across America. I'm helping him, and just gave him a check for that purpose." His check was made out to William Pierce, for fifty grand. In the memo was written, "loan", which Pierce knew he'd never have to repay. But the guy could later deduct it on his taxes as an uncollected debt.

As he spoke, a 60ish, mustachioed man in a lime green jacket picked out clay pigeons embossed with the faces of Jesse Jackson, Barbra Streisand, and Al Sharpton. "Pull," he ordered, as he brought his .12 gauge Weatherby Orion up and across, pulling the trigger. In rapid succession, he obliterated all three. "Great shots," another man said. "Too bad we're not doing this for real."

A short, mustachioed man in a light blue golf shirt told a nasty joke which involved a rabbi, a black man, a Hispanic, and a lesbian. The hatred these racists openly expressed in their private enclave was as vitriolic as anything I heard at Klan meetings, Aryan Nations conferences, Resistance Records concerts, and Holocaust Denial conventions. These articulate old guys just spoke better English and wore tailor- made jackets, trousers and shirts.

Not unlike drug addiction, hatred crosses all socioeconomic and class lines. Junkies and bigots can be well-educated, or sixth-grade drop-outs; they may have $350 million or be in hock to a pawn shop for eighty bucks. They may wear $8,500 bespoke suits and drive shiny new Bentleys, or own only one pair of torn jeans from Goodwill and live in a stolen car while they evade the police and bounty hunters. After another few hours, Pierce and I were chauffeured back to his compound near Mill Point, West Virginia. Throughout the drive, he pressed me hard to follow up on the university outreach project that the rich SAE alum wanted to fund. I took a pragmatic approach and walked a fine line.

Ticking Pierce off wasn't an option. But I didn't want my name associated with an "outreach" effort that involved neo-Nazis permeating college Republican organizations. "Sir, this could backfire on you," I told him. "It might cause more grief than good." Pierce knew this, but he wasn't about to leave millions of dollars on the table. The armed, bearded Nazi driver kept glancing back at me in the rear-view mirror, clearly viewing me with suspicion.

As we made our way back to his compound, Pierce said, "let's kick this around, and at least do some- thing. I want that money." The professional haters I dealt with were always money-oriented. As we drove through the gate of what I nicknamed the 'Nazi nest', Pierce said, "Get some sleep. Tomorrow, at 12 Noon, I'd like you to attend a birthday party. It's in honor of the Fuehrer." I spent that night in a single-wide trailer that Pierce used for guests. The quilt atop my twin bed was adorned with Swastikas.

German time is six hours ahead of West Virginia's, and the party would begin at 6 pm in Germany. An international long-distance call, on speakerphone, would be made to Rochus Misch, in Berlin. Misch was Adolf Hitler's bodyguard during WW II, and was then an 82-year-old, unrepentant Nazi. "We'll all sing 'Happy Birthday' in German to our Savior," Pierce said. "If you don't know German (I didn't, and don't), just listen, and enjoy. Or, if you want, my assistant typed up some phonetically-spelled German lyrics. They'll be passed out prior to making the call so everyone can sing along." This was like a long-distance, international, Nazi version of Karaoke.

Pierce later told me that singing Happy Birthday via long-distance to old buddies of Adolf Hitler was a tradition he began in the 1980s. Among Pierce's loyal fans was a pro-Nazi banker named Francois Genoud. As referenced earlier, Genoud was also a close associate of Willis Carto. He earned $650,000 from Carto in 1991-93 to help procure over seven million dollars from the estate of a Holocaust denier and Carto admirer who gave the IHR $17 million. These phone calls to old Nazis were made possible via Genoud's contacts. Anyone who thinks 21st century Holocaust deniers haven't dealt, and don't deal, directly, with friends and associates of the long-deceased Adolf Hitler is flat wrong.

In 2002, Swiss authorities shut down a bank based in Lugano, Switzerland, which they believed was founded by Francois Genoud. This financial institution, the al Teqwa bank, was believed to have functioned as a funding conduit for al Queda, Hamas, and other terrorist organizations. Mr. Genoud made international news in 2015, posthumously, when a German court ruled in favor of a daughter of another Genoud ally – Hjalmar Schacht – who was Hitler's Minister of Economics and President of the Reichsbank. Genoud, along with Carto, made a fortune publishing the diaries of various Nazi leaders, including Josef Goebbels and Martin Bormann. He spent the last 41 years of his life aiding those he viewed as natural heirs to the Third Reich's wealthy, professional anti-Semites: Arab terrorists.

Pierce and Carto got money from several other Nazis, all arranged by the talented Mr. Genoud. As Pierce spoke, my mind went back to a cute Jewish girl who had been a high school crush for me. Her name is Beth Holzman, and her parents and mine were good friends. I took her out a few times. Beth had relatives who perished in the Holocaust. What would Beth, Sam and Barb Holzman think if they knew that the kid who was crazy for their daughter was about to join some Holocaust Deniers in celebrating Adolf Hitler's birthday, via a phone call to his bodyguard in Berlin? I wanted to fire up an 8-ball of crack and smoke it all.

I also wanted to get a few of my black buddies to stomp the crap out of these racist sickos. "Sounds good," I replied. "I've never sung Happy Birthday to a Fuehrer." Until that night, I also hadn't known his bodyguard was still alive. "I assume," I said to Pierce, "that after 1945, this former bodyguard found another line of work, right?" Frowning, Pierce arched his eyebrow and said, "that's not funny."

The birthday celebration commenced in the Lecture Hall of Pierce's largest building at his headquarters. An enormous white cake with a Swastika, etched in bright red and blue frosting, was brought in by two beautiful, blonde, big-busted Aryan-looking chicks. The red and blue banner draped across the front of the table read, 'HAPPY BIRTHDAY, to our FUEHRER'. The party was more like a séance, with lit candles encased in brass sconces affixed to the walls of the great hall. As one neo-Nazi after another toasted their hero, they looked toward the ceiling and acted as though they were speaking directly to Adolf Hitler. Finally, the call was made to Berlin, where several Hitler fanatics were with Rochus Misch.

Both English and German were spoken by those attending Pierce's party, depending on whom they addressed. But the only language I knew besides English was Ebonics. Finally, William Pierce, acting like Ryan Seacrest introducing an act on American Idol, announced that 'Happy Birthday' would be sung. A lady who volunteered in Pierce's office got a chair, stood on it, and kissed a larger-than-life-sized poster of der Fuerher. For these Germans to waste time on such wretched nonsense was dumb. No wonder they lost the war.

"Alles Gute Zum, Geburtstag; alles gute Zum, Geburstag …" came the chorus, and refrain, followed by the English version. I sang along with that. "Hap-py Birth-day, mein Fue-rher' … hap-py birth-day toooo yoouuuu" weren't lyrics I liked singing, however. At that point, I REALLY wanted to get some of my black and Hispanic buddies to stomp these guys. No job was perfect, I reminded myself. But how many jobs require singing Happy Birthday to history's most vile monster? In February of 1986, I had joined several fellow White House staff members to sing Happy Birthday to President Reagan on his 75th, in the White House press Briefing Room. Had I just become the only person ever to sing Happy Birthday to Adolf Hitler and Ronald Reagan? Creepy.

After the call, Pierce asked us all to sign a large, custom-made Birthday card for the old bodyguard. It was already postmarked, on a National Alliance postage meter, that day – April 20, 2001. Hitler's birthday. Rochus Misch died in September, 2013, aged 96, and had remained the same, unrepentant Nazi he had been when he had protected Adolf Hitler.

The summer of 2001 was busy for me, as the FBI continued sending me to events and meetings across the USA. By this time, I'd flown to California, Nevada, Louisiana, Alabama, South Carolina, Florida, North Carolina, Georgia, Ohio, New York, Montana, Indiana, and Arizona. That summer, the agents informed me that the bureau would be sending me to Grand Cayman. A white supremacist had secured tax-exempt status for a charitable entity, based on claims that the organization's purpose was educational and research was conducted. He wanted to open an account at a Caymanian bank with several hundred thousand dollars. In the early 1990s, while on a family vacation to Grand Cayman, I'd opened a private account at the British American Bank in Grand Cayman. It wasn't much; I think I deposited $25,000, and later added another $50,000. As required by U. S. law, I always checked the box on my federal income tax forms which acknowledged the account. I never tried to hide its existence. An IRS agent asked me about my BAB (British American Bank) account shortly after I began working for the FBI. After checking with a JTTF honcho, the agent told me that this I could mention my BAB account in conversations with targets I was assigned to surveil. This wouldn't constitute entrapment. The hope was that the targets would ask for more information, and at some point, express interest in opening such accounts. That's what happened in the case of this White Supremacist, whom I got to know while working with Mark Cotterill, David Duke and Willis Carto. In 1996, 1997 and '98, Carto sent me to Grand Cayman to meet supporters who were signatories to bank accounts of corporations he controlled. He knew I'd visited that island nation several times, with my family, beginning in the early 1980s. In the case of this lesser-capitalized White supremacist, the bureau wanted account numbers and other information.

Getting that info proved trickier than I initially thought, but with some friendly assistance, I delivered. I met with two FBI agents, again on the grounds of the Smithsonian Institute, at the old Pension building now known as the Building Museum. Per our usual routine, I took the stairs to the third level, and, after checking to make sure no one was watching, knocked on the door of the room with the agents inside. The meeting was brief, about 15 minutes. I left first, and – since I'd be flying in less than 20 hours, decided to not try to cop a fix. The effects of cocaine in one's system and high altitudes don't mix.

As I got into my car, my cell phone rang. It was a junkie who had started dealing crack to support his habit. "My baby mama," he said, "she tell me 'dat y'all be the onlyest dude we both knows 'dat we trust." I accepted the compliment, and he asked me to meet him at his apartment, which was about ten minutes away. As I pulled up, I carefully looked around, then pulled my .380 from under the drivers' seat. The federal agents I'd just seen wouldn't approve, but in the hoods, why take chances? Once inside my buddy's crib, he handed me $600 in cash, all in fifties. "What's this for?," I asked.

Reaching into his sock, he pulled out a meatball of crack – a $100 rock – wrapped in cellophane. He put it in my hand, atop the 12 fifty-dollar bills. "Take it to da bitch, Tawd. It be fo' she child support. Fo' months' worth, plus two hundid I owes her fo' a TV set."

"You can't take it to her? Need a ride?"

"Nope. Bitch done got a judge slap a restrainin' order on my black ass. Can't even see my fuck trophies." I'd not heard that term before, and asked what those were. "My kids," he replied. He explained that the meatball was for my trouble in taking his Baby Mama the money. Fifteen minutes later, I was in a cheap hotel room on New York avenue, N.E., where the gal lived. After I gave her the money she poured me a glass of Grape Kool-Aid. The glass was a jelly jar. "We was homeless fo' a minute," the pretty young black lady told me. "Now, we livin' here. It be hard, Todd, 'specially at meal times." Pointing to an ancient Microwave, she said, "Try cookin' a good, balanced meal wiff dat."

Her three-year-old daughter, a beautiful, happy child, suddenly climbed up and sat on my leg, nearly making me spill my Kool-Aid. This sweet little girl was, apparently, affection-deprived.

"Latasha!," her mother yelled. "Y'all ain't axed Mister Todd if him want you in he lap. Get down."

I told Flavonda it was okay. The little girl was clinging hard to me, hugging my neck, and had the cutest smile. Looking down at the threadbare carpet, the tired, stressed-out mother of three youngsters said,

"My kids be as starved fo' a good male role model as they is fo' some decent clothes and a real home." This saddened me, because it was true. "I'm not sure that a drug addict is a good role model, Flavonda." The three-year-old high-fived me, and started to giggle. Then she kissed my cheek, and I returned her kiss. What a sweetheart. "Y'all still be better than any man been 'round here," her mother replied, which wasn't saying much. Driving home, I thought about that little girl and her two siblings, and being raised that way. JFK said life isn't fair, and anyone who thinks it is should meet some kids who live in America's hoods.

My alarm was set for 4 a.m. 40 minutes later, I drove to Washington, D.C's Ronald Reagan National Airport and met up with the racist, pretending to not notice the two FBI agents already there. We flew to Miami and, from there, to Puerto Rico. From there, to Grand Cayman. By the time we were cleared through and at the hotel, it was nearly 4 p.m. There are many great hotels and resorts on Grand Cayman, but as the FBI was paying, the racist, whom I'll call 'Guy' (his real first name), and I stayed at a Days Inn. Not extravagant. As we'd meet the next morning with a banker from the British American Bank, I rented a car. I drove Guy around the island. Having first visited Cayman with my family in 1982, I knew it well; this trip was my twelfth. Upon checking in to the hotel, I put both rooms in my name, and paid. "You can reimburse me," I told the target. "You don't need any records of your credit cards used here." He thanked me for helping to keep him off of law enforcement's radar without realizing there was already a record of his flight.

As we ate dinner at the 'Grand Old House' restaurant, I formulated my plan. It was imperative I obtain copies of the documents he'd get, relating to the BAB accounts he would open. That's where Jack, Jose', and Jim came in.

As in, Jack Daniels, Jose' Quervo, and Jim Beam. Guy was a drinker, but not a big one. But I'd make sure he'd tie one on tomorrow night, with enough booze to make Dean Martin look like Pat Boone. Luckily, I had kept in contact with some buddies on the island. I called one of them, and asked him to meet me after Guy – who was an early-to-bed type, was asleep in his hotel room. Earlier, Guy and I agreed to meet for breakfast in the lobby at seven and go to the bank at nine.

My buddy Quentin was from Newport, Rhode Island. He'd moved to Cayman after graduating from Brown university and worked as a sailing instructor and bartender while awaiting an inheritance that came through about two years later. He and his girlfriend lived in a condo on Seven-mile Beach. Quintin and I met for drinks at the Marriott Resort bar at 10:30. "So," he asked, "you want me to line up a bartender who'll mix you light drinks and go heavy on Everclear, to get this dude blotto?"

"Yeah," I replied. He agreed to arrange this and I slipped him $50 Caymanian money for his trouble. Fifty bucks Caymanian, incidentally, was, and still is, worth more than $50 U.S. "Tell your bartender buddy he'll earn a nice tip for his trouble, which may include having to help me carry the guy to my rental car." Obtaining account numbers, U.S. addresses and the amounts deposited, and other info, sometimes meant resorting to unorthodox means.

The next morning, a Friday, went as planned. Guy and I drove to the British American Bank, met with a banker, and he opened two accounts. The checking account was in the name of his tax-exempt entity; the savings account was in his name. He deposited $125,000 in each. For each deposit, he brought Cashiers checks, drawn on a Virginia bank. Until after 9/11, Grand Cayman was considered a sunny place for shady people, a repository of hundreds of billions of dollars, some of it dirty. Since then, it's actually easier to hide money right in the USA. High-limit debit cards, for example, work just fine. A Costa Rican Bank's debit cards permit up to $250,000 to be on deposit, with no limit on how many such these cards clients can own. The OffShoreProGroup, inc., with offices in Switzerland, Panama and the

Caribbean, offers no-limit, premium debit cards. These cards are used to buy expensive jewelry, real estate, vehicles and other high-end items, or to just park funds.

The outdoor Caribbean bar featured a live band comprised of island natives. They were playing 'Yellow Bird' as Quentin's bartender buddy led us to a reserved table ten feet from the musicians. Guy liked Pina Colodas, which made it all the easier to get him drunk on high-proof rum, mixed with Everclear. "Do you like black licorice?," I asked. He said, "yeah, that and coffee are the only things I like that are black." I advised him that at a Caribbean night club in Grand Cayman, he shouldn't express such views.

"You gotta try Jagermeister", I said. "Tastes like black licorice." After two shots of Jager, he asked for a third. Then he had a fourth. He never asked for a fifth or sixth shot, but I made sure he had them. Within two hours after drinking Jagermeister for the first time, he quaffed three Pina Coladas, all turbocharged. He also had downed two double Jack Daniels, poured neat, and a Mimosa that was about 60 percent alcohol. The bartender made sure our food was delayed, which made my job even easier. I signaled the bartender for the check. I paid the tab and tipped him with a Caymanian C-note. He didn't even ask if I needed help getting my target to the car. It was obvious.

We got back to the Days Inn around 11, just as the front desk clerk was being relieved by the night staffer. For $20, he helped me get Guy into his hotel room, to which I had a swipe key, since both rooms were registered in my name. The two of us gently lifted him onto his bed, removed his shoes, and covered him with a light blanket.

"Ah don tink dot dees mon gonna be comin' down fo' da brick-fizz," the Caymanian said. "Sumpin' tell me dot him gonna hafta sleep eet off unteel WAAAYYY pazz da lunch time. Ummm-hmmm. Heem maybe not wakin' up even befo da deener time, yah." When the clerk left I opened the briefcase. On the flight down to Cayman, I had noticed that his four-digit combo was 1-4-8-8. Surprise, surprise. I took the folder from the BAB down to the hotel's business center. Fifteen minutes later, I had two copies of every document.

Also listed were numbers for the ATM card, which was to be mailed to his home in Virginia. His cell phone was listed as a contact number, and his email address. Until then, the FBI didn't have his cell phone info, as it was billed to a third party. All of this would be invaluable in helping the bureau track his financial and political activities.

The methods I used to gain this information weren't suggested by the FBI agents. The bureau didn't approve or condone such, but I was given an assignment, and knew that the target wasn't ever in any real danger at any time. This was a healthy 45-year-old nonsmoker who'd be just fine in 24 hours. And he was. Just to make sure he'd be okay, I slept that night in the other bed in his room. Aside from me stepping barefoot in his vomit the next morning, all went well, and he never suspected a thing. On the flight back, though, he repeatedly bitched that his saliva tasted like black licorice.

A few months after I accompanied the money-laundering white supremacist to Grand Cayman, the 9/11 attacks occurred. One of the lasting repercussions of these terrorist acts was the Patriot Act, which Congress passed, and President Bush signed into law, in October, 2001. The Patriot Act's anti-money laundering provisions affect every person who holds a bank account in the United States. This is because the terrorists who perpetrated the 9/11 attacks had no trouble opening American bank accounts in the U.S. They also got credit cards by using fake Social Security numbers. The Patriot Act doesn't require banks to notify account holders that they're being investigated for suspicious activity, and U.S. banks can freeze anyone's account without telling them why.

These factors and other stringent requirements have made it far more difficult for foreign banks to service, and do business with, American clients. It's also made U.S. clients about as popular with overseas banks as Hillary Clinton was with NRA members and blue-collar men in 2016. The Obama administration offered amnesty from criminal prosecution to Americans holding offshore accounts who had evaded U.S. taxes. While this program brought billions of dollars to the U.S. Treasury, most high-flying abusers had, by then, transferred their funds out of Caymanian banks.

Under President George W. Bush, the FATF began pressuring the Caymanians to loosen up on bank confidentiality. This came after the U.S., under President Clinton, held the feet of Swiss bankers to the fire over account information relating to descendants of Holocaust victims. For decades, Caymanian bankers knew that many of their clients were hiding assets and not reporting income to their countries. Banks began advising clients that they, the bankers, would report such income to the respective nations.

Caymanian banking clients now must sign a document stating they've been so advised, which acknowledges that a Caymanian court can order production of their bank records at the insistence of a foreign government agency that has reasonable grounds. Drug traffickers, manufacturers, and wholesalers, along with the mob, have known for years that if your objective is to scrub dirty cash, Grand Cayman isn't the place to do it. Nor, now, is Switzerland. In 2010, the government of Germany launched an all-out, tactical and rhetorical assault on the Swiss banking system and on Germans holding Swiss accounts. When German Finance Minister Wolfgang Schauble declared, "there's no future for bank secrecy." He meant it. Germany had just paid nearly $3.5 million to obtain bank records and information, including the names of suspected tax evaders, to informants who upped the ante with even more detailed offers of additional, thought-to-be-confidential information from financial institutions.

Stealthy, nondescript computer hackers work overtime to produce and sell such records, with a level of expertise that makes Julian Assaunge and his team of Wikileaks hackers look like amateurs. Wealthy white supremacists, informed neo-Nazis, and well-placed Holocaust deniers aren't confused about these changes in bank secrecy, and have reacted accordingly. Such people and their financial advisors probably know more about how to hide money in 2017 than most lawyers.

Placement. Layering. Integration.

These are the three steps to laundering dirty cash. Long before I met drug suppliers like Antwan, Dino Cassini, and others, I learned about money-laundering from Willis Carto, William Pierce, David Duke, Chris Temple and other white supremacists and Holocaust deniers. Carto was especially skillful at cleaning up dirty money. In some instances, he – with the advice of Mark Lane – used the IRS code to illicitly enrich himself and his financial backers. In the summer of 1998, Willis and I delivered $350,000 in hundred-dollar bills to the Georgetown home of a very wealthy, elderly anti-Semitic couple. This constituted the placement of their cash.

The old man then wrote a check out to one of Carto's tax-exempt corporate entities for $450,000, in return for the 3,500 C-Notes that Willis gave the man. This constituted layering. The value of that four hundred fifty large to the donors, once deducted on their joint federal income tax return, exceeded the extra hundred grand that he wrote the check for, in excess of the amount of cash that Carto gave him. Here's how it worked: if their annual income, before deductions and credits, was $1 million, then that placed them in what was, and is, the top tax bracket. Deducting four hundred fifty grand against that amount netted them a savings of over $145,000 on their tax return.

Effectively, the man put up one hundred large to realize tax savings worth approximately $145,000. So, the couple netted out a $45,000 profit, and Carto's Foundation for Economic Liberty (it may have been the Foundation to Defend the First Amendment, or another entity; I no longer recall) showed a $450,000 gift on its books. Once the check was cashed and the funds were deposited into the account of Carto's tax-exempt, nonprofit organization, the money was cleaned up – laundered. It was then integrated into the U.S. economy. Carto made a hundred grand on the deal and his supporter netted $45,000. Willis Carto got back all of his cash, with the losers being American taxpayers. Often, in Carto's larger deals, cash was delivered instead of funds being wired to avoid creating a paper trail or electronic evidence.

Carto William Pierce made extensive usage of registered corporate agents in Delaware, to function as the 'front' for shell corporations in which they were shareholders. Once these corporate entities were up and running, Carto would authorize the opening of bank accounts in Costa Rica, Panama, and Grand Cayman, to hold his laundered money. Debit cards were issued under the names of those corporations with Willis as the authorized card holder. He wasn't always the signatory to the accounts, but whoever was had been authorized and designated by him. Willis Carto and Mark Lane obtained secondary debit cards for each account, with the aliases E. L. Anderson, Frank Tompkins, and others. Pierce and Carto also regularly sent employees and trusted associates to remit funds to neo-Nazis worldwide.

Some wealthy Carto backers laundered money via rare art. Art and collectible antiquities are often used to facilitate tax evasion and outright avoidance. Money launderers aren't trying to make profits on their ill-gotten gains, and don't mind overpaying for assets which enable them to hide dirty cash. Such transactions drive up the value of the rare art, coins and collectables. Art dealers and purveyors of pricey collectables were exempted from The Bank Secrecy Act of 1970, which opened the door to such fraudulent activity. In 2012, German police found nearly $1 Billion worth of rare art, mostly oil paintings, in the modest apartment of 79-year-old Cornelius Gurlitt. While in power, the Nazis systematically plundered property from people in every territory they occupied. Some of these cultural treasures were sold, but many were hoarded. The Nazis also burned books and destroyed art that they considered to be degenerate. However, some Germans with direct ties to the Nazis who administered this desecration realized the value of such art, most of which had been stolen from Jews. A former museum director named Hildebrand Gurlitt became, effectively, Adolf Hitler's art dealer, and did rather well for himself. By 1945, Herr Gurlitt had managed to stash well away well over 1,500 pieces of this rare booty. His son, Cornelius, had 1,406 of them in his apartment near Munich.

At his home in Austria, Gurlitt kept about 60 more pieces of rare art. Investigators estimated that Gurlitt had probably sold approximately 100 to 150 paintings between 1956, when his father died, and 2010. Cornelius Gurlitt was only one of hundreds of Europeans whose direct ties to Hitler's deceased associates have brought them riches. Through his friend Francois Genoud, Willis Carto also had ties to such individuals. But after late 1996, he feared being nabbed by European authorities and jailed if he ever went back across the pond. Indeed, after a California Judge ruled Carto had embezzled millions of dollars from the Institute for Historical Review, Swiss authorities issued a warrant for his arrest.

Among these authorities was prosecutor Nicolas Cruchet in Laussannne, who also issued a warrant for Carto accomplice Henri Fischer. But by then, Willis was way, way ahead of the law, in Switzerland and in the United States. In early 1997, Carto sent me to Zurich, Switzerland and Vienna, Austria. This was about eight months after Genoud had killed himself. I was initially afraid to go over there, representing Carto, for obvious reasons. But Willis paid me thirty grand, paid for round trip, first-class airfare, and for two days of alpine skiing in Zermat and another two days at Patscherkofel, in Innsbruck.

I met with an art dealer at Vienna's Palais Schwarzenberg hotel, who gave me a packet of bearer bonds worth $3.75 million USD. Acting on Carto's directive, I then delivered them to a former Genoud associate in Zurich, who converted them to cash and wired the funds to a Carto-controlled, numbered bank account in Costa Rica. Carto, who rarely trusted anyone but his wife, sent me on his behalf because I had proven, consistently, my trustworthiness.

While on the return flight to the USA, I remember thinking that I knew how a whore must feel. Years later, I ran into Mike Piper at the bar in the Monaco hotel, in the Penn Quarter section of D.C. He was drunk, and told me that Willis had twice flown him to Europe to take delivery of, and return to the states with, "some flawless diamonds that were worth millions." On each trip, rich Nazi sympathizers in Liechtenstein gave Piper some large tubes of toothpaste, inside of which were the perfect gems. This was around 1994 and '95, Piper told me. For his efforts, Carto paid him ten grand for each trip, plus all expenses. Those rocks were later stashed in some safe deposit boxes in a bank in the Florida Keys.

A disproportionately high number of currency exchanges in the USA and Canada are owned and/or operated by Muslims. Mainly, Muslims then operated three types of businesses in large U.S. cities: currency exchanges, newsstands, and convenience stores. In many subway stations and at the exits and entrances to many public transit bus stops and METRO stations, newsstands are still owned by Muslims.

Generally speaking, most of them are ethical, and not likely involved in laundering money. But some operators of check-cashing services and Pay Day loans businesses are another story. More on that later.

For usurious rates of interest, such establishments loan poor people money against paychecks. Many impoverished folks, particularly those on various forms of Welfare, don't have bank accounts. But they often cash checks, including welfare checks, at such enterprises.

I knew crackheads who received checks from the federal government and the government of the District of Columbia who, for various reasons, avoided banks and credit unions. For a rate which was usually 20 percent of the amount of the check, these junkies cashed their welfare checks at such establishments. This cheats honest taxpayers, and the exorbitant rates charged – which, for practical purposes, can be as high as operators want and recipients will pay. Bank tellers aren't as suspicious of checks, especially government checks, presented for deposit than they are of the same amount of cash being deposited.

I've seen such checks cashed at bars, liquor stores, and even by crack dealers who operate out of their cars. Those who cashed them ALWAYS took at least 20 percent off the top. In taking unfair advantage of economically disadvantaged Americans, including drug addicts, some people are shameless. As far as employees of the banks or credit unions knew, these unethical operators of businesses that cashed such checks provided either cash or products to the payees equal to the amounts listed on the checks.

Effectively, the financial institutions where such funds are deposited have unknowingly participated in the facilitation of fraudulent economic activity.

Just because negotiable financial instruments like checks and money orders don't raise as many eyebrows when they're presented for deposit at banks and credit unions doesn't mean that the freshly cleaned-up money wasn't dirty. Money laundering has a long and sordid history, but it first came to the attention of the masses – at least, in the USA - during the Prohibition era. Bootleggers hid profits from illegal alcohol production and distribution by mingling that cash with monies from legitimate businesses. Once the illicit income was on the books, and reported on tax returns, it effectively was legitimate.

One of these money launderers back in the day – whose fortune was based in illicit liquor sales – was a Boston banker who served as FDR's ambassador to Great Britain and his chairman of the Securities and Exchange Commission. That money launderer was the father of President John F. Kennedy. During the Watergate scandal, it was learned that members of President Richard Nixon's re-election committee had laundered substantial funds. The President who served between Kennedy and Nixon, Lyndon Johnson, authorized the laundering of money during his 1948 campaign for the U.S. Senate. According to LBJ biographers Robert A. Caro and Roger Stone, Johnson kept laundering money as Senate Majority Leader, and as Vice President and President.

In 1994, a Republican operative who had worked with me at the 1988 Republican National convention in New Orleans, Joe Waldholtz, laundered over $1.5 million to help his then-wife, Enid Greene Waldholtz, defeat an incumbent member of the U.S. House. I had drinks with Joe Waldholtz in New Orleans, during the 1988 Republican National Convention, at Pat O'Brien's bar in the French Quarter. Characteristically, he stuck me with the bill. The AUSA (Assistant U. S. Attorney) who prosecuted Mr. Waldholtz was Craig Iscoe, whom President George W. Bush later tapped to serve as an Associate Judge on the Superior Court of Washington, D.C. The same Judge Iscoe who, in 2006, presided over my case and sentenced me to serve time in the DC Jail and probation. Money laundering techniques have become aggressively more sophisticated since I first learned of Carto's financial deviousness in the mid-1990s.

By the time I left the drug scene in 2006, the internet had already created new methodology, which feature even more ways to clean up dirty cash – which are now in place around the globe. PayPal, anonymous online payment services, internet banking operations, and virtual currencies such as Bitcoin have accelerated such activity and made detection of illicitly transferring funds harder than ever. Proxy servers and specialty software designed to anonymize users allows the integrated, cleaned-up cash to become nearly impossible to discover. That's because transferring and withdrawing money can now be facilitated with no evidence of an IP (Internet Protocol) address.

Gambling websites, online auctions, and virtual gaming websites also enable laundering, with deposits which are refunded to players. Just as with casinos, players can falsely claim that refunds represent winnings, pay tax on them, and clean up dirty cash in the process. Such scammers also can cash out in person, and later claim that the entire amount they spent on chips was lost. A cocaine wholesaler I knew bought $500,000 worth of gift cards, at five hundred bucks each, from a restauranteur whose café was about to go out of business. Not only was the money laundered, but the $500,000 was deductible as a loss once the establishment folded and the restaurant owner filed for personal bankruptcy. The café owner got fifty grand for facilitating this transaction, which was off the books.

Those gift cards were worthless from the time of purchase, as both parties to the transaction knew. Any crook who owns a cash business, especially one that folds and whose owner files for bankruptcy, can readily cite how cash was purportedly spent. A similar deal was done in the name of this drug supplier's son, who owned a landscaping business, two bars, a car wash and a rental equipment operation. The son then claimed losses and took deductions on each entity's tax returns. Documents he provided as back-up were the receipts for the five hundred grand his father had fronted. In the event of an IRS audit, the chiselers only had to show receipts which substantiated the deduction, and tell auditors that they had planned to give the gift cards to their customers and hold raffles. It was just bad luck that the business went under, was their story.

From the time the FBI first retained me in March of 2000, I apprised them of the money laundering schemes and techniques perpetrated by organized white supremacists, and Holocaust deniers. FBI and IRS agents said that a few months earlier, the United States attorney in New Orleans, Louisiana, had formally requested that U.S. Postal Inspectors join a federal Task Force investigating David Duke for money laundering, tax evasion, and mail fraud. By early 2002, federal authorities dropped the hammer. In December, 2002, Duke entered guilty pleas on the charges of tax evasion and mail fraud. U.S. Postal Inspector Bill Bonney speculated that Mr. Duke had "agreed to the plea to avoid harsher money laundering charges." My years of dealing with David Duke convinced me that Inspector Bonney was correct. Duke was sentenced March, 2003 to 15 months in federal prison and reported to prison in Big Spring, Texas, on April 15, 2003 to being serving his sentence. Given that tax evasion brought him down, it was ironic that he began serving his sentence on April 15.

The day after returning from Grand Cayman, my parents hosted Linda and I for dinner at the National Press club in downtown D.C. There, at the club's bar, sat reporter Jim Tucker, a long-time neo-Nazi sympathizer who wrote for Willis Carto's new weekly publication, the American Free Press. Tucker beckoned me over to the empty seat next to him. "I heard you were a-skeet-shootin' awhile back," Tucker said. I asked how he knew. "Because some of those same ol' fat cats a-dolin' out the big bucks to Doc Pierce have been a-backin' Willis for years." Tucker offered to buy me a drink, which I declined. "Thanks, but I'm with my wife and my parents." As I returned to our table, I realized that the tight network of wealthy anti-Semites went far deeper than I'd previously thought. I made a mental note to apprise the FBI agents of this when we met to go over the information I gleaned in Grand Cayman.

At dinner that night, my parents talked about their five grandchildren – my brother's and sister's kids. The oldest would start kindergarten that fall. My brother and his wife were expecting their third child; my parents, and Linda's, wanted us to make them a grandchild. We were trying, but the long hours I worked, and my frequent travel for the bureau, and my increasing usage of crack cocaine, complicated matters. What I didn't know then was that sustained cocaine usage can and does significantly damage a man's little swimmers – sperm – and lower his chances of being able to father children.

Cocaine narrows blood vessels and causes a condition called vasoconstriction, which leads to erectile dysfunction. It can also degenerate testicular tissue, and cause lowered potency in the hormones used to produce sperm. When addicts stop using coke, the body requires three to four weeks to clear itself of the affected sperm. It then takes approximately six months more for the sperm production of most men to return to normal levels. Many males, however, take YEARS for their sperm production, counts and quality to return to normal.

For the remaining three years of our marriage, I never kicked the cocaine habit. That's probably why I'm only the third Blodgett in our family line to father no children since before my ancestors arrived in north America in the early 1630s. Addicts who want kids should consider the price I paid for using drugs.

Around this time, I got to know a drug dealer who called himself Antwan. He'd once been affiliated with Rayful Edmond, whom the authorities blamed for bringing crack to D.C. At his trial, the prosecutor showed that in the early 1990s, Edmond's organization was bringing 2,000 kilos of cocaine each week to D.C. This figure was probably an underestimation of the actual amount. Antwan was about my age and a natural entrepreneur, like many drug pushers.

The Edmond organization employed 150 people and its annual income was estimated at over $300 Million. At least 30 people were murdered by Edmond's known associates, some on his orders. He was directly connected to the murderous Medellin drug cartel. Antwan was allegedly with Rayful Edmund when he dropped $457,619 at a Georgetown clothing store. Mr. Edmond later became a government informant, and is imprisoned as part of the federal witness protection program. Where he's locked up is confidential, for good reason. Following Edmond's demise, Antwan affiliated with yet another major coke supplier, Randy 'Alpo' Martinez. For his role in the

1990 murder of New York city crack supplier Rich Porter, who sold $50,000 of crack each week, Martinez was sentenced to 35 years in prison, also under federal witness protection.

By the mid-1990s, Antwan ventured out on his own, supplying high-quality crack to select dealers in DC and Baltimore. The quality of crack is determined by how much cocaine (purity) it contains. Crack with high levels of level pure cocaine gets users high quickly, and it's an intense high. However, when the cocaine content – and this also applies to powder – is diluted, which is known as being "cut", it loses potency and the 'high' doesn't last for nearly as long.

Like a watered-down highball with too many ice cubes and low grade mixer, severely 'cut' cocaine in any form isn't satisfying. Snorted coke will get users high in about one to five minutes, and hits its peak effect within 20 to 30 minutes, which lasts about 45 minutes. But a 'high' feeling from crack, or injected cocaine, hits in about 15 to 30 seconds, and will be at its peak within three minutes. It lasts for about 20 minutes. For these reasons, inhaling or injecting coke renders users far more susceptible to its addictive effects. By the time I met Antwan in early 2001, he was regularly supplying about 60 DC street dealers. He knew I regularly smoked crack and my money was "good and plenty", as he described it.

Appealing to my addictive personality, Antwan pointed out that what he sold was "further upstream" of the dealers who would 'cut' his product. "Why don't you buy directly from me?" When I said I didn't know he sold directly to users, he replied, "That's true, mostly. But I make exceptions." So, I became exceptional and often bought from him. We hung out for years, and Antwan told me about the various businesses he owned, money-laundering, tax-evading vehicles, all. Included were a hair salon his wife ran, a dry cleaning establishment, a half-interest in a two bars, and a recording studio. The few clients who got hair styles, hair weaves, and pedicures were amazed at the rock-bottom prices.

That's how money laundering operates. Antwan also set up landscaping businesses for his two sons, neither of which did much actual business. Of course, the tax returns indicated otherwise. Any IRS auditor would've concluded that satisfied customers, not dirty cash, floated those businesses. Antwan's recording studio catered to aspiring rappers who hoped that their hip-hop – which in their world passes for music – would make them rich and famous. The cost for each two-hour recording session was $600; the studio featured four sound-proof, state-of-the-art box studios with the best acoustics and equipment. Claiming that each studio was booked for 50 hours a week enabled him to claim annual gross income of approximately $3 million. And that was before deducting salaries, maintenance, rent, and other operating expenses. Drug revenue facilitated, as it does many other commercial enterprises.

I once asked Antwan about the two bars in which he held a half-interest, and the implications for the bar's legitimate competitors. Antwan said he'd also parked about $650,000 on gift cards from Target, WalMart, Home Depot, Walgreens, and other major retail chains. Money launderers will either sell or use such cards. Antwan dismissed my concerns about the effect that his businesses were having on their legitimate competition. He said the U. S. government "owed" him, because his ancestors were slaves. "Jews do 'dis shit all da time," Antwan told me, "and whiteys do it, too." It was tragic to hear a black man who probably didn't even know any Jewish people condemn them for the very crimes he was committing. He also believed that Jews, somehow, are not white. No wonder that Antwan was an ardent admirer of, and contributor to, the so-called Rev. Louis Farrakhan and his anti-Semitic Nation of Islam. Antwan, incidentally, wasn't the only black anti-Semite I encountered.

At several white supremacist functions I attended, a black man named Robert Brock spoke. Brock was a black separatist who hated Jews, for whom be blamed for delivering his ancestors to enslavement. When I told my wife that a black man was a featured speaker at a conference attended by members of the KKK and Aryan Nations, Linda thought I was joking. But in the milieu of white supremacy, the truth can often be stranger than fiction, as shown in

2019's 'BlacKKKlansman', movie. That's also true with drug pushers, junkies and the entire realm of substance abuse and addiction.

Around this time, the Holocaust-denying pseudo-historian David Irving came to America to raise funds to pay his attorney's fees, court costs, and the lawyer's fees incurred by a lawsuit in which he was the plaintiff. The legitimate historian that he had sued in a British court, Prof. Deborah Lipstadt, had won, and now Irving faced financial ruin. Mark Cotterill asked me to join him and Irving for dinner in DC the following evening. David Irving's pro-Hitler version of history was as nasty, and inaccurate as it was controversial. But it was highly profitable for him, his publishers, and to various professional anti-Semites like Carto, Pierce, David Duke, and others, who promoted Irving's books via their publications, websites, and at meetings.

Throughout the 1990s, Irving regaled his audiences with crude jokes and snide lies about the Holocaust. Among his standard lines: "I'm going to form an association of Auschwitz Survivors, Survivors of the Holocaust and Other Liars: ASSHOLS." When his daughter was born, Irving penned an anti-Jewish, racist ditty which he sung to his baby girl, and later taught to her:

"I'm a baby Aryan, not Jewish or Sectarian I've no plans to marry an ape or Rastafarian"

Among Irving's crowd-pleasing lines was that more people died as passengers in Senator Ted Kennedy's car than in gas chambers at Auschwitz. The three of us met for dinner at Billy Martin's Tavern. We sat in the same back booth where William Pierce and I had sat. Democrat Chris Matthews, the host of TV's popular HardBall, was seated at a booth with someone as I entered. Matthews was deeply engaged in his conversation, and he didn't notice that David Irving was seated 15 feet from his booth. Had Chris Matthews recognized Irving, it could've been disastrous for me, just as my hosting William Pierce at the University club had been. I recorded our discussion and gave it the next day to the FBI. Irving offered me a 20 percent commission on whatever money I could line up for him. I called no one to help him.

Later that summer, Linda and I flew to Iowa for a week to be with her parents and mine. Her father still practiced law in Mason City, and her parents and mine had many mutual friends. We joined them and two other couples for dinner at the Mason City country club. My dad had represented Mason City in the state Legislature for four terms, and has been a member of that club since 1967. Our table was beset by people who congratulated him on his presidential appointment.

The next day my dad played golf, and my mother and Linda, and her mother, drove to Minneapolis to shop at the Mall of America. I took my dad's boat out that morning, alone, for a spin around the lake, which took about an hour. As I hoisted the boat into the lift, my addiction kicked in: I needed some crack. But I didn't know any Iowa drug dealers. Later, sitting alone on the deck of my in-law's house, I tried to think of a way to get a fix. I finally drove to Mason City, which is nine miles east of Clear lake. I stopped at the home of an old buddy I'd known since seventh grade. Jim Burgess had just split up with his longtime girlfriend and now lived alone. I knew he'd know some users of illegal drugs, which meant he'd know where to get what I wanted. When I told him of my addiction, he thought I was joking. "That's a good one, Todd!", he said. Realizing I was serious, he cautioned me. "That shit will ruin your life. How can someone so smart be so damned dumb?"

"I'm addicted, Jim," I replied. "Are you gonna help me get a fix?" Handing him a fifty-dollar bill, I said, "Tell whoever you call that I'll need a pipe, and a filter." This was like a bad dream to my friend, who was shocked to see the depths to which I'd fallen. He called someone who knew someone. 10 minutes later, a dealer called Jim's cell phone and said she was on her way. Not long after that, a pretty girl arrived and the deal was done. As I lit the crack pipe to take a hit, Jim – who knew my parents, and Linda, and my siblings – asked me what my family would think if they knew I was an addict. "Here you are, Todd, back in your home town, and you can't go without crack cocaine," my old friend practically yelled. I didn't reply, and kept on taking hits.

When the crack was gone, I went into 'carpet-surfing' mode. That's when junkies drop to their hands and knees, and scour the carpet for crack they may have dropped. When I first began using crack, I laughed at addicts who did this. Now, I was doing it, too. But this was too much for my old buddy. As I searched the floor for crack, Jim grabbed the pipe, threw it to the floor and stomped it. "Get the fuck outta my house," he said, pointing toward his front door. "It kills me to see you smokin' that shit. We're still friends, but don't come back 'till you're done with this crap!"

I drove back to Clear Lake. Linda and I joined our parents that evening for drinks and dinner with Congressman Tom Latham and his wife. Following church services on Sunday, we flew from Mason City's airport to Minneapolis, and then back to D.C. While my cell phone was turned off during the flight from Minneapolis to DC, two drug dealers left messages. There were also messages from David Duke and Dr. Ed Fields. Ed Fields was a retired Georgia chiropractor who owned a popular, racist monthly newspaper and website called 'The Truth at LAST'. These two professional anti-Semites were to be in DC in a few weeks for an event being organized by Mark Cotterill, which would take place in Arlington, Virginia. I notified the FBI about this function, which I was asked to attend.

Cotterill had rented both floors of a large restaurant. The entire place, including the bar area, would be overrun with haters for over four hours. The restaurant was called The Mayan Grille, which, ironically, was owned by an El Salvadoran named Edgar Gomez. The place served Mexican and Central American food. The confab commenced with everyone singing 'God Bless America', followed by 'God Save the Queen'. Then, buckets were passed around, which were quickly filled with tens, twenties, fifties, and hundred dollar bills. David Duke and others addressed the throng. I spoke, too, to promote Resistance Records. About 180 racists packed the place, on both floors.

Members and leaders of the Council of Conservative Citizens, the National Alliance, American Renaissance, Liberty Lobby, the Knights of the Ku Klux Klan, White Aryan Resistance (W.A.R.), the American Friends of the British National party (the AF-BNP), and several other organizations were out in force. A lawyer named Victor Gerhard, whose clients included Dr. William Pierce and his National Alliance, addressed the crowd on the importance of making, and keeping, top-level contacts. Gerhard also dispensed legal advice and urged the attendees to write and submit news releases to their local media at least once per month, to promote their "cause".

The costs were underwritten by those groups, and by the owners of anti-Semitic publications like Media Bypass, The Jubilee, The NATIONAL INVESTOR, The Free American, and The Resistor. Several active-duty soldiers who subscribed to The Resistor were present, proving that the organized, racist Far Right had permeated the U.S. military. Paul Hall, Jr., spoke, asking for donations to fund subscriptions to his Christian-Identity newspaper, The Jubilee, for imprisoned haters whom he called "incarcerated Saints in tribulation." Fields, who also hosted a short-wave radio program called 'America First Radio', told the group of his admiration for the recently-deceased Byron de La Beckwith, the convicted assassin of civil rights leader Medgar Evers. Sam Van Rensburg, a pro-apartheid South African anti-Semite, warned of the racial carnage he foresaw, based on what had happened in his native country.

Van Rensburg was the deputy national membership coordinator for the National Alliance. He had served as a Special Forces officer in the former South African military, and he delighted the crowd with his war stories and "being paid to kill jigaboos." Van Rensburg was a dashing figure who knew how to use his cultured, classic South African accent to impress women. "By the time I turned 25," he said, "I'd already lost count of all the niggers I'd killed. It was well into the hundreds, maybe over a thousand."

This resonated with everyone, many of whom were openly envious. Even the women present wanted to do what he claimed to have done. "Nothing is quite so enjoyable as killing niggers and being paid for it," he said. "It'd be even more fun to gun down Jews," he said, "but it'll be awhile before that's legal." William Pierce introduced Steve Barry as the National Alliance's military unit Liaison. Barry – who'd been featured on the CBS program, '60 MINUTES', and was educated at West Point – had served as a Special Forces instructor in the U. S. Army in the 1980s.

A father of nine children spoke next, and said that teachers in public schools are "teaching white kids to hate their own flesh". The thunderous applause he received from those 180 attendees felt as though it had emanated from thousands.

Among the sought-after items for sale were bottles of 'Holocaust HOT SAUCE' – the tag line of which was, "Over 6 Million Served". Some 800 bottles were sold that day, at $3 each. A vendor told me that orders were taken for another 1,500 bottles, for delivery to the faithful. At various intervals, wallets and purses were opened and checks written, and cash was stuffed into straw baskets being passed around by members of the audience. While no one who attended this event was poor, most were just average, middle-class Americans. This wasn't a gathering of the organized elite of Holocaust Denial. Eight or 10 speakers addressed this gathering, which lasted for about four hours. Pierce later told me that between the sales of his books, magazines, Resistance Records CDs, DVDs, and magazine subscriptions, and sales of back issues, and donations to the National Alliance, and orders for Vanguard Books, he had grossed nearly $30,000. I never learned what the others collected, but it had to be considerable. Of greater concern was how the leaders of these groups skillfully assigned their minions to utilize the more violence-inclined sympathizers who attend such functions. William Pierce, Willis Carto, Richard Butler, David Lane, John Tyndall, Tom Metzger, and other racist honchos identified among their fans those who were willing to destroy property and end lives in the name of hatred. Such fools were even willing to lose their own life if it advanced the so-called movement. Trusted supporters were assigned to stay in touch with the unstable creeps, to whom Byron de La Beckwith was a hero.

Some such self-destructive kooks were low on dough, or altogether broke. This made earning their loyalty easy, by providing free subscriptions to publications, free admission to Holocaust Denial confabs, hate-rock concerts, and other functions, and hiring them to perform menial tasks, including at their offices and at rallies. They also gave them cash, and sometimes paid their rent and utility bills.

"Walking-around money", as Richard Butler called it. In certain cases, racist skinheads land jobs due to their penchant for violence. Eric 'the Butcher' Fairburn was one of those. Another racist sociopath was the Holocaust denier Jamie Von Brunn, whom Carto knew to be extremely violent. Carto hired him as a distributor of The SPOLIGHT and The Barnes Review, with a forgivable monthly draw of $1,250 plus expenses. Dr. Pierce knew Hendrik Mobus was a vicious killer long before he invited him to live for nearly three months on his West Virginia property.

Pierce also correctly perceived that Wade Michael Page was capable of wiping out minorities, and said so. While he didn't sign Page to a recording deal with Resistance records, Pierce insisted that the National Alliance maintain cordiality with him. Richard Butler, the so-called 'Pastor' of the Aryan Nations, and WAR's Tom Metzger, also reached out to such weirdos, whose propensity for violence and destruction was evident. When such creeps kill, it's rarely on orders from the likes of a Carto or William Pierce, or Richard Butler, or Tom Metzger. But once such troubled loners are noted, and subsequently funded, they're stoked. Efforts are made to feed and capitalize on their anger. And when these losers – and other, like-minded creeps, like Timothy McVeigh – finally lose it, and wreak havoc against Jews, blacks, Hispanics, gays, or others they hate, it satisfies those who fuel bigotry's anger-fired flames.

White supremacists will sometimes physically attack other violent bigots. I and several others watched Eric 'The Butcher' Fairburn administer such a severe beatdown on a middle-aged Holocaust denier named Bob Hoy that the victim had to be taken by ambulance to a northern Virginia hospital's

Emergency Room. It took six of us to pull Fairburn off of Hoy. His injuries required multiple surgeries and extensive re-hab, and kept him hospitalized for weeks. Fairburn once fortified a wooden baseball bat with dozens of 8-inch carpet nails. After pummeling two blacks into unconsciousness, he repeatedly pounded them with his homemade weapon. When Robert Hoy awakened in the hospital after being comatose for two days, he turned to his nurse and said, "I picked a fight with the wrong Nazi."

A few months later, I flew to California to meet with several neo-Nazis, including Paul Hall, Jr., who published the Jubilee. At a reception, I met a smooth-talking young racist named Corey Lamons. He was then in his early 20s and affiliated with several white supremacist groups in California and elsewhere. Less than five years after we met, Corey Lamons was beaten to death by members of the pro-KKK gang 'Public Enemy Number One', with claw hammers. His body was loaded into the trunk of a Ford F-150, which was owned by one of the killers. They planned to burn his body and then bury the remains in a remote location on property owned by a Holocaust denier. But on the way there, the driver was pulled over for a routine traffic violation. A police officer searched the vehicle, and discovered the bloodied body of Corey Lamons. He died because a stripper who called herself 'Wild Kitten' accused him of stealing 12 grand from her. One of Corey's killers, Billy Joe Johnson, had already murdered – by axe handle – two other racists, Clyde Nordeen, and Scott 'Scottish' Miller.

The death rate of white supremacists dying by non-natural causes rivals that of drug dealers, rappers, and people who find themselves on the wrong side of the Clintons. From California, I flew to Reno, Nevada, for a meeting of what was called the American Media Association. This was in either the spring or summer of 2001. The meetings were comprised of the publishers of 32 racist and anti-Semitic magazines, newspapers and Newsletters, most of which owned accompanying websites. All were profitable due to paid subscriptions, sales at gun shows and at other events, and paid advertising. The owners of these publications wanted to increase their ad revenues, including for that of their websites.

They asked me to present a plan of action, and I apprised the FBI of their request. The agents were delighted that in my facilitating it, they'd have direct access to the records of revenues of each and every publication, press run totals, advertising revenue figures, actual numbers of paid subscribers, mailing list trades, and contact information for their distributors and distribution networks and other relevant facts relating to these nefarious operations.

The conference began on a Thursday morning and concluded on Sunday afternoon. All of the major publishers and website owners were either present or represented. Don Black's presentation on creating a web presence was as professional as anything that the top-shelf website engineers back then were doing. As their advertising co-op representative, I brokered deals between these guys to exchange mailing lists of donors, subscribers, distributors and important (read: well-to-do) supporters.

What made my sales pitch so effective was the proven record of success my agency had racked up with The SPOTLIGHT. Carto sent a representative named Michael Collins Piper to this confab. The obese, heavy-drinking Piper was a pro-Nazi, gay author of anti-Jewish books. His books blamed the Mossad for the assassinations of JFK and Dr. Martin Luther King, Jr. They were primarily sold online and via ads in The SPOTLIGHT, The American Free Press, The Barnes Review and other such publications.

Confabs like this one also had his books on display and hundreds of copies were sold at such gatherings of the faithful. Piper knew that the acrimonious dispute between Carto and I precluded any advertising agreement involving Liberty Lobby, but he was nonetheless cordial to me. On the second day of the confab, Mike spoke to a standing room only audience in a large banquet room. Along the walls of both sides were folding chairs to accommodate the overflow. Everyone focused on the professional anti-Semite whose lectures were a staple at such events. "You can identify problems that truly concern everyone," he said. "So, write some letters to editors blaming Israel, AIPAC, and every Jew, for these troubles. Call in to talk radio, and blame

Israel and AIPAC," he urged, "convince people that there's nearly always a Jewish connection to these problems. And if not, then just invent one."

My college fraternity brother Phillip Canale, III, is the son of the distinguished Memphis attorney who had prosecuted Dr. King's assassin, James Earl Ray. I knew Piper's claims were rubbish, from having talked, at length, with Phil about the MLK case back when we were students at Drake University. Still, nothing ever surprises me whenever I hear of the half-baked, phony claims of alleged Jewish conspiracies manufactured by full-time, well-paid, professional anti-Semites like Piper. He said that "Jews have wreaked havoc on America, and it's time to hold them accountable." He gave examples of what he called "dialogue starters" for the purpose of recruitment. "When you're standing on line at a fast food restaurant, or sitting on a bus, or a subway train," he advised, "have a newspaper or magazine that features an article about crime, or the Middle East quagmire, or affirmative action, or government waste, high taxes, or anti-gun politicians and policies. People fear crime, detest high taxes and wasteful spending, and illegal immigration. They fear America being drawn into a war and going down the tubes. They're also worried that the next generations won't live as well as they do."

Piper told the audience that they can help to "finally solve the Jewish problem" by blaming nearly all their problems – and those of America - on the Jews. This line got big laughs, as everyone realized what "finally solve" meant; Final Solution. Piper was a skilled propagandist.

After the conference ended Sunday afternoon, I called Linda and then parked myself in the hotel bar. My flight back to DC would leave the following morning. I just wanted to chill. A few drinks in, I looked up; there was Michael Piper. "There's talk you might've gone over to the dark side and that you're now a Fed", Piper said. "People can talk all they want," I replied. "Doesn't make it true." He added he didn't think such was the case, but if it was and became known, I could be killed. "My grandfather's 92," I said. "So, I plan to be around for a long time." Satisfied with my reply, Piper asked if I knew about the extensive role of racist bikers, skinhead gangs, and organized white supremacists in the southern California drug trade.

Yeah, I told him I knew many of the under-age-35 Holocaust Deniers were crystal meth addicts and sold meth, coke, heroin and weed. I also knew that members of Richard Butler's Aryan Nations and some Ku Klux Klan members had traded AK-47's and some military-style, shoulder-fired mini-rocket launchers and Colt .45 pistols, for crystal meth at a Kentucky gun show in the summer of 1998. Piper knew that some proceeds from the sale of those firearms had found their way into Liberty Lobby's coffers. "Maybe write a book about this?", I asked, jokingly. "Are you crazy,?" he said. "That would guarantee I'd end up like that Jewish shock jock that David Lane and his boys ventilated."

Piper was referring to Alan Berg, the Jewish Denver radio talk show host gunned down by Holocaust deniers in 1984. He feared reprisal from the organized racist Far Right, but reporter Kimberly Edds doesn't. This gutsy California journalist filed an eye-opening article with The Orange County Register that was published Dec. 12, 2006. Here's an excerpt: 'A highly organized and corrupt leadership helped Public Enemy Number ONE evolve over the past quarter-decade from music fans and casual drug users to a violent Skinhead gang that has mauled and killed its way through the methamphetamine trade across much of southern California.' She also disclosed dangers posed by these racist gangs:

'On Thursday hundreds of local, state, and federal investigators rounded up 57 members of the gang and affiliates, law enforcement officials said, after threats were made to assault and kill several local police officers and at least one Orange county prosecutor who tried to crack down on the gang's drug, counterfeiting, and white-collar criminal operations.' Many Americans have been conditioned to think that the drug trade is mostly operated by blacks and Hispanics. Not true, as the above referenced article proves. Minorities are often merely only the front lines of America's problem with drugs.

Like Pavlov's dogs, the talk about drugs made me want to get high. I was 'Jonesing'. But where does a junkie find crack cocaine in a strange city, where he knows no one? Then I remembered that as I drove my rental car from the airport to the hotel, there were some trailer courts and low-rent apartment buildings just west of the airport. Some of the structures there looked like public housing, or Section 8 units. I drove out to this area, desperately looking for a 'Drug-Free Zone' sign, which would be a clear indication that illegal drugs were available.

I parked my car on a street that was littered with boarded-up businesses, a bail bonds operation, and a 7-Eleven that had bars on the windows. A liquor store was at the end of the block. I got out of my car and walked into the 7-Eleven. Some young black dudes milled around as I asked the clerk – deliberately speaking loudly - if she sold 'roses' and 'Chore-Boy'. "We sell Chore-Boy. Lighters, too. But we don't sell roses no more." These Roses were encased in glass tubes, which, once they were removed, functioned as crack pipes. 'Chore-Boy' is the copper wire which becomes the pipe's filter.

"Well, where can I buy roses around here?" She told me that the liquor store down the street sold roses. I thanked her and turned around. Four or five of these young black dudes had heard every word of our conversation, as I'd intended. "How's it going, fellas?", I asked. "It be good," one replied. I exited, lit a Marlboro Light and smoked it directly outside the 7-Eleven. When I finished, I threw down the butt and walked to my rental car. As I fastened my seat belt, the kid I'd spoken with exited the 7-Eleven, and walked toward the car. Leaning in, he gently tapped on the passenger window, which I lowered. "Yeah?", I asked.

"Word up?"

"Not much. You?"

"Y'all be a PO-leece?"

"Nope. You?" Ignoring my question, he asked me if I was all right. "I could be better", I replied. Scanning the street as we spoke, he said, "So what you want, and how much?"

"Crack. Good stuff. I'll go up to fifty bucks for now. If it's good, I'll get more."

"I can get dat. Gimme fifty, and I be back in a minute."

"How long is a minute here in Reno?"

"I'm talkin' ten minutes. Tops." I pulled a General Grant from my pocket, and folded it. Reaching over to shake his hand, I said, "Ten minutes, tops. If you're not back by then, I'll figure you cheated me, and I'm outta here. But if it's good, I'll buy more. Understand?" He nodded, and suggested I buy the Chore-Boy and rose while he was gone. Five minutes later, I was back in my car. Three minutes later, the kid reappeared. I lowered the window, and he asked if he could get in. He got in and told me the crack was in his left sock. "I be reachin' fo da shit," he said. This street-wise dude said this to not worry me that he might've been going for a gun. We made the hand-off, and he asked if I needed a place to smoke.

"I've got one, at my hotel. If it's good, can I call you? Will you deliver?" He handed me a piece of paper with a number on it. "I gots me some wheels. How about I lines y'all up wiff a bitch, or two?" I thanked him for the offer, told him I was married, and said that the crack was all I wanted. Back at my hotel, I rolled up a bath towel and ran water over it. I placed it on the floor, alongside the base of the door, to prevent smoke from escaping. I fired up the pipe and took my first hit of crack in nearly five days. The kid was right: it was really potent. 45 minutes later, I wanted more. Using my cell phone, I called the young dealer's number. When junkies are high on crack, they shouldn't even try to drive. If it's possible, the best way to obtain more drugs is having them delivered. I told the pusher my hotel room number.

30 minutes later, he knocked on my door. I bought $200 worth – 20 dime bags. This young dealer was nice and very personable. He pulled out a Zip-Loc bag containing the twenty bags and dumped them on the hotel room desk. I gave him his two C-Notes, and we briefly chatted. Suddenly, his broad smile became a frown. I followed his eyes over to the TV, upon which a Confederate flag T-Shirt was draped. It was given to me by the head

of a pro-Confederate organization, and would be given to the agents when we met in D. C., in two days. The kid's mouth was agape. "That – that's, uh," I said, "it's a GIFT."

My ruse wasn't working. "See, I know this dude that's sort of a redneck." This young pusher was a gentleman about it, but was ticked off. As I opened the door for him, he said, "When y'all checks outta here, is you takin' dem bed sheets wiff ya? Maybe cut some holes in 'em, so ya'all can see, when you go burnin' some fuckin' crosses in people's yards?"

When I finished smoking, I typed a memo on my laptop computer for the FBI about the conference. I then watched two movies and packed. Ordered breakfast via room service, ate, and showered. My 'high' had sufficiently worn off by then to drive to the airport. On the long flight back to Dulles airport, in Virginia, I downed one Jack Daniels and Coke after another, wishing I could fire up a crack pipe. Even as I monitored these evil, dangerous racists for the world's most famous investigative bureau, my goal was to get high, and stay high.

CHAPTER EIGHT

In the late Spring of 2000, William Pierce asked me to travel to the United Kingdom on behalf of Resistance Records. He wanted to go there, but Great Britain's Hate laws prohibited him from entering the country. A major reason for this trip was to promote Resistance Records, LLC, and inform the label's British, Scottish, Welsh and Irish fans that Pierce was negotiating to purchase NordLand, the Swedish counterpart to Resistance Records. Another reason was to recruit distributors for Resistance Records products and announce the coming DVD game, 'Ethnic Cleansing'. A third reason was to meet with John Tyndall, who for decades had been a leading British neo-Nazi. Tyndall had recently been deposed by a former protégé, Nick Griffin, whom I'd met in 1999, at a Roger Pearson-sponsored gathering in Chevy Chase, Maryland. One of the hosts of the meeting in Chevy Chase was a member of the exclusive Chevy Chase country club, which – along with Burning Tree – is among Washington's finest.

To organize these meetings, Pierce turned to Mark Cotterill, whose connections spanned from the USA to England, to South Africa, to Canada, to Germany, to New Zealand. I notified my FBI handlers of this development. Once the dates were set, FBI travel personnel made airline and hotel reservations for four agents to accompany me. The agents – two from the FBI, one from the IRS, and one from the JTTF – arrived about 36 hours prior to my arrival in the U. K. I landed at London's Heathrow airport, and took a taxi to the Hilton Mews, where I stayed for the five nights I was there. Pierce budgeted $15,000 for the trip, which included my flights, hotel and restaurant tabs, and the costs of entertaining the targets I was to surveil and record. Before I left, a courier delivered 50 one hundred dollar bills to my office, which Pierce directed me to "spread around, generously" to the overseas haters with whom I'd meet.

After checking in, I called the agents at their hotel, which was in another part of London. We met in the bar of their hotel for about two hours. The next morning, the agents and I met with two agents from the MI-5, which is the FBI's British counterpart, of sorts. While most people would agree that the only place where the United Kingdom is still a major world power is a James Bond movie, try telling that to an MI-5 agent. They're as proud as they are professional. This meeting took place in a small conference room at the hotel where the agents stayed,and lasted about an hour. The Mi-5 agents gave me a cell phone, which they instructed me to use throughout my time in the country.

I wasn't wired for this trip, which may have had something to do with conflicting laws regarding electronic surveillance by law enforcement between the two countries. Jet lag had set in, so after the meeting, I returned to my hotel for a nap. Upon awakening, I called Nick Griffin, who'd lined up one of his top lieutenants, Stevie Cartwright, to make arrangements for what would be about a three-hour gathering at an old pub which was located a few blocks off of the Strand, in downtown London. Cartwright, a native of Scotland, would arrive the following afternoon. I had met him in the USA in 1998, when my advertising agency represented the SPOTLIGHT.

The proprietor of this pub wanted a 100-Pound damage deposit and an additional, advance payment of 200 pounds for the three hours. Food would be ordered from the menu, and I was to be presented with a tab when all was done. Griffin and a racist from Leeds met me at a pub about two blocks from the Hilton Mews. After a liquid lunch, we drove over to the pub where the meeting would take place the next afternoon.

I paid the three hundred pounds to the pub's proprietor, for the rent and deposit. He assured me that the full deposit would be credited against the charges as long as nothing was damaged. Little did he know that the crowd the next day would be comprised of those to whom violence is second nature. The gathering was held in a large room in the basement of the pub. The place was musty, and had seen better days. There was a bar, but no bartender. Over the next three hours, three, maybe four different waiters came down to take orders for appetizers, drinks, entrees, drinks, desserts, and drinks, and more drinks. By the scheduled time of the meeting, about 16 or 17 had arrived.

Just before we brought matters to order, two more came in. One of them was named Tommy Mair, who came alone and sat down without introducing himself. Nick Griffin, who introduced me, was well-known to this crowd. But I'd not met most of the racists who attended until that afternoon. The presentation, which included 'Movement updates', lasted about an hour. I extended greetings from William Pierce to them all, and answered questions relating to Pierce's recent activities. There were complaints voiced about some British members, who charged far higher prices for books and other items from Vanguard Books, Resistance Records and the National Alliance, than were priced in Pierce's catalogs. The term, "Jew" was repeatedly spoken as a verb.

Following the presentation, everyone ordered more food. Four or five tables were about the floor, and people sat at all of them. I made it a point to sit at each table for awhile, as political candidates do when they're campaigning. After the dishes and cutlery were removed, more alcohol was ordered and served. This kept on for another hour after we had finished eating. Several of these low-life leeches ordered additional food, strictly for take-out purposes, and the guys from Scotland asked me for they called "petrol cash". I paid for their extra food, and handed out their damned gas money.

As they learned about 'Ethnic Cleansing' – Pierce's DVD game where blacks, Hispanics, gays, and Jews are killed in a simulated New York city Subway station – they were giddy. They laughed at the premise of 'Ethnic Cleansing', high-fiving one another. They grinned like four-year-olds on Christmas morning, upon discovering the toys Santa Claus had left them. One especially rough Brit said he'd buy a dozen DVDs of this computer game, for all of his nieces and nephews. Some of these activists were members of

Combat 18, known as C-18. Combat 18 was a pro-Nazi paramilitary group formed to protect Europe's Holocaust deniers and racists from physical attacks. Ostensibly defensive, members of C-18 were quite aggressive, and came under MI-5's radar hundreds of times. By about 2012, C-18 had effectively been supplanted by the British Ku Klux Klan, of which by late 2019, featured at least five chapters in and around London. These weren't just violent people; some were killers.

At one table, the talk was about David Copeland, AKA the 'London nail bomber'. Copeland is a militant British neo-Nazi whose 13-day bombing campaign had injured over 100 people and killed three others. Copeland's targets were London's blacks, Asians, Gays, and Jews. He was also a member of Cotterill's British National Party and the Holocaust-denying National Socialist Movement. These fellows all were highly sympathetic to Copeland and upset he'd been caught. During his prosecutors learned he had read 'The Turner Diaries' and admired William Pierce. Six weeks after this UK gathering, Copeland was convicted of murder and given six concurrent life sentences. Several of us were at the bar when a Scottish chap introduced me to the quiet, shy dude named Tommy Mair. Mair was articulate, well-mannered, and self-educated. Someone asked if on this trip I had taken time to see the sights of London. No, I replied, explaining that this was my eighth or ninth time in the city, and I'd previously seen such attractions. One tourist attraction I mentioned was Chartwell, which is the historic home of Sir Winston Churchill. Upon hearing this, Mair grimaced. "Churchill was a kike-loving bastard," he blurted, to his fellow haters' agreement.

When I said nothing, Mair asked me if I had read a book by the famous, Holocaust-denying pseudo-historian David Irving. When I said I'd not read it, he cited passages from it and recommended it to me. From there, the talk drifted to the influx of Asians and other minorities into the United Kingdom, and what they thought should be done about it. In June, 2016, Tommy Mair would shoot, stomp, and stab to death Mrs. Jo Cox, who was a Laborite member of Parliament.

As the event wound down, the proprietor came downstairs, and I announced last call. A final round was served, whereupon I told the manager to close out the tab. The bill came to around 700 or 800 pounds. I paid in cash, and left a 100 pound tip for the wait staff. Prior to flying to England, William Pierce sent me $5,000 to cover my costs, so I didn't ask the FBI to reimburse me. Outside, I joined several attendees on the sidewalk. Four guys from Scotland were getting into the same car. Three of them had asked for, and received, gas money from me. The moochers had implied that they all drove separately.

Regardless of where they are in the world, I thought, these Holocaust deniers are all con artists. I returned to the Hilton Mews via taxi. En route, I called the JTTF agent who was my lead contact on this trip. He and I met in Green Park, in west London. We then met with two MI-5 agents in the St. James neighborhood, where I debriefed them on what transpired at the pub. Back at the Hilton Mews, John Tyndall called my room to confirm our meeting the next morning.

Tyndall had for decades been the very public face of organized racism and anti-Semitism in the U.K. He and William Pierce were friends, and Pierce wanted me to meet him. The next morning, I took the tube (that's British for subway train) to either the Didcot or Oxfordshire station; I can't recall which. From there, I took a cab to Tyndall's estate. The house was an old mansion that he said had belonged to his mother-in-law. I didn't meet Mrs. Tyndall. Tyndall had prepared tea for my visit, which we drank in front of the fireplace in his elegant sitting room. For the next 90 minutes, I was subjected to a tirade about blacks, Asians, and eastern Europeans invading his country, and the Jews facilitating it all. Tyndall described how, twenty years earlier, he secured funding to develop and administer semi-annual para-military training encampments in the United Kingdom. The purpose of these week-long camps was to indoctrinate young attendees into neo-Nazi ideology and teach them fighting skills.

At its peak, this organization – which was named SPEARHEAD – consisted of over 50 ex-military trainers of young British men. For nearly 15 years, thousands of young Brits were trained in weaponry, including explosives, and brainwashed into hatred. They were even given Nazi-style uniforms, which were paid for, Tyndall told me, by a donation from a close friend of the Duke of Windsor, who'd previously been King of England. As I left, Tyndall asked me for my address in America. I wrote it down and handed it to him. He said I'd be given a free, one-year subscription to his newsletter, and added to his mailing list.

From the UK, I flew to Switzerland, but not on FBI business. I met up with my old buddy Peter Burri. We played Squash, had dinner, and spent an enjoyable evening in a bar. Later, I took to the ski slopes at Zermatt. After three days, feeling refreshed, I flew home.

I was unpacking when Linda got home from work. But it didn't take long for me to notice that something was different. Between my work and the frequent travel it required, and my rapidly-worsening addiction to crack cocaine, my marriage was suffering. It's precisely at such stressful times that addicts use drugs more than ever. Usage masks the pain, emotional distress, and the worries which are innate to being alive. Drugs also make users feel more alive, even as souls are being damaged and destroyed. I foolishly thought I could handle it.

I was becoming more adept at sneaking around to buy crack and get high. Developing these skills meant spending much time in the hoods. There, I bought drugs from, and smoked and socialized with, people from backgrounds of which I'd never before come in contact. Some tried to rob me, but such attempts rarely went well for them. At a crack house in DC's Petworth neighborhood, a crackhead and his lady friend set me up. We had met while buying from the same dealer, who went by the name of 'Skillet'. They seemed nice, and we had some mutual friends from the hood. Then they invited me back to their rented townhouse to drink and smoke. The gal offered to make a fried chicken dinner, so I accepted their invitation. Little did I know what they had planned. Before we started smoking, the chick excused herself, and went into the kitchen. I was seated, alone, on a couch that was positioned about ten feet from the kitchen entrance. The dude sat across from me, with a low table between us. On this coffee table was a large, heavy, lit red candle, the aroma of which smelled like cinnamon.

Experienced junkies often use candles to disguise the odor of smoked drugs. Just as I lifted my pipe to my mouth, the chick – who was good-sized – grabbed me from behind, going for a headlock. My crack pipe was in my left hand; the butane lighter in my right. As her strong arms encircled my neck, I jerked the lighter straight back, behind me, with the flame still going. Simultaneously, I jabbed the crack pipe backwards, hitting her face. The impact of the glass punctured her skin, breaking the pipe. I jabbed, hard, with the jagged pipe, slicing her repeatedly, as the flame blazed her right ear.

In under three seconds, her ear, cheek, lower neck, earlobe, and afro were all torched. Screaming, she let go and ran into the bathroom. Her friend reared up, maneuvered around the table between us, and lunged at me. The broken crack pipe was his downfall. With most of it still firmly in my hand, I cut his face. Severely. He dropped to his knees, taking his face into his hands, which now was embedded with glass shards. While he was down, I adjusted the lighter to high flame. I stood, flicking the blaze directly onto his ear and afro, and, with my left hand, poured hot wax from the candle onto his head and neck.

The thug screamed, pushed off from the table, and was on his knees on the floor, dripping blood like a stuck pig. As he tried to rise, I slammed the heavy candle – which was about four inches in diameter, and ten inches tall, encased in glass – straight into his temple. I heard a thud, resulting from the weighty candle bashing his skull. The glass cracked, but – like his skull – it didn't break. But the thug was down for the count. As I caught my breath, the chick returned. I said, "Things got heated, eh? Your friend, here, will need about two bottles of aspirin." She said, "take yo shit and leave da fuck out mah house."

"Look, bitch," I replied, "I'll leave on my terms and on my time."

"Say whahh?", she asked.

"When you and your thug jumped me, it scattered my stuff." Pointing to an 8-ball that I'd bought, I said, "And this rock's coated with candle wax now. You're paying for that. You'll also pay for my broken crack pipe and the monogrammed shirt my wife bought me in New York. It's from Paul Stuart."

"We ain't doin' shit," she replied.

"You already did, bitch." As she advanced toward me, I pulled out my .380, flicked off the safety, chambered a round and aimed straight at her. "I detest thieves, and you and your thug assaulted me. You tried to rob me. Shut up and sit down. And keep your hands where I can see 'em." While she sat, I reached into the back pocket of her unconscious thug and removed his billfold. It contained twelve, maybe 15, hundred-dollar bills. "You're lucky I'm honest, sweetie," I told her as I removed four C-notes. "Most folks that get attacked like this would take ALL this money. I'm taking only what's rightly mine."

Tossing the wallet to the floor, I stepped over the crumpled hulk of unconscious thug. "You know, I was raised to never hit ladies. But you left me with no choice. Incidentally, that's quite a grip you've got. You might consider going into the Mixed Martial Arts, if you ever decide to work. You'd might win their heavyweight championship." The stupid skank had likely not encountered an armed white crackhead, especially not one who turned the tables on her and her accomplice's thuggery. Her expression changed from fear and anger to befuddlement.

"You and your pallie should take up a collection from your fellow hood rats," I said. "Then you won't have to steal. You can call it the Ignited Negro Fund."

I silently walked toward their front door and headed straight to my car. I decided to postpone smoking the crack that had survived their assault. As I drove away, my cell phone rang. It was my buddy Simon Jacobsen. Simon lived in Georgetown, and was an architect in his father's firm. We disagreed on politics, but always enjoyed debating. Simon invited me over to his house for some drinks. His wife was out with some girlfriends, so he and I caught up with each other for a couple of hours.

While driving to Georgetown, I realized that while my moves in the crack house were purely defensive, and that I hadn't instigated the fight, it wasn't appropriate to feel so exhilarated. Slamming that heavy candle into that thug's temple could've been fatal. And while it was done in self-defense, I didn't want anyone's blood on my hands, not even that of a violent, drug-addicted thief who had assaulted me. It was great to spend a few hours with Simon. But as we knocked the drinks back on his bricked-in, back patio, I wasn't, deep-down, happy. I got home late, and went straight to my den in our basement. I hid the crack, and put my gun in the center drawer of my desk. A few minutes later, I climbed into bed. I thought Linda was asleep. "You've been drinking," she said, once the light was out.

This wasn't a question. My wife knew I was drunk. "Yeah," I answered, "I was at Simon's place." She began to ask me more questions, I didn't want to answer. I got out of bed and walked out of our bedroom. Our house had six bedrooms. I headed straight down the hall, to the guest room that Senator Jepsen always stayed in when he came to visit. We called it the "Senator's room". I slammed the door, which was uncharacteristic of me.

Linda followed me into the bedroom. "Todd, what's going on? Why are you acting this way?" I shifted to my right side, facing the window on the wall, not responding. The entire time, I remember thinking: I've come home drunk before. I've come home after using crack cocaine before. But I was at least civil. But now, I didn't care about anything. I just wanted to be left alone. Finally, she gave up, left the room, and went back to bed. I wasn't raised to treat women this way, and I felt terrible about having been so damn disrespectful to my wife, of all people. I knew I should apologize, and return to our bedroom, and try to make peace. Or, better, yet, make peace and then make love. No, forget that - at least, for now, anyway. That wasn't going to happen, not in my present state.

The cocaine in my system, plus the alcohol, and my lack of sleep - on top of jet lag - would render me about as competent at making love as politicians are at telling the truth. When I awakened, Linda was back in the Senator's room, checking on me. At first, I thought she'd just gotten up and was about to go to work. But it was nearly six p.m. She worked while I slept the entire day.

Something was wrong, very wrong, and it wasn't just my drug addiction, or my excessive drinking. So what WAS it? Why was I feeling so exhilarated one day, and so down in the dumps the next? Why did I sometimes feel like I could do anything, and then, just hours later, I'd want to pull the covers over my face and stay in bed? Why'd I not want to get up? As these thoughts raced through my head, I had to pee. But I couldn't engage my mind in order to climb out of bed, and go to the bathroom. Such thoughts and reactions were symptomatic of the bipolar II disorder I would later be diagnosed with at the Sheppard-Pratt hospital in Baltimore, Maryland.

But as I experienced these feelings, it creeped me out something awful. Looking back, I was damn lucky. My feelings of despair never led to any suicidal thoughts. But more than once, I became extremely aggressive, to the point of violence. But I had no idea of what the hell was happening. Was I going crazy? Had this aspect of my thinking been dormant for years? Did drugs trigger it? What, if anything, could be done? The following morning, Linda made an appointment for me to see a psychologist in DC who specialized in bipolar disorders. I was to meet with Dr. Ron Weiner the following week. As is the case with bipolar disorder, I bounced back the next morning. Linda was scheduled for a seven a.m. surgery. She was an RN, with a Masters degree in bone marrow transplantation technology.

By the time I awakened, she had left for Fairfax INOVA hospital. I felt good, but with nothing scheduled, I just wanted to get high. But not many drug pushers are up and doing business at 9 a.m. After several attempts, I finally reached one, and made arrangements to pick up two 8-balls. I drove to DC, to the hood where I was to meet my contact, whose name was J.R. He was a black dude in his mid-thirties from whom I'd bought many times.

As I got out of my Range Rover, I noticed a kindly-looking, elderly black man sitting on the front porch of the townhouse where J. R. often stayed. He was over six feet tall, and dignified. J.R. was to meet me a block away, and I was right on time. As I crossed the street, the old man left the porch and walked toward me. Pointing to my vehicle, he said, "nice car." I thanked him, and he asked, "Are you Todd?"

His question stopped me cold. Eyeing him suspiciously, I replied, "Yeah. And you, sir?" Introducing him-self as Charles Jackson, Sr., we shook hands. His grip was firm, his gaze steady. "I'd like a word with you, Mr. Blodgett."

"What's this about, Mr. Jackson?"

"It's about your drug addiction." My guard was up now. "Are you a cop, or a police informant?", I asked. No, he replied. I asked him if he was with the government. "I was," he said, "for 35 years – GSA. Before that, I served for 12 years in the U. S. Army." He came right to the point. "My daughter tells me that you buy crack from my grandson. Unless she's wrong, you and I need to talk." We locked eyes for five or so seconds before I responded. "Your grandson is … ?"

"My grandson is Jamal Renfro. You know him as J.R." This old man was on to me. He emanated sincerity, composure, and genial authority. "There's a little cafe two blocks from here. Why don't we walk over there, and I'll treat you to some of DC's best soul food?" As I listened, my eyes were focused on the sidewalk. I looked at the house where the old man had been sitting on the porch, the place his grandson often stayed. I saw a black lady peering at us from behind the curtains in the window. I offered to drive. "Oh, thank you, but no. I'm 75 years old, but I love walking."

As we walked to the Florida Avenue Grille, Mr. Jackson told me he'd been a Sergeant in the Army, and became certified as an electrician. He also said he still played "a pretty mean jazz piano." We sat in a wooden booth with plastic seat cushions near the middle of the café. Directly across the aisle from us was a long service bar, of which every stool was occupied. After ordering sweet iced tea, half smokes, collard greens, fried chicken and butter beans, my host wasted no time.

"Regarding your drug problem, I'm sorry you're afflicted. I'm also sorry that my grandson is mixed up in it. I'm not going to lecture you, and I know you're aware of the evils of addiction." He asked me how old I was. I told him I'd turn 41 in two weeks. This was in late August, 2001. "You're wearing a wedding ring, Todd. Does your wife know about your drug issues?"

"No, and I'd like to keep it that way." He asked if my parents knew about my addiction. "Not so far," I told him. "Well, if you keep it up, they'll know," he admonished. "As will your friends – that is, the few friends you'll have left, if you continue down this dark road. But that's on you." I nodded, as the waitress refilled my tea. The old guy's eyes then focused on a very heavyset black man whose back was to us, as he sat on a stool facing the bar. This customer needed about three stools, and his blue jeans weren't pulled up. Mr. Jackson looked disdainfully at the man, because the top half of his buttocks were in pain view of everyone. "Well," I told him, "this is a crack neighborhood!"

He said, "I'm respectfully asking you to stop associating with Jamal, effective immediately. Okay?"

"Well, Mr. Jackson, if that's what you – "

"Is that a yes, Mr. Blodgett?" Damn, I thought. This old guy is sharp, and means business. He even knows my full name. What the Hell else did he know? Damn that internet. "Yes, sir, I responded. "Good. Thank you. Now it's YOUR turn. I'm all ears," he said, smiling, as he began eating. This good man was Godly; a smart, kind soul, whose moral authority sprung from his innate decency, intelligence, and compassion. He loved his family, and was being protective. He also cared about me. I decided right then and there I'd not disappoint him. "Mr. Jackson, J.R. is a good dad to his kids, and he tries to support them. He's even honest in his dealings, and never cheats me."

"He may not cheat you in that respect. But don't tell me he's a good father when he deals drugs." The soul food was tasty, and he asked if this was the first soul food I'd eaten. "Hardly. I have lots of black friends. I've eaten soul food many times." Mr. Jackson remained serious. "I assume you're a college graduate?" Yes, I answered. "Todd, you've had many blessings, including opportunities most folks never get. You're well-spoken, well-mannered, well-dressed, well-educated, well-bred; you own a fine automobile. You're from a good family that's highly respected, and, I presume, your wife also does. Your parents have helped you, and will always be there for you." I was stunned that he knew all of this, but shouldn't have been. This old guy was smart and perceptive.

"I know." Unconsciously, I had shredded two paper napkins into about 30 shreds. The check arrived, which my host paid with a twenty. We walked, mostly in silence, back to my car. As I approached my parked vehicle, the old man looked me straight in the eye, and extended his right hand. "I'm trusting you, Todd. Please don't let me down." I assured him I wouldn't. "One more thing," he said, before turning away. "Don't let yourself down, either. You can still get out of jail, son. You know that, right?"

JAIL? "What? What jail, Mr. Jackson?"

"I'm referring to the jail you've built around your life, with your addiction. Look at how you have to live; sneaking around, having to look over your shoulder, fearful of being robbed, beaten up, straying further from your wife, your parents, family members and friends. This risky, destructive existence you've carved out is destroying relationships, and your present, and your future. And if that's not self-imposed incarceration, I don't know what is." As I acknowledged his point, the old man walked back toward the porch of the house from where he emerged 90 minutes earlier. I kept my word, and avoided his grandson. JR stayed away from me, too – obviously on his grandfather's orders.

But it would be another four-and-a-half long, hard years before I'd finally kick my drug addiction. And this would happen only AFTER my wife divorced me, and I'd been in some drug re-habs and real jails. Around this time, Antwan introduced me to a man who owned some Chop Shops. These illicit businesses exist to rapidly dismantle stolen vehicles and sell them for parts, or to be reassembled elsewhere. The guy I met – who, incidentally, was white – used terms like "vehicle rebirthing", and "JIT" projects. 'JIT' means 'just-in-time' theft, where thieves will effectively steal autos to order. There are professional thieves in D.C., New York City, Philadelphia, Baltimore, and other large American cities who specialize in such custom thefts. Such criminals are usually tied in with the owners of Chop Shops.

Car rebirthing experts know all of the places in and on vehicles where the VIN (Vehicle Identification Number) is located. Within two hours of a stolen car appearing at a Chop Shop, it can be completely disassembled, down to its chassis. This guy's shop's main location was in a remote, nondescript, old warehouse in western Maryland. Had I told the FBI agents about him and his businesses, it would've probably been traced back to me - and you wouldn't be reading this book, because I'd be dead.

Each year, millions of dollars of stolen vehicles were taken apart there and at his other shop in northern Virginia. Relatively speaking, this operation was small-time. He told me he had bought the two chop shops from a syndicate comprised of hundreds of such illegal enterprises. Those who say crime doesn't pay have probably never been in a chop shop. One of the chop shopworkers was an on-again, off-again junkie I'll call Derek. He sold crack on the side to fund his drugging and pick up a couple of extra thousand bucks every few weeks. One evening, Derek and I and his lady friend, a cute, twenty-something black chick named Minolta, were returning from buying six 8-balls from a dealer in S.E. Washington. We were less than three miles from the crack house where we had planned to get high, and Derek got careless. A beat-up Cadillac El Dorado had suddenly run a stop sign and pulled out about forty feet in front of us. Derek swerved, avoiding a collision, and flipped off the driver.

He then blasted his horn, three times, over about 10 seconds. He was doing 42 in a 30 mph zone. His reflexes were as superb his judgment was lousy. In the car's rear-view mirror suddenly appeared a DC police cruiser, with its blue and white lights rolling atop. No siren yet, but the cop immediately sped up in pursuit of Derek's borrowed Buick Skylark. Based on probabilities, this cop had reason to suspect that we were driving dirty – that is, with drugs. This could've been avoided had Derek not foolishly blasted his damn horn at the beat-up El Dorado.

"DAMNIT," Derek yelled, as he gunned the Buick to 60, while still in the 30 mph zone. "Todd, get out da car when Ah stops, and run y'all white ass into da METRO station." Derek handed me the $900 worth of crack, which I stuffed in my coat pocket. Not that he wanted to give it up, and he wasn't making sure I could use it later. But he knew that DC's Finest would soon be locking him up. When junkies know they're about to be busted, avoiding a possession charge becomes the name of the game. And with the large amount of crack he possessed, his charge would include intent to distribute. Derek and Minolta would share the possession charge. She fired up her pipe as soon as the cop gave chase.

Knowing that being arrested was only minutes away, she blazed a few hits. Addicts have priorities. As Minolta smoked away in the back seat, we approached the station. Derek said, "only one Po-Po in dat cop-mobile, Todd. Him gonna hafta letcha go. Dat fuckin' donut junkie want me more den he want you." Such clarity of thought came quickly to those accustomed to dealing with, and running from, the police. Derek slowed the vehicle, which I bolted from before it came to a complete stop. I didn't shut the passenger door. "I've got your back," I said to Derek as I bolted from the car. I covered the 25 yards from the curb to the main entrance to the Petworth METRO station in six seconds, tops. Racing down the escalator three steps at a time, I fumbled for my wallet and retrieved my METRO card. Then, panic.

My card had only 45 cents left on it, and 95 cents was the minimum required to board. Such minimum requirements enabled the DC Metro Authority to keep their facilities free of drug addicts and other low- lifes like me, who run from cops while carrying drugs. In front of the only operational card dispensing machine, an elderly black man, somewhat confused, fumbled for change. Out of breath, I gently nudged him aside. With a careful sweep of my hand, I gave a him a twenty dollar bill. "Sorry, sir, but I'm in a big hurry. This twenty's for your inconvenience." I stuffed my METRO card and another twenty into the machine. Seconds later, my card – now worth $20.45 – popped out. I inserted it into the slot in the turnstile and passed through to the other side of the station, where the train would soon arrive.

Glancing back, I saw the old codger smiling at his good fortune, and gratefully thanking "sweet Jesus" for his unexpected windfall. As he looked up at the overhead fluorescent lights, hands clasped, prayer-style, it almost seemed like he expected "sweet Jesus" to reply, "you're welcome, bro."

I also prayed to sweet Jesus for the incoming Green METRO Line train to be on time, if not early. To not be seen by anyone on the escalator, I positioned myself and leaned, way back, on a cement bench attached to a 3-foot-wide cement bulkhead. The train arrived on schedule. After checking the escalator for cops or suspicious METRO personnel, I boarded. As the recorded voice said, "doors closing". I sat down, relieved, my heart pounding. As the train began moving, I realized I had peed my pants for the first time since pre-school. A black teenaged girl noticed this, too. As she exited the subway, she said, "Y'all need some DEPENDS", referring to the special diapers for people who are incontinent.

The next morning, my cell phone awakened me at 7 a.m. It was Shontell, Derek's brother. He said Derek needed five grand. "Bail's that high?", I asked him. "It ain't be da bail, Mister Todd. Derek getting' out on he own re-con-science." I asked Shontell about Minolta. He said, "Dat bitch goin' down fo' a minute. She gots priors." I asked him if Derek could be assigned a public defender. "Him gots one. Him some kinda Chinese. Dem slant-eyes be smart," he told me. "But Derek need dat five Large 'cause dat wheel weren't his. Da PO-leece, dem's keepin' it."

"Wheel? What wheel?"

"Da wheel, dude! Da car." I asked Shontell why the cops were holding the car. "Tickets. Somethin' like forty-nine hundid bucks worth on dat joint. Da nigga who wheel it be, him be rollin' up here in a minute. Him say he comin' to my crib, fo' he money."

"Will this minute be more or less than three days, Shontell?"

"It be some time today. We ain't talkin' no drug pusher minutes." I told him I'd get the cash to him by three that afternoon, and kept my word. The adage, "If the drugs don't get you, the lifestyle will" came to mind as I delivered 50 C-notes to Derek's brother. He may have lied to me about the alleged tickets, but it was worth five grand to ensure that Derek wouldn't implicate me. Derek also knew that once he'd been paid, betraying me wasn't an option. I don't screw people over, I keep my word, and I'm loyal. But no rules apply when someone deliberately causes me harm, as Derek knew. Not long after this close call, I found myself in a crackhouse off of Bladensburg Road, in D.C. I'd gone there after being invited by a crackhead I knew, who dealt drugs to support his habit. This black man's nickname was Hootchy.

After about an hour, he left the drug den to go 're-up'. In his absence, an argument ensued between three other addicts over a girl who wasn't there. Two crack whores and I took hits of crack as the three argued over the chick to whom each laid claim. Atop a credenza were bottles of Mad-Dog 20/20, Ripple wine, and Hennessey cognac. All but two were full. Just before Hootchy knocked on the door, their argument became violent. One of the junkies turned his anger on the mouthier of the other two, picked up an empty bottle, and broke it against the counter. As he approached his prey, he said, "which ear y'all want me to cut off first, mutha fuckuh?" From behind, one of the crack whores slammed a full bottle of Hennessey against the back of his head. The big black guy instantly crumpled to the floor as I stared in disbelief. He wasn't dead, but after he recovered, the young lady who struck him may well be, I thought. The other crack whore, oblivious to this, kept right on smoking crack.

Racing to the door, I let Hootchy back inside. After nearly tripping over the unconscious crackhead, he said, "Dat nigga be dead?" I bent down and checked. "No. He's got a strong pulse and his breathing is steady." Hootchy was glad the guy was alive because, he said, "dis dude owe me two hundid." The crack whore who smacked the big guy knew she'd face a painful reprisal once he was back on his feet. She claimed that the unconscious addict had "disrespected" us all, including Hootchy. Removing a folded-up switchblade from his boot, Hootchie handed it to the attacker. "Here, bitch. If y'all want 'dis nigga dead, all it gonna take be one slit to him throat."

Hesitating, the gal said, "it's been a minute since I done sliced anybody." The other chick said, "You go, girl. It's better safe den sorry. If I was y'all, I'd a-took him out already. Go ahead, girl, get it over wiff – slice da movva fuck. Ain't nobody here be sayin' nothin'."

I grabbed the switchblade from her hand, and then grabbed Hootchy by the arm, and said, "are you nuts? Providing a weapon – an ILLEGAL knife – to a cracked-out junkie, and egging her on to commit murder?" As our eyes locked, I said, "What the hell's wrong with you? Come on, Hootch, let's go. This isn't what we came for. Let's go. Now."

Hootchy told me to wait outside, while he sold the last of his drug stash. For the three minutes I was on the front porch, I prayed there would be no more violence inside that crack house, at least not until we had gone. Hootchy drove to an all-night Denny's on, I think, New York avenue, N.E., where we ate breakfast and drank coffee.

It dawned on me that ghetto logic, and justice in America's hoods, isn't any different from what takes place among members of the KKK, the Aryan Nations, and violent, racist Skinheads. A few days later, I was back in Dr. Weiner's office in downtown D.C. Like all competent therapists, he sensed that something was amiss. "You're way edgier than usual," he told me. "Anything you want to tell me about?" His compassion showed in his eyes, and if anyone should hear about what happened with Hootchy, it was this psychologist. "I'm – I'm just, uh, well ... no, let's just ... "

Interrupting me, he said that if at any point during our session I wanted "to discuss whatever it is that's clearly affecting your thoughts", to "feel free to bring it up."

"Let's just say that certain people I know, and have hung out with, and done business with, engage in some really nasty shit – sometimes on a professional, paid basis." Smiling, Weiner replied, "Are you talking about Republicans?"

CHAPTER NINE

The racist, anti-Semitic publication 'The Jubilee' sponsored a four-day convention at a resort near Scottsdale, Arizona in 2000, called The Jubilation. This was about three weeks after the FBI agents had assigned me to attend a two-day confab hosted by American Renaissance, in Reston, Virginia. I had attended the 1998 Jubilation, also in Arizona. In 2000, over 300 Christian "identitarians", as they called themselves, showed up for seminars, lectures, exhibits, and the opportunity to meet fellow haters. The Council of Conservative Citizens, Liberty Lobby, and other far right, racist organizations also participated.

Absent was Jared Taylor, whose American Renaissance group eschewed anything he deemed to be anti-Semitic. Not having Taylor and his fans at the Jubilation lowered the average IQ of the attendees by probably 30 points. William Pierce wasn't there due to scheduling conflicts, so I was there in his stead. After attending the 2000 Jubilation, I filed a lengthy report on it. In 2001, the agents assigned me to attend that year's event.

At least 30 National Alliance members were present and recruiting efforts were in full swing. About 75 white supremacists and Holocaust deniers sat in the air-conditioned cabana near a huge pool, behind the brick and stone mansion of a Pierce supporter in Scottsdale, just off of Camelback Drive. Barry Goldwater's home was two miles from this impressive house. On the first night of the conclave, a racist country music band entertained. The lead singer sounded like Johnny Cash. One of his most popular tunes was a reworked version of Cash's bit hit, 'Ring of Fire'. Among the lyrics:

"Jews – they're a wicked bunch, whose bones, I'd like to crunch; Pa-tri-ots like us aspire - to toss 'em in-

to a Ring of Fire. Down, down, down, in a burn-in' Ring of Fire; them Jews burned up, as the flames got

higher - Evil Hebes all baked, in a Ring of Fire; a Ring of Fire… Them nasty Jews all burned, in a Ring of

Fire, to my heart's de-sire; in a Ring of Fire, a Ring of Fire, a Ring of Fire, a Ring of Fire … "

Another crowd-pleaser was a bigoted version of 'Tie a Yellow Ribbon 'round the old Oak Tree':

'I'm comin' home; done my time… A Jew-boy Judge said killin' a spick's a crime; Bein' locked up with

them Jig-a-boos was really tough to take – Luck-i-ly for me, I found some fag-got heads to break … and

Mus-lim necks to break … So, hang some kikes and nig-gers from the ole Oak Tree; 'cause when I get

home, it'll sure please me … "

Then there was, 'Who likes a Nigger', which opened this way:

'Billy Jeff Clinton was a-flyin' one morn, over south Loose-ee-anna, a-feelin' forlorn

So, he looks down below, and what does he see? But two Cajuns pullin' a nigger on skis

So he lands, says thanks fer helpin' yer black brother,

Well, them two Cajuns just looked at each other, said,

He might be smart, but I'll tell you sumpin' – he don't know a thing about

Aaallll-li-ga-tor huntin'

Whop, whop, bam, bam, who likes a nigger?

Whop, whop, bam, bam, who likes a nigger?

Whop, whop, bam, bam, who likes a nigger"

'Cause hatin' on niggers is a-gettin' much bigger'

To the tune of Bobby Darin's 'Mack the Knife' was this number:

"Jig-a-boos, and Guat-e-mal-lans, and the fag-gots, and He-brews ... It's time to line 'em, up and shoot

'em; when they're all dead, ahh, what great news ... "

Then, there was this one, to the tune of Dean Martin's 'That's Amore':

"When a Jew comes your way, what do you have to say – Heil, Hitler;

When a coon robs your place, blast him to outer space – Heil, Hitler –

Spicks and Queers, make 'em disappear; we don't want 'em here, and you'll shout,

Heil Hitler; Help your race; it's our place, Heil, Hitler –

When they're gone, then we'll see ... just how great life can be, Heil, Hi-it-ler;

Fight the fight, do what's right, 'cause we're proud to be white, Heil, Hi-it-ler ... "

To say the crowd tremendously enjoyed the floor show is an understatement. Predictably, everyone laughed uproariously and enthusiastically applauded. I wrote the lyrics down (excerpted here), and recorded them with my cell phone. Witnessing this audience, many of whom were well-educated, high-income professionals and small business owners, enjoy such disgusting entertainment was absolutely surreal. I wondered what their customers, clients, employers, and neighbors, or golf partners, would think if they knew that these folks were clapping to the beat of, and humming along with, such vile, despicable music. There were plenty of school age children there that weekend, as well as college students. The following day, at the resort where these Christian Identity adherents met, I spoke with a lawyer. She practiced law near Philadelphia, was very well dressed, and wore some very expensive jewelry. She also understood the importance of not being associated with this event.

"I'm here with my parents," she said, "and I don't necessarily agree with everything that's said." Then, lowering her voice, she said, "but the Jews have too much power. Any white Christian in Philly knows that, even Democrats who used to vote for Mayor Rizzo." The former mayor, Frank Rizzo, had previously served as Philadelphia's Police Commissioner. Rizzo was basically a Philly version of George Wallace, a blue-collar politician who bragged that his governing style made "Attila the Hun look like a faggot." I also spoke with a charming young mom and her husband.

They were in their early twenties, with young twins, in a double-stroller. "We're here for these two," she said, pointing to the children. "They've just turned two. We're worried about their future. Jews, blacks, homos, and these Illegals," she insisted, "must go. They're destroying our country." Her husband – who was in medical school - added, "It's our nation, not theirs." Their rants reminded me of Willis Carto, who frequently bemoaned what he called America's "niggerfication."

The sheer sense of entitlement that these young, professional couples exhibited didn't give me much hope for the future. Would their children be raised with such thoughts? Most likely, the answer is yes. In advance of this trip, the FBI agents I worked with provided me with the contact information for agents from their Phoenix office, who knew I was there. But for this trip, on-site back-up wasn't necessary. Three weeks later, I was in Cleveland, Ohio, with William Pierce, for a National Alliance conference. The Cleveland chapter was the largest in the organization, with about 75 dues-paying members, and another 125 or so casual supporters. During my years with Pierce, I was in Cleveland three, maybe four times.

Pierce arranged for me to meet with a man who recruited young adults. This recruiter was as adept as any chair of any county or state political party operation I've met in the U.S., of either party. "I don't care if these younger prospects are loners, weirdos, geeks, or popular with their peers," he told me. "Our movement accommodates every type of student and working-class young adult, male or female," he said. "Nerds can help with our websites;

geeks can write propaganda, and the grunts and bullies can do the heavy lifting. These emotionally constipated young people need a substitute family; we provide it. When we land some popular kids, their friends often follow them. Once we instill pride in them, and prove to them that our issues are their issues, and that our movement is for them, they'll sign up. We also build up the self-esteem of the less-popular teenagers and young adults, by instilling in them pride in their race, and heritage." I asked him where he learned to identify and recruit.

He had worked in sales and his manager had once been an Army recruiter. It freaked me out that the recruiting techniques and sales tactics which had been developed for military recruitment purposes were now utilized to draw vulnerable young adults into the ranks of racial hatred, anti-Semitism, white supremacy, and Holocaust denial.

Then there was the music, particularly the Hate Metal, racist Country, and other genres, being produced and distributed by Resistance Records. "Our websites, brochures, pamphlets, and other recruitment materials aren't nearly as effective as music. They dig the lyrics, love the sounds and the beat, vocals – everything. It speaks to them. They play it in their cars, on their Walkmans, and at home, and with their friends. They dance to it, sing along. Once it permeates their minds," he said, we got 'em." The tune, 'Who Likes a Nigger?' was his personal favorite. On the spot, he sang a few bars:

"Ain't much difference 'tween a nigger and a donkey; about as much as 'tween an ape and a monkey. A mule earns his livin' by the sweat of his neck; a nigger lives high on a government check –

Now, a nig-ger should be smar-ter, as a gen-e-ral rule; but in a spel-lin' con-test - I'd pick the mule."

I realized how damaging this music truly was. I was also relieved to be retained by the FBI, monitoring this nastiness, and not trafficking in it, as the co-owner of Resistance Records. I may have once sold my soul to the Devil, but now I was helping the good guys. As we concluded our meeting, the recruiter said a major benefactor of 'The Movement' – a very wealthy

South African anti-Semite – had offered several million dollars to permanently fund four or five Militia-style training and indoctrination camps in the U.K., America and Switzerland.

When he told me about these plans to brainwash new recruits, and instill the ways of hatred into their souls, I wasn't only dismayed, but felt guilty, knowing that Resistance Records had played a role in it.

"When people ask me what problem I have with Jews," the man said, "I say, it's because they EXIST."

Just like the British anti-Semites I encountered while in London, this dude was a fan of the militant, British neo-Nazi David Copeland, referenced earlier. Copeland was called the 'Brixton Nail bomber', who subjected London to a 13-day campaign of violent assaults on the city's Gays, Muslims, blacks, and

South Asians. Copeland injured over 100 victims and killed three innocent people in 1999. It came as no surprise to me when Copeland became a hero to anti-Semites, violent skinheads, white supremacists and Holocaust deniers, and other racists throughout the U.S. and Europe.

Later, I met Tom Metzger for breakfast. Metzger believed violence strengthened the movement. He wasn't interested in waiting for a race war: he wanted one now, and said it was long overdue. Metzger's recruitment tactics weren't subtle; he was more of a 'Be a Man; Join the Klan' kind of guy. His group, 'WAR' – for White Aryan Resistance – raised funds selling items like T-shirts which featured hooded Klansmen above the words: 'The Original Boys in the Hood'. American flag decals featuring 13 stars surrounding a Swastika were also popular at the Ohio event and the vendors made small fortunes. One lady ordered 500 such T-shirts and 500 decals on the spot. This woman was the chairman of her local School Board, an elected position, and her husband was the Vice President of a bank.

Tom Metzger advocated what he called "leaderless resistance", which he said could be achieved via "lone wolves" engaging in "meaningful violence" designed to "send a message that whites are fed up." He added that, "our cause is best served by going underground. The government is becoming more oppressive … many people are alive simply because it's illegal to kill them." While we were eating, a young man approached our table. He introduced himself as an employee of Anthony Pierpont, a Minnesotan who owned Panzerfaust Records. Panzerfaust – which was the name of a Nazi anti-tank rocket – was then the only real rival to Resistance Records. This young man, who had recently graduated from the University of Minnesota, was working on what Pierpont called 'Project School yard'.

The project was launched a couple of years later, with the goal of distributing free racist and anti-Semitic CDs and DVDs to 100,000 elementary, middle-school, and high school students, all across America. By the time Panzerfaust folded in 2005, over 50,000 students had been given these sampler DVDs and CDs.

He wanted to know if Resistance Records was interested in joining forces with Panzerfaust in these efforts. Had that happened, it would provide the FBI with new sources of information about the so- called movement, including the players involved. But I knew that Pierce would say no, because his company then covered 75 to 80 percent of the white power music market. Any joint efforts would disproportionately benefit this rival, with Resistance records splitting the cost. "Nice try," I told

Pierpont's rep. From the bureau's perspective, I wanted to accept his offer, and wished Pierce would've agreed. I recall thinking, as we talked, that had Panzerfaust been as well capitalized as Resistance, they wouldn't need a partner.

On the final night of the conclave, about 180 to 200 hard-core anti-Semites and racists gathered on a large tract of property owned by a Cleveland racist. This place was about 20 miles from Cleveland and each invitee was given a map with directions. I drove alone in my rental car. As each vehicle approached the property, men and women in Nazi-like brown uniforms required stops at three points before being admitted. Upon presenting my credentials and being waved through, I parked among about 60 other vehicles.

The weather cooperated beautifully for the evening. It was about 60 degrees under a moonlit sky, with no wind.

Folding chairs were arranged in a semi-circle around a bonfire which was surrounded by four burning Crosses. The logs and kindling comprising the bonfire were arranged in the shape of a Swastika. This presentation was no recruitment seminar or indoctrination lecture. Tonight's event was the for the True Believers, totally committed to the cause of Hatred.

"Hail, victory, my brothers and sisters in racial unity, and cultural solidarity," said the man who wore a Swastika armband on his left arm as he gave a Nazi salute. The audience heard about his neighbor's daughter, who brought home her out-of-wedlock, mixed-race child. "Just because this child contains your blood, your DNA," he told the group, "doesn't mean you should accept it as a worthy member of your family." From there, he segued to "Christ killers" – meaning, Jews – who "aren't like us." Jews were also denigrated as "deck stackers", and "global elitists" whose goal, he said, was "total world domination." He closed by lamenting the state of the United States, and Europe. "It's a sick world that condemns, instead of celebrates, the extermination of Jews." The applause was thunderous.

"We must educate the scores of millions of Caucasians in America and in Europe who can be considered favorable to our cause," he told the crowd. Heads nodded in agreement, with attendees yelling, "damn straight", and "right on". It was a white equivalent of parishioners in a black church, reacting favorably to the preacher's words. "Our opponents say we're paranoid, but enlightened vigilance isn't paranoia," he told his followers. Four 50-ish, barbershop quartet-style singers entertained the crowd with a bastardized version of the 1963 classic, 'Up on the Roof'. This hit song has been performed by many artists and bands, most notably by the Drifters. Their acapella, neo-Nazi version went like this:

"When Spicks, Coons, Kikes, and Queers get me down, I take my baseball bat out in the street –

when the time is right, I swing my bat hard, and on their heads, I start to really beat …

One by one, they fall down, to the … ground – and on their homely heads, I pound, and pound …

Well, lemme tell ya now, when I get home, the wife hugs me tight, 'cause white gals love a man

who fights the fight … Patriots know evil's ugly face; we do what's right for our Caucasian race …

Us Klansmen know just what we must do … shoot all wetbacks, Jews, Fags and jigaboos

I keep a-tellin' you, the Holocaust is just one big lie, but soon, it will become reality …

Spicks, Coons, Kikes, and Queers, will disappear – and then us whites won't have to live in fear …

Well, lemme tell ya, now, our Fuehrer would be so proud of us all, for pre-serv-in' racial pur-i-ty

And fixin' things for all eee-ter-ni-teey … "

Another bastardized tune they warbled was this version of Doris Day's 'Que, Sara, Sara':

"Niggers and Jews, and Spicks and Queers

Have wrecked our country, so, they must go

Ban 'em forever, they'll stay out, for good

That's how it must be, you know

Que, Sara, Sara, the Hebes will be gone, someday

Because that's the only way –

Que, Sara, Sara

Death to those evil Jews

Que Sara, Sara"

The late Doris Day would not have approved. But the audience adored these reworked songs and their racist lyrics. Three wicker baskets were passed and stuffed within 10 minutes. Nearly everyone had dropped twenties, fifties, even hundreds, into them. The planners of this event knew this audience the way Hollywood executives, political consultants and program directors understood how to appeal to their targeted demographic for maximum profitability.

Just as I returned to my hotel room, one of my FBI handlers called. He asked me why I hadn't notified him or his partner of a 'Spiritual and Enlightenment' seminar, which was scheduled to begin the following day. This event was in either North Carolina, or Georgia; I now don't recall. Attending so many such gatherings over the years somewhat blurred my memory. I remembered being invited, but it slipped my mind. The FBI wanted "coverage" at this event, so I flew there the following day. 25 or 30 of those present were members of the Confederate Hammer Skins, a group of young Skinheads and Hate Metal music fans to whom violence seemed to be second nature.

Local members of the National Alliance helped to organize this function, supervised by a fourth generation Klansman named Chester Doles. Regional Ku Klux Klan chapters were well represented, as were various Aryan Nations cells and other Holocaust denying organizations. Anti-Semitic publications were on display, as were books written by David Irving, David Duke, and Gregory Douglas.

The first speaker was well turned out, and she was ravishing. This lady was about 30-35 years old and dressed in all white. Her appearance was striking, and her remarks were dynamite to her admirers. She was as curvy as the gorgeous models who appear each year in the SPORTS ILLUSTRATED famed Swimsuit Issue. Her teeth were straight, white, and polished; her hair, light blonde. Her hair may not have been any more natural than her bosoms, but it made no difference to me, or anyone else. Her uncle was an influential member of the Council of Conservative Citizens, and was paid ten grand for her appearance.

Her provocative rhetoric elicited audience responses about every two minutes.

Here's an excerpt, along with the responses: "Jews rig the system to their advantage. Is that fair?"

NO

"When anyone gets unfair advantages, others get short-changed. You're the victims. Now, we all know that blacks get special privileges, just for being black. Do you like that?"

NO

"Shouldn't we stop racial quotas, affirmative action, and other anti-white nonsense that harms whites?"

YES

"Do YOU like being victimized by Jews who control the bans, media, the schools, and our government?"

NO

"Will you help to fight the Jews who've turned America into a Hell-fired, multicultural cesspool?"

YES

"The bible states that Jews won't go to Heaven. We all know that Hell is where they belong, and deserve to go, and WILL end up. When your earthly life is over, do YOU wish to go to Heaven?"

YES

"Do we want Jews and mud people up with us in Heaven, when our time comes?"

NO

"As Americans who love our country, and as PATRIOTS, will you help the cause of your fellow whites?"

YES

"Will you help us to expose the LIE known worldwide as the Holocaust?"

YES

"Y'all are just great people, and it invigorates me to be with you. You've restored my faith in the good old U S of A; you give me hope for the future. I love you." She blew a kiss to her fans, who she played like a fiddle. A beefy Skinhead whose .45 was holstered to her hip stayed at her side as she mingled with her fans. This was wise, as two guys flirted so blatantly with her that they were ordered to go outside.

One of them complied, but the other pushed his luck. He was promptly removed and told to exit the premises. Out in the parking area, he objected, and was pummeled in the face, and elsewhere. Three Skinheads then knocked him to the ground, stomped him hard, then tossed him, unconscious, into the back of his own pickup truck. No charges were filed, as doing so would have meant certain death for the complainants.

The July 22, 2003 edition of The Atlanta Journal-Constitution reported that Chester Doles was under investigation for 20 months by federal authorities, including the FBI. An informant was assigned to befriend Doles, and information he provided to the bureau helped to bring about a federal raid of his home. Doles was do dedicated to Nazism that he named his son Pierce, in honor of William L. Pierce, and named his daughter Aryana. Nearly 70 federal agents, according to neighbors, converged on the Doles home when he was arrested on weapons charges. Most of the agents wore bullet-proof jackets. Within days of Doles being locked up, a website was set up: www. freechesterdoles.com. It didn't take long for nearly eighty grand to be raised via this site.

I flew back to DC the next morning, which was Sunday. Linda met me at the Ronald Reagan airport. We met my parents for brunch at Martin's Tavern. Everyone noticed how preoccupied I was. But I couldn't discuss the specifics of what I'd seen and heard.

That night, I dreamed I was surrounded by uniformed Nazi guards at a German Concentration Camp. The nightmare ended as I was face to face with Adolf Hitler, who called me a race traitor and said I would hang from my neck until dead. When I awakened, Linda was as scared as I was. "You were yelling in your sleep, Todd" she told me. My pajamas were drenched in sweat. We got out of bed, and Linda changed the sheets. But I still couldn't sleep and went downstairs to sit by the fireplace in our den. I was shutting down emotionally, believing that the only way to deal with my stress was to get high.

I later learned that this response to the pressures of life is common among drug addicts. It prolongs addiction, and destroys friendships, careers, marriages, relationships with family members, and lives. In my case, violence had become as much a part of my life as my work for the bureau, and my drug usage. The following afternoon, I realized I'd not smoked crack in five days. Linda had gone to a co- worker's baby shower. By early evening, I wanted to get high. So I drove into DC, and called a junkie named Juanita, who I'd met about a year into my addiction. Juanita lived with her sister, LaTasha, in Sersum Corda, which was a public housing community in Washington, D.C.

It was known as "the Quarters" to many locals. Juanita was a great cook, and kept her place clean. The manager of her building knew she used drugs, but allowed it, as she did with other residents. Juanita also had superb connections with pushers whose product was consistently first rate. When I would send her out with $300 for crack, she always returned promptly and, as far as I knew, she never skimmed any coke off the top before bringing it to me.

When I arrived at her place, a dealer named Marquette was already there. He was a black man whose nickname was 'Corleone', and while he was cordial – as drug dealers go - he looked menacing. I don't use this term lightly, and not many people of any type intimidate me. But this dude was scary; his potential for violence was as evident as it was with any racist skinhead I was monitoring. Just as with certain white thugs, I sensed this guy could kill without thinking twice about it. It turned out I was right.

Thuggery comes in all colors, races, and backgrounds. Ghetto thugs, hateful Skinheads, and money-laundering, pedigreed white guys in suits are basically all the same. Greed, violence, and control are what these narcissists are all about. The nickname 'Corleone' also spoke volumes which confirmed my impression of him. Marquette, whose last name was Ward, sold me two 8-balls and took off. Juanita was right: the stuff was top-notch. I bought crack from Corleone several more times over the next two years. In January, 2004, Marquette 'Corleone' Ward hired a thug named Frank Thompson to kill a 14- year-old black resident of Sersum Corda. Jahkema 'Princess' Hansen had witnessed Ward fatally shoot a rival drug dealer named Mario Evans. Marquette Ward was afraid that she'd "snitch" to the police and hired Thompson to take her out.

Her murder took place on the same floor of the same building where Juanita lived – the very place I'd smoked crack with her and LaTasha. On the night I got high with these two sisters, our crack-smoking session was interrupted by a loud knock on their door. LaTasha opened the door to an ex-boyfriend of hers, a black man whose nickname was 'Night Latch'. Before he even sat down, he demanded a crack pipe, and asked for a lighter, saying, "Ahh needs me a hit!" His arrival definitely shattered the mood of the evening. Juanita later told me her sister let Night Latch in their apartment because she feared that not doing so could result in him shouting profane obscenities and loudly pounding on their door.

Such behavior could've attracted the attention of neighbors, who may have called the cops. So there we were. "Ah'm sayin', Ah wants me 'dat pipe, bitch! Gimme some hits and a lighter." We all offered him our pipes. "Why y'all in such a bad mood, Latch?", LaTasha asked. After he took his hit, Night Latch said he'd just "offed da wrong dude" a couple of hours earlier. But that didn't bother him. He was upset because the lady who hired him for the job refused to pay. "Bitch ain't gonna pay me now," he said, "and Ah needs 'dat money." He scooped up three ten-dollar-sized rocks from the coffee table and stuffed them in the pocket of his hoodie. "Well," Juanita replied, "Y'all can't blame nobody fo' bein' mad. I'm sayin, y'all s'pose to do a job. Bitch gots a right to expect you to not fuck it up."

Turning to Night Latch, LaTasha said, "'customer satisfaction' important, nigga. 'Dis be on y'all. You done messed up. Mmm-hmmm."

"Whatevuh" Latch mumbled, as he loaded another dime-sized rock into his pipe and took another blast.

LaTasha suggested Night Latch go back out and "get it right" – meaning, hunt down the man he agreed to take out, kill him, and collect his fee. "Ain't happ'nin' now", he replied "Nigga done leff outta town. Him runnin' scared, so him and he lady friend done skipped out. It be too late. Him gone." Juanita then said, "Y'all best hope yo parole officer don't find out what y'all done. I'm thinkin' 'dat killin' some nigga could be a violation. That P.O. finds out, Latch, and 'yo black ass goin' back to da big house."

LaTasha asked him if he'd been neglecting his court-ordered anger management classes. "Maybe Night Latch were thinkin' dem anger management classes would bend he mind in a way dat keep him from doin' he job," Juanita said. "Maybe him were thinkin' he might assault da teacher, so he just tryin' to do what bess for ever-body, umm-hmmm, and stay away," LaTasha replied.

Ghetto logic is in a class all by itself.

I asked Night Latch how much he was offered to kill the man. He said five grand. Another dealer later told me that Night Latch was friends with Marquette 'Corleone' Ward, who paid $8,000 to have the teenaged witness murdered. The price was higher on her head because she'd witnessed a murder which implicated Marquette.

Ironically, the Latin meaning of Sersum Corda is: Lift up your Hearts. In my years there, I saw broken hearts. Even the Feds were reluctant to set foot inside Sersum Corda, a fear which worsened when federal prosecutors were shot at while trying to interview witnesses to crimes. When the then-Mayor of D.C., Anthony Williams, visited the mother of the 14-year-old victim of Marquette Ward, a drug buy transpired within 30 feet of a police car. Elderly residents would help hide drug pushers out of fear of reprisal, and DC Police Sergeant John Brennan openly expressed his fear of having to send officers to Sersum Corda. The Peace Room was a Community center across the street from Sersum Corda.

Art work created by children is displayed there on what's called the Dream Wall. One of the banners read, "I have a dream of a world without guns." Sister Helen McCulloch was a nun who moved to Sersum Corda in the 1980s to try to help the poor community. But she moved out in the 1990s after her unit was burglarized and her car stolen. Nearly everything she owned was stolen – including CDs of religious music and her panty hose. Many of her personal items were sold in a parking lot a few blocks from Sersum Corda.

Sister Helen said she left because "the evil was becoming insurmountable." Two assistant U. S. attorneys and a police detective were fired upon by a cocaine dealer after they photographed a drug transaction. A drug dealer from whom I bought crack told me matter-of-factly that his then-girlfriend had been the shooter, and I had no reason to disbelieve him. Juanita knew a Sersum Corda resident, Antonio Davis, who was shot and killed at Sersum Corda in May, 2003, over a PlayStation video game. His killer, Felix Wood, shot Davis 13 times with a rifle. Wood then beat the victim so hard with the gun that it broke its wooden stock.

Marquette Ward and his buddy Frank Thompson went on trial for murder, and were convicted in 2006. During the trial, a key government witness was safely ensconced in jail. But when he was brought to testify against Ward and his accomplice, he was so high on marijuana that the defense moved to strike his testimony. Part of the problem in cases like this is what's called the anti-snitching attitude among residents of America's inner cities. These people learn from an early age not to cooperate with the authorities. In some cases, they're paid off. In others, they're threatened. Sometimes, witnesses knew people who snitched and died soon after as a direct result. As a member of D.C's Narcotics Anonymous program told me years later, "Snitches be bitches that needs stitches – or, they ends up in ditches."

That pretty well sums it up.

Marquette Ward and Frank Thompson were sentenced in January, 2007, to 196 years in prison. I was at Sersum Corda at least 50 times during the seven years of my addiction. I twice faced violence there, and in both instances, turned the tables on my would-be attackers. But the memory of my evening with Night Latch, Juanita, and LaTasha still haunts me. Especially troubling is what Night Latch told me as our crack smoking session ended. He said. "Just 'cause Is kill people for a livin' don't make me a bad dude."

The next evening, my wife and I joined my parents and U.S. Senator Chuck Grassley, and his wife, Barb, for dinner on Capitol hill at a restaurant called the Monocle. Also at our table was Congressman Tom Latham. The Directors of the Chambers of Commerce of Mason City and Clear Lake, Iowa, were in D.C. Our party occupied five tables in the back of the restaurant. Senator Grassley, on whose campaign I once worked, sat next to me. He'd known me since he was a state Representative running for the U.S. House. He asked how things were going. "You don't seem to be yourself tonight, Todd. Is everything okay?", Senator Grassley asked. I nodded, and said, "I'm okay, Senator."

Everyone suspected otherwise. What kind of person was I becoming? I wasn't raised to be part of anything which was hateful or racist, or to associate with murderers and Nazis. My parents, my brother, sister, grandparents, and great-grandparents (whom I knew), and aunts, uncles, and cousins, were and are good people. My upbringing was solid. I regularly attended church, and was a Boy Scout. I played Little League baseball, ran on the high school Track team, and had a newspaper route. I was a good kid who was raised right. But to judge from those with whom I was associating and my activities, I was as much of a low-life as any racist skinhead, or drug thug.

I personified downward mobility, and due to my addiction, I didn't care. At this point, I no longer enjoyed working for the FBI. My chief concern was getting high. That night, I realized that my marriage was in serious jeopardy. A drug addiction is like a jealous mistress, demanding of time, emotion, money, effort, and affection. It's also like cancer that insidiously destroys its victims – inside, and out.

The offices of Dr. Ronald Weiner, in downtown D. C., were on the 8th floor of what, by DC standards, is a high-rise building. Unlike every other major city in America, DC has no buildings which are over about thirteen or fourteen stories. By law, no building can exceed 130 feet tall.

"I'm Jewish, Dr. Weiner said. "Does this bother you?"

"No."

"Then we're off to a good start, aren't we? But I read newspapers and watch TV, and I've seen what's on the internet. You've got a rather interesting history."

"Are you here because you want to be, or because your wife and your parents want you to be?"

"Both."

"Your wife thinks you may have a mild bipolar disorder. You're clearly under stress, and I can see you're skillful at hiding it. What we discuss here stays here. It's doctor-patient privilege, which is legally and professionally protected." That was a relief, which helped me to open up to this good man. After an awkward silence, he asked, "Okay, Todd, what are you thinking right now?"

"I'm really fucked up."

"On that, we agree. So, let's get to work, shall we?" This initial session with the Doc ended after an hour. I drove home to Virginia, where Linda and I enjoyed a quiet dinner and discussed my first appointment with my therapist. That night, I wondered if I'd ever be able to tell my psychologist about my addiction. If I did, could he help me? Could anyone? I drifted off to an uneasy sleep.

The next day agent Jones called my office. "We need a list of Resistance Records customers", he said. I told him I'd look for it, and try to get it to him. The only copy of that list – which was on a disc – was at Liberty Lobby head-quarters on Capitol hill, in an old safe Carto kept in a small apartment on the third floor. I knew the combination, but Carto had banned me from the building after our acrimonious break-up. I had to find some way to get inside.

I enlisted the assistance of a Liberty Lobby employee with the unlikely name of Dallas Texas Naylor. Aside from being intellectually challenged and physically clumsy, he weighed 350 pounds. He drove a red pick-up truck and wore rodeo boots and NASCAR caps. He was Liberty Lobby's custodian, and also picked up from and took mail to the Post office and ran other errands. He had the keys to the place. Dallas Texas Naylor's favorite restaurant was an all-you-can-eat place called Bob's Big Boy. These family-style, unpretentious restaurants were in Virginia and Maryland, and other states. I'm sure that after Dallas wiped out those buffets, the managers prayed he'd never show up again.

Carto paid Dallas Naylor a pittance, which, given his food addiction, gave me an ace in the hole. I played that card when I took him out to dinner at a dive in Arlington, Virginia called 'Whitey's', on Washington boulevard. Dallas and I had remained on good terms, and it paid off that night. The five hundred bucks I would offer him for his assistance in getting those computer disks would tempt him. We met at DC's Union Station. Completed in 1907, Union Station is on Massachusetts avenue, just a few blocks from the United States Capitol. During World War II, over 200,000 people regularly passed through Union Station every day. Beautifully restored in 1988, it is today one of America's major railway stations and transportation hubs. AMTRAK is headquartered there, and it is that line's second-busiest station.

Union Station also serves the MARC line, commercial bus lines, and Washington, D.C's METRO subway system, and commuter buses. It also features a large shopping mall. Each year, approximately 40 million people visit Union Station. Dallas Naylor's 400+ pounds were stuffed in some extra-large bib overalls, covering a bright red shirt. He wore heavy boots and a cap on which was emblazoned the Confederate battle flag. After trying to climb into my Range Rover, he finally chose to sit in the back seat, which accommodated him more comfortably. I jokingly told Dallas that it appeared he'd lost weight. He said he had, and he was serious. "Todd," he replied, "I can lose three pounds by a-brushin' my teeth." I wondered if the cost of tonight's dinner might be higher than my monthly health insurance premiums, which were about $300.

Whitey's was an old, blue-collar, neighborhood dive which served food that wouldn't make it on anyone's list of healthful fare. It was a noisy, greasy spoon kind of place, with regulars in nearly every booth. Being from Iowa, I was long accustomed to such spots.

That evening, Dallas Naylor polished off seven hamburgers, all with French fries. Then he scarfed up three four-piece fried chicken dinners – each with a salad, and rolls. He then wiped out an entire apple pie, straight from the pan, and two big dishes of vanilla ice cream. He drank eight or ten large glasses of Dr. Pepper, plus three or four cups of coffee. Dallas asked our waitress for six take-out containers of baked beans. "Midnight snack food," he told her. It was a relief that he didn't eat those beans there. Watching him eat was like seeing a human version of a hog feeding at the trough. "Dallas, how much does the buffet cost at Bob's Big Boy?"

Between bites of food, he said it was something like eight bucks for all you can eat. Once I explained that five hundred dollars would pay for 60 trips to Bob's Big Boy, he agreed to help me. On the way back to the District of Columbia, Dallas asked to stop at a Dairy Queen for some chocolate malts. "That apple pie was good, Todd" he said, "but it didn't fill me up."

As he slurped down three jumbo-size chocolate malts, I explained the plan. I knew that the combination to Carto's safe was 4-20-18-89: Adolf Hitler's birthday, April 20, 1889. The problem was going to be getting into the Liberty Lobby headquarters, and into Carto's private bunker on the third floor. Video cameras were positioned throughout the building, but none were in the apartment. The Liberty Lobby compound was comprised of two separate, three-level structures. No elevators. Willis Carto paid an anti-Semitic, drug-addicted black separatist named Greg Garnett to watch the place at night. The safe was in a locked room in Carto's private quarters.

Carto and Dallas Naylor possessed the only two keys, so I had to wait until Carto was at Liberty Lobby's California offices to make my move. As it turned out, Carto had left DC the day before Naylor and I met in Arlington, and wouldn't return for another week. There still remained the problem of the video cameras, especially inside. There was no way Dallas could turn them off or tape over the lenses. Ever since Carto's California offices were fire-bombed in 1984, he took extraordinary precautions to ensure safety and security at Liberty Lobby's Capitol hill headquarters. So Dallas, who died in 2004, came up with a brilliant idea. "Todd", he said, "I'm gonna build a shipping crate. You'll be inside of it for about 20 minutes, going in and going out. You climb inside the crate and I'll nail it shut. If anybody sees me wheel the crate inside, or coming back out, they won't suspect a gosh darn thing."

Sometimes, simple minds come up with some damn good ideas - especially when a 350-pound glutton is motivated by 60 paid trips to his favorite, all-you-can-eat buffet. Dallas asked me for a hundred and fifty dollars to solve the problem of the Louis Farrakhan fanatic, Greg Garnett. As it happened, the drug of choice of this black Nationalist was crack. Dallas said once Garnett got the cash, "he'd be as gone as a wild goose in the winter, and won't be back till tomorrow morning."

The crate was about five feet tall, by three feet wide, by four feet long. Dallas had constructed a small, built-in bench for me to sit on as I made the trip. Needless to say, sitting inside that hot, uncomfortably tight wooden crate was no picnic. But it was well-made and strong. The ride to Capitol hill was bumpy, and when we arrived at Liberty Lobby, Dallas hooked a metal truck on to the back of his pickup. Once the crate was on the sidewalk, Naylor tipped it onto a four-wheeled steel cart.

Air wasn't a problem; oxygen freely permeated my confines. He then went inside and gave Greg Garnett the money, telling him it represented what Dallas had recently remembered he owed him, from a long-ago bet on a Washington Redskins game. The Farrakhan fan was out the door in less time than it took Dallas to suck down his three Jumbo malts at the Dairy Queen; about 90 seconds.

My cell phone clock showed I'd been inside that thing for about 25 minutes when we arrived at Carto's headquarters. It was about 8 p.m., and Liberty Lobby was empty. Once inside, Dallas said he'd check to make sure no one was there. Meanwhile, I remained inside the crate. Ten minutes later, he was back in the receptionist area. The trip to the third floor began then.

Referring to Greg Garnett's drug addiction, Dallas said "that damn nigger loves smokin' that crack. How can anybody be so stupid, usin' that shit?" At the base of the first stairwell, Dallas transferred the crate from his four-wheeled cart to a two-wheeler. Then he tipped the crate backwards, and, one step at a time, lugged the crate up the stairs. The same process was repeated as he pulled me up the second flight of stairs. This was an old structure with 12-foot ceilings. That meant lots of steps on each stairwell. As we traversed each step, I was knocked around pretty good.

To get me back downstairs, he said, he'd position the cart against his back side and guide it down, one bumpy step at a time. Ten minutes later, I heard a door slam shut, and its lock clicked. "Okay, Todd, we're in the bunker," Dallas announced. Using the claw end of a hammer, he removed the top of the crate and I got out. Going directly to Carto's safe room, Naylor unlocked the metal door and waved me inside. By this time, I was wearing thick Latex gloves. 30 seconds later, the old safe was open. It was a late 1930s, or early '40s model, manufactured by MEILINK. It stood about four feet tall, and maybe 30 inches wide and three feet deep. Among other items, there were hundreds of plastic, airtight coin tubes, each holding about 30 Krugerrands. A Krugerrand is a one ounce gold coin issued by South Africa.

For many white supremacists, owning them is paying homage to apartheid. Each tube contained about worth $25,000 of gold. In today's dollars, a single Krugerrand is worth about $1,350. So, my eyes were focused, initially, on about $2.5 million worth of gold coins. In the upper left, on the middle tier shelf, were several computer disks. Among them were two which were marked, RESISTANCE RECORDS customer file: August, 1998. I took them both, because Carto had no legitimate claim to either one.

Also inside the safe were stacks upon stacks of uncirculated U. S. currency. Packets of $50 and $100 bills, like those that William Pierce brought to my office. Did this money also come from the ill-gotten stash of Bob Matthews? It was time to climb back in the crate and make the trip down. Before Dallas nailed me back in, he pointed to a nice, upholstered chair in the corner. "See that chair, Todd?"

"Yeah, what about it?"

He told me that a Carto admirer had shipped it to him a few days earlier, but it had been down in the Shipping and Receiving area on the first floor. Dallas had waited until Willis Carto had left Liberty Lobby earlier that day to bring it up to the third floor. "If Willis asks me what I hauled up here," Dallas told me, "I'll tell him that it was this here chair." After a bumpy ride down the stairs, Dallas loaded the crate – with me inside - back onto the bed of his pickup truck. He then drove me back to the Kennedy-Warren.

Once in the underground parking garage, he pried open the top of the crate, and I climbed out. The experience made me feel like a dog or a cat that someone had shipped via U P S. He got his five hundred cash, and I placed the disks in the safe in my office. I then called the JTTF agent who had asked for a disk, and left him a voicemail message. "I've got the disk you want. Let me know where to meet." I also said on the recording that the next day wouldn't work for me. Now that my clandestine chore was completed, I wanted to buy some crack and smoke away.

By ten that evening, I had parked my Range Rover in the nearly empty parking lot of the GIANT grocery store where 'O' Street Northwest intersects with the 1400 block of 7th Street, N. W. I was to meet Andre', a twenty-some-thing coke dealer who specialized in top-quality crack. Right on time, Andre' pulled up in his beat-up Buick. Unlike other pushers, Andre' wasn't flashy. He knew that as a black man often on DC's streets after dark, and into the wee hours, the cops suspected him of selling drugs.

By not wearing fancy threads and driving an expensive car, he didn't flip the police off, figuratively speaking. Showing off their drug profits has landed many drug dealers in prison, so Andre' didn't provide law enforcement officers any extra reasons to despise him. Andre' got in my car and told me to drive around the block. He scanned the streets carefully as he slid his left hand down toward his high-top Air Jordan basketball shoes, talking the whole time. He pulled out two small Zip-Loc baggies, each about two inches square. Then he reached over and placed them into the outside right front pocket of my coat. I already had four Benjamins in my hand, which he palmed into his. "Y'all done hear about Quinteesha?"

She was a crack whore who used to live with a dealer we knew, who'd been sentenced to prison. The dude was serving time in the DC jail on what's called a Marshall's hold. The time served in jails following sentencing is usually, but not always, applied to the required sentence while it is determined to which prison the inmate is sent. "Quinteesha done messed wiff da wrong nigga. Now, she dead." As this crack whore destroyed her once-beautiful body and looks with drugs, her customers found her less satisfying. They switched to others who provided the same services who weren't junkies. At the same time, her dealer boyfriend was locked up.

His incarceration ended Quinteesha's steady, easy supply of crack cocaine. She agreed to buy fifty bucks worth of crack cocaine with her EBT (Electronic Benefits Transfer) card – Food Stamps, in effect. This type of transaction is very common in the hoods. All it requires is for the welfare recipient to call the 800 number which is on the back of the card. The drug-addict then punches in the numbers on the front of the card. A computerized voice states the amount of money which corresponds to the account that's available for purchases. This confirms to the drug dealer that the card is worth X dollars.

The addict then is given half of this amount in exchange for the EBT card. The dealer will later take the card to a grocery store and use it to buy groceries. But Quinteesha got greedy. Stupid, as well. Once the drug pusher left her apartment, she called the number on the back of the EBT card and declared it stolen. Two days later, a replacement EBT card was shipped to her via the U. S. Postal Service. She effectively cheated the dealer out of crack with a street value of $50, which, for him, was a $100 loss.

When the dealer tried to use the EBT card, a check-out clerk at the grocery store told him it was used up. Worthless. The next day, Quinteesha's grandmother found her dead in the tiny kitchen of her apartment. A 12-inch screwdriver had been pounded through her ear and completely through her head. The sharp tip of the shank was pierced clear through to her other ear, and then into the wooden top of her kitchen table. "The nigga 'dat done kill Quinteesha," Andre' told me. "Him done it wiff one of 'dem steam irons. Him swing dat joint like a damn sledgehammer, stabbed her, den him pounded da bidness end of dat screwdriver wiff dat steam iron right into she head."

By the time Andre' finished telling me about Quinteesha's painful demise, we were back in the GIANT parking lot. "Looky here, lightskin," Andre' said, as he handed me his cell phone. There, on the screen, was a photo of the dead junkie. Her head was on its side, impaled, in to the table. Her eyes were wide open, her mouth agape, with blood was pooled on the table. The red handle of the screwdriver pointed straight up from her ear. It looked like someone had affixed a candle atop the victim's head, directly onto her ear. I won't ever forget that horrific photo.

As Andre' got out, he said, "If y'all gonna keep smokin' this stuff, you gonna hear lots of 'dis kinda shit, my man. Get used to it." I asked Andre' when he thought Quinteesha's killer would be apprehended.

"Is you crazy, lightskin?", he asked. "That nigga ain't catchin' no charge."

"Why not? He brutally murdered someone over a small amount of crack cocaine, didn't he?"

"If she momma call da cops, da nigga dat done kilt Quinteesha be sendin' some niggas to do even worser" to she fam [family]. Dem peoples ain't doin' shit." I sat in stunned, disgusted silence.

"Later, dude. I'se gone."

I drove home and went straight to my downstairs den, and hid the $400 worth of crack in a corner of my desk drawer. I was too nauseated to even try to get high. After showering in the basement bathroom, I went upstairs to bed. Quinteesha never had a funeral, and her body wasn't viewed by any mourners. Anyone who thinks that this is unusual doesn't understand how things operate in the evil underbelly of America's hoods. Even cops fear certain gangs and the violence of which they're capable, and known to perpetrate. As of 2010, there were 3,479 unsolved homicides – open cases – in Washington, D.C., according to Thomas Hargrove, a reporter for the Scripps-Howard News service. The Washington Post reported on July 24, 2018 that of the 1,345 tracked homicides in DC between 2008 and 2018, 44 percent of these killings resulted in no one being arrested. Since 2010, FBI sources estimate, another 500 DC murders have gone unsolved. Each year in the U.S., 6,000 killers get away with murder, and since 1980, 211,000 homicides are still unsolved, according to the Scripps News service. Homicides are less likely to be solved in 2019 than they were in 1975. Nowadays, police don't make arrests in about one-third of such cases. Cleared cases, according to the U. S. Department of Justice, are those in which arrests were made and someone is handed over to the courts for trial. According to the FBI, the U.S. homicide clearance rate in 1976 was 90 percent. In 2012, it was 64 percent.

NPR reported in 2015 that "since at least the 1980s, police have complained about a growing 'no snitch' culture, especially in minority communities. The reluctance of potential witnesses makes it hard to identify suspects." No kidding.

By this time, I had met several times with Dr. Weiner. Seeing a therapist is like stripping naked for a physical examination while being cross-examined. This guy was so good at his profession that he often knew what I'd say before I even got the words out. "You began using coke because you were unhappy with your life, and with yourself. Your habit became an addiction, which is extremely dangerous, especially for someone who is bipolar. Every time you use, or venture into the hoods to cop your fixes, you're risking your life." I told him I knew this, but wasn't ready to quit. "Well, what about your parents, and your wife? Have you even considered how your sudden death would affect them?"

"Not really."

"That's typical, self-centered, addictive thinking," he said. "You've caused them heartache and misery, You've wasted years of their lives. Effectively, you've stolen from them, even if you've not taken money. You're NOT the only one who's suffering because you're a crackhead." After about thirty seconds of silence, he said, "if it doesn't bother you that people who love you are suffering, then I can't help you."

The no-nonsense Dr. Weiner meant what he said, and couldn't have been more adamant.

"My time's valuable," he told me, "and I prefer to spend it on patients who are at least willing to listen to my advice, and make the effort to improve their lives. That's because resolving their problems can also help others – innocent victims – to live happier, more productive, better lives."

Those words of wisdom truly resonated, and have remained with me to this day.

But I still kept smoking crack cocaine.

CHAPTER TEN

About a week later, I wanted to get high again. Linda was visiting her sister in Minnesota. I called Andre', whose stuff was among the most potent I'd ever used. We didn't meet until around 1:30 a.m. I had attended a reception with my parents on Capitol hill, and then joined them for a late dinner at the Jockey club. We left the place around 10 p.m., and I drove them to the Lansburgh. My mother and I talked for another hour, after my dad went to bed. She was concerned about the state of my marriage. I drove to a bar called Tryst, in the Adams-Morgan hood, and met J. Ralph for drinks. He knew I was using regularly, and lectured me for nearly two hours about the need to get help with my addiction. I dropped J. Ralph off at his apartment on 14th Street, N.W. While driving the twelve blocks to the GIANT store, at the corner of 7th and 'O' Streets, N. W. I called Andre'.

Andre' lived two blocks from the grocery store, and got there as I arrived. He was smoking a KOOL, and knew he couldn't smoke in my Range Rover. I walked over to him and fired up a cigarette. When we finished chatting, we each reached into our pockets. In my hand were four hundred dollar bills. Andre's hand held two good-sized bags of crack, each one containing ten smaller bags, each with a value of $20. They're called 'Dubs' because – as I've mentioned - each bag is worth twenty dollars. Andre' walked back home as I went back to my car. Unlocking it with my remote, I opened the door and sat down in the driver's seat. Turning on the ignition, I geared it into reverse. It was time to go get high.

At least, that was the plan. But in the hood, plans often go awry.

I was about to press the lock button when a black man opened my door, and stood in the space in between the open door and my vehicle. "Who the hell are you?", I asked . "Gimme some stuff, dude, and I be on my happy way." This guy obviously had seen my drug purchase go down, and was Jonesing. It was 2:50 a.m., according to the clock on my dashboard, and the last thing I needed was to be extorted by an enterprising, sneaky crackhead. "Leave. Now." He grinned at me, and made it clear he wasn't moving until he got some crack. I reached into my pocket, pulled out my .380, and aimed it at his chest.

"Dude," he told me, "y'all gots lots to lose. You not riskin' it by shootin' me." He was right, and wasn't scared. "Besides," he correctly said, "they ain't no silencer on 'dat piece. Y'all ain't killin' no nigga over fo' dime bags of crack."

"Four? That's your price?"

"I'll settle fo' three."

"You get nothing. Now, move." The jerk smiled at me, crossed his arms, and said, "Ain't goin' nowhere, dude, not till y'all gimme three dime bags. Den I'se gone." I had already shifted into reverse while he made his threat. All I had to do was remove my foot from the brake pedal and hit the gas. "That's your final warning." I said. "You've got five seconds to get outta my face" He didn't move, but the car did.

Fast.

With my gun still in my right hand, I slammed the pedal to the floor, which jerked the vehicle 15 or 20 yards backward. The homey never stood a chance. I planted had my left foot against the car door while accelerating, and pushed out my left arm to make sure it didn't close. So, instead of the car door swinging shut on him, it stayed in place as the vehicle reversed, knocking him to the blacktop in under two seconds. Due to the height of the Range Rover, the base of the door was at least two and a half feet above the ground. He hit the asphalt face-down, with no time to break his fall, and stayed down as the car kept going.

Two seconds later, I braked and then slammed the car into forward. I pulled the door shut, hit the lock button, and drove right past him. From my rear-view mirror, I watched him get up as I drove away. He brushed himself off and waved to me with both hands, with one finger of each. While driving to the Braxton hotel, the thought hit me: I'd just risked injuring, or possibly killing, a junkie, over thirty bucks worth of crack. What did that say about me? Just because I wasn't a thief or a ruthless hitman didn't mean I couldn't turn into a bad person. Was I dooming myself to an eternity in Hell, with Adolf Hitler?

A couple of weeks later, I feared I was in a Hell on earth, and about to die, at the hands of a corpulent, seedy bigot. The fat, racist hillbilly who had organized the gathering was missing about half his teeth. He had obviously lived fast, and hard. He wore a NASCAR cap and spoke with a cigarette dangling from his lips. "C'mere," he said, pointing at me. "Me and my boys wanna talk to y'all." This was in North Carolina in the midsummer of 2001. The JTTF had sent me there to monitor the attendees of an all-day picnic, followed by a cross-burning, and then a speech the next morning. These events were sponsored by several regional chapters of various Hate groups. As I walked toward this fellow and a few others, the picnic had just begun. I had no idea of what they wanted. Once we were apart from the crowd, the man came right to the point. "We hear tell President Bush done give yore Daddy some sorta fancy Judge title, in Washington, DEE-cee", he said, with the accent on the 'D'.

As he spoke, one of his cronies squirted a load of tobacco juice from the side of his mouth. The National Alliance member to his left, with lightning bolts inked on both forearms, dragged on a cigar. That dude said, "some of us is a-thinkin' yore just a little too uppity fer us folks."

"Foll-uh me," another said, with a wide sweep of his arms. As we walked about 50 yards toward an old, unpainted barn, two more members joined us, each well over six feet tall and at least 250 pounds. I did my best to appear as cool as possible. "What's up?," I asked. "We'll deal with that when we-all's behind them there closed doors," the ringleader replied, without looking back at me. The inside of the dusty barn reeked of mold, and cobwebs were throughout the place. As the bearded guy flicked the light on, the sound of the switch reminded me of those from my grandmother's house in Pleasantville, Iowa.

"We been suspectin' y'all might be a motherfuckin' FED, and we're gonna find out, one way or t'other," one of the beefy creeps said. "We ain't a-sayin' that y'all ARE a damn rat, a-spyin' on us. But if that's the case, well, we'll deal with it," the shortest one told me. With five sets of suspicious, beady eyes on me, I said something along the lines of, hey, that's crazy, guys. I then asked them where they'd heard this. "It don't matter none. That's our bidness," the other fat racist said.

After I'd made it clear I wasn't a 'Fed', I hoped they believed my lie. I detest dishonesty, and I'm not a good liar. Lying makes me uncomfortable and I feared they were unconvinced. A redneck then removed a switchblade from his front pocket. "Well, now," one of them replied, "ain't that nice?" While they exchanged glances, the guy with the NASCAR cap said, "Assumin' yore tellin' the truth, then y'all won't have no problem with what we goin' make ya do." He then nodded to the guy standing next to him. Reaching into the front pocket of his striped overalls, that one pulled out a bag of powder cocaine. "Well, then, boy - since you ain't no Fed, why, we wanna see y'all snort a few lines of this here.

'Cause no Feds ever gets away with a-snortin' coke", he said, looking directly at me.

"Yessiree, this here's the moment a-truth," another said, nodding his head up and down. He handed his buddy a one dollar bill. The man rolled it, and handed it to me. He then poured the cocaine out on the table between us. As he poured, two of his buddies positioned themselves on each side of me. One of the fat dudes got in front of the door. The guy at the table pulled out a bank card and neatly chopped the small pile of powder coke into three lines. Each line was about four inches long and maybe three millimeters wide, approximately an inch and a half apart. "You want me to snort this?"

They all silently nodded. The ringleader said, "All. Three. Lines."

With my left index pressing against my left nostril, I bent down to the table. Upon inserting the rolled-up dollar bill inside my right nostril, I inhaled. After making the first line of powder vanish, I looked up at my hosts. They were exchanging glances as a snorted up the remaining two lines. By the time I finished, my nose tingled. The effects of the drug were slower in taking effect than when free-basing, or smoking crack, but I convinced my hillbilly skeptics I wasn't a 'Fed', despite my being one. I probably came closer to convincing them I was a cocaine fiend. By being accustomed to smoking so much crack, the powder cocaine's effect on me was minimal. "Buford, he ain't no Fed," was the verdict.

"Okay, let's get back to the party," said another, as we walked toward the door.

Later, I became slightly jumpy, and felt an instant jolt of energy. But snorting coke was nothing like crack; its effect was milder, and wore off in about 20 minutes. The quick dissipation of the euphoric feeling created by cocaine is a major factor in the high financial cost of coke addiction. The same amount of crystal meth costs about half as much as crack, and about one-fourth as much as powder cocaine, and the effects last far longer.

Due to the massive amounts of crack that my body was then acclimated to, I remained in full control of myself after snorting their cocaine. I was also relieved that in my hurry to get to the picnic, I had left my recording device back at the hotel. "He sure as fuck AIN'T no Fed," the ringleader told a man who was outside, awaiting the verdict. Later, we shook hands and they apologized for having suspected me. The picnic was in full swing, with a five-musician band playing a cross of racist bluegrass and rockabilly-style music. This band showcased what were called 'hate-billy' tunes. The sponsors featured no heavy metal or rock music, as that would've alienated this crowd, which was primarily older, more rural, and with several members who likely used Poli-Grip.

About 15 minutes into the picnic, an enormous woman with a beehive hair style suddenly stuck her fingers in her mouth and wolf-whistled. Her loud, shrill whistle got everyone's attention. "Listen, up, y'all", she began, and announced a "moment a-silence" to honor Byron de la Beckwith. This was the third event that year I had attended since his death in 2001 where this murderer was so honored.

An even more obese, middle-aged lady with bleached blonde hair wept during the two-three minute silent tribute to the killer. When the silence ended, this gal, who wore Swastika earrings, raised both of her arms toward the blue sky. She shouted, "We love ya, Byron. When I get up there, I'm huggin' ya, darlin'. Y'all done real good fer yore race, sugar plum; the Lord loves ya fer what you done. That's why yore up there in Heaven, instead of in Hell, with LBJ and Martin Lucifer Coon."

This racist mourned someone she'd never met, and expressed love for him for killing a good, innocent man in cold blood in front of his wife and their small children. It apparently didn't occur to her that wherever De la Beckwith was, it wasn't heaven. And it was rather smug of her to assume that she'd someday go to Heaven. I wanted to tell her where to go, but I knew she'd get there, unless she changed her ways and thinking.

Plans were made for a protest in front of the Israeli Embassy in Washington, D.C. The protest, in which over 250 neo-Nazis would participate, was scheduled for early January, 2002. I committed to attend the protest. One of the activists planning this protest was an elderly, longtime anti-Semite named Jamie Von Brunn. He was 80 years old and had served time in federal prison.

With his index finger and thumb an inch apart, Von Brunn said, "I came this close to knocking off every damn member of the Federal Reserve Board. The Jews arranged for me to be sentenced to prison for that." Fulfilling my role as a sympathetic fellow racist, I replied, "Leave it to Jews to screw up our efforts to take back OUR country." His aged face instantly crinkled into a smile as he said, "I like you, Todd! Haven't we met?" I reminded him we'd met many times. He was a distributor of two Liberty Lobby publications, The SPOTLIGHT weekly newspaper, and The Barnes Review monthly magazine. I learned early on that people will talk if you agree with them, or at least appear to, and bring humor into the discussion. Von Brunn told me all about himself, and cracked jokes about blacks, Gays and Mexicans.

At this picnic, everyone else listened to the speaker, a wealthy Atlanta lawyer and investor with some longstanding movement ties. "Our goal is to take revenge on the forces – people – who've destroyed the America that's best for white people," he said. "We must focus on the long-term picture, and plan accordingly." The so-called long-term picture he referenced meant organizing outraged, anti-Semites to perpetrate violence against the U. S. government. If this meant bombings, assassinations, and sabotaging municipal water supplies, that was fine with him.

It was fine with his listeners, too, who lapped up his message. "Our Wal-Mart economy progressively swallows up tens of millions more working-class white people. We don't want a nanny state, and we will stop our government from dividing up our birthright and redistributing it to blacks and other minorities, including Illegal aliens, and those whom Hitler called 'useless eaters'," he told the crowd.

"Laid-off factory workers, displaced white families, and enlightened activists like all of you," he said, "are in need of a permanent solution. The Jews, with help from the blacks, have neutered your chances to achieve the American Dream to which white people are entitled. Politicians don't care about you, and won't ever restore America for you, or your children, or grandchildren. We must take responsibility for our destiny, and alter the political terrain." After a brief pause, he went in for the kill. He said, "the only way to bend the course of history to our liking is to drastically alter America's demographics. We must destroy this multi-racial, Jew-ordained cesspool of multiculturalism."

He meant every word, and the audience agreed with all of it. This speaker wasn't referring to deporting Hispanics who are illegally on U. S. soil, and keeping Illegal aliens out. He was saying that all minorities, including some U. S. citizens, should be eliminated – and the sooner, the better.

After the speech, I sat among several younger men and three women. The average age was about 35. They explicitly voiced their fears, some of which were actually valid. "I can barely feed my family on our income, after payin' my mortgage and taxes," one guy told me. "The wife, she's a-working. Gots to, ain't no two ways of it," he complained. His voice's bitter tone was of disappointment, dashed hopes and feeling exempted from The American Dream. It was impossible to not feel sorry for these people, who truly comprise the backbone of America. It's also easy to see why they are so disillusioned about politics, government, their leaders, and their own futures. But they don't realize, or seem to care, that throwing in with evil is an inappropriate response to their fears.

Affiliating with the violent, racist far right is, for these worried, pessimistic American men, is almost a way of reclaiming their manhood. "Bein' here," one twenty-something racist told me, "sorta makes me feel like I'm a man that stands up for myself, my woman, and our two boys. And ain't that what a man's s'posed to do, 'specially if he's hitched to a woman that's done popped out his kids?"

While I condemn all unjust violence, racism, and hatred, and detest those who exploit such fears, it's easy to understand the paleo-conservative view of today's USA. History proves that the United States has been the best nation on earth for minorities. As Muhammad Ali said, as he left Africa on a plane: "I'm glad my ancestors didn't miss the boat," referring to slave ships. A young man I sat with began singing a few bars from a song called, 'No crime being White'. The band which recorded it was called 'Day of the Sword', and Resistance Records was its distributor. The tune's lyrics, while obstreperous, specifically address his concerns:

"The birthplace is the death of our race; our brothers bein' laid off is truth we must face – Take my job, it's Equal Opportunity; after all, your people were oppressed by me. I put in twenty years, but my country favors gooks, niggers, and queers - well, what about me, and my so-called Golden Years?" The young racist then said, "we've had our nuts cut off by Jews, niggers, spicks, and queers. The politicians, the laws and the judges ain't on our side. That's why we'll shake things up," he promised. "Once we get started, Jews and niggers will last about as long here as grasshoppers in a hen house. You'll see."

It was as like these haters were playing a bigoted version of 'Pick a card, any card', in which all problems, once identified, were blame on Jewish people. To them, Jews are causal to all of their troubles, and the only way to solve such problems is to eliminate them. A reformed ex-bigot named T. J. Leyden left the realm of hatred in the late 1990s. Interviewed about his former life as a full-time, professional anti-Semite, Leyden said, "our main goal became the elimination of the Jew from the world. We included other enemies, like blacks, homosexuals and physically challenged people… ", but Jews were always their chief target. Regarding those who funded the HATE milieu, Mr. Leyden observed: "Another interesting and compelling fact to me was that white power wasn't backed by a bunch of rednecks in the woods. There were doctors, lawyers, ministers, and even software moguls behind the cause; it's about suits, not boots!"

When a reporter asked about the important role played by the internet and racist music in recruitment of young HATE activists, Leyden said, "if I filled a room with 1,000 neo-Nazi Skinheads and asked them, 'what's the single most important thing that influenced you to join the neo-Nazi Skinhead movement?', probably 900 of them would say the music." Experience proved Leyden correct. Toward the end of this gathering, several college kids who were National Alliance members appealed for funds. A well-spoken, clean-cut young man who looked about 21 years old said he needed to raise $1,000 to print 250 posters for distribution on his campus. A very attractive young lady of about his age then displayed a 3.5' X 3' poster featuring an early 1940s era black and white likeness of dozens of Hitler Youth kids.

Each teenager in the photo held a canister of Zyklon-B gas, which was used to exterminate Jews and others deemed by the Nazis as undesirable. The banner below the enlarged photo read, in bold letters, 'GOT JEWS?' The young lady then told the crowd about computer mouse pads. She wanted to raise $1,200 to produce 500 mouse pads – an inflated price, incidentally - featuring a likeness of Adolf Hitler, with the caption, "I was RIGHT!" Three baskets were then passed among the crowd. In under ten minutes, the students raised enough cash to print the posters and produce their mouse pads.

The weekend ended with an encore performance by the 'Hate-billy' band. One of their songs was to the tune of 'Silver Bells', which is a popular Christmas song. The lyrics included these stanzas:

'Burning Jews, burning Jews; it's Holocaust in the city – I'll blaze a few, just for you; we'll snuff out every He-brew … Hitler warned us, made some Jews dust, but too many went free; us white Chris-tians must now save our country … Jimmy Carter, Bush, and Reagan, and 'ol slick Wil-ly, too; they love Jews, but they care not for you… Burning Jews, Burning Jews, your race is countin' on you …'

A couple who appeared to be in their sixties held hands as the band played. As the song ended, the lady told her husband she wished "Burl Ives was still alive", so that the folk singer could record this version of "that lovely song." Several people asked the bandleader if they could buy a CD of their music. Some of the songs were available on CD, the lead vocalist told them. But 'Burning Jews' wasn't, because the original lyrics to, and melody of, 'Silver Bells' was owned by songwriter Ray Evans and protected by U.S. copyright law. "Ahh betcha he's a Jew," a lady sneered. As she spoke, her upper dentures came loose.

A few days later, back home in Virginia, Linda reminded me of my appointment with Dr. Weiner the following afternoon. As we talked, my cell phone rang. A DC-based JTTF agent asked to meet with me later on the same afternoon I was to see Weiner. Our house in Annandale featured a paneled den with a fireplace and built-in bookshelves lined with over 3,000 books, where I spent much time. Linda, who often rose early, for her job at Fairfax hospital, often went to bed early. By 10:30, she was asleep while I was downstairs. By that time, I was Jonesing, needing some crack, and wanted to get high. I had learned to park my car either in our driveway or on the street, and not in our garage.

That way, my departure would go unnoticed by Linda. On the way to DC, I called Kenny, who usually had the best stuff at all hours. We agreed to meet in Anacostia. 30 minutes later, Kenny and I met up by some trash dumpsters in an alley which was about a half block long. The exchange took place behind three dumpsters, as we kept our eyes peeled for anyone who might see us.

Seeing no one, Kenny handed me two 8-balls of crack and took my three C-Notes. Ten seconds later, we silently bumped fists, and then went our separate ways without a word. I was about 50 yards from where the alley ended and met with the side street where I'd parked my Range Rover when three young punks – all wearing hoodies – appeared from behind some large trash receptacles. I instinctively placed my right hand over my front pants pocket. As they were 20 feet in front of me, they stopped, and so did "Y'all know what 'dis be, right?" I said nothing.

"Give it up, dude." This spokes-thug demanded my watch, cash, cell phone, car keys, wedding ring and wallet. Another said, "give us 'dem drugs we done seen y'all buy from da nigga. Dey's in yo' pocket."

I said, "Seriously?" It was clear that between them, they had no weapon, with the possible exception of a switchblade. Another said, "Give us yo shit, and maybe you ain't gotta go to da E.R. We not playin'." The spokes-thug then added, "Him know we serious." Facing me, he said, "Dis here be for real." These dumb malefactors thought they'd hit a payday. The spokes-thug added, "Don't makes us teach you how things works in dis hood. Dey's three of us."

"There won't be," I warned, with a .22 caliber Fabrique Nationale aimed their way. This Belgian-made handgun was loaded with hollow-point, 'cop-killer' rounds that explode on impact. I flicked off the safety as the chrome handgun flashed before them in the dim lights. Then I pulled back the slide, chambering a round. Looking directly at the mouthiest one, the ringleader, I ordered them to step back and shut up. "Put your hands on top of your heads if you want to keep 'em," I said. They all complied. The

279

shocked, open-mouthed expressions on their wide-eyed, suddenly silent faces reminded me of some clueless JEOPARDY contestants who were stumped by the Daily Double.

There was no chance they'd get shot, but they didn't know that. With their hands on their heads, I told them to turn around, face the brick wall, and "Stay put." I walked backwards about 100 yards to the side street where my vehicle was parked. Once I got to the street, my .22 was safely back inside my pocket. I turned around, and shouted, "Go home, boys. You'll live longer." I also thanked them for teaching me how things work in the hood, and told them that I'd heard "this hood's dangerous."

Driving away, I decided against getting high that night. I'd had enough excitement for one evening. I drove back to Virginia and got home shortly after midnight. I stored the two 8-balls behind some books in my basement office. I learned the next day I'd forgotten to remove my gun from my pants pocket. Our cleaning lady found it as she loaded the washing machine. She wasn't pleased. Even on minor things, I was messing up my life. Now, even our cleaning lady was upset with me.

Most FBI informants aren't paid, and don't provide full-time service to the bureau. Most paid FBI informants who work full-time today still aren't compensated at the level I was. In many instances, informants work to get a lighter sentence, or have charges dropped, altogether. The attractive offer I received was made, in part, because of my surveillance-ready contacts within the realm of white supremacy, hatred, and Holocaust denial. Of added interest to the bureau was the fact that I had no criminal record, and had already been granted a top-level security clearance by the FBI and the U.S. Secret service for my position on the White House staff. I also had the extra advantage of not being under indictment, and didn't have to cut any kind of deal with prosecutors.

They also knew I knew most of the tricks of the trade concerning funding of the movement, and how the top players laundered dirty cash, evaded taxes, and bilked their contributors. David Duke, in late 2000, was in the DC area for several days. He made appearances before Cotterill's organization, 'The American Friends of the British National Party', and met with several members of the National Alliance.

I notified the agents of Duke's impending visit a few days before he arrived in Washington. On his first evening in town, I took Duke and Cotterill to dinner at the Palm, in downtown D.C. The three of us sat in a booth near the back. The manager, Tommy Jacomo, was a longtime buddy of mine. Tommy is a great guy who always got me a good table at his restaurant. At one point, I left the table to take a cell phone call outside the Palm. As I walked back in, Tommy took me aside and asked if that was David Duke who was at my booth. I said it was. Tommy shot me look of disapproval, and shook his head from side to side. He said nothing, and didn't need to. Things like that were what made my life as an informant very hard. But I couldn't reveal that hosting the infamous KKK leader was part of my job.

Shortly after signing on with the FBI and JTTF, an IRS agent with whom I became good friends, took me to dinner. We discussed many topics, and he repeatedly urged me to take good care of myself, and to not let my work interfere with my marriage, or relations with my parents, friends, and family. How I wish I could've done that. In my view, if people who are recruited by the FBI to work as full-time, paid confidential informants already lead troubled personal lives, they should decline the bureau's offer.

This is particularly timely since the bureau became so politicized after James Comey became its director in 2013. I followed this closely, and have since it became known that under President Obama, the FBI, IRS, and the Department of Labor, also were chronically political. In 2016, the FBI received information compiled by informants with connections to former British intelligence agent Christopher Steele. Mr. Steele's spies had gathered and furnished to him information about Donald Trump. Steele was then a private investigator whose services were retained by a Trump business rival. As is now known, in an effort to undermine Trump's campaign, he provided the documents gathered by informants to an FBI contact in London in the summer of 2016.

As a former Moscow-based MI6 undercover agent, Mr. Steele – who'd also worked with the FBI and CIA - had impressive Russian ties. My bureau contacts told me that the FBI authorized a $50,000 payment to Steele in return for release of the documents he gave his FBI contact and for providing additional reports along the same lines. However, the additional reports never materialized. The realm of professional, FBI and CIA full-time informants is murky, dark and fraught with danger. I'm glad it's over, but I don't regret the years I spent doing it. But the fact that I wasn't fired during my first month as an addict still amazes me.

The offices of George F. Baker, III, were at Baker-Nye Investments, Inc., in midtown Manhattan, near Central Park. I had met Mr. Baker in 1993, through some mutual friends. He and I hit it off, and in early 1999, he invested $50,000 in a direct mail venture in which I and my dad were the other two investors.

The company was called Donor List, L.L.C., a limited-liability corporation. It had no employees, and did well financially; by late 2000, the three of us had recouped our initial investment. From there on, it was pure profit. Donor List was profitable because it owned mailing lists which were rented to commercial, political, and charitable mailers. The files were managed by a northern Virginia-based direct marketing firm called Diamond List.

Twice a year, usually in February, and in August, I would visit Mr. Baker's offices and he would take me to lunch. George Baker was a family man, and was the namesake of his great-grandfather, George Fisher Baker, who was an industrialist and a prominent banker in the early 20th century. George F. Baker, III, was very conservative and adamantly opposed political correctness. In August, 2001 – just before 9/11 – I took AMTRAK to New York City, and met with George Baker in his office. I called the New York Athletic club and reserved a guest room there, under my dad's name. My parents were members of a club in Iowa, The Embassy Club, and the University club of DC, which had reciprocity with NYAC, as the New York Athletic club is known. The club's location was ideal, and I liked its food.

Its rooms were less costly than at the Essex House and other hotels. Its library was extensive and the drinks poured by the old bartenders were stiff. Its thick carpets, oak-paneled walls, musty books on the shelves, and brass sconces brought back memories of my fraternity house, where I had lived as a student at Drake university in the 1980s. As far as anyone there knew, my dad would be staying there with me. Upon arrival, I was given a key to the room. Shortly after checking in, my cell phone rang. It was a drug dealer named Pinball, who consistently sold some of the most potent crack cocaine I'd ever smoked. Seeing his number appear on my cell phone made me want to get high.

Addiction can be almost Pavlovian, in how things trigger junkies, causing a direct reaction to the stimulus. Hearing Pinball's familiar voice increased my desire to get high. "Yo, Mist Todd, 'dis here be Pinball. Ahh gots me some of da bess damn shit y'all ever goin' gets. 'Dis here shit be da bomb." I told Pinball I wasn't anywhere near the DC housing project where he lived. "I'm in New York," I said. "Well, lightskin, it just happen 'dat 'dis stuff done come here from New Yoak city. Does ya'll wants me to tell my boy to call him supplier, so's you can get ya some?" Pinball was offering to have local DC supplier contact the wholesaler in New York. That sounded good. "How much ya'll wants, dawg?"

I said I'd take an 8-ball, which he said would cost $200. I agreed. He asked for the club's address, phone number and my room number. He said he'd call back on the land line. Ten minutes later, Pinball called; the supplier was on the way. The guy would call me from the club's lobby. No fucking way, I said.

A drug dealer at the New York Athletic club would fit in like Rush Limbaugh at a dinner party hosted by Nancy Pelosi. Pinball called the pusher back and told him to meet me outside the club. "I'm-a gives you a password," Pinball said. "He gonna axe ya what it be. Y'all say Iced Tea." I didn't know then that Iced Tea was the name of a black rap artist and TV star. Pinball asked me what I was wearing, so he could tell the drug pusher. "Plaid jacket, khaki pants, light blue, button-down shirt, red necktie, argyle socks and brown loafers," I replied. "Hey, Lightskin," he replied, "don't every whitey at 'dat club wearin' dat? A few minutes later, the pusher called. "Who 'dis?," he asked. Upon identifying myself, he asked me the password. Upon my saying, 'Iced Tea', he said, "Okay. I just done crossed me Seventh avenue. I'se on 58th street. Where y'all is?" I told him I'd be down in five minutes. He was near the back entrance of the NYAC, about a half block from Central Park south. He was driving a black Honda Accord with New Jersey license plates and spinners. 'Spinners' are the fancy, solid chrome, shiny hubcap covers which rotate as the car moves. They're popular with drug dealers, pretentious, middle-aged owners of high-end vehicles and white guys in their twenties who think they're rebels. A rotating outer plate is encased over the hubcap which spins in an eye-catching way, guaranteed to draw attention.

Riding in a drug dealer's car with spinners spinning, as I bought crack cocaine in the heart of midtown Manhattan, wasn't smart. But as I was Jonesing, nothing would to stop me from getting my fix. One of these days, I thought, I'll get busted by the cops, and go to jail. Hopefully, it wouldn't happen today. I got the drugs, and the equipment. The pusher let me out of his vehicle about a block from the club. Back in my room, I grabbed a towel off the rack, and placed it in the bathroom lavatory. Once it was wet, I carefully arranged it along the space between the door to the room and the carpeted floor.

This was to prevent the aroma of crack smoke from escaping. I turned off my cell phone and smoked crack for the next six hours. Before meeting Mr. Baker for lunch, I downed a third of a bottle – a fifth – of Jack Daniel's. If George Baker noticed anything wrong, he didn't mention it. He was a classy man.

Upon returning to D.C., my travel schedule was packed. The bureau sent me to white supremacist's cook-outs, religious services, three-day conferences and seminars, and to meet with benefactors whose donations funded these events. Such interactions provided me with the perspective of these haters, and their reasons. Consistently, they said that they truly believed that blacks, Jews, and other minorities were fundamentally different from whites.

As such, went their thinking, they simply weren't entitled to the same treatment. As one rich racist told me, at his country club in Savannah, Georgia, "we can't have equal rights when not everyone's equal." Many of these people were still upset that the Confederacy lost the War between the States, and some were clearly irate that the Nazis had lost World War II.

The influence of wealthy backers of White Supremacy, Holocaust Denial, and organized hatred cannot be overlooked. Without such support, the reach, influence, and power of Hate groups wouldn't be any- where near the level it became, and still is. Willis Carto, William Pierce, David Duke, and other leaders in this milieu were highly adept at financial schemes which either scammed their supporters, or the IRS, or both. Effectively, they finagled ways to force U. S. taxpayers to subsidize their activities.

William Pierce's wealthy supporters would write substantial checks to churches whose ministers were friendly with pseudo preachers whose views mirrored Pastor Richard Butler's. The benefactor would then take the tax deduction, with the ministers splitting the funds, 75-25, with racist preachers, in favor of the neo-Nazis. In some instances where this scam was perpetrated, the donors of record didn't put a dime of their one money into the scam.

Pierce would provide the funds to a willing facilitator, whose check would be made to out the church. Once these ministers got the money, they'd turn over to a neo-Nazi pastor 75 percent. The cash then wound up wherever Pierce designated. The recipients included bands who were under contract to Resistance Records and smaller, newer local chapters of various white supremacist organizations. There were even times when such monies were used to bail skinheads out of jail, and purchase firearms, knives, and other weapons.

A young Alabama Klansman who stole, and the squandered a few thousand dollars on hookers and crystal meth was punished, severely, following a trial of his peers, in a KKK Tribunal. Three of his fingers removed. Without any anesthetics. He had been sentenced to lose only two fingers. But then he spat in the face of the brute who was removing them, with wire cutters. So he lost a third finger, in a post-sentencing action abruptly undertaken by the enforcer. Needless to say, this man no longer belongs to the Klan. He also never notified the law about what occurred, because he knows that ratting out his attackers means a sudden, certain, and violent death.

Obviously, violence – or, the threat thereof – plays a major role in racist politics. This includes some among the Black Lives Matter crowd, and some anti-Trump protesters. It's also a big part of the drug world. This results from the mentalities of those who operate in these realms. Environmental factors, life experiences, and interactions with others, all influence such thinking. But how do illegal drugs impact the thought processes of addicts?

Neurologists know that drug addictions affect the frontal lobe of the brain, which is the part that controls judgment. Looking back on my years of drug use, it's easy to realize how badly my judgment was impacted. Once the minds – cerebrums - of drug addicts are permeated with the effects of consistent drug usage, it alters the chemistry and structure of the brain. Over time, these changes lead to what's known as addictive thinking. This makes it difficult for junkies to kick their addiction.

The thought process of addicts is severely impaired, which can adversely affect nearly every decision they make, and actions they take. It goes with the territory. Trust me. The good news is that recovery from addiction can restore parts of the brain which were adversely impacted. Such cerebral parts regulate analytical ability and impulsivity. This means that while an addict uses drugs, making poor decisions with no regard to their consequences will be commonplace.

Cocaine addicts and meth junkies consistently show increased activity in the ventral striatum, which governs part of the brain's reward circuits. This is where the pre-frontal cortex comes into play, along with what are called nucleus accumbens. When stimulated – as in, activated by a perceived reward, such as water, sex, food, money, votes, and other stimuli - information makes its way to the nucleus accumbens. This information then travels to the prefrontal cortex. Regardless of how cocaine is ingested – smoking, snorting, or by injection – the drug travels to the brain through the bloodstream.

It reaches all sections of the brain, but the euphoria users feel is facilitated by the so-called reward pathway, or circuits. The after-effects of this euphoria is what causes behavioral disruption, mood swings, and bad choices made by drug addicts.

Chemical substances known as neurotransmitters communicate information within the brain. An array of chemicals form such neurotransmitters. One neurotransmitter is called dopamine, which is released by a neuron into a small gap between neurons called a synapse. Dopamine binds with proteins called dopamine receptors, which send signals to the neurons. These signals are then carried throughout the brain via dopamine transporters. This creates a build-up of dopamine, which causes a continuous stimulation of receiving neurons that are responsible for the euphoria created by using cocaine.

The longer a junkie uses cocaine or crystal meth, the more their brain is altered. That's why addicts who use drugs for five or more years often have a harder time kicking their habit than those who have been addicted for less time. Cocaine addiction is not a physical dependence, although physical dependence often accompanies drug addiction. This knowledge helped me and other addicts to realize that recovery was possible. There's another important factor to successful recovery: how the brain reacts to success and failure. Scientists studying the part of the brain called the habenula have discovered why success often breeds more success, and failure more failure. Researcher Sam Golden, who is with the Mount Sinai School of Medicine, investigated the habenular switch. This so-called switch regulates inputs from the region of the brain that sends signals relating to anticipation and reward.

Animals who ward off danger, win fights against aggressors, catch their prey, simultaneously boost their testosterone level and mitigate stress hormone levels. This also applies to humans. Such success positively reinforces an animal's sense of well-being, and helps to engender a mindset that provides an edge in future encounters with danger, or involve risk, or continuous effort. This is the neuro-biological reason why it feels good to win and bad to lose. The brain's reward circuitry becomes conditioned, over time, to associate positive experiences with feeling good, and negative experiences and associations with feeling bad.

Dr. Robert Sapolsky is a Professor of Neurology and Neurosurgery at Stanford University. He has studied what he calls the 'Winner Effect', and its application to our lives. In a 2017 column in The Wall Street Journal, Dr. Sapolsky wrote that "victory increases confidence and risk-taking. Winning boosts the secretion of testosterone and suppresses stress hormones like cortisol. This increases confidence and risk-taking, and it changes the biochemical makeup of pheromones," while "losing has the opposite endocrine effects. It prompts subordination behavior, risk aversion and the production of fear pheromones – which function as a kind of olfactory 'kick me' sign."

Poverty also alters the brain, in ways which make addiction more likely and recovery more difficult. A 2014 study, funded by Economic Mobility Pathways (EMPath), established the effects of growing up in poverty on the brain. Poverty is conducive to stress which leads to making unwise decisions, regardless of intellectual capacity. Obviously, this problem is worse for stupid people, but even individuals of high intelligence who are impoverished fall victim to this unfortunate reality. The outcomes of these bad choices compound other difficulties, which cause poor people to believe they can't improve their lives. Exposure to such 24/7 stress actually alters the brains of these people. Al Race is the deputy director of Harvard University's Center on the Developing Child. Mr. Race correctly claims that impoverished kids who remain poor are doubly doomed. Societal disintegration will result if this problem isn't eradicated.

EMPath's programs and counseling services have lifted people out of poverty and into jobs which pay enough to support entire families. But more like-minded organizations are needed, and needed now. Poverty impedes the development of a sense of control over one's destiny.

That's because when an inordinate level of brain bandwidth is devoted to dealing with issues of poverty, there's often not enough left to enable impoverished individuals to move forward. But doing so will lower drug addiction and race-based hatred in the USA and other nations. Junkies who want to kick their addiction must resolve to change. As a successful, former crack addict told me, "I stopped waitin' fo' light at da end of 'da tunnel, so I done lit 'dat bitch up, m'self." This author knows that not everyone can do this. But with proper assistance, nearly all drug addicts can. Stress caused by particularly intense experiences also adversely affects the brain's neurochemistry, and such trauma can also impact brain structure. Experts know that trauma – which would certainly include drug addiction, and that which goes with it – can, and does, alter the way brains function.

Neurosurgeons know that brains feature a sort of elasticity, which can be modified via intense life experiences. Genetic predispositions can play out within the brain during, and following, powerful occurrences. Psychologically, and physiologically, stress caused by drug addiction can, directly, and indirectly, basically reconfigure the brain. As addicts begin their recovery efforts, it's crucial for them to realize that they have the ability to positively change their how their brain functions, by self-imposing such changes. As their brain reverts to its normal status it becomes easier for junkies to avoid using.

This, in turn, facilitates their recovery efforts, and increases their chances of staying clean. Classifying addiction as a disease impedes recovery, and can prevent it altogether. Addiction is an unintended result of people who turn to drugs for some form of satisfaction. This satisfaction may be the desire for pleasure, or the need to stay alert, energetic, to raise productivity. It could be a diversion from an unfulfilling life, or relief from boredom from a routine job. Treatment based on the disease model of addiction often fails, as statistics have conclusively substantiated. This is largely the logical result of rehab programs which are predicated on the false premise that drug addiction is a disease.

This observation is not intended to discount the value of attending Narcotics Anonymous meetings, or rehab facilities based on the 12-step model, or clinicians whose approach is disease-based. Most of what such programs and professionals emphasize is helpful. But how addiction is perceived is crucial to how it's treated, and believing that addiction is a disease can, in my view, undermine recovery efforts.

Addition is a poor choice made by people with underlying problems. Whether they're depressed, angry, or simply can't cope with stress or deal with life's ups and downs, they're not diseased. Their problem is addiction. If left untreated, diseases worsen. Sepsis, cancer, Parkinson's, Schizophrenia, all spread if the patient is simply locked in a cell. But taking away booze from alcoholics enables them to stay sober. While there is a medical aspect to addiction, it's a social problem which requires social intervention. Those who claim it's a disease are effectively perpetuating a political statement while ignoring reason, facts, logic and sound arguments.

Perhaps the worst effect of addiction-as-a-disease is the self-victimization philosophy it instills in those who believe it. Many addicts already feel powerless. This includes minorities, the poor, women, and junkies who come from dysfunctional families. The LAST thing they need to believe is that they have no power. Those recovering from addiction and the Hate Movement know that by empowering themselves to take control of, and responsibility for, their destiny, they can reject their feelings of powerlessness.

This is critical to their success. Re-branding oneself as having power, even if that power is limited to oneself, enables them to exit such destructive thoughts and leaving these realms behind.

During my years of using, and since getting clean, I've known hundreds of junkies who served time in prison. While they paid their debt to society, many weren't well served by society. Recovery for incarcerated drug addicts is at least theoretically easier than for junkies on the outside. But the buying, selling, and using of drugs in prison, and many jails, occurs every day in America. How? To begin with, someone brings those drugs into the detention facility. Those people are often staffers. Guards, cooks, processing personnel, maintenance workers, and other employees, either smuggle drugs into these facilities or allowing others to sneak them in. I knew dealers who supplied prisons with cocaine, crystal meth, pot, and heroin. They relied on staff members to facilitate entry of such contraband.

Once it's there, staffers sell it to inmates, who then distribute it to incarcerated addicts. Junkies in lock-up pay for drugs with cash, cigarettes, errands, or sex. Cash always finds its way to the employees who facilitated its entry.

Jailed junkies who aren't flush with cash perform services for those who provide them with their fix. This includes braiding hair, or even physically assaulting – or killing – inmates on whom others have put out contracts. I also knew a middle-aged crackhead whose ex-husband was knifed while in prison for informing the deputy warden's assistant of a drug ring operating inside the facility. She told me that her ex's mistake was in not knowing that the staffer he snitched to was in on the operation. A week after the dude ratted the culprits out to the deputy warden's assistant, the inmate was attacked by four inmates and stabbed nearly to death. After that, he kept his mouth shut.

For drug addicts, there are pitfalls to returning to society, even under court-monitored supervision. In many cases, addicts who are released from prison are remanded to halfway houses. These government-sanctioned, taxpayer-funded facilities are theoretically ideal. Most are effective in helping residents re-adjust to living and working in civilized society. But some aren't only not helpful, but they actually kick- start, and effectuate, bad habits and lifestyles, and can undermine, or prevent recovery.

The District of Columbia's halfway houses were plagued by serious problems when I was addicted to crack cocaine. I saw this, myself, because I smoked crack in such facilities – at times, with paid staffers who ran the places. DC's Hope Village is one such establishment where recently-released prisoners are often sent. The Washington Post chronicled the post-prison life of Joseph Willis, who was remanded to Hope Village. Mr. Willis told The Washington Post that Hope Village's "job-training services and access to mental health services" were "anemic." He said "it was difficult to get money to ride METRO to job interviews," and claimed that the facility lacked Internet access. Joe Willis calls it "Hopeless Village."

A thick 2013 report issued by the DC Corrections Information Council (CIC) found that the staff at Hope Village and other district-based halfway houses didn't know how to help residents find employment and housing. Staff members "hindered them from accessing mental health services," and "residents said they felt unsafe." Several residents also said that "the facilities lacked an effective system to handle grievances." That's an understatement. Beat downs frequently occur in halfway houses; I saw some.

The report also concluded that, "on multiple occasions, incarcerated DC residents would prefer to stay at secure [Bureau of Prisons] facilities than to reenter through Hope Village." Michelle Bonner, who then chaired the CIC told reporters that, "there are some things that are obviously dysfunctional." I learned that some DC halfway houses were great places to score crack, use drugs, and hook up with women who traded sex for drugs. In many ways, halfway houses are as secure for drug addicts to buy and use drugs as any safe house. This didn't surprise me any more than it surprised those who compiled the report I referenced earlier, because l bought and smoked crack in such establishments.

In some cases, resident directors accept cash or drugs, in return for allowing this to take place on the premises. I was present at a halfway house in northwest DC when a drug runner showed up to deliver crack. While the kid was on the third floor transacting business, a resident ran up the stairs. He told the drug runner that the car he'd driven to the halfway house was in the process of being repossessed. The young black man raced down two flights of stairs, leaving bags of rock and cash in his wake. Several residents and I watched from the windows the interaction between the drug runner and the two men who were hooking up chains to the vehicle. One of the repo men warned the runner, "Keep away or you'll get pepper sprayed." Profanity followed from both sides.

Minutes later, the young drug runner re-entered the halfway house madder than an incontinent Klansman who'd peed his sheets. His anger ramped up more when he realized his drugs and cash were gone. "Where be my shit?", he asked, clearly fearing the consequences he'd suffer from his employer.

"That guy took your money", I replied, pointing at the culprit. "And this dude has your rocks," I said, identifying his accomplice. Neither thief denied stealing, and weren't upset over being ratted out. We knew the drug runner wouldn't call the cops. I said I was leaving, and no one blocked me. If they had, they'd have quickly backed off, as I was armed. A few days after this incident took place, the drug runner's employer – the dealer – ordered hits on the two thieves. Both ended up hospitalized in critical condition. A rival crack dealer told me that one of them suffered permanent brain damage and the other had more than ten broken bones. Nobody proffered charges against anyone. The three guys who nearly killed the two thieves each earned $150, a carton of KOOLs, and a 40 liter bottle of Mad Dog-20/20 malt liquor. By ghetto standards, those two were well compensated.

Inferior halfway houses and recovery facilities operate far outside of the District of Columbia. In March, 2017, the owner of drug treatment centers, Kenny Chapman, admitted that he'd threatened patients, turned them into prostitutes, and allowed addicts under his care to continue using drugs. Chapman also confessed to insurance fraud and money laundering in the operation of his treatment centers in Florida.

The Palm Beach Post verified that at least two patients in Chapman-operated drug rehab centers died while they were patients at treatment facilities Medical doctors and other professionals were also implicated in Kenny Chapman's scams, as co-defendants, and co-conspirators.

In May, 2017, two addictions counselors who worked at the Freedom Ridge Recovery Lodge in West Chester, Pennsylvania overdosed and died.

These men lived at the home, where they were found, dead, in their bedrooms. They were working as certified, on-site counselors whose duties included keeping medications under lock-and-key, and dispensing them.

The problems that these recovering addicts face, resulting from the hiring of blatantly unqualified workers, continues to plague even non-junkies and other innocent victims. In October, 2016, an addictions counselor named Brian Craig Webster broke into two homes on Capitol Hill. Once inside, Webster held male occupants at gunpoint and duct-taped their hands and feet. He then sexually assaulted them. One of Webster's victims broke free of these restraints, and fought with him. After a brief struggle, the victim grabbed the attacker's gun. He and his roommate – who'd also been assaulted – held the perp until police arrived.

At the time of this attack, Webster was working at Community Connections, a DC health clinic which helps clients who suffer from addiction, depression, mental illness, and homelessness. Webster had earlier assaulted at least two other victims before being arrested in October. He had worked at Community Connections for two and a half years at the time of his arrest, and was immediately fired.

Not long after this travesty occurred, seven police officers in Baltimore were indicted for crimes ranging from armed robbery to racketeering, to helping a drug dealer being tracked by law enforcement to remove a GPS tracking device that the Drug Enforcement Administration had attached to the pusher's vehicle. Four officers were charged with stealing $200,000 in cash and a watch valued at $4,000. Three others were indicted for impersonating a federal officer so they could steal $20,000 in cash. An officer was alleged to have said that working for the police department is "easy money."

Four other officers who arrested a man during a traffic stop stole his stash of drugs, and took $21,500 in cash. Three of these cops illegally stopped a man on the street, searched his car without a warrant, and then shook him down for $1,500. Baltimore Police Commissioner Kevin Davis described these cops as "robbers wearing police uniforms", who operated like 1930s-style gangsters." Federal investigators said that the crooked officers began their criminal enterprises in 2015.

The concerns of some residents of Baltimore, and Washington, D.C., however, are more focused on specious suspicions of alleged racism. A DC firefighter, Norm Brooks, advocated online that "PIGS" – whom he considered "racist" – "deserve nothing short of a bullet in their heads." He said that "crooked-ass racist cops" "deserve" to be shot.

CHAPTER ELEVEN

A pageant of Euro-American bigotry was on full display, for a fee. A drum and pipe corps consisting of 48 musicians, all dressed as Scotsman, played Scottish folk songs, as twelve costumed ladies in traditional Irish clothing danced their gigs 20 feet in front of them. 50 teenaged girls decked out in 1930s Ukrainian dresses followed, dancing from one end of the massive hall to the other, and then twice back again. A Slovak singer crooned Yugoslavian drinking tunes, backed up by a 12-piece orchestra. 355 pro-white people had paid $20 each, or $35 per couple, to attend the Euro-American Cultural Society extravaganza, held in Parma, Ohio. The event was hosted at Parma's German-American Central Hall, which is about 15 miles from the Cleveland airport.

Following the event, another 200 Euro-Americans joined the 355 already there for a dinner of home-cooked Nordic, German, Swiss, Irish, Polish, Lithuanian, Slavic, Baltic, Latvian, Russian, and Estonian cuisine. Each meal ticket cost an additional $20. The receipts for just those two functions, along with donations from wealthy backers, totaled just under $75,000. I know this, because William Pierce – who attended the extravaganza – had sent me there a full week in advance. It was back to Cleveland, again. "You did advance work for Reagan and Bush," he told me. "So now, you can apply your front-man skills on my behalf." He mentioned this to me on Sunday, April 4, 1999 – it was Easter.

Even more distressing than working on Easter Sunday was the fact that Pierce hosted a catered dinner party that evening for his staff and about 15 or 20 local supporters. But they weren't celebrating Easter. They were celebrating the 31st anniversary of the assassination of Dr. Martin Luther King, Jr.

"Because of the Jews," Pierce said that evening, "Martin Lucifer Coon's birthday is a federal holiday. But we give thanks for that commie nigger having had his brains obliterated." He then raised his glass and made a toast to James Earl Ray – Dr. King's convicted assassin – who had died in 1998. All told, nearly 700 Euro activists swarmed this hall and the grounds that evening, in late April of 1999. Over a 10-hour period the following day, 2,000 people – many of whom had been there the previous night – came to see exhibits, hear lectures, and participate in various presentations. Each person paid $25 to attend those events. The $125,000 raised in those two days, which including more donations on day two - more than covered the approximately $25,000 cost.

Nearly all of the food and entertainment were donated. The exception was The Stanley Mujac band, which performed at its standard rate. Following the opening dances by the costumed performers, the Master of Ceremonies invited anyone who wished to Square Dance to take part. In Iowa, such MCs are known as callers, because they 'call' the prompts to which the dancers dance. But first, about 50 or 60 well-practiced Square-dancers formed a human Swastika on the wooden dance floor.

Among the disgusting calls that evening, I wrote these down on the back of a paper napkin:

"Swing your partner off to the side; Dose some Jews with Cyanide," the MC announced. "Twirl her around, off to the right; stomp your feet, cuz yer proud yer White."

From there, it got worse.

"Help yourself to a rifle, or two; Go and shoot a Jigaboo. What we do is in-still fear, in every Muslim, Spick, and Queer. Lost your partner; what'll you do? Run down Kikes, and Bull Dykes, too. Swing your partner; twirl her around – Then, kick some fairies to the ground."

And then, there was this:

"Find your partner, there's lots to do; shoot a Filipino, and a Haitian, too – It's all in the name of the red, white, and blue; build a fire, and roast a Jew."

Normal people find this despicable. But the dancers who sashayed around that floor were smiling, even laughing, as the caller shouted their prompts. The prompts the caller shouted were horrific, but seeing the smiling dancers enjoying them was even worse. While growing up in Iowa, I attended some Square Dances with my grandparents in their quaint, little town, called Pleasantville. Both sides of my mother's and father's families have roots there which date to the 1850s. The farmers and townspeople Square-danced to the "calls" of a local Master of Ceremonies. But the dances held in those barns in rural Marion county, Iowa were nothing like this one.

The National Alliance took in grand total of $165,000, net of expenses, in about 60 hours. And while the ostensible purpose was to broaden its base, the behind-closed-doors dealings involved the funding of organized neo-Nazi hatred, by way of Resistance Records. Parma, Ohio, is where John D. Rockefeller began his career, in the 1850s. It's also the hometown of Erich Gliebe, the virulent, neo-Nazi, ex-pro boxer who fought under the name of the Aryan Barbarian. As one of the National Alliance's top local organizers, Gliebe (pronounced as 'Glee-bee') proved his value to Dr. Pierce by tirelessly building the Cleveland unit – units being referred to as 'cells' in the National Alliance – into one of the most effective in his organization.

William Pierce, like Willis Carto, knew that wealthy, influential bene-factors would never let themselves be seen with the likes of crude brutes like Erich Gliebe. That's where they both utilized me.

Five Republican Presidents since 1872 have been members of the Cleveland Union club: Grant, Hayes, Garfield, McKinley, and Taft. Events have been hosted there by Presidents, U.S. Supreme Court Justices, Cabinet members, U.S. Senators, Governors, and Ambassadors. But during that last week of April, 1999, some well-tailored, wealthy Holocaust deniers hosted meetings there over lunch, and dinner. I was there for the luncheon and dinner, representing William Pierce in advance of his arrival.

Upon landing at the Cleveland airport, I checked into the University club of Cleveland, which is near the campus of Case Western Reserve University. Two hours later, I drove to Cleveland's Union club, where I was to meet some shadowy benefactors of William Pierce's empire of Hate. In the club's lobby, I stated the name of the National Alliance supporter – a Union club member – who was hosting me. The clerk replied, "he's awaiting you in the Reading Room. Please follow me." My host was sitting with another gentleman who was smoking a cigar. They looked about 70 years old, and in good shape for their age.

We shook hands as I gazed up at the high-ceilinged room, with oak-paneled walls, marble fireplace mantel, Persian rugs, and thick draperies.

They invited me to join them in the club's bar, which was like an old-time men's grille, with ox blood leather seats at each table. As we sat at a corner table, my host handed me a small card. On it was printed, "You must train harder than the enemy who is trying to kill you. You will get all the rest you need in the grave." On the card's flip side was my host's name, address, and phone number.

Beneath the quote was the name of Leon De Grelle. "General De Grelle was the last surviving General of the Third Reich," the man told me. "We were friends", he added. Leon De Grelle had been dead for only five years when this meeting occurred. His memory was still vibrant in this old neo-Nazi's mind. I mentioned that De Grelle also knew Willis Carto, and he was writing his memoirs for Carto's NoonTide Press – with a $100,000 publisher's advance - when he died in 1994. The other gentleman then said that after another round, we'd eat in the club's formal dining room.

It was called the Wedgewood Room and it was ritzy. These old geezers held their liquor well. As they ordered another round, I told the waiter to make mine a root beer. I would need all my brain cells firing at full strength for this discussion. "We agree that what's discussed at this table stays between us and Dr. Pierce," the other gent said. "Tell us about this, this – is it Renaissance Records?" Correcting him on the company's name, I explained the appeal of Resistance Records in terms of outreach, and profitability. "What's ironic," my host said, "is that the fans of this type of music are precisely the kind of white people that Adolf Hitler, himself, wouldn't have ever admired, or even liked." True, that, I replied. But one need not admire, or like, those whose support is needed, and whose cash is desired.

"It's our understanding that Resistance Records is a for-profit corporation, unlike the National Alliance, or Vanguard Books. Is that correct?" Yes, I answered. "However, it's owned by the National Alliance, which is a nonprofit entity." They asked how much of the company I owned. "None, actually. Recently, I sold my shares to Dr. Pierce." They knew that my contract required me to consult to the company. "My wife's best friend is a liberal, pro-Clinton, Jewess," one of them said. The other man complained that his next door neighbors were Jewish, and that Howard Metzenbaum had been "right here in this very room" the previous week. Metzenbaum was the long-time U.S. Senator from Cleveland. This guy referred to Mr. Metzenbaum as Senator 'Matzo Ball'. Howard Metzenbaum had left office in 1995, but the antipathy these two felt for him was still fervent. "That damn, nigger-lovin' kike's a fuckin' commie," the other man said. Over the course of the next two hours, I answered all of their questions, and then offered my opinions on how making a contribution to Resistance Records would help further the cause they so staunchly supported: the cause of hatred.

"Okay, we'll both donate $50,000 to a charity of our choice," one of them told me. "Twenty-five grand out of each donation will be wired to Pierce, by each recipient. This way, we'll get the full benefits of tax deductibility and simultaneously help the National Alliance."

"Sounds like a plan, gentlemen," I said.

I later learned that the Union club didn't admit women until 1983, and blacks weren't allowed to be members until 1989. In 2015, the Union club of Cleveland elected its first black President. A world-renowned architect who lives in Cleveland, Robert Madison, is black. Mr. Madison, who was elected President of his graduating class at Harvard, began his business career in

Cleveland in 1954. He told The Cleveland Plain Dealer that when he first visited the Union club, the staff "pointed me to the kitchen."

The following evening, I met with three other Pierce supporters at the Union club. This time, the host brought along his wife, and a friend from his hunting lodge near Cincinnati. They each gave me a sealed envelope, which I was to turn over to Pierce. Each envelope contained bank drafts for $15,000. The $95,000 that was raised, and committed to, at those two meetings, was in advance of the $125,000 net that would be raised at Parma's German-American center three days later. That's when I realized I should've held out for more money when William Pierce offered to buy my Resistance Records shares.

He wasn't merely making big bucks on it, he was using it to RAISE even more.

Pierce flew into the Cleveland airport early on the following afternoon, before the festival began. Gliebe met him at the airport, accompanied by the winner of a drawing held among members of the Cleveland cell for the chance to ride with Pierce to Parma. This wasn't William Pierce's first trip to Parma. He spoke there in November, 1996, and again in the Spring of 1998. A video of the 1998 speech is on YouTube. That speech and the question-and-answer follow-up prove how effective Pierce was at communicating his agenda to his followers. He was introduced by Erich Gliebe. Tom Metzger spoke immediately after Pierce, and served up an even darker, more violent, view of what he hoped and believed was on the way.

Around 90 people attended the event that's on YouTube. Every seat was filled. Many were standing in the back of the room and along the side walls. But that audience was nowhere near as large as many of the Pierce speeches and seminars I had seen over the years. Pierce also spoke of the "young men and women that we are recruiting on university campuses now," and about the inroads that the National Alliance was making in Chicago, Dallas, Milwaukee, Seattle, Los Angeles, Boston, and Houston, and other "big cities." He said, "to reach our goal, we must have organization, and effective, fully committed new leaders, who have a sense of mission." We want those "who feel a calling to do exceptional things."

Pierce also said efforts were underway to attract what he called the country club societal subset. The head of WAR, Tom Metzger, said on that day some things which could've just as easily been spoken in 2019. The audience is comprised mostly of well-dressed, articulate, intelligent activists. "I represent the White Aryan Resistance," Metzger told them. "It's sort of a blue collar National Alliance," he said. "I'm a white racist. Our entire idea is the salvation of our race, and the environment that the race has to live in. Things are looking great, 'cause everything's fallin' apart." The room rocked with laughter. "We're very happy with the disintegration of Washington, D.C., and the U.S. Economy. We cheer when we see bad headlines. We've gotta save this country. Lookin' around, I don't see much I want to save. We're certainly happy to have the representatives from the Special Forces here today, too. They certainly need to be guided in the right direction. Race-mixing and integration lead to racism. Great."

Metzger concluded by saying, "my pitch is very easy... we are anti-elitists. We talk about Civil War and Revolution," because that's what WAR is all about." Erich Gliebe then reminded the crowd that in two months, the pseudo-historian David Irving would address the cell members. Guests were welcome. So, is white supremacy exclusively the province of bigoted haters who advocate violence against minorities, or is it to some degree a systemic aspect of the innate structure of the United States? It's both. Who can deny that historically significant imbalances of money, power, resources, and political influence have overwhelmingly benefited whites since America's inception? Pretending otherwise is ludicrous, as is ignoring the symbiosis of law enforcement and other societal institutions that played roles in precluding blacks from becoming full participants in the American Dream. Just as Sheriffs, Judges and police officers used to aid slave owners in capturing runaway slaves, modern societal factors beyond the direct control of the victims have effectively barred many blacks from attaining their full potential. In the process, tens of millions of Americans were wrongfully short-changed. But try telling that to people like Tom Metzger, David Duke, Ed Fields, and Don Black.

Richard Butler was actually far less offensive than many other Holocaust-denying preachers. Reverend James 'Jim' Wickstrom held crowds in the palm of his hand as he advocated the extermination of Jews, blacks, feminists, gays, and Hispanics. In the summer of 2000, I attended a sermon in which he said, "I have a dream! If that goddamn nigger can have a dream, by God, then I can have one, too. And my dream is that in the days to come, there won't be anyone who isn't white living in America." Wickstrom told me he looked forward to when he "can walk down the roads all across America, and see nigger heads, Jew heads, spick heads, and Queer heads on fence posts."

I was also in the audience when, in 2002, he said he wanted to "bring the Jews to V. A. hospitals, and tie 'em to chairs, out on the lawn. Then bring in some veterans who've been mutilated, and give 'em some baseball bats. Then, let those vets beat the Jews to death! All of 'em. Take the chairs with the dead, strapped-in Jews, and throw 'em in a wood-chipper! Toss their remains into an incinerator and burn 'em. That'll be the Holocaust the Jews never got, but which they all still rightly deserve." As he spoke, I realized that not even Adolf Hitler was this blunt about his hatred. Wickstrom later hosted a radio show called, 'The Lyin' Jews' which was broadcast on the Turner Radio network. As of 2017, it's still being aired on shortwave radio, and online. In the early 1990s, Jimmy Wickstrom was sentenced to 38 months in federal prison, for distributing counterfeit cash at the Aryan Nations World Congress. He and his intended recipients had agreed that the fake bills were to be used to fund paramilitary and militia activities. Upon his 1994 release, he jumped right back into white Supremacy, Holocaust denial, and advocating the violent murder of minorities.

A few weeks later, I was on the receiving end of racism, as I got kicked out of a DC crack house. The junkie who lived there was a black separatist who hated whites. He said, "Ah ain't havin' me no Cheerio in my bowl of Cocoa Puffs." On his ceiling was painted a life-sized image of Malcolm X, posed with a black separatist, who was a big fan of Rev. Louis Farrakhan. Had I tried to stay, it would've been violent. As there were witnesses, and my gun wasn't equipped with a silencer, I left. I was drunk, high on crack, and didn't want to be arrested for public intoxication while armed and carrying drug paraphernalia and crack. Feeling woozy, I took refuge behind a couple of dumpsters in a darkened alley. With my back up against a brick wall, I dozed off for what turned out to be about an hour. I was awakened by an enormous rat, who decided to crawl up onto my left leg. The light from the street lamp enabled me to make eye contact with this big rodent, just as I moved my leg to rise from the asphalt pavement. As it scurried toward this alley's opposite wall, I felt well enough to return to my car and get the hell out of there. While getting into my vehicle, my buddy Willie Mack called. He was a crack dealer and a U.S. Army veteran whose company I much preferred to that of the Beltway Barnacles I'd socialized with for years. "Whazzup, white boy?", he asked. I told him what had just gone down.

"Well, dat be da thing about bein' a white junkie in da hoods," he told me. "Y'all meets dudes dat don't want nothin' to do wiff ya, even if you gots money." Willie Mack said he knew of a place where I could safely get high, in the company of some nice junkies, who were friends of his. I said, "I'm in! Let's go, homey." These addicts lived in the Barry Farm. The Barry Farm dwellings public housing project is home to thousands of residents in the southeast quadrant of the District of Columbia. Apartments there range from two to six bedrooms, and it featured a nice recreation center for residents and their guests. Barry Farm's 432 households each pay 30 percent of their income to live there. The land is adjacent to the Anacostia METRO station and is bordered by Martin Luther King avenue, and Sheridan road. I drove to an underground parking garage in downtown D.C., and got into Willie Mack's. He was blasting a Tupak Shakur CD, the volume of which made it impossible to understand anything he said.

Turning it down, he reminded me he'd heard music in my Range Rover which wasn't to his liking. "Y'all like Tupak about as much as I like Johnny Cash, which ain't much. Y'all be da whitest white dude I know," he said. "No,

I'm just the whitest white dude you know who smokes crack," I replied. This apartment was on the ground floor of one of the buildings. Willie Mack's friends were nice, and glad to meet a friend of a friend who had money. The lady lived there with her boyfriend, Roosevelt, and her son from a previous relationship. Another junkie, whose name was Trayshon, was also there when we arrived. We smoked crack for the next hour and a half, as Willie drank beer. Around 9:30 p.m., my hostess's son arrived. "Isaiah," his mother said, "meet Mister Todd. Him be friends wiff Willie."

This kid was about 16, and was carrying notebooks and a textbook. He had a backpack with him, which he set down as I rose from the sofa. As he politely introduced himself, I said it looked like he'd been studying. "That's right, sir," he said. "I've been at the Martin Luther King library. Took METRO home." This kid knew what had been going on; it was obvious, from his dejected expression. He was as serious as he was shy, and understood that life had dealt him some bad cards. Growing up in a dangerous hood in a family of crackheads doesn't infuse self-confidence, or a desire to study. "Isaiah be a straight-A student," his mom told me. "He be a honors student at one of 'dem magnet schools. Him rides three different buses, twice, every mornin' and every evenin'," his mother said. I asked him about his post high school plans. He said he'd like to become an addictive disorders counselor. The big fellow who'd let me in a few hours earlier rose from his chair, grabbed the kid by the shoulders, and slammed him against the wall. "Listen up, y'all little, bitch-ass mothafucka," the man yelled, shaking the boy.

"Don't never be talkin' dat kinda shit 'round 'dis place, hear?" The anger in the dude's eyes was as intense as the fear on the teen's face. He was help-lessly pinned to the wall. "Yes, sir", came the reply, barely above a whisper. "Y'all best LOSE 'dat punk-ass shit, boy, or I'll knock yo' nigga butt into next week," the man screamed. The kid tried to apologize, but the big dude slapped him to the floor.

Cowering in fear, the boy tried to make eye contact with his mother, who was too high, and helpless, to be of any use. The dude wasn't finished, though.

He picked the kid up and threw him against the big-screen, older model TV set, scattering a small collection of candles and knick-knacks. "I didn't come here to see anyone assaulted," I told the big guy. Roosevelt raised his fist, and the two of us locked eyes. "Knock it off. Now." The kid covered his face, was inching over to a corner of the room. As the big dude advanced toward me, he pointed toward his lady. "Ahh done brought 'dis here bitch and her snot-nosed kid into a whole 'nuther world." With my .380 aimed it at his face, I replied, "back off, or you'll be in another world Right quick." My words must have registered with this huge, violent junkie, because he said, "Okay, okay. Ahh'm a-let it go 'dis time." Turning to the boy, he said, "Get da fuck in yo' room, ya damn faggot." His mom stared blankly at the torn carpeting, shaking her head. She was looking for pieces of crack, not thinking about this attack on her child.

The lease for the apartment was in the name of Roosevelt's mother. As the kid scampered off to his bedroom, his attacker said, "Ahh ain't likes him attitude. He thinkin' him cool. But Ahh'm a-tell ya, 'dat boy ain't shit." I set down my pipe on the cheap table as the big guy said, "y'know, him looks down on me, and on he mama, and ever-body here, 'cept fo' dis white dude," Roosevelt said, nodding in my direction. He fired up a KOOL and mumbled, between drags, on the cigarette. Realizing that a more severe beat down had been averted, I got up to leave. "I'm a-walk y'all to yo' car," the brute said. I accepted because white guys walking after dark in DC public housing projects can be risky. Though I was armed, being seen with a big black man was a better deterrent.

He put on his coat, which was at least a size 50, and we left. Willie Mack reminded me that he was my ride. "Then I'll get a cab, unless you're ready to go," I replied. As the three of us walked the half block to Willie's old Thunderbird, Roosevelt asked me where I lived, and if I was married. I told him that Linda and I lived in northern Virginia. "Do she know y'all be smokin' crack?" No, I said, "she has no idea."

Laughing, he replied, "Well, she be findin' out, sooner or later. Once you into 'dis, it only gets worser. You'll see." Several people, all of them black, passed us as we walked to Willie Mack's car. We had no problems. We shook hands as I silently promised myself to never set foot in that place again.

Driving home to Virginia, I felt bad for that kid, and realized how lucky I was – not only for my present situation, but also for the advantageous manner in which I'd been raised. Getting knocked around, and verbally abused, by his mom's ignorant, live-in boyfriend. Being ridiculed in his own home because he studies, and sets laudable goals. Being unable to express opinions without fear of violent reprisal, and being insulted, and called a faggot, by the male authority figure in the home. I had never seen such abuse heaped on an innocent teenager by any adult. How this high school student was managing to get straight A's, and keep his bright hopes alive for a positive future, was testament to his determination to better himself. His desire to help junkies overcome addiction, I realized, may well have resulted from what he'd seen in his home. I want to believe that this kid made it.

It's been nearly 20 years since this happened, and I never saw him again. But while driving home, I prayed for that kid. I wondered: what if white supremacists could see how these kids have to live, amidst such misery, squalor, and violence, right in their own homes? Would it change their thinking? Would they become compassionate, and understanding, if they were exposed to situations like this? Don't bet on it.

It was also around this time that I first realized that many people – and this is particularly true with addicts, and white supremacists – don't like themselves. In the years since I kicked addiction, this became more apparent to me. People who are unhappy with their lives are far more susceptible to becoming junkies, and white supremacists, than those who are pleased with life. But being displeased with life shouldn't be confused with not liking oneself. Everyone experiences unhappy, even unpleasant, times. But to not like yourself? That's got to be horrific.

In recent years, I've met, and spoken with, people who simply didn't like themselves. Tragically, most are decent people; in some cases, they're actually far nicer, and kinder, than any narcissist. It seems that self-esteem is directly linked to ones' upbringing. Kids who grow up in homes with intelligent, happily married, well-educated, well-adjusted parents, where money isn't a problem, and where hard work, self-discipline, and respect for others is taught and nurtured, will like and respect themselves. It also helps to have loving, dedicated grandparents who are involved in the lives of their grandchildren, and provide a sense of where they came from, and their purpose on God's earth. To truly understand the causes of drug addiction and racial hatred, one must first take into account what makes people unhappy, and – in some cases – to not like themselves.

Dealing with unhappiness by using drugs is bad enough, but when unhappy people dislike themselves, it's a recipe for disaster. This holds true for addiction, and being susceptible to becoming a White Supremacist. Given the disintegration of scores of millions of modern American families, and the destruction of the societal institutions which provided the glue that molded our citizens and bound Americans together as one, unified people, the future doesn't appear promising. But most Rotarians and Masons don't become crackheads, and supporters of the United Way and the Salvation Army aren't Holocaust deniers.

Misguided government policies that destroy incentives and reward imprudent behavior are also causal to societal destruction, and institutional disintegration. When I began my recovery, my parents bought some drug-testing kits designed for home usage. They required testing of me every other day – when I was 45 years old – and monitored each and every result. This lasted for 12 full months, until June 1, 2007. They kept paying the fees of Dr. Ron Weinier, the renowned DC psychologist for our weekly sessions. They also enrolled me in an outpatient re-hab facility that was staffed by highly qualified drug abuse counselors. They even paid for a membership in a private health club at the Watergate, and also let me use the health center, pool, and other amenities at the Lansburgh, where they lived. At times, my mother even attended Narcotics Anonymous meetings with me, in D.C., and back in Iowa.

Most parents of junkies can't provide such attention, dedication, and resources to the recovering drug addicts. Elected officials, and judges, must implement policies which are conducive to helping people, not harming them. Specifically, welfare recipients must be randomly drug-tested as a condition of getting benefits. Able-bodied people on welfare should be required to work, at least part-time, in return for Food Stamps, Section 8 vouchers, subsidized day care, Medicaid, free or reduced school lunches for their children, EBT cards, and to be eligible to live in public housing. Taxpayer-funded lawyers shouldn't be allowed to challenge such policies, and judges who side with any plaintiffs should be recalled or impeached. Politicians who oppose random, mandatory drug-testing of welfare recipients should be targeted for defeat. Abraham Lincoln said, "America will never be destroyed from the outside. If we falter and lose our freedoms, it will be because we destroyed ourselves." We're doing that now.

This hands-off attitude on drug-testing of welfare recipients by our otherwise paternalistic government will, unless corrected, cause further erosion of our society. Along with formulating constructive policies to prevent and combat addiction, the notion that addiction is a disease must be dispelled, in my view.

Governments and medical establishments in every nation have falsely claimed for decades that addiction – whether to drugs, gambling, alcohol, or whatever – is a disease. Partly, this classification dispels the societal stigmatization of junkies. Partly, it's to facilitate insurance payments to the rehab profession. Science and facts prove that addiction is not a progressive, chronic disease. Yes, it can be a progressive and chronic addiction, and often is. But since when can anyone, using only will power, keep at bay, or cure, any disease? Try willing away cancer, TB, diabetes, dementia, or heart disease. It won't happen. So what makes people think that they can "will" away ANY disease? The answer is they've been brainwashed into believing that addiction is a disease.

Addition can cease via applied will power. Recovering addicts who don't view their addiction as a disease are enormously relieved to know that while drug usage made their brain operate in ways which are harmful, their brains – while changed - nonetheless still function in normal ways. While the term 'recovery' has positive connotations, it can also be self-limiting. This isn't to devalue psychiatry, or treatment specialists, psychology, or medications. However, in my view, addiction is no more a disease than Holocaust Denial, which can also be dispelled, avoided, banished, and prevented.

The anti-Jewish, bigoted followers of these well-financed neo-Nazi organizations in the U. S. and Europe believe whatever nonsense is published, as long as blame is heaped on minorities, and, chiefly, on Jews. William Pierce, David Duke, Richard Butler, Sam Dickson, Willis Carto, and other leaders of the racist Far Right all told me they knew that the Holocaust had taken place. But there were tens of millions of dollars available via Holocaust denial, which they wanted. They fanned the flames of hateful dishonesty via writers who penned anti-Semitic books, brochures, articles, pamphlets, and website content, all providing propaganda, faked evidence, that the Holocaust was a fraud, dreamed up by rich Jewish people and the Jewish lobby to enrich themselves, and Israel.

For the entire four years I was directly associated with Liberty Lobby, and for the nearly three years I worked for the FBI, and until about 2011, a shadowy, anti-Semitic sociopath who called himself Gregory Douglas produced and disseminated lies about Jews to a worldwide audience. "Douglas" – whom I met probably 20, or 30 times - cranked out dozens of books, hundreds of articles and essays that were regularly published in various Carto-owned publications, and posted to websites, and linked online.

William Pierce also sold this pseudo historian's stuff, as did other racist, anti-Semitic groups. The FBI agents I worked with said Douglas had at least a dozen different aliases. One of them was as a Nazi memorabilia dealer known as Arthur D. Royster. Another is Peter Stahl. Others he uses are Peter Norton Birch, Douglas Gregory, Samuel Prescott Bush, Peter Norwood Burch, Dr. George S. McAllister, Gregory Douglas Alford, Michael Suslov, Ph. D., Prof. Friedrich Hasek, Walter Storch, Karl Kolchak, and Freiherr Von Mollendorf, among others. Because wealthy anti-Semites would believe whatever Carto and his German-born wife, Elisabeth, told them, Douglas (as an alias) would fly around the USA, Canada, and western Europe, to sell forged documents which were purportedly signed by Adolf Hitler, Hermann Goering, Joseph Goebbels, and others.

Using yet another alias, Douglas defrauded Holocaust deniers who had more money than brains by selling counterfeit sculptures, which he claimed were created by the famed French artist Auguste Rodin'. Carto's scams involving Gregory Douglas knew no limits, even for con artists. An old anti-Jewish lady once gave Carto 500 uncirculated Krugerrands for a fake Rodin' statuette of the German composer Richard Wagner. The thing was made of plaster, dipped in brass, gold-plated, and mounted on a faux marble base. No self-respecting operator of a flea market would've asked for more than twenty bucks for it. But once Carto vouched for its authenticity, this old bigoted gal drove over to the Riggs National Bank with him, where they opened her safe deposit box. Each of the one ounce, uncirculated gold coins was worth approximately $950, which made all 500 worth nearly half a million dollars.

Many Carto fans and supporters also subscribed to William Pierce's 'Attack' magazine, and bought books, tapes, and CDs from the National Alliance, and from Pierce's Vanguard Books division. Much like Dr. Pierce, Liberty Lobby, and other Carto-controlled entities regularly sponsored three-day conferences, at which hundreds of Holocaust deniers, white supremacists, and virulent anti-Semites would gather. "Israel is always involved in everything!", Gregory Douglas told an audience of a June, 2002 Carto-sponsored convention on Capitol Hill, which drew about 120 attendees.

Seated between former FBI agent Ted Gunderson and retired U. S. Air Force General Benton Partin, Douglas told the group he possessed a top-secret document, issued by Germany's then-Chancellor, Gerhard Schroder. He claimed the document proved the Bush administration and Israel orchestrated the 9/11 attacks in New York city. Following up on this line of disinformation, a Holocaust denier from Arizona then told the crowd that no planes ever crashed into the Pentagon on September 11, 2001. What the world saw on TV, he said, was a faked videotape. No one even asked the basis of his theory. He and his trusted investigative partner had visited "the alleged crash site" in early 2002, he said. Upon checking, he said, they found no metal revealing any "markings" of American airlines. "A criminal regime," he told the enthralled audience, "has taken control of the United States government for at least the last 100 years." As this crackpot spoke, heads nodded in agreement, and several said, "yes." And everyone there unquestioningly believed everything he said.

On the final evening, a raffle was held. The prize was two original editions of a late 1960s anti-Jewish comic book. The main character in this comic book series was called 'WhiteMan', and was based on 'Superman'. 'WhiteMan' resembled 'Superman' and wore a red and blue uniform. The man of steel's had a large letter 'S' emblazoned on it. The uniform worn by 'WhiteMan' featured a Swastika. In the copy of 'WhiteMan', the Aryan super hero was fighting two villains: 'The Jew from Outer Space' and 'Super Coon'. Readers can guess which character kills the other two with his bare hands. The raffle was not without controversy. The Holocaust denier who created 'WhiteMan' in 1967 – John Patler - later shot and killed the then-head of the American Nazi Party, George Lincoln Rockwell.

Several Holocaust deniers present wanted nothing to do with comic books featuring a character created by Rockwell's killer. The lady who won the raffle wanted to give the 'WhiteMan' comic books to her grandchildren. The many books Gregory Douglas wrote sold hundreds of thousands of copies. A Douglas book titled 'Gestapo Chief', sold over 70,000 copies between 1995 and 2001. Such propaganda poisons the minds of trusting readers, whose hatred is reinforced by what they believe to be true history. Willis Carto and William Pierce told me they knew that writers like Gregory Douglas were dishonest. But they provided to their gullible, ignorant customers what they wanted, while making money and widening their sphere of influence. In 1997, Carto said, "Todd, most people on our side are stupid." But he was as cordial and accommodating as could be when veterans visited him in his office, many of whom designated Liberty Lobby as a beneficiary to their life insurance policies, or designated Wills and Elisabeth Carto as heirs to their trusts and estates.

The old, stately house in Cincinnati's Indian Hills neighborhood was home to a wealthy couple who loved Willis Carto and all he represented. Carto and I met with his supporters in Canton, Ohio, and then drove to Cincinnati for the reception. Over 300 activists had turned out to meet Carto in Canton, with checks and cash that totaled nearly $90,000. The couple hosting the Cincinnati house party handed Willis a check for $50,000 upon our arrival. A longtime Carto ally, Kirkpatrick Dilling, was a successful lawyer in Chicago. He made the arrangements for this meet-and-greet, and arranged for Carto and I to stay in rooms at the city's Union club. Kirk Dilling, a World War II veteran, had once directed a de-Nazification program for German POWs in the U.S., for the U. S. government. Dilling's late mother, Liz Dilling, had been an anti-Semitic author of books blaming the Jews for Communism and the decline of Western Civilization. Mr. Dilling's 2003 obituary states he "spent much of his free time at St. Elizabeth's Episcopal church, where he served in the vestry for more than 40 years."

Nearly everyone there had their photo taken with Willis Carto. They fawned over him and were thrilled to be in his presence. Having been with Ronald Reagan and the first President Bush at private functions in homes of supporters, I saw that the adoration for Carto was every bit as enthusiastic as it was for those revered Presidents.

"I sure hope you'll be ready to succeed Willis when he retires," an attractive, matronly, blue-haired lady told me. "Jews have ruined our country, and must be stopped. America needs a fourth Reich," she said. I wondered if this old gal had indoctrinated her children and grandchildren with hate, as

Kirk Dilling's mother had. Memories of the lady who won the raffle for the 'WhiteMan' comic books flooded my mind. Anti-Semitism and racial hatred can be multi-generational, which was on full display. In the library of this gorgeous home, religious books lined the built-in shelves, including some by Billy Graham and the Rev. Norman Vincent Peale. But, somehow, these devout Jesus lovers detested Jews, Blacks, Hispanics, Gays, and everyone else who wasn't white, Christian, and straight.

As Carto and I were leaving, some guests were talking on the front porch. An old man said, "everybody knows the Jews had John Kennedy killed." Another guy replied, "they sure did. It's the only good thing they've ever done." That night, Carto and I met in his room – which was across the hall from mine, at the Union club - to count up the receipts from the house party. The total came to slightly over $100,000 in checks and cash. He also had ten or twelve pledge cards in which supporters collectively committed another forty-five thousand. We then went down for drinks in the club's bar.

Carto told me that this Ohio trip had been "a gold mine for us." The following week, he converted the cash and checks to Canadian Maple Leaf gold coins, Krugerrands, and U.S. Double Eagles. Gold coins are completely untraceable, which Willis had learned in the 1950s from FDR's son-in-law, Curtis Dall. That trip was worth an extra 25 grand to me, based on the 20 percent commission that Willis paid me on donations in which my efforts played a role.

Not long after, Linda and I saw 'Traffic', a film which was set in Indian Hills and Washington, D.C. 'Traffic' is about a crackhead whose father holds public office and is appointed by a President as his Administration's Drug Czar. As we watched that movie, my then-wife didn't know of its applicability to her husband. Talk about Déjà vu. My marriage kept deteriorating due to my drug usage. But I knew I was powerless over my addiction. What mattered to me was getting and using drugs. It was clear that my addiction was destroying my life, marriage, career, and my relationships with my parents, my siblings and their children, and my friends. I cared, but not as much as I did about getting high.

Between 1991 and 2001, a Holocaust denier named Bradley Smith paid for hundreds of advertisements placed in over 350 student newspapers on university campuses in nearly every state in the U.S.A. His organization was called CODOH: the Committee for Open Debate On the Holocaust. Mr. Smith founded CODOH in 1987, while he was working for the Institute for Historical Review (IHR). These ads ran under the auspices of what was called The Campus Project, sponsored by CODOH. A wealthy member of Washington, DC's Cosmos club, a retired international banker named Andrew Grey, was keenly interested in CODOH and its efforts on America's university campuses.

These advertisements generated little interest on the part of students or faculty, or anyone who was affiliated with any university, to attend debates about the Holocaust. But Smith's goal – which, sadly, he achieved – wasn't to host debates as much as it was to cast doubt. Smith, who died in 2016, was still at it, even in the last two years of his life. Well-to-do Holocaust deniers in the USA underwrote his expenses, which included his travel to college campuses, and flying students to DC to attend functions hosted by Liberty Lobby, the Institute for Historical Review, and The Barnes Review.

Polls taken by the Roper Center for Public Opinion and Research show that in 1945, 93 percent of Americans believed that the Germans killed or starved many people in concentration camps. Of this 93 percent, nine percent said that while they believed this to be true, they felt that claims may have been somewhat exaggerated. Only three percent of those polled said that the claims were false, and only one percent expressed doubt about them. Canadian researcher and author Jerry Amernic wrote in 2015 an article citing a recent Gallup poll in which 30 percent of Americans didn't know what the Holocaust was.

In the United Kingdom, the same poll showed, 28 percent of the respondents who were between the ages of 18 and 29 also knew nothing about the

Holocaust. Clearly, Bradley Smith, Andrew Gray, and Gregory Douglas and their backers understood very well that such ignorance among college students represented, and represents, a tremendous opportunity for their cause.

The purpose of those ads was to get people talking. College students talk to lots of people. The CODOH ads generated buzz, and people who took offense at them often were accused of wanting to silence free speech. These Holocaust deniers knew exactly what they were doing, and judging from the polls, they largely achieved their objective. Their ad campaign instilled doubt, skepticism, and hostility. Smith said that "students are empty vessels to be filled", and knew his audience. In his 2002 autobiography, Smith wrote he "was ten thousand dollars in debt … I mailed out a solicitation begging for money, promising I would use part of it to get college speaking dates to talk about Holocaust revisionism. Within a month I'd gotten enough money to pay off my debts."

The title of Smith's autobiography, incidentally, is: 'Break his bones.' Smith's wife was Hispanic, and his ex-wife was Jewish. These two spouses enabled him to claim that he wasn't anti-Semitic. For decades, Andrew Gray had hosted meetings at the Cosmos club which featured David Irving, Gregory Douglas, Willis Carto, Roger Pearson, and other anti-Semites whose goal was to promote Holocaust Denial. I was present at four such gatherings between 1995 and 1998, all held in a private room at the Cosmos club. Readers should note that Andrew Gray always made sure to not have David Irving and Gregory Douglas at the Cosmos club at the same time.

Among the luminaries there was retired Admiral Thomas Moorer, who had served as the chairman of the Joint Chiefs of Staff under President Nixon. A retired, high-ranking CIA official named Fletcher Prouty also frequently attended such functions. When Andrew Gray died in 2001, David Irving wrote a tribute to him entitled, 'Real history loses a friend in Andrew Gray'.

David Irving still makes the news, and still has his supporters. In 2017, The London Guardian reported that Irving claimed to have found "a new generation of 'Holocaust Skeptics'." Irving said that "interest in my work has risen exponentially in the last two years," largely via the internet. "It's mostly young people," he said. "I'm getting messages from 14, 15, 16-year-olds in America. They find me on You Tube. There are 220 of my lectures on YouTube," Irving said, and "I'm getting up to 300 to 400 emails a day." Irving told The Guardian that he answers every email, and "I build a relationship with them." One of the lawyers who defended Deborah Lipstadt against Irving's libel lawsuit is James Libson.

"We really thought the verdict marked Holocaust denial as a done subject," Libson said. "We'd proven it, conclusively, in a court of law." Lamenting the massive increase in Holocaust denial online activity since 2016, Mr. Libson added, "we naively thought that the internet would help" expose the fraud behind Holocaust denial. But "the internet has actually done the opposite", Libson told The Guardian, and expressed remorse at the level of donations that Irving now receives from online contributors. "It used to be small amounts," Irving said, "and those still come in. But people are now giving me verylarge sums, indeed – five figure sums. I now drive a Rolls-Royce."

David Irving also now lives in a 40-room mansion in Scotland, provided to him by a wealthy benefactor.

As Willis Carto, William Pierce, and David Duke all learned, Holocaust deniers take care of their own, and many anti-Semites are extremely generous with the producers and distributors of hatred. Gregory Douglas viewed Andrew Gray just as David Irving did, because Gray was also his benefactor and a tireless promoter of his hateful fiction.

At these dinner meetings, Bradley Smith – whom had once been a member of Liberty Lobby's Board of Directors – distributed a three-ring binder to everyone at the table. Reports, timetables, budgets, updates on CODOH activities, along with projects slated for the future, including grant requests and proposals and scheduled campus visits, were listed. Over after-dinner liqueurs and highballs, and martinis, these participants committed funds, wrote checks, and gave cash directly to Smith. Bradley Smith raised so much money for Holocaust denial that in early 1999, he escrowed $250,000 and offered it to anyone who could arrange for a prime-time debate with an ADL (Anti-Defamation League of B'nai B'rith) official on any TV network.

Among CODOH's financial backers were several of William L. Pierce's closeted major contributors, supporters of Carto's Institute for Historical Review, his Holocaust-denying monthly magazine, The Barnes Review. These benefactors paid for extensive, expensive promotional campaigns. A Carto staffer bribed a member of the Board of Directors of the American Historical Association – with $2,500, in cash – to obtain a copy of that organization's mailing list. Over 12,000 members of the A.H.A. received free, three-month subscriptions to the Journal of Historical Review. The AHA denounced this mailing, and only about four percent of their members who received the free issues chose to subscribe. But that two percent meant 480 people paid $59 a year, for twelve issues of The Barnes Review.

Do the math: 480 X $59 = $30,320 in just one year. The AHA would never have allowed their private, internal mailing list to be used to promote any vile, monthly magazine. But the Holocaust Deniers found ways to promote and distribute their propaganda and generate profits. Also around this time, every senior who graduated from four private high schools in Atlanta, Georgia, received a graduation gift from the IHR. They all received, by U.S. mail, a hardback copy of 'The Dispossessed Majority', an anti-Semitic, racist book. ROTC cadets in every class level at Auburn University also received the books, courtesy of the Institute for Historical Review.

These Holocaust denial honchos knew that Gregory Douglas was a liar, and that David Irving and other hired propagandists had no credibility outside their narrow sphere. But as long as their lies promoted Holocaust Denial, they were well paid for their dirty work. These well-financed efforts were not entirely unsuccessful. A Colorado teacher, Dorothy Grotluschen, told students in her history classes that the Holocaust was a Holohoax. She passed around copies of an article titled, 'Swindlers of the Crematoria'. When she was reprimanded by the school district, she sued, and won a settlement. A Perdue University Professor named Don Hiner basically told his students the same thing in the 1990s.

By using the first amendment and academic freedom, free speech rights, and open debate demands as a pretext, Holocaust deniers have made headway in the halls of universities in the USA and Europe. On several occasions during my years with Carto, while at my office at the Liberty Lobby headquarters on Capitol Hill, college students would visit the place.

If Willis was there, they got to shake his hand or spend a few minutes with him in his private office. These students were enthralled to find themselves in the presence of the person they regarded as the Godfather of Revisionism. The classic 1991 movie, 'Never Forget' starring Leonard Nimoy, is about Willis Carto's legal fight with Mel Mermelstein, the famed Holocaust survivor. This excellent film is now on YouTube and worth watching. The scenes in 'Never Forget' where the actor who plays Carto speaking to a room full of young Holocaust deniers are eerily accurate. I know this because I was present at some of the actual functions depicted in the movie.

Attending those dinners at the Cosmos club showed me that Holocaust denial isn't merely the result of ignorance and apathy. It's highly organized, coordinated, and well-financed by shadowy, dishonest - but intelligent – successful, well-connected bigots. Their deep hatred of Jewish people is why they foment, maintain, and continue these lies, with an eye to the future. Except for me, the only attendees of those meeting who are alive in 2019 are Gregory Douglas, Roger Pearson, and David Irving.

Holocaust Denial has outlasted its founders, and, sadly, will likely outlast everyone reading this book. After attending one such event in the fall of 1996, I called the lawyer for Liberty Lobby, Mark Lane, and asked to meet with him. Lane, who was also Willis Carto's personal lawyer, had been with Liberty Lobby since 1980. Prior to that, he was the lawyer for the Reverend Jim Jones, of the Peoples Temple in Jones-town, Guyana infamy. I asked Lane to keep our conversation between us. He broke his promise.

We met in Lane's private office, at his townhouse on Capitol Hill. On the walls were photos of him with John F. Kennedy, Jane Fonda, Jim Jones, comedian Dick Gregory, William F. Buckley, Jr., and the late U.S. Congressman Leo Ryan – who was shot and killed on the same day that nearly 1,400 Jones followers drank the cyanide-laced Kool-Aid that ended their lives. Incidentally, the Jonestown tragedy is how the phrase, 'drank the Kool-Aid' entered the American lexicon. There were photos of Lane with Leonardo DiCaprio and the actor's father, and Eleanor Roosevelt, author Norman Mailer, and several other celebrities and politicians. There was a signed photo of Lane with Lee Harvey Oswald's widow, and another taken with his mother. There was a photo with former President Gerald Ford.

I knew, from talking with President Ford at the 1996 Republican National convention, that he detested Lane – as did lawyer Phil Buchen, who was Ford's White House counsel. Mr. Buchen was a member of the University club, and became exasperated at the mere mention of Lane's name. Lane had been infamous since his days as a crusading state Legislator in New York. As he faced me, he clearly felt that he held the high cards in this encounter. That's how it turned out. Turning directly to me, Lane said, "Todd, are you aware of how I managed to get out of Jonestown alive in 1978?"

He said as two armed guards held rifles on him and another attorney, while they were being held on orders of Jim Jones in a shack in the jungle, he made them a promise. Lane told me he said, "I'll tell the truth about what happens here." His voice then lowered to an ominous tone as he looked me straight in the eyes. "I'll expose your extensive involvement here at Liberty Lobby, with Willis, and others. Documentation proves you've colluded with Willis on tax fraud, money laundering and mail fraud. You've sent receipts, on your ad agency's stationary, to advertisers enabling them to take illegal tax write-offs for checks sent to our non-tax-deductible entities. You've signed memos to the purchasers of such ads, falsely claiming that their checks were tax-deductible, as donations to tax-exempt entities. Which they weren't." But Lane wasn't through. Continuing, he said, "we have proof, including your ad agency's invoices, that irrefutably show your guilt on several counts, in more than a few ways." I wanted to leap out of my chair and choke him. As he kept up his verbal volleys, I tossed in one of mine.

"I know more about what Willis – with your help, sir – has done, than everyone except you, and Mrs. Carto. We both know that the Internal Revenue Service would be most interested in that info." Lane wasn't cowed. "True, that," he agreed. "But if you go after Willis, or any of his enterprises, you'll bring yourself down, and heap shame and embarrassment on your wife and family. Your name will be mud. Then there's the matter of your father's political career, and his reputation, the ruination of which will result from such disclosures about his wayward son, the fundraiser for neo-Nazis.

Referencing a possible future GOP administration, he warned that "no one named Blodgett will have a chance of being named to any cushy position once this hits the media. Abandoning Willis in his time of need will rain down on you like a ton of bricks." I was legalistically checkmated by a savvy grandmaster. "You know that I at all times acted on Willis's orders, Mark. You were involved in some of it. Neither I or my ad agency were paid any money that was inappropriate." Lane smirked, replying, "That, young man, will be for the media, the courts, the IRS, and the public to decide." Mark Lane was a superb manipulator of the news media, who for decades had been a bona fide celebrity in the eyes of no small number of journalists in print and electronic media. And he had me over a barrel.

He understood I realized that against him, I'd not stand a chance. But then he abruptly became somewhat magnanimous. Willis Carto's "time of need" that Lane mentioned was a reference to the ten million dollar judgment that a California Judge, Runston Maino, had imposed against Carto and Liberty Lobby a week before this ill-fated meeting. As Lane got up from his chair, he said he'd "make a call that will put a nice chunk of change in your ad agency's coffers, and your pocket." The next day, Liberty Lobby's accountant, Blayne Hutzel, called me at my office.

"Todd, you're to meet with a man we'll call Mr. Gray. Be at the Metro bus stop in front of the National Zoo at One p.m. Willis is in California, and Mr.

Gray is authorized to convey an offer to you." Before I could say anything, Hutzel hung up. Arriving a few minutes early, I sat down on the Metro Stop's bench. Almost immediately, a sleek, black Lincoln Continental pulled up. The front passenger window slid down, and a man seated in that seat said, "hop in, Mr. Blodgett."

He looked tough, and on his right little finger was a gold pinky ring, adorned with a ruby that was nearly the circumference of a dime. He was smoking, and kept at it for the entire 20-25 minutes I was in the car. As I joined Mr. Gray in the back seat, he said Carto had agreed that for the next three months, my agency's commission rate would increase from 20 percent to 35 percent, and I could discount all ad sales by up to 25 percent and be paid commissions on the full, posted rate. This offer amounted to an 80 percent, 90-day raise, which would apply to 13 issues of the newspaper, Gray said. "It'll result in about a ninety grand windfall for your ad agency, Mr. Blodgett."

In America's capital city, politicians aren't the only ones who are offered bribes, or payments for silence. "Of course, Willis won't expect you to threaten resigning once this agreement takes effect. And Mark

[Lane] will be apprised on what we discuss," Gray said. Had Lane, somehow, thought I still might talk? As Gray was silent, the driver added his two cents.

"Mistuh Gray, heah, has laid it all out for youse real good. Youse best see things to his likin', and take dis deal. Do youse get it, Mistuh B?" That's when the big, menacing man in the front passenger seat turned around and looked at me. As the driver spoke, he looked at me, via the rear-view mirror. I said nothing as I watched the pedestrians walking around Dupont Circle. The big guy then said, "and if dat ain't da case, den youse gonna get a meetin', an involuntary meetin'." Looking at me via the mirror, he said, "with some real convincin' goombahs, in da very neah futuh, if youse say no before we drop ya back off. Youse unduhstand?"

I looked at Gray, and then up at the driver's hard, cold eyes, staring at me in the car's rear-view mirror. "Cuz lemme tellya," the big dude warned, "deze dudes will leave youse with no doubt dat you should accept dis offuh. It's best for youse, and for 'dat pretty little wifey, Linda Marie Blodgett. Capiche?"

This was no negotiation. It was undisguised extortion, combined with a bribe, and blackmail, sealed with implied violence. By having their minions threaten me, and Linda, Mark Lane and Willis won. But at least they were charitable in victory – even if they weren't nice. The driver pulled into the half-circle front driveway of the Kennedy-Warren. Pulling to a stop, the big guy got out and opened my door. "Thanks for your time, young man," Mr. Gray said, as I turned to enter the building. As I entered the lobby, my cell phone rang. It was my dad, who was co-hosting a reception for Senate Majority Leader Bob Dole, who was seeking the GOP presidential nomination. He asked me how I was doing. I said fine.

A few days later, I ran into my friend Dr. Alfred Lilienthal, at the University club. Lilienthal was Jewish and a leading opponent of Israel. In the club's upstairs bar, I told him about meeting with Mark Lane. As a well-known Jew whose anti-Zionist views received lots of publicity, Lilienthal was controversial. He seemed to revel in this. He knew I was no anti-Semite, and described Mark Lane as a "scoundrel". The next day an envelope awaited me at the club's front desk. Inside was an encouraging note from Alfred E. Lilienthal, and a copy of an article by the respected reporter Steven Brill, from the Feb. 13, 1979 issue of Esquire magazine. The article's headline: 'The case against Mark Lane' was instructive; the content was even more damning. Brill concluded that Mark Lane "has only two motives: Profit and headlines."

Brill also wrote that, "Mark Lane is as utterly truthless as any who has ever moved across our headlines." Reading Brill's story of his time spent with Lane in 1979 caused me to me realize that Mark Lane was a greedy, sociopathic monster. But why was I surprised? The New York Times reporter Anthony Lewis also wrote about Lane, very unfavorably, as had numerous other journalists.

The Yiddish term, 'Judenrat 'refers to Jewish people who betrayed their fellow Jews during the Third Reich. Several Jewish friends of mine used this term in describing Mark Lane. 'Lie down with dogs, wake up with fleas' doesn't only apply to drug addicts. It's also applicable to associating with white supremacists, Holocaust deniers, and racist conspiracy theorists. Then there's the canny, brazen, credentialed, well-paid, well-connected professionals they hire to do their dirty work.

This latter category now included me.

Three years later, in mid-1999, I was subpoenaed by lawyers representing the Institute for Historical Review, which was then the world's premiere Holocaust-denying organization. Lane and a team of other lawyers, all representing Carto and Liberty Lobby, were all there as I was questioned on the stand by one of the IHR's attorneys. Willis Carto was about 25 feet in front of me as I testified under oath in the courtroom of Judge Martin Teel, Jr., in the U.S. Bankruptcy Court in Washington, D. C.

When I was asked about many of the very things that Lane had threatened to expose, I calmly told the truth. Eyebrows were raised, and audible gasps heard, when I admitted my role in Carto's scams to illegally direct large advertisers to pay for ads with checks payable to his nonprofit entities, rather than to Liberty Lobby, or to the SPOTLIGHT. According to 'Blood Politics', which is a 2009 book about the White Nationalist movement, my testimony was decisive. As author Leonard Zeskind wrote, "The hearing, particularly Blodgett's testimony, apparently convinced Carto that his best path was to avoid the reporting that bankruptcy court required. Within the next month … an agreement was reached and ratified by Judge Teel." That night, I received an anonymous death threat.

Some coward called my cell phone, and threatened to cut my head off. The coward had blocked his phone number, so tracing the source was impossible. Linda and I were watching TV when the dude called. When she asked who had called, I replied, "Not a friend."

A few weeks later, a process server handed me a subpoena, issued by the law offices of Mark Lane. Willis Carto was preparing to sue me, for $580,000. This lawsuit was without any basis, as Carto and Lane knew. With my lawyer,

Jack Fornaciari, I sat for two depositions with Lane, and another Carto attorney, Tom Stanton. They tried to force a settlement, which I refused. After I paid about $35,000 in legal fees in about three months, Lane and Carto backed off. By that time, I had Fornaciari file suit against the University club – which was the start of $450,000 I paid in legal fees to three attorneys and three law firms, over the next six years. But Willis Carto and Mark Lane weren't yet done with me.

Much like Mark Lane, the Holocaust deniers I associated with were also after headlines and profit. But at their core, what motivates them to use the Holocaust to spread their hatred toward Jewish people? What makes them detest blacks, Hispanics, and Gays? As William Pierce said, "we cannot just go out and yell about how much we hate Jews. Practically speaking," said Pierce, "we must use salient issues to get others to hate them." That's what they do, when they lie about proven history and dispute the valid claims of the survivors of Nazi atrocities. Pierce, Willis Carto, David Irving, Gregory Douglas, David Duke, Don Black, Chris Temple, Paul Hall, Richard Butler, Ed Fields, Jamie Von Brunn, and other prominent, intelligent deniers, all privately acknowledged that millions of innocent Jews were either exterminated, tortured to death, or left to die, or overworked, until they dropped dead.

But by denying, or disputing, irrefutable facts, they turn people against Israel, and against Jewish culture, and against Jews. They also make racist, fascism and other radical ideas more palatable to certain people. Their over-riding desire to slam all Jews as selfish, money-hungry, dishonest conspirators fits the negative stereotypes which, tragically, have poisoned tens of millions of minds over hundreds of years. "People used to think the world was flat, or that man would never set foot on the moon," Pierce told skeptics he sought to convert into Aryan warriors. Then he'd segue into "the so-called Holocaust", and convert the skeptics into True Believers.

Believing such lies means ignoring the more than 50,000 interviews, taken in 56 nations and in 32 languages, with Jewish survivors of, and witnesses to, the Holocaust. It requires ignoring the reality that Germans have never denied their atrocities. It ignores judicial records from the Nuremberg trials. It ignores the fact that there were nearly six million fewer Jews in Europe in 1946 than there had been in 1939. It ignores film, photographs, news reels, and aerial surveillance of concentration camps and other evidence substantiating one of the most fully documented events in all of history.

Holocaust deniers and white supremacists speaking at seminars advise their audiences to turn charges of hatred to their advantage. Dr. Ed Fields and David Duke were particularly skillful at this. They and other speakers urged followers to deny claims of hate, by stating that they love their race, and their dissatisfaction with the present state of their country, and the mess it had become. The contrast between the racist radical right and normal holders of public office couldn't be more striking. Liberals and conservatives, and Republicans and Democrats, hold divergent views. But at base, most of them promote what they believe is in the best interests of their constituents and the country.

That's why I respect candidates and elected officials like Donald Trump, Ronald Reagan, my Dad, and others of both parties who don't go into government to enrich themselves. Many public servants – elected, and appointed, and at all levels – sacrifice to serve. My father's political career didn't come cheap. During the 16 years he served in elective and appointive office, he gave up $10 million in income, based on what he made as a successful orthodontist. As a Legislator his annual salary averaged $25,000 – down from $650,000 he'd earned from as an orthodontist. His out-of-pocket costs were also considerable, in Des Moines and in D.C. Each of the eight years he served in the Bush administration set him back $150,000 over and above his annual salary as a federal administrative Judge.

Overall, my dad's political career set him back nearly $12 million in out-of-pocket expenses and the substantial income he chose to forgo. He and my mother also nearly lost a son, to my drug addiction and the dangerous lifestyle that goes with it. But in my view, I was feeding and maintaining a developmental disorder as I learned to be a junkie. A false consciousness overtook my thought process, and had become my new 'normal'. I recall thinking I could overcome my addiction if and when I chose. Years later, when I was finally ready, that's what occurred.

Since joining Narcotics Anonymous in early 2005 – when I was still smoking crack but knew that not stopping meant either going to prison, or dying – I've tried to carry the message to addicts that if they want to get clean, and stay off of drugs, they can.

This also applies to organized white supremacy, Holocaust denial, and racist hatred. Where there's a will, there's a way. To prevent sociopathic behavior – and this applies also to drug addicts – parents, teachers, and others can try to obviate the onset of self-entitled thinking among children, teenagers, and young adults. Self-entitled thinking can lead to sociopathy, and it did among people who became drug addicts and hateful racists. In my case, some good Samaritans and guardian angels helped me. If there was anyone who saved my life, and more than once, it would be the late J. Ralph Whitehead. Ralph was a black man 15 years older than I, with a son who is nearly my age. We became friends in 1990, when he began working at the Kennedy-Warren building, where I had lived since 1987. He was also a veteran of the United States Army, and a resident of the District of Columbia since the late 1960s.

"Come to da Cat; buy a nigga a drink, or six," spoke the familiar voice on the phone. It was J. Ralph, inviting me to pick up the tab for some double Hennesseys on the rocks. He was walking to the Black Cat, a downscale bar on upper 14th street, NW, in D.C. Upon my arrival, J. Ralph said, "Here come Captain Save-a-Ho! Whassup, Mighty Whitey?"

"Why do you say that?"

" 'Cause dat what you is," he answered. J. Ralph then referenced my throwing down with the ghetto rat who tried to rape our mutual friend Tamika. "Remember 'dat nigga 'dat y'all done stopped from rapin' Tamika? He done left outta DC. Word in the hoods travels faster than on Capitol Hill."

"Whatever became of that scumbag?," I asked. "Spent three weeks in DC General," Ralph replied, referring to the district hospital the creep was taken to after Rollo rearranged his face, broke three of his limbs and bit off part of his lower lip and an earlobe. "Rollo lay into 'dat cat like a damn buzz saw." "Dat nigga were damn lucky Tamika neighbor lady done called 9-11, befo' Rollo could finish him off", J. Ralph said. "I told Rollo to not kill the dude," I replied. "He didn't," J. Ralph said. He added that after the perp "moved down to South Carolina, to be with he peoples", out of fear. The waitress brought us drinks, which Ralph had ordered in advance of my arrival. I told Ralph I wasn't surprised that Rollo had torn the guy halfway to pieces. "Yeah, 'dem am-bull-ance peoples didn't think he were gonna make it."

"That bad, huh?"

"Rollo ain't one for showin' mercy. Y'all done picked da right homey to stomp dat nigga." Taking a strong pull on my Jack and Coke, I said nothing. "I ain't sayin' dat asshole ain't deserve what he get," J. Ralph said. "I'm down with it, for real. But you Republicans, y'all be hypocrites."

"How's that?"

"Y'all always bitchin' about you taxes bein' so damn high."

"Taxes ARE too high."

"Maybe. But siccin' dat crazy mofo onto dat low-life mean SOMEBODY had to pay he hospital bill. That's how you a hypocrite. Dat ass-kickin' 'dat y'all done lined up make taxes even higher."

"How's it my fault that the law won't allow citizens to shoot rapists? Liberals made that illegal."

"Oh, I gets it. Shoot now, and axe questions later?"

"Why ask questions?"

"Now you soundin' less like a Republican than a fascist. Probably on count of dem Nazis y'all knows."

"You're saying I'm a Nazi?"

"I ain't say 'dat. Y'all a Republican."

"Okay."

"Course, most Republicans just be Klansmen without they robes!"

"That's B.S."

"I ain't so sure. But YOU ain't 'dat way. That's why we friends. We make a Democrat outta y'all, yet!"

There was no chance of that. "I'd have to smoke a shit load of crack for that to happen."

"Well, you be well on yo' way. Anybody carry loaded guns in DC ain't zackly smart. Get y'self busted with one of 'dem pieces, even dat Republican livin' in dat big, white house at 16th and Pennsylvania won't sympathize with yo' pistol-packin', crazy, white ass."

"You have more faith in the alleged crime-busting abilities of DC's finest than I do. I'll take my chances."

"That's what you was BORN to do, dawg. But don't worry. When y'all be in lock-up fo' five to ten, I'll visit ya. I'll tell 'dem niggas in da joint to not let nobody makes you be they bitch."

"That's nice of you, Ralph. But it won't be necessary."

"That's what dem all says, till they gets busted by da PO-lice. Thazz for real. Mmm-hmm." When the DC cops busted me a few years later, I realized J. Ralph had been right all along. Violence that's such an integral part of addiction was becoming, ever more, a frequent occurrence in my life. A few months after J. Ralph warned me about where addiction was taking me, I was in a basement in Anacostia, DC, with with two black men, two white guys, and a black lady – junkies, all. Lacking a crack pipe, one of the black guys walked outside, broke off a car antenna, and brought it back inside to use as a pipe. Upon disassembling the antenna, he washed it out in the bathroom lavatory, and then dried it by threading some Q-Tips through it. He then had the stem – a crack pipe.

But an argument ensued over the crack on the table, with the two white dudes and the black chick throwing down against the two black fellows. After two minutes of loud name-calling, including violent threats in which every-one called everyone a nigga, the white guy who owned the place ordered one of the black dudes – a drug pusher, who went by the name of 'Q' – to leave. The dealer rose and began gathering up his unsold rocks, which were on a low table facing the couch. The other black guy, Charles, wasn't kicked out. One of the whites, realizing the drugs would vanish once 'Q' was gone, told the pusher to leave. As in, immediately.

'Q' was still carefully dropping his unsold rocks into a large Tylenol container. "Gimme a minute," he replied, "Lemme finish puttin' my shit back in 'dis bottle." The junkie repeated his demand as I walked toward the staircase leading to the ground level. 'Q' reiterated that he'd be done "in just a minute."

The white crackhead, whom I'll call Mark, then swept his arm across the low table, scattering about four hundred bucks worth of crack onto the shag carpet. Some of it even flew into the bathroom, and at the landing where I stood. If Mark thought 'Q' would leave, right there and then, he was mistaken. The dealer sprung to his feet and backhanded the junkie so hard that it broke his jaw. His jaw dropped about two inches below its normal level. His buddy, whom I'll call Jeff, yelled at 'Q' and threatened to call the cops.

Just what we need, I thought: police at this crack house, where the only person who'd pass a drug test is the dealer. 'Q', astonished at Jeff's 911 threat, said, "feel free." Charles, sensing danger, administered an ultra-swift kick to Jeff's stomach, knocking him to the floor. Gasping for air, sprawled on the carpet, Jeff held his midsection, groaning like an actor on a 1970s Alka-Selt-zer commercial. The crack whore, Trishondra, said, "Todd, help me find they rocks." When 'Q' heard this, he looked directly at Trishondra and warned, "Steal any my rocks, bitch, I will braid yo titties."

As Trishondra unlocked the door to let them out, Charles turned toward Mark. "Don't never keep no nigga away from his shit." I drove Jeff and Mark to the Howard University hospital Emergency Room, where their injuries were treated. Mark's jaw was wired shut for three months. But for the entire time, he continued to get high. With junkies, where there's a will, there's always a way.

Shattuck-St. Marys school hosted an all-class reunion in June, 2002. One of my old roommates called and urged me to attend. As I was to be in Iowa for the month of June, I attended. Linda remained in North Iowa for the two days I was in Faribault Minnesota, at the campus. While driving to Minnesota, I wasn't looking forward to telling my old buddies – over a dozen of whom had attended our wedding nine years earlier – of my situation. But at least I didn't have to let on that I was hopelessly addicted to crack cocaine, and my marriage was on the rocks.

The Shattuck school campus, by now called Shattuck-St. Mary's, has since 1858 been situated high on a bluff overlooking the bucolic little town of Faribault, Minnesota. The original buildings, most of which still exist, are in a sort of gothic architectural style, which reminds many first-time visitors of a medieval cathedral community, with some 1920s art-deco tossed in. Driving onto the main entrance of campus requires passing under a massive marble arch, known as the Whitney Arch. It was given to the school by the Shattuck class of 1921. As I walked over to the massive tent set up on the enormous front lawn, a couple of alums beckoned me over to where they were gathered.

"Blodgett! C'mere, you crazy Republican!," one yelled. Within 20 minutes, I downed three double gin and tonics, but was still sober. A man I didn't recognize walked up and introduced me to his son, who'd just completed his freshman year. "This is Mr. Blodgett, son. He was the wildest guy in Whipple dorm, in our day. After that, he was the wildest dude in Dobbin dorm. Todd's certifiably crazy, but that didn't stop two Presidents from hiring him."

As I shook hands with the kid, a familiar voice from behind me joined the conversation. "Blodgett was the craziest kid in this entire school!," a former dorm mate said, shaking my hand as he walked up. "I should know," yet another man said, "I lived in the room right next to him, for a summer session." The kid asked me, "who was the President when you went to school here,?"

I replied, "Gerald Ford and then Jimmy Carter." The boy's father wasted no time in putting that information to good use. He told his boy, "Mr. Blodgett had to take a summer session here, after he was kicked out. But he graduated from college and then worked for two Presidents. So maybe it won't be so bad for you next week when you begin your summer session." The unimpressed kid didn't seem to agree.

CHAPTER TWELVE

The lawsuit I filed against the University club of DC was ten times as costly as I'd anticipated. Even after I had paid my attorneys $200,000 in legal fees, there was no end in sight. Depositions, hearings, and the discovery process aren't cheap. I made an appointment with my dad to see him at his office, to ask him for some financial assistance. As I sat across his desk from him, he was sympathetic, but skeptical. "I'll help you, Todd, but where does all your money go?" My Dad knew I had netted over $1 million from my years with Liberty Lobby and that in 1998-99, I had inherited $675,000. Because my sale of the shares of Resistance Records stock was reported in the news, he also knew that another $300,000+ had come my way. He also knew what the FBI was paying me, and that Linda was highly paid for her work as an oncological surgical Registered Nurse. But he didn't know I was a drug addict whose addiction – and its related expenses - had already cost me over $500,000. He agreed to pay all of the remaining legal bills related to my lawsuit, which ended up being approximately $350,000.

William Pierce called me that later that same day. He said a supporter of his wanted me to meet with two of his associates, who might be able to influence the outcome of my case. Cryptically, he said he didn't "always recommend the methods utilized" by these so-called associates. Days later, I found out that their proposal involved killing James Bond. These associates of Dr. Pierce's benefactor met with me in a guest room of DC's Metropolitan club. A member of a private club from another city was the guest of record in this room. His club had reciprocity with the Met club, and the National Alliance supporter who belonged to that club paid for their two rooms. Had I not known they were affiliated with anti-Semitism, White Supremacy, Holocaust denial, and racist violence, I'd have assumed – based on their appearance and demeanor – that they were professionals of another sort.

They could've passed for successful bankers, M.D's, partners in a top law firm, real estate developers, or even lobbyists. They were, however, way too well-dressed to have passed for members of Congress. They appeared to be about the same age, around 50. They wore expensively tailored suits, silk neckties, and gold wristwatches. One of them wore alligator shoes, and the other had on black brogues, polished to a high gloss. These two, whom I'll call 'Lou', and 'Nate', were as smooth as they were well-spoken.

"As you're aware," Lou said, "one of our clients is a very generous supporter of Dr. Pierce. This client is very interested in making sure your legal action will result in a favorable outcome for Caucasians. He's fully supportive of your efforts to battle against the Jews and their useful idiots, who got you expelled from the University club." At that point, Nate asked me if I needed a refill on the Jack Daniels he had poured me five minutes earlier. I did. Nate, referencing that my attorney had filed my lawsuit in D.C., told me I needed "a change of venue."

"A change to where?" Smirking, he replied, "to outside the law." Lou said, "we know who the Board members are who've caused you all this misery. We also know where they live, work, and socialize."

"You fellas are into research," I replied. "Our client is particularly upset with Mr. Goldman, Milton

Kotler, Susan Neely Jones, Bernie Casey, Tim Sullivan, and James Bond," Nate told me. "Of secondary importance are Mark Tuohey, and Judge Loren Smith." These people were all University club members, and all held leadership positions. Susan Neely, an Iowa native, was on the club's Board of Governors.

I'd known her since 1982, when she was Lt. Governor Terry Branstad's press secretary in Des Moines. Judge Loren Smith, who was Jewish, was an early supporter of Ronald Reagan, dating back to his 1976 campaign. He was now the Chief Judge of the U.S. Court of Claims. Smith had also served on President Nixon's Legal Defense Team during the Watergate investigation. Yet, to these guys, Judge Smith merely represented a payday, and they wanted me to wish Mr. Smith dead. Mark Tuohey is the son of a late, legendary FBI special agent and was a prominent DC lawyer who had served as a counsel to President Clinton during the Monica Lewinsky scandal. Bernie Casey, a former President of the club, was a well-known attorney, as was Sullivan. James Bond was a member of the Board of Governors, and a very well-connected Washington lobbyist. "We understand that Mr. Bond has longstanding ties to AIPAC," Lou said, "from his years on Capitol Hill, with Senator Packwood."

AIPAC is the American Israel Public Affairs Committee, an influential political entity. I later found out that their findings were spot-on correct. This was way beyond creepy. Over the next 15 minutes, Nate and Lou said no action would be taken absent my approval. "Our client won't authorize anything which you feel might adversely impact your lawsuit, or anything you don't wish to occur," Nate told me. "But as a member of Ronald Reagan's White House staff, you surely know that one of Reagan's greatest strengths was his ability to delegate tasks to competent professionals," Lou said. "I know," I replied.

"You know Jamie Von Brunn," Nate said. "Yeah, what about him?" Nate said that Von Brunn would be the liaison between me and these two killers. The mere mention of Von Brunn's name left no doubt in my mind that these guys were deadly serious. As a violent racist who served prison time for attempting – while armed – to take hostage the members of the Federal Reserve Board of Governors, he was on a first name basis with known murderers. He often spoke of his desire to gun down Jews, blacks, and other minorities. An avid reader, Jamie Von Brunn had referenced my ouster by the University club, and how it had angered him. "Let us know by the end of next week if you wish to retain our services," Lou said. "If and when you give the go-ahead, things will go much better for you," Nate said, smiling.

They told me this wouldn't cost me a dime; the rich neo-Nazi would pay their fee and all expenses. "Not having this facilitated could mean you won't get back into your fancy private club," Lou warned me. "But even if you lose your lawsuit," he said, "the results of our services would mean that at the very least, you'll receive a substantial financial settlement. Fear is a truly wonderful motivator, and our client wants these politically correct scumbags to suffer, if you agree." Nate assured me that no aspect of this would be even remotely traceable to me, or to Pierce. "We're here to help, because that's what we do", he said, smiling. Lou said, "totally professional, Mr. B, with satisfaction assured." It was then I noticed the gold, diamond pinky ring on the little finger of Lou's left hand. They weren't hinting at breaking jaws, arms and legs, or windpipes. They were offering to commit multiple homicides, which they discussed it as casually as golfers at the 19th hole bitch about taxes over drinks. If I agreed to their proposition, it meant that murders would take place.

Chills tingled down my spine, and I suspected that my breathing, and facial expression, conveyed fear. I wiped sweat from my forehead, and could feel sweat in my armpits. I wanted to guzzle my third straight Jack Daniels even quicker than I'd slammed the first. But I didn't. As I approached the door to exit the room, it was implied and understood that nothing would ever be said about what we had discussed. "Remember," Nate told me, "we're here to help. That's what we do. And everything is to go through Von Brunn, regardless of what you decide. Nice meeting you. Thanks for stopping by, Mr. B."

"Thanks for your time, guys," I said, before walking down the hall to the elevator. I was shaking, despite having just downed three Jack Daniels on the rocks, with no mixer. In the Met club's lobby, I ran into an old friend, John Arundel. John's family was originally from Iowa, and his older brother, Peter, was also a buddy of mine. He was just arriving, and invited me to the upstairs bar for a drink. It was the last thing I needed, but at the same time, more alcohol seemed in order. We sat at a table near the bar on the second floor. John noticed right away that something was awry. "Is everything okay,

Todd?", he asked. "Yeah, I'm good, thanks," I replied, as I signaled the waiter for a Jack and Coke, this one a double.

By the time I left, an hour later, I wanted a different kind of coke. So I drove to Fairmont Street, N.W., and called a drug pusher who lived nearby.

The next day I called Von Brunn and told him I wanted nothing to do with the hit men or their offer. Pierce called me an hour later from his West Virginia Nazi nest. He said Nate and Lou were "sincere, dedicated, highly competent professionals who can efficaciously and permanently resolve this damned, Jew-induced problem. Their expertise", he told me, "is indisputable. They're exceptionally efficient and creative. They're consistent, reliable experts; among the best and the brightest in their field. Retaining their services is risk-free, and their clients – some of whom I know, personally - are extremely satisfied with their efficient, alternative methods of achieving conflict resolution, and obtaining lucrative financial settlements," he said. I thought that these had to be about the most elegant words anybody ever used to describe professional killers.

My world was a real-life version of the film 'Traffic', juxtaposed with 'American History X' and 'The Informant'. But, now, 'The Sopranos', 'The Godfather', and Goodfellas' were mixed in. Their demeanor conveyed their complete confidence in knowing I'd never report them or their proposed actions to law enforcement. This wasn't their first rodeo, which they knew I had sensed. I later learned that their hits included lacing a target's cigar with nicotine sulfate. After only a few puffs, he was dead.

They knew that those who are privy to what they do for a living fully understand that ratting them out means certain, sudden, violent death. While I risking dying from a drug overdose every time I used crack, I wasn't willing to place a bullseye on my back for some murderers to whom killing is like playing a quick nine holes before dinner. Given the corrupt nature of many DC cops and police in Maryland, it wouldn't have surprised me if Lou and Nate had allies within law enforcement in the Washington area and in other jurisdictions.

How would they have offed my University club detractors? Slip polo-
nium-210 in their coffee? Thallium? Shoot them, and make it look like a
robbery gone bad? Cut their brake lines? As I thought about these various
means, my head ached. Would they have smeared VX nerve agent powder
or cream on the faces or hands of their targets? Maybe poisoned them with
acute radiation, or plant car bombs in their vehicles? Smear a deadly nerve
agent cream on their faces? Most people only know about hit men from TV,
newspapers and movies, but I'd just knocked back drinks with them. Would
they have used Ricin powder, or Fentanyl-laced food? Perhaps done drive-by
shooting, or maybe used cyanide, or pentobarbital? Mail bombs? Arsenic?
Dosed them with a toxic level of digitalis? What?

How they'd have done it mattered not. I was relieved to obviate it and
horrified that I'd encountered such thugs. These dudes were far scarier than
Timothy McVeigh, Wade Page, or Eric Fairburn, Hendrik Mobus, Buford
Furrow, or Tommy Mair, or other killers I had met. These eminently presentable guys could've passed for realtors, ambassadors, bankers, executives,
insurance agents, stockbrokers, MDs, or corporate CEOs. For years now, I
had associated with people who placed no value on the lives of those they
hated. As far as I knew, Nate and Lou may not have even been neo-Nazis.
To them it was just business. As Lou said, "we're here to help, because that's
what we do. We love helping people."

My world was getting crazier and scarier every week. I hadn't left Iowa
to become part of this sordid milieu. But I was deep into it now. Would the
worst fears of my wife and my parents of me being killed as a result of these
associations come true? It might be preferable to dying of a drug OD, or
being killed in the hoods. Researchers at the Center for Applied Criminology at Birmingham City University in the United Kingdom studied contract
killers and how these professionals operate. Their findings, published in The
Howard Journal of Justice in 2014, confirmed what I had sensed: the best-
paid hit men are low-key, operate with no drama; to them, it's all about the
money. They make no mistakes, often have paramilitary experience, and are
as skilled at evading justice as they are at their criminality. They also never

reside in the same general area as their victims, which thwarts local law enforcement efforts to even investigate efficaciously, let alone bring them to justice. The report concludes that it's probable that "some hit men are so adept as killers that the deaths of their victims does not even raise suspicion and are, instead, simply thought to be the result of natural causes?" The average payment per hit in the UK was $25,000, said Professor David Wilson, and a comprehensive study by the Australian Institute of Criminology found that murders for hire in Australia averaged a cost of $16,500.

From sociopathic drug dealers and crazy junkies in the hoods, to violent, racist Skinheads, to these hit men whose wealthy, pro-Hitler client was a benefactor to the world's leading neo-Nazi, I was hanging out with people who made John Gotti look like John Kerry, or John Goodman. Worse, it was all going down as I was working for the Federal Bureau of Investigation in Washington, D.C., where my dad was working for the President of the United States, and my mother volunteered in the Bush White House.

My cell phone contained the personal cell phone numbers of several FBI agents, and agents from the JTTF, and the IRS. I was meeting with federal law enforcement agents at least every month; sometimes, I'd see them three or four times a month. But informing them of these two well-paid, professional killers would be signing my own death warrant. I didn't even want to think about any harm which might find its way to my wife, or to my parents. I was in a daze. This wasn't only real; it was surreal.

Hiring hit men to kill people isn't uncommon in the realm of the racist far right. Not long after I met those two professional killers, a 31-year-old lawyer named Matt Hale was arrested in Wisconsin for soliciting an undercover FBI informant to murder a federal Judge.

Between 1995 and 2002, I spoke with Hale at functions I attended. On one occasion, the two of us addressed the same audience. Matt Hale styled himself as the Pontifex Maximus of a neo-Nazi organization called the World Church of the Creator. Pontifex Maximus is Latin for 'highest priest', which is how Hale saw himself. For Matt Hale, hatred began as a teenager, in East

Peoria, Illinois. His father was a respected police officer; Hale told me that while growing up, he regularly attended church.

According to the Southern Poverty Law Center, Hale's brother was also actively involved in organized hate. Their father allowed Matt to operate the World Church of the Creator from a guest bedroom in their home. Mr. Hale was a friend of Benjamin Smith, a neo-Nazi who was enamored with publications distributed by Liberty Lobby and the National Alliance. In the summer of 1998, Ben Smith visited the offices of Willis Carto. At the time, he was a student at Indiana University. Carto, a native of Fort Wayne, Indiana, instructed Blayne Hutzel, Liberty Lobby's accountant, to reimburse Smith for his travel and lodging expenses. Mike Piper said that Smith also got a check for $5,000 from Willis.

Ben Smith brought two three-ring binders to Liberty Lobby on that day. Both scrapbooks were filled with articles and editorials about his anti-Semitic activities, which had been published in newspapers and magazines throughout the Midwest, and mainly in Illinois, and Indiana. Carto was extremely impressed with this young man, and the two spent over an hour taking in his office, with the door shut. When their meeting was over, they both walked past the office of my assistant. Benjamin Smith stood at the doorway, fired off a Hitler salute, and said, "death to Jews." Earlier, while he was waiting to be shown in to see Willis, Smith asked me if the SPOTLIGHT and The Barnes Review could run some print ads to promote what he called his "campus crusade against Jews."

Knowing that Willis Carto always liked to accommodate what he termed "the next generation", I told Smith – who wanted a substantial discount – that I would discuss his request with Carto. Before I could get around to it, Liberty Lobby and I had parted ways.

A year later, when Ben Smith was 21 years old, he went on a three-day shooting spree in the summer of 1999. He killed nine orthodox Jews, a Korean-American graduate student, and Ricky Byrdsong, the former head basketball coach of Northwestern university. Benjamin Nathaniel Smith also fired shots at nine other people, but missed. When Smith murdered Mr. Byrdsong, he was a successful insurance executive. Smith shot Byrdsong, who was black, as he jogged near his home with his 8-year-old son and 10-year-old daughter. His wife and the couple's other daughter were at home when the tragedy struck. Slowing his stolen van to a near-stop, Smith calmly took aim and began shooting. He didn't harm the two children. They were riding their bicycles behind their dad when the attack occurred, remaining with him as he drew his last breath. Byrdsong was widely known for his faith in God and his integrity. He also wrote a bestseller, the title of which was, 'Coaching your kids in the Game of Life'.

As Linda and I watched the news reports on TV about this heinous crime, I told her what a shame it was that this book wasn't around for Ben Smith's parents to read while their son was growing up. I never told Linda that Ben Smith had been in my office, and maybe she'd not have been surprised.

Ironically, had Ricky Byrdsong had the opportunity to meet Benjamin Nathaniel Smith, his first inclination probably would've been to try to help him.

An FBI analyst told me that Smith's crimes were directly related to his membership in the World Church of the Creator. For trying to arrange for the murder of federal judge Joan Lefkow, Matt Hale in 2005 was sentenced to 40 years in federal prison. He is scheduled to be released in December, 2037, when he'll be 66 years old. In September of 2000, Linda and I flew to Paris for ten days. I turned 40 years old while there, and we took in all the sights of the City of Light. But our trip didn't improve our marriage.

In late August of 2001, we flew to Paris again, and then to Florence, Italy, for the wedding of my buddy Kevin Bailey. While it was great to get away, I had too much on my mind to truly enjoy myself. On the flight back to Dulles airport, I sensed that my marriage was doomed. I also was sick of dealing with professional anti-Semites, Klansmen, and organized, racist haters.

In 2002, the late Whitney Houston said, "crack is whack. Crack is cheap. I make too much money to ever smoke crack." Regardless of whether the lovely Miss Houston smoked crack, for addicts, it's not cheap. And with no disrespect to Whitney Houston, no one makes too much money to smoke crack. Upper-middle-class, well-bred, college-educated, and even wealthy junkies aren't unique. Jeb Bush's daughter, Noelle, was addicted to crack for years. Thankfully, she's now clean. Law enforcement statistics often don't accurately reflect the amount of crack cocaine consumed by the demographic that I'll label here as 'Republican crackheads'. Partly, it's because such junkies – and/or their families – can retain the services of superior lawyers, and have influential contacts, which helps in dealing with courts.

It's easier to get a charge dropped, or reduced, or an arrest record expunged, when the addict's father plays golf with the district attorney, or the junkie's mom plays bridge with the judge's wife. Even some nouveau riche families who may lack formal education credentials have the cash to buy access to those with useful connections. While it may be true that white guys can't jump, they can, and do, pull strings.

Most drug addicts in America's inner cities lack the money, lawyers, contacts, and resources, to game the legal process in their favor. They're not infrequently stuck with overworked, underpaid public defenders, whose caseloads are so backlogged that the best they'll do for their clients is convince them to plead guilty a lesser charge, which may not be acceptable to the prosecutor, or Judge. A stockbroker I knew, whom I'll call Chip, was a crackhead with a substantial trust fund. After he was let go from his job, his wife – who also used drugs, occasionally – became the breadwinner. When Chip's parents found out he was still smoking crack, they cut him off, completely. By this time, his wife was pregnant with their first child. To support his habit, Chip stole luggage. He'd steal pricey baggage from DC's Reagan National airport and Dulles international airport.

At the same time, he stole luggage from the Baltimore-Washington airport, Boston's Logan airport, and, eventually, New York's LaGuardia and JFK airports. Several times, he made trips to Philadelphia's international airport for the sole purpose of stealing expensive suitcase, duffel bags, and other luggage. In about 24 months, Chip was able to fence – that is, sell to a third party – that luggage and its contents for nearly $500,000. In one single heist, Chip snagged three brand new Gucci suitcases, all containing high-end, new clothing and leather goods from Europe. He also snagged an Alpha Tumi suitcase, and an Andiamo. This scam was easier to pull off than most people imagine, back in the first five years of the 21st century. In 2010, a Phoenix couple was charged with taking more than "1,000 pieces of stolen luggage and belongings piled floor-to-ceiling in their home. The pair had been lifting bags off carousels at the airport," according to reporter Scott McCartney of The Wall Street Journal.

Most airline passengers simply won't suspect a nice-looking, white, well-dressed, preppy young man, wearing $500 Brooks Brothers cordovan loafers, shirts from Paul Stuart, and a three-button sport coat from J. Press, of being a high-end thief. Back then, the Transportation Security Administration (TSA) didn't require airlines to report baggage theft statistics, and sometimes have no idea if luggage was stolen or simply lost. Chip was never caught stealing baggage, or busted for drugs. By the time his third child came along, he'd been clean for several years. He has since mended his relationships with his parents and siblings. Airline passengers collectively lost a half million dollars because of his thefts.

Chip's drug addiction was as emotionally devastating to his parents and grandparents as mine was to my loved ones. Because his family name is well-known, he lived in constant fear of being busted, and the shame and embarrassment he knew would result. But that didn't stop him from committing larceny. Then there were the five junkies from D.C's Georgetown set, who devised a creative, yet illicit, way to fund their habit. A crooked attorney and a crooked realtor masterminded this scam, which also involved a stockbroker, a Lobbyist and a PR executive. These guys would negotiate short-sales of high-end homes, which involved getting banks to allow the sale of residences for less money than was owed on the properties. This was done to partially recover their investments.

When they'd buy these homes via short-sales, none of the men had enough money on deposit in the bank to cover the checks that they wrote to purchase the properties. In obtaining mortgage loans for these houses, they lied to the lenders regarding the fair market value. In reality, these properties were worth considerably more. So when the sales closed, these buyers then sold the homes, at far higher prices – often on the following day. This was done absent the knowledge of the lenders. Money from the later sales were deposited into their accounts, to cover the checks they wrote for the first purchase. Their illegal profits resulted from them pocketing the discrepancy.

Two of these guys were from highly prominent families whose names are well-known in DC and the surrounding area. They lived in constant fear of being caught, busted, arrested, charged, and then sentenced, for their multiple crimes. I could relate well to such fear, because I shared it.

Anyone who Googles my name or my father's name can see what I mean. Longtime Iowa political reporter John Skipper covered my father during his four terms in the Iowa Legislature, and while he served in the Bush administration in Washington. In a 2014 column, Mr. Skipper described my dad as, "almost the perfect example of the Republican stereotype: the retired Orthodontist is an unbending, ultraconservative country-clubber who did very well in his professional life before he entered politics." "Dr. Blodgett uses his money and influence to make sure his people get elected." Skipper described my dad as north Iowa's "Republican patriarch, who regularly introduces Gov. Terry Branstad and other GOP dignitaries when they" visit north Iowa. Skipper accurately described my dad, especially as an 'unbending, ultraconservative'. Another Iowa publication, North Iowa Today, referred to my father as "north Iowa's Republican Kingmaker." I dreaded the thought of my drug addiction ever being made public. But being an unbending ultraconservative only made it more difficult for my dad to understand drug addiction or accept the fact that his oldest son had become a junkie."

For my parents, my addiction was confirmed when an alert staffer working at the Lansburgh's front desk – a black lady, who was a good friend of my mother's, whose husband was a recovering crackhead – became suspicious and voiced her concerns to my mom. When my parents confronted me about it, I confessed. My mother was heartbroken and started crying. She immediately wanted to help me.

My dad glared at me, yellling, "You smoke crack? Crack? Damnit, even I know that that's a goddamned GHETTO drug! What the Hell's WRONG with you? Dangerous people use that stuff, most of whom are black. You could go to prison, or get yourself killed, just by associating with such losers. Stop it, STOP it, STOP it NOW. Do you hear me? You weren't raised to hang out with junkies, or use drugs. No more drugs, of any kind. Never. Got it? If you don't understand me, you will when you're out of my will."

He then asked my mom when dinner would be ready. Before I left, I pleaded with my parents to not tell my wife, or anyone, of my problem. They said they wouldn't hide it, but agreed to not inform Linda, or anyone else, about it. My father added that this promise was conditional, upon my ceasing with crack cocaine, and disassociating myself from those he referred to as "the druggies." I left their apartment after dinner, and drove home. Linda was there, watching TV and drinking a martini. She'd never been a big drinker and didn't particularly like martinis. But lately, she'd been drinking way more than usual. Husbands can drive their wives to drink, and my activities were having that effect.

It turned out that this was her second martini. We drove over to Pistone's Italian inn, an old line restaurant in Falls Church. Linda said that while she still loved me, she was worried something was very wrong, and it wasn't only my work for the bureau. She ordered a gin martini and picked at her food. Before she could order another, I asked for the check. Back home, she went straight to bed, while I went to my basement office and put my head down on my desk. Addiction was running my life and ruining it at the same time, and harming Linda, as well.

I was increasingly witnessing the downsides of addiction while continuing to use drugs. One night, my buddy Chip sent me a text inviting me over to his condo to join him and his wife for dinner and drugs. I never introduced Linda to Chip and his wife, because Linda wasn't a crack head. Before I arrived, some unexpected guests invited themselves to Chip's place. As I knocked on the door to their snazzy pent-house unit, something felt weird. Once inside, I encountered four big thugs I'd never seen. They were working for a Baltimore-based drug dealer to whom Chip owed money – lots of it.

As this nice, well-dressed couple with a baby on the way sat nervously on their sofa, their personal belongings were being carted off in lieu of payment. Chip and his wife, Kelsey, sat helplessly, as their flat screen TVs, stereo, speakers, and DVD players were unplugged, and hauled away. They took their microwave, toaster oven, Kitchen-Aid mixer, and some of Chip's suits, blazers, and even shoes.

Wedding presents, family heirlooms (Chip's great-grandfather had been a famous WW II General under the command of Dwight Eisenhower), and golf clubs which had belonged to Kelsey's grandfather, and three sets of skis, and two snowboards, were walked out of their home. "Blodg, this is what's called making good on a drug debt," was Chip's way of explaining it. I realized that what was happening was standard procedure, and a far less painful alternative to what awaited less affluent junkies. "Do dis be a kid's tennis racquet?", asked one. "It's my squash racquet, dude," Chip replied. "Just take it."

Shrugging his shoulders, the thug tossed the Head racquet into a box. "I gots me a nephew 'dat play tennis. I'm a-see if him want it," he said, as he re-zipped the leather cover. The moving crew left about 40 minutes after my arrival. Chip was crestfallen, and Krissy was in tears. I ordered two pizzas from Domino's for our dinner. That was because the thugs had taken the ribeye steaks, Caesar salad, baked potatoes, wine, chocolate pudding, and brownies that Kelsey had planned to serve that evening.

As I left their place, it was clear to me that Karma was real. Karma remembered that Chip had stolen luggage and valuables to support his drug habit, and now she was making him pay. Those who have met the bitch called

Karma know to stay on her good side. Those who stray are always ready for an unexpected, painful slap on the back of the head from Karma.

The next day, I met with two FBI agents before I drove to Baltimore to meet with William Pierce. He had met with his lawyer, of the firm of Piper and Marbury. Pierce and I met at an old, Italian restaurant in Little Italy. Baltimore's Little Italy section is in the heart of its downtown, not far from the inner harbor. Pierce informed me that a skinhead, Wade Michael Page, whom I described earlier, drove to his compound and pestered the Resistance Records staff about signing him to a contract. Page had no talent whatsoever, I told Pierce. He'd been a perennial presence in the Hate Metal music scene for years, and was mentally unstable. Among his many tattoos, Page was especially proud of the Celtic cross on his left bicep, which encircled the number 14 - as in David Lane's 14 words.

I told Pierce that Page should be banned from having any further contact with Resistance. "He seems to have some loose screws," Pierce replied, and "he also has the capacity for violence." Pierce added that Page had been discharged from the U. S. Army for misconduct. It was while in the military that Wade Michael Page became active in organized Hate. In 2012, Wade Page walked into a Sikh temple in Milwaukee and shot the place up, killing six parishioners.

Pierce then said he'd fired Sam Van Rensburg, the South African Holocaust denier I had worked with several times. Van Rensberg had bragged about being "paid to kill niggers", as a sniper with the Afrikaners. Van Rensburg, Pierce said, had been harassing girls, including some who weren't yet 18. William Pierce was also obsessed with sex, and he described – in vivid detail – his experiences with several women he said he'd recently bedded. There was no doubt he was telling the truth, which I had already learned from a part-time staffer who worked in the shipping department.

In one case, a very attractive Nazi chick in her late twenties wanted to bear his child. Pierce eagerly accepted her invitation, despite being married to his fifth wife. When the woman found out that Pierce had had a vasectomy years earlier, she threatened to have him killed. Pierce told me that he was armed at all times. Had the Baltimore police known of this, we'd have both been arrested, and faced prison time for illegally carrying loaded weapons. How I managed to avoid getting arrested for violating so many laws, so many times, I don't know. But it made me more appreciative of the role that luck plays in all of our lives. Among my friends are drug addicts, drug dealers, and petty thieves, who were busted, arrested, charged, convicted, and sentenced, for crimes not nearly as serious as some I committed.

It's impossible to ascribe my good fortune to mere luck. God watched over me. As a college-educated white guy who dressed well and owned a Range Rover, I was cut much slack, even by cops. This wasn't accorded my fellow junkies who were black, and/or poor. Life is unfair. Unlike drug dealers, suppliers, and wholesalers, high-level white supremacists tend not to be flashy with money. They fly under the radar. William Pierce's successors in the so-called White Power movement aren't nearly as intelligent as he was. However, that hasn't stopped them from coming up with some rather diabolical ideas.

I learned of the concept of 'ghost skins' in the fall of 2001, following a meeting with Chris Temple and Steven Berry. Operation 'Ghost Skins' was a plan – which was, and is, successful – to infiltrate all of the branches of the U.S. military, police forces, Sheriff's departments, and other U. S. law enforcement entities. There are over 18,000 law enforcement agencies in the USA, but no centralized recruitment process, or even guidelines, exists. Because of this, Sheriff's departments, and local and state police, are ripe for infiltration by white supremacists, via their fellow members being hired by these entities.

At a weekend seminar in the Spring of 2002 which I attended, I took a break and called and FBI agent to whom I'll refer, here, as Tim Connors. I told agent Connors of these plans being discussed by Steve Berry, Lawrence Myers, Mark Cotterill, Chris Temple, and a top aide to Rev. Richard Butler. "Take them to dinner, Rommel", agent Connors said, and "record everything." When I met with this agent, and his partner at the National Building Museum a few days later, I gave them the cartridge containing the audio record of that conversation. While the information I provided wasn't news to the bureau, it was taken seriously, and investigative efforts were stepped up.

The FBI found that a Skinhead gang was actively encouraging its members and supporters to seek employment with police departments, so Ghost Skins would be able to warn the crews of any investigative efforts. Three years after my efforts on behalf of the FBI ended, in early 2006, a JTTF/U.S. Department of Homeland Security report referenced the term, 'Ghost Skins', and efforts by such organizations to infiltrate the military and civilian law enforcement entities. A 2009 report authored by the FBI and the Department of Homeland Security noted a "resurgence" of organized hatred, in which participants are "focusing their efforts to recruit new members, mobilize existing supports, and broaden their scope and appeal through propaganda."

This report specifically cited "disgruntled veterans" as a major source of concern, and likely recruitment targets. Racist, anti-Semitic "right wing extremists will attempt to recruit and radicalize returning veterans, in order to exploit their skills and knowledge derived from military training and combat."

Conservatives and some Tea Party activists were incensed over these claims in this report, and vented their anger with the report's allegations, particularly the implication that veterans may be involved. The then-DHS Secretary, Janet Napolitano, apologized to veterans and disavowed the entire report. The investigators who had authored the report were reassigned to other tasks, and their efforts came to a screeching halt. The unit's chief was retired, and all of the professionals involved were told to not publicly discuss their findings or how the investigation was abruptly ended.

My friend Heidi Beirich of the Southern Poverty Law Center said, "they stopped doing Intel ... and that was that." The lead analyst on the report was a former Department of Homeland Security researcher named Daryl Johnson. Mr. Johnson said, "federal law enforcement agencies, in general - the FBI, the Marshalls, the ATF – are aware that extremists have infiltrated state and local law enforcement agencies that may be sympathetic to these groups." Since then, Johnson, said, the problem has become "a lot more troublesome." Among the Skinheads I knew, several were veterans, and many younger Skinheads expressed a desire to enter military service, and later become cops, so they could "help the cause." Clearly, this will be a problem for years to come if nothing is done about it. These groups are now recruiting active and retired law enforcement officers, according to Johnson.

Along with other experts in the anti-terrorism field, he claims that local police and county Sheriffs departments aren't making any efforts to even address this problem. "There's not even any training now to make state and local police aware of these groups and how they could infiltrate their ranks," Daryl Johnson told reporters in July, 2015.

I was dismayed to learn that Conservatives, in 2010, largely caused the deep-sixing of an important report that had correctly exposed, and warned of, the efforts of members of organized hate groups to infiltrate the U.S. military and various civilian law enforcement agencies and departments. That's politics. Like some politicians, drug dealers are often their own worst enemies. In the fall of 2016, a pusher named Levi Watson was busted for his role in a drug ring which supplied cocaine and heroin.

Watson told the cops that he lacked a steady income and lived in subsidized housing. However, he had posted on Instagram some photos of his Ferrari and some Lamborghinis, for which he'd paid cash. He also bragged online about his top-of-the-line Rolex watches, posted photos of him wearing over $250,000 worth of gold chains and other jewelry, and pricey accoutrements of his ostentatious lifestyle. Watson also posted photographs of himself sitting in a bathtub, where the tub was filled with $250,000 in U.S. $100 bills and Jamaican $1,000 bills. This fool has a black belt in dumb-assery. Conspicuous consumption and lavish lifestyles have brought down many drug dealers, and not only in the United Kingdom, where Watson operated.

I knew at least twenty drug dealers, distributors, and wholesalers, who lived even more exotically than Levi Watson. I asked a multimillionaire drug wholesaler why he felt so compelled to show off his riches, when most people he was trying to impress knew the source of his money. He said it was important to him that others were aware of his success. Whereas drug dealers flash their wealth around for attention, the more intellectually challenged white supremacists and Holocaust deniers seek notice of a different sort. These racist knuckleheads want to be seen as tough, even if it means committing murder.

In early 2017, a 29-year-old, self-proclaimed Christian nationalist named Ben McDowell made plans to massacre Jews at a South Carolina synagogue. McDowell is a big fan of Dylann Roof, the white supremacist who in 2015 killed nine blacks in a South Carolina church. He was arrested when he tried to buy guns from an FBI agent posing as a hit man for the Aryan Nations. For months prior to meeting the undercover agent, McDowell posted on Facebook praise for Dylann Roof, for having murdered blacks.

The FBI said his online activity also included indications he had set his sights on a synagogue in Myrtle Beach. On the internet, McDowell blamed Jews for bringing illegal drugs to America, in order to destroy whites. He also wrote, "if you ain't got the heart to fight like Dylann Roof did, then you need to shut the f**k up… " He was irate about "white people running their f***ing mouth," and "not doing nothing." McDowell described his aim as eliminating what he called "world jewelry" – meaning, Jewry – "in the name of Yahweh."

Yahweh, which is pronounced as "yahh-way", is a name for God expressed by members of the white supremacist faith known as Christian Identity. This pseudo religion is popular among racists, and its followers believe that Jews are the children of the devil. McDowell referenced Jews as "sumbitches" and suggested that for a successful race war, racists needed to [do it] "in a smart away [sic], "and White Warriors like we was born to be like Dylann Roof." In another post, he wrote, "I seen what Dylann Roof did. In my heart, I reckon I got a little bit of hatred … I want to do that shit."

For someone whose stated desire was to be "smart", Benjamin McDowell failed. He met the man he thought was an Aryan Nations hit man on Feb.

15, at a Myrtle Beach hotel. McDowell had $109 on him, for the purpose of buying a gun. Instead, he found himself surrounded by FBI agents who busted him. McDowell's criminal record made it illegal for him to own a gun, as he has prior convictions for burglary and assault. He borrowed the $109 for the gun from his grandfather. Outside the courthouse, his mom told reporters that her "wonderful son is a good man, and innocent until proven guilty."

Every time a racist-perpetrated hate crime is reported, I remind myself of what William Pierce used to say. Hundreds of times, I heard him say, "Ultimately, we will win the war only by killing our enemies." That's what Pierce wanted, and even now, 17 years after he died, that's what's happening. I last met with William Pierce in March of 2002, at the Nazi nest. Although he didn't know it, he had four months to live. He mentioned two events that the National Alliance would sponsor. The first – his annual Leadership Conference – was to be his last. It was scheduled for April 20, which was Hitler's birthday.

The second was to take place in August. Upon my return to DC, I passed this info along to the FBI agents who debriefed me. William Pierce died July 23, at his mountaintop compound in West Virginia. He would've turned 69 on September 11. A few months before he died, his fifth wife called it quits and left him. Pierce left nothing to his two sons. He bequeathed his entire estate to the National Alliance. Even as death knocked on his door, Pierce chose hatred over family.

During our last meeting, which took place in his private office, we spoke privately for nearly three hours. William Pierce sounded off on familiar themes, but also made three remarkable statements. He said that Watergate's 'Deep Throat' character was an ex-FBI man named Mark Felt, and that Donald Trump – whom he denigrated as a "kosher Conservative" – would someday be the President of the United States. Pierce castigated Mr. Trump as a "Jew lover" who "would out-do Ronald Reagan in backing Israel and move the goddamned American embassy to Jerusalem." A few years later, W. Mark Felt admitted he was 'Deep Throat', and his admission was confirmed by Watergate chronicler Bob Woodward. And in 2017, U.S. President Donald J. Trump ordered the U.S. Embassy moved from Tel Aviv to Jerusalem. Mr. Trump's detractors should think long and hard about how America's leading neo-Nazi was repulsed at even the mere thought of Donald Trump ever becoming America's chief executive.

"Todd," he said, "once the kikes, niggers, queers, and spicks have been exterminated, the race mixers, and race traitors, and stupid, lazy white freaks, should be rounded up. About 10,000 railroad cattle cars can be commandeered, and by the millions, those losers should be loaded onto those cars. They can then be double-timed, and dumped into abandoned coal mines, and even into Mount Saint Helens."

Pierce then told me that "our opponents" were "dead men." He said they were "marching, in lockstep, toward their own graves." But four months later, William Pierce beat those he despised to the grave. In August, 2002, at the FBI's request, I attended this protest at the U. S. Capitol building. It was called 'Taxpayers against Terrorism', and sponsored by the National Alliance. Other Hate organizations also contributed funds, and manpower, to organizing the event. Over 1,000 DC cops, U.S. Park Police officers, and the National Capitol police, and other law enforcement officers were present.

Several hundred neo-Nazis, most of them masquerading as conventional conservatives – swarmed the Capitol grounds, along with about 250 counter-demonstrators. It felt weird being there, and I stayed as much in the background as I could. TV reporters, news photographers, and other journalists covered the protest. I avoided them like a crackhead stays away from drug dealers to whom he owes big bucks.

The entire lawn of the United States capitol was filled. Some cops were on horseback. When the two opposing crowds got within about 80 feet of each other, the mounted police formed a line to keep them separate. The official count of the protesters was 444. A U. S. Park Police officer estimated that there were about 300 counter-demonstrators, along with the more than 1,000 law enforcement officers. The coordinator for this was a William Pierce disciple named Billy Roper. I had met Roper on several other occasions when I was with Pierce. For awhile, Roper lived on the grounds of the National Alliance, as he worked 14 hours a day spreading Holocaust denial and white supremacy. Billy Roper, Shaun Walker, and Kevin Strom, followed Erich Gliebe's orders in orchestrating this protest.

Referring to the counter-demonstrators on the Capitol lawn, Walker said they were no different from "other Jew-loving creeps." He then equated visitors to DC's U. S. Holocaust Museum, and to Europe's concentration camps, with tourists who visit the Haunted Mansion at Walt Disney World. "They go to these places to get scared," he told me. "It's all about money, with the Jews." Even if Shaun Walker had been correct, which he wasn't, he apparently was OK with a gentile named Walt Disney making money with Disneyland. As Pierce was on his deathbed, I told FBI agents, a JTTF policy analyst, and a journalist from the Southern Poverty Law Center that his Hate empire wouldn't long survive him, and it didn't.

This protest was ostensibly organized and funded by a group that called itself Taxpayers against Terrorism. And while that was the actual name of the organization, it was a front, the strings of which were being pulled by the National Alliance. William Pierce's followers had learned their lessons well, and were now applying them to do what public relations professionals call controlling the message. Prior to the demonstration, some National Alliance members met in a Capitol Hill townhouse, with some Blacks who were members of Louis Farrakhan's Nation of Islam. Hatred of Israel, and of Jewish people and culture, is what brought them together. While most of the counter-demonstrators were white, there were probably 50 or 60 blacks, and some Hispanics. Among those 50 or 60 black people were those Farrakhan supporters. They later provided information relating to the organizers of the counter-demonstration to their hateful white counterparts. The FBI isn't the only entity that utilizes informants.

Had Pierce been alive in the aftermath of this protest, there would've been tremendously successful follow-up efforts to maximize the return on investment by the National Alliance. But the ineptitude of Erich Gliebe, and the impending exclusion of Mark Cotterill from the U. S., severely impeded what remained of Pierce's empire to expand, and to even sustain itself. The FBI agents notified me of the legal efforts underway to deport Cotterill just after Pierce died. These efforts began after a Judge in Arlington, Virginia, issued an order to ban Cotterill from the United States for 10 years. He was given ninety days to get out. Cotterill's exclusion from the USA took effect in October, 2002.

Even prior to William Pierce's death, Cotterill was trying to unify the major Hate organizations in America. As an AFBNP (American Friends of the British National Party) supporter said at the time, "I particularly like [how] the AFBNP seems to operate as an 'umbrella group' for a number of other racial nationalist organizations." According to the Southern Poverty Law Center's Intelligence Report, "the AFBNP ... raised $85,000 – and very likely, much more." With Cotterill gone, William Pierce dead, Willis Carto bankrupt, and Liberty Lobby non-existent, my FBI work was coming to an end. This was fine with me, because my marriage was on the ropes, and getting high had become my top priority.

My buddy Myles was one of those perpetually confused souls of the Lost Generation of the late 1960s and early '70s. After becoming a pot head, he graduated to hashish. From there, it was then cocaine, and then LSD, acid, and Heroin. This affluent bibliophile detested Ronald Reagan, guns, and Republicans. We had nothing in common but crack cocaine. Intellectuals can be trapped into drug addition, as this most literate crackhead proved, as we argued politics, and discussed women, pro boxing, and books, when we got high together. We had met at a crack dealer's apartment, several years earlier. We smoked crack together at his co-op, where our conversations were always interesting.

I ran into him, by chance, at the Trio café, near DC's Dupont Circle. The Trio has been in the same spot since 1950, and Myles saw me sitting at the bar, alone. "Well, if it isn't DC's version of a modern, middle-aged Holden

Caulfield," he said. "What problems is our overprivileged, opinionated misfit running away from today?" When I didn't answer, Myles said, "Still blowing through your trust fund, trying to find yourself? Judging everyone you meet, and still cynical as ever, Todd?"

"Fuck off," I replied. "I may be cynical and conflicted, and sometimes overly judgmental," I told him, referencing the J.D. Salinger character. "And I was booted out of boarding school back in the day, as was Holden. But unlike him," I said, stubbing out a smoke, "I'm not rich, and I don't think everyone's a phony." Myles laughed as I said that there was much in my life to be negative about. "I'm negative, as well", he replied, "but like you, Todd, I'm not phony." He looked around to make sure no one else could hear, and said, softly, "and neither is the stuff I've just arranged to have delivered in twenty minutes."

My interest piqued, I asked, "are we talking twenty real minutes, or twenty drug dealer minutes?" "Finish your drink and settle your tab, you right-wing nut. Then come with me," Myles said. "You're gonna love this shit." What junkie could decline that invitation?

Being compared to Salinger's tormented, confused character wasn't new. Over the years, many others – including some of my fraternity brothers - said the same. But it's one thing to be cynical and conflicted as a teenager, or in your twenties. But after age 30, normal people shouldn't be that way. And if they are, well, they sure as Hell shouldn't be. At least, that's how I see it. But unlike Holden, I'm an upbeat cynic; knowing that the world is infested with sickos won't keep me from making light of it. We walked the three blocks from Trio to Myles's place, at the Rutland Court apartments on 17th Street. His co-op unit was way in the back, and because he was depressed for much of the time, it was a damned shambles. Even well-to-do, Shakespeare-quoting intellectuals can live like pigs if they're crackheads.

The combined housekeeping staffs of DC's Mayflower Hotel, the two Hiltons, the Monaco, and the Omni Shoreham would've taken days to make it livable for normal people. But junkies don't care about their surroundings, as long as drugs are there. The room in Myles's co-op where we got high was, basically, a memorial to his deceased son and wife. Framed photos were on every wall, including the two that were covered by the built-in bookshelves, which sagged from the weight of his books. In some ways, talking with him was almost as beneficial as were my weekly sessions with Dr. Weiner.

Myles asked about the state of my marriage, which he suspected wasn't good. Not being in the mood for a contemplative discussion, I deflected. "I like being married," I told him, "we'll see what happens." He then said, "there's something special about coming home to a hug and a kiss; a smile, and a kind word." As I blazed a rock, he reiterated how nice it is "to be able to experience that, because it truly means something." Exhaling smoke, I replied, "these days, it would mean I'm in the wrong house."

Myles's phone rang. Someone was outside the building and wanted to be buzzed in to his apartment. Myles punched the buttons to admit his visitor, who was a hooker. "I know you're faithful to your wife, Todd," he said. "I'll leave some stuff here in the den. When you're done, the door will lock behind you."

The hooker, a gorgeous black chick, was no older than 25. Myles then was then 55. The hooker told me she had a friend who was available, if I desired her company. When I displayed my wedding ring on my left hand, she said, "So? Most of my clients are married, and so am I. What matters?" Myles, in typical smart-alec fashion, said, "Keep smoking crack, and before you know it, that ring goes in a dresser drawer and stays there. Or, you'll sell it for drug money, if your habit eats away your cash reserves."

Being married mattered to me, and I left – but only after smoking the rocks that Myles gave me. Rocks were also what my marriage was on. My parents had just celebrated their 45th anniversary, and my grandparents their 69th. But my drug addiction, and working for the bureau, had created misery, especially for my wife. As Myles had said earlier that afternoon, "no lady should ever have to compete with drugs for her man's love." This applies to anyone in a relationship. Addiction has undermined and destroyed millions of relationships. Even then, three years before our divorce was decreed, I knew that crack cocaine would win.

Looking back, I realize that this is where I should have applied some of the lessons I learned from my long association with Ronald Reagan. The 40th President was among the most optimistic individuals who ever lived. Not only was Reagan innately positive, but he was equally determined and extraordinarily persistent. This helped him to be resilient. Reagan also firmly believed in God, and the power of the almighty to improve the lives of those who ask for help. Being positive, determined, optimistic, and persistent, and a belief in a higher power, helps drug addicts to set themselves on a course to recovery.

In the stirrings of recovery efforts, the addictive mind must be re-ordered and conditioned for the coming battle. Given that addiction is in the mind, then it can be ended by application of proper thoughts. Will power and belief in a higher power are major components, but not the only ones.

Not long after smoking crack with Myles, I ran into Tamika and Corey on 17th Street, N.W., near the Safeway grocery store. While his mom shopped for food, I took Corey across the street to McDonalds, where I bought him a Happy Meal. As we ate, Corey told me he wished I was his dad. He also said he wished that he was white.

When I asked him why, he said he believed that if he was white, his life would be easier and he'd be happier. My attempts to challenge him went nowhere. Looking me straight in the eye, this boy asked, "Todd, would you rather stay white and live to be sixty, or be black and live to a hundred?"

His simple question blindsided me, and I didn't know how to respond. After an uncomfortable eight or ten seconds, Corey said, "see what I'm sayin'?"

My cell phone rang. It was Tamika, ready to take her groceries home. At her car, she thanked me for keeping her son company while she shopped. That was the last time I saw them. Years later, Ralph Whitehead told me that Tamika and her two children had moved to South Carolina, where she died of lung cancer. I don't know what became of Corey and his sister, Shaveeka, following their mother's death. I think of them from time to time, and if they're reading this, I hope they'll contact me.

CHAPTER THIRTEEN

In March, 2017, federal agents in San Diego arrested the attorney general for the Mexican state of Nayarit on charges of drug smuggling. Edgar Veytia was the top law enforcement official in Nayarit, which is near Puerto Vallarta. FBI agents uncovered ties between Veytia and the Jalisco New Generation cartel, which they reported to the DEA and to the Department of Homeland Security. His federal indictment stated that beginning in 2013, upon becoming attorney general, Veytia conspired to manufacture and distribute heroin, cocaine, and crystal meth, until February, 2017. His alias was 'Diablo', which means devil in Spanish. But he wasn't the same Diablo who sold crack in D.C.

Mr. Veytia told voters that he was "a lawyer with a pistol on his belt", and presented himself as the "terror" of criminals. He said, "in Nayarit, there is no room for organized crime." The Los Angeles Times reported that survivors of "disappeared" cartel victims complained that Veytia wasn't interested in trying to find their missing relatives. But Mexican politicians and government officials have American counterparts who make big profits by selling drugs. High-ranking bureaucrats – kleptocrats - are getting on this lucrative gravy train. The New York Daily News reported on February 1, 2017, that a respected lawyer serving on the staff of the IRS in Washington, D.C., who also was a Professor at the Georgetown University Law School, was arrested for dealing crystal methamphetamine.

Mr. Jack Vitayanon, the well-paid professional who was moonlighting as a drug dealer, was busted when authorities confiscated a FedEx package sent by Mr. Vitayanon which contained 460 grams of crystal meth. Prosecutors said that when Vitayanon's home was searched, drugs, drug paraphernalia, packaging supplies, and drug ledgers were found.

Since 2011, Mr. Vitayanon's responsibilities included investigating attorneys, CPSs, IRS agents, and other professionals who were suspected of misconduct. Six months before Professor Vitayanon was arrested, another well-known political figure in the DC area was busted by Virginia police, in a drugs-for-sex sting operation. The mayor of Fairfax city, Virginia, Richard 'Scott' Silverthorne, went on trial the same week that Mr. Vitayanon's arrest was made public. As Mayor, Mr. Silverthorne promoted 'Quality of Life' issues, and also served as a substitute school teacher in Fairfax county. Of the USA's 3,144 counties, Fairfax country, Virginia has the second-highest median income. 50 days before his arrest, Silverthorne was sworn in for a third mayoral term. During the campaign, he promised "greater transparency".

These two recent examples of the drug culture in Washington, DC and its surrounding area aren't at all unique. Congressional aides, lobbyists, lawyers, bankers, and other professionals like Silverthorne and Vitayanon buy, sell, and use, illegal drugs in DC and the communities which surround it. In 2016, and 2015, staffers who worked for U.S. Senators Thad Cochran and Chuck Schumer were arrested on drug charges. In 2014, U.S. Representative Trey Radel, a Florida Republican, resigned from Congress after he pleaded guilty to cocaine possession. "My struggles had serious consequences," Rep. Radel wrote, in his resignation letter to then-Speaker John Boehner.

All of these well-connected druggies were either fired, or they resigned from their positions.

But if these offenders were black, lacked influential friends and contacts, and were represented by a public defender, their struggles would have had far harsher consequences. They'd also have had a far rougher time putting their lives back together. In Washington, D.C., part of the drug problem there is the composition of its police force. As mentioned in an earlier chapter, nearly 500 of the recruited officers in 1990 had criminal records. As of 2014, over

200 such officers had been arrested. Many had lengthy felony records and some could barely read or write, according to Richard W. Carlson, the former director of the Voice of America, and the father of journalist Tucker Carlson.

Some recruits who graduated in the class of '90 never even learned to properly handcuff suspects, and others insisted on keeping their sunglasses on while testifying in court. An officer arrived in court to testify at a jury trial wearing a T shirt, untied tennis shoes, low-hanging baggy shorts and six gold chains adorning his neck. A drug dealer who sold crack and PCP was incarcerated when, in 1989, he received a letter informing him of his acceptance into the DC Metropolitan Police academy.

While in the process of becoming a cop, Mr. Smith was a member of a notorious street gang called the R Street crew. A year after Smith graduated from the Police Academy, he was arrested for selling PCP and then fired. The recruitment program under which Charles Smith and other criminals were allowed to become cops was signed into law by Marion Barry, Jr., the crack head who served four terms as DC's mayor between 1979 and 1999. Mr. Barry served as a member of DC's City Council until 2014, and was still in office when he died. Louis Farrakhan spoke at his funeral. Barry's son, Marion Barry, III, died in 2016 of a PCP overdose. He was 36 years old.

For the most part, I kept my druggie associates away from Linda. But in the fall of 2002, she found out about some of them. She was in Atlanta, Georgia, for an oncology nurses conference. During this time, my parents – who were by then had lived in downtown DC for nearly two years – were in Florida, to see my niece play in a youth soccer tournament. For four nights and five days, I was alone at our house in Virginia. Early on the second evening, the urge to get high materialized when an addict I knew called my cell phone. His girlfriend had bought an eight ball of crack, and they offered to share it. I invited them over. After about two hours, we called a dealer who delivered three more eight balls to my house.

After that was gone, we drank until we were sloshed.

I began peeking through the curtains in our living room, dining room, and den, fearing the police were outside. I thought that burglars were about to break into the house. I ran upstairs, frantically looking for the key to my gun safe, which, I'd forgotten, was behind a framed picture in one of the guest rooms. Being unable to locate the key, I ran out to the garage and got an axe. I hacked away the door to the gun safe – which was made of solid walnut - and retrieved a Sig Sauer P-226 with a 15-round magazine.

I then went outside with my fully-loaded gun to confront whoever was on my property. Seeing no one, I went back inside the house, had more Bourbon, and collapsed in an overstuffed leather chair in the den. When I awakened about six hours later, the junkies had left. Nothing appeared to be missing, but how would I explain to Linda about the obliterated wall? An hour later, I called the junkie who had partied at my house. He and his girl had called a dealer they knew, who drove to my house while I was passed out.

He drove them back to D.C., and took one of my guns, a .38 Smith & Wesson, and ammunition. I noticed later that this gun was missing. I knew of this drug pusher, and would've never allowed him to even know where I lived, let alone allow him inside my house. But not wanting have one of my guns used in a crime, I called J. Ralph. He didn't know the dealer, but assured me he'd find him.

Five hours later, J. Ralph called. He had tracked down the thief and retrieved my .38. When J. Ralph arrived at my home an hour later, he was roughed up. The thief only gave up my piece after J. Ralph and another dude kicked the crap out of him. At one point, when the thief called J. Ralph an Uncle Tom, for being friends with 'whitey' (that would be me), J. Ralph's accomplice grabbed him by the afro and repeatedly slammed his forehead into the sidewalk. "That thievin' nigga," J. Ralph said, "he definitely gots his self a concussion. Him missin' half his 'fro, now, and he lucky him still breathin.'" The banged-up thief never pressed any charges against J. Ralph or his accomplice. He knew better than to even consider doing that. The stress of what occurred made me want more crack.

Later, Linda discovered that a bottle of Valium in her medicine cabinet in the master bathroom was missing. Someone had stolen it, along with her wedding ring – which she had kept in that bottle. This was a beautiful, $18,000, 2.75 carat, six-pronged platinum ring, custom-made for me by north Iowa jeweler Ross Caniglia.

I called another dealer, Remfronius, who told me to come straight to his apartment. He had to watch his kids while his Baby Mama met with her probation officer. Remfronius was a dealer who, to minimize risk, never sold crack to anyone who resided in the subsidized apartment building where he lived. His unique name was a ghetto amalgamation of his mother's name, Frondriffa, and his dad's favorite Disney character, Uncle Remus. Remfronius was pronounced as "Rem-FROW-nee-us". I called him Remy. He only dealt with junkies who lived nowhere near him, and usually, he delivered. On the elevator I ran into the renowned Father Christian Mendenhall, formerly of the DC Roman Catholic diocese.

Christian was about 15 years older than I, and a native Iowan. We'd met years earlier, at a Capitol Hill reception sponsored by an organization called Iowans in Washington. 'Mendy', or 'Father Christian', as he was known, was also a full-time Professor at DC's American University. He was gay, and by comparison made Milo Yiannopolous, Liberace and other flamboyant homosexuals look masculine. Sometime before 2000, when I met him, Mendenhall had become addicted to crack cocaine, crystal meth and PCP. His sideline was drug dealing, and his enterprise wasn't restricted to delivering stuff to clients. He made even more substantial profits by shipping powder coke, crack, and crystal meth via Federal Express. He and a dealer I knew, Diablo, had once been partners in this enterprise, as herein referenced. But after Diablo realized that Mendy was skimming profits, he called it quits. Christian paid him thirty grand to go his separate way and became a sole proprietor.

Using high-end microwave ovens, he melted large, scented candles encased in lidded glass jars. Inside his posh apartment at 4000 Massachusetts avenue, N. W., there must've been 25 top-of-the-line microwaves. The machines were scattered throughout the place, even in closets. Some were stacked atop others, and all were plugged into electrical outlets, and into multi-units plugged into outlets.

Mendenhall would melt the candle wax, then drop small, Zip-Loc bags of crack, powder cocaine, and crystal meth into the glass dish which contained the melted wax. Using dental floss, he positioned the wick in the exact spot where it was before the melting took place. Once it re-solidified, the drugs were undetectable, even to trained dogs used by police to sniff out drugs. His method was ingenious, in that he always first poured a full inch of melted wax, and, after it hardened, he added the solidified wax that contained the drugs. This piece was placed near the middle of the candle dish, below the wick.

The original labels were removed from the containers, replaced with one designed for 'Father Christian', the candlemaker. As referenced earlier, Christian wasn't the only drug supplier or dealer who used this creative method of distribution.

He also delivered drugs – mostly, crack, and crystal meth, which he called 'Tina" – to customers while in his priest's uniform. Inside Father Mendenhall's white cleric's collar were small, zippered pockets which could hold varying sizes of drug-filled, Zip-Loc baggies. The same applied to a long, white stole he would drape over his black, formal, priestly uniform. Father Christian also used bibles with pages excised in the middle of the book to conceal the drugs. Even his zucchetto hat, which he often wore while making what he called "house calls", featured tiny, inside, zippered pockets, for storing illicit drugs.

As the elevator doors in Remfronius's building opened, Mendenhall was the only person aboard. To most anyone who saw him, he looked like he was about to celebrate a mass, or on his way to visit members of his parish. "When you're all done, padre," I asked, "will you hear your own confession?"

"Please, my child", he replied, "you know I'm just serving people's needs." When I smirked, he said,

"Show some respect, honey, or you just might go to Hell." I said, "don't call me honey. As to Hell? As a junkie, I'm already there."

"That you are," he answered. "I've got some wonderful rock. Blessed it myself. Interested?"

When I didn't respond, Mendy said, "Gosh, I adore your blazer, and that necktie's lovely. Silk, right?"

Drug pushers – like Holocaust deniers - are sort of like members of the Hare Krishna, in that they seldom waste opportunities to spread the word and shake people down. They're salesmen of the first order, whose game includes deceit, flattery, lies, and more BS than what's heard at the national conventions of America's two major political parties. A few years later, Christian Mendenhall, Ph. D., received a six-figure settlement from the American University in DC. He had sued the institution for what he claimed was unfair dismissal. Six months later, he was busted by the DC Metropolitan police for possession of narcotics, with intent to distribute.

When his neighbors complained, he was forced to vacate his luxury apartment near the American University campus. He liquidated most of his possessions and moved into a cheap, one bedroom apartment on Georgetown's 'R' Street, N.W. Upon being evicted, he called me and asked if I'd "keep an eye" on his possessions – which were then piled outside the building – while he went down the block to use a pay phone near the Safeway grocery. Even his cell phone service had been terminated, for non-payment. He squandered his remaining dough on crack. Mendy briefly returned to Iowa, then moved to Rhode Island, and then to New Jersey. He died in 2013 of drug-induced liver and kidney damage. Remfronius opened the door to his apartment while holding his 20-month-old son. His three-year-old daughter was playing with some black Barbie dolls in front of the TV. Remy was a high-tech buff, and had the latest laptop computers, printers, and other electronic equipment in his apartment. There was a stack of WIRED magazines on the kitchen counter. As he excused himself to go back to the room where he kept his product, his little girl smiled at me. He lifted his son into his high chair, and handed him a bottle. On Remy's refrigerator were several photos, held in place by magnets.

There also were some clipped-out news articles. The one which caught my eye came from WIRED. It was published in 2002, and its headline was, 'Games Elevate Hate to Next Level'. It read, in part, "The most sophisticated of these new games is Ethnic Cleansing ... "

I was glad Remy didn't ask me about that when he returned to his kitchen with my fix. Once I was hooked up, I got the hell out of there.

A few days later found me back in Dr. Weiner's office. This Doc was direct, honest, and effective. He forced me to be honest with myself, which ticked me off. With five minutes left in our session, I said, "Damnit, maybe I should just call it quits with these fucking therapy sessions." Looking a me with pity, he replied, "why not? This wasn't the response I expected.

"Yeah? So, Doc, do you think that maybe I could just - "

"Sure," he told me. Then he shifted his voice to a low enough tone that nearly put me to sleep. Waving his hand to the side, he paused for a moment. Then, smiling, he said, "after all, aside from being a seriously troubled, bipolar, severely addicted junkie, with anger issues that frequently manifest themselves in violence, you're doing just fine. Then good luck to you."

Exhaling deeply, I said, "well, then, maybe we should keep going, for the time being."

Winking at me, Weiner said, "See ya next week."

Google 'Most racist game ever', and 'Ethnic Cleansing' will pop up. Then click on to Google Images. 'Ethnic Cleansing' can also be found online via YouTube. Once the video begins playing, the voiceover is William L. Pierce, himself. Dr. Pierce can be heard saying, "White Revolution is the ONLY Solution." From there, it gets even more abysmal. Viewers who watch the full length version see this introduction:

The Race War has begun. Your skin is your uniform in this battle for the survival of your kind. The White Race depends upon you to secure its existence. Enemies surround you, in a sea of decay and filth that they have brought to your once clean and white nation. Not one of their numbers will be spared."

Resistance Records released Ethnic Cleansing in January of 2002: Martin Luther King, Jr. Day. A few minutes into the video, William Pierce's image appears, as he speaks these words:

"The only way to make a revolution in this technological era is from inside the gates. If our aim is to gain control of the machinery of power, then we must recruit people who already are part of the machinery. We need the technicians, the engineers, and the scientists; we need the programmers, and the system administrators. We need the Professors, the military officers, and police officials. We need the writers, editors, and newspaper reporters – and the lawyers. We need at least some of the people who already have their hands on the levers of power. People who can throw open the gates at the right moment."

William Pierce's unexpected death in July, 2002 effectively marked the beginning of the end of his empire of hatred. It's horrifying to even speculate about the further damage he could have, and would have done, had he had more time. Had William Pierce lived for as long as Willis Carto, he would've been alive until 2022. As long as evil exists, Holocaust deniers and violent racists will fan its flames. To them, To these people, Hitler's defeat was only a temporary setback. They're in this fight for the long haul.

While I often agree with much of what is exposed by the Southern Poverty Law Center concerning racist thuggery, anti-Semitism, and organized hatred, this organization sometimes overstates their case. In doing so, opponents of bigotry, and violence against minorities, and Holocaust denial dilute their efficacy and undermine their otherwise good works. People are not hateful merely because they oppose affirmative action programs, racial quotas, or predetermined, race-based, or gender-specific outcomes. Dr. Martin Luther King, Jr., said he wanted all people judged not on their skin color, but on the content of their character. But increasingly, liberals today inadvertently foment hatred by siding with racist, conniving, liberal policy makers.

Adding insult to injury, they then lash out against those who justifiably condemn race-based programs and policies where outcomes are often preordained. Some liberals conflate the views of America's 45th President with those of David Duke and his sorry band of followers. The baselessness of these charges, however, hasn't stopped these agitators or their allies in the media from pushing their absurd, anti-Trump smears. The 45th President has not only condemned anti-Semitism, race-based violence, and Holocaust deniers, but he's mindful of the fact that he could not have been elected absent the votes of minorities. Had the votes that Donald Trump received from Jews, blacks, Hispanics and Gays in Pennsylvania, Michigan, and Wisconsin flipped to Hillary, she'd have won.

Needless quarrels based on the wrongful accusations that Donald Trump is a bigot only hinder efforts to deal with, and stop, the threats posed by neo-Nazis, anti-Semites, Ku Klux Klan members, and violent, racist Skinheads. Labeling as bigots those who aren't helps haters spread their vile message, recruit new members, raise funds, and claim they're wrongfully portrayed. It's not racist to agree with the immortal words of Martin Luther King.

In recent decades, Louis Farrakhan has tried to co-opt Dr. King's mantle. But Farrakhan peddles snake oil, spiced with anti-Semitism and threats of violence. A member of Farrakhan's DC chapter of the Nation of Islam organization was every bit as anti-Jewish as any white Holocaust denier I encountered. The man, Robert Brock, whom I referenced earlier, was funded by Willis Carto. Brock, who wore a dashiki, told me that, "the black Holocaust was a million times worse" than what he termed as "that so-called Jew Holocaust." Ignoring that he was claiming more black deaths than the total number of the world's inhabitants, Brock cited Farrakhan's vile statements about Israel. These included his claim that "Israel practices a dirty, gutter religion, for their nasty, nefarious purposes."

When I diplomatically reminded him that, historically, Jewish people have been very supportive of civil rights and efforts to improve the lives of blacks, he became downright vitriolic. "Jews want a master-slave relation-ship with us," he said. "Jews are wicked! Deceitful! They con the American people, and they're blood suckers - just like Minister Farrakhan says." Also citing Farrakhan another man told me that "Jews worship at the synagogue of Satan, and they've wrapped their tentacles around the U.S. government. Jews are evil, and they are sending our nation straight to Hell." During this discussion, about 30-35 black Muslims were present. All of them took Robert Brock's side, with some yelling, "you tell 'em, brother!", and offering other, supportive rejoinders as Brock and his comrade made their case.

When yet another participant said, "someday, we gonna BURN they greedy, Jew asses, just like Hitler done", people clapped, and shouted, "Yeah, YEAH." Another said, "ain't no Jew ever got Holocausted. That's a Jewish LIE. Y'all stop talkin' that shit." Just as with white anti-Semites, facts and history were irrelevant to these Farrakhan fanatics. Referring to Kivie Kaplan, the first president of the NAACP, Brock said that "Jews have been using us black folks for decades. That's why kikes like Kivie Kaplan take over groups that's supposed to be for blacks, only." Another man claimed that Kivie Kaplan was "only in it for the money", which ignored the fact that Kaplan was a philan-thropist who contributed millions of dollars to universities, hospitals, and organizations like the NAACP.

In 'Hating Whitey', author David Horowitz noted in 1999 that "the level of Jew-hatred is higher today than it has been in my entire lifetime, thanks largely to its legitimation through the poisonous rantings of Louis Farra-khan and his followers, and the tolerance of these views by large sections of the black intelligentsia." If anything, that level of hatred has only accelerated since Mr. Horowitz wrote those words in 1999. Mr. Horowitz, whom I've long admired, also wrote that, "no conservative politician would be seen in the company of David Duke, but a wide spectrum of liberal black politicians have embraced Farrakhan." Then there's liberal pundit Al Sharpton, whose history of anti-Semitic insults is well documented. Taunting Jewish people, Sharp-ton said, in 1991, "if the Jews want to get it on, tell them to pin their yarmul-kes back and come over to my house." He now has a paid gig with MSNBC.

In 2019, Minnesota U.S. Representative Ilhan Omar tweeted that Congressional support for Israel is "all about the Benjamins" – a double entendre', referencing $100 bills and Israeli Prime Minister Ben Netanyahu. Ms. Omar's rant was condemned by Democrats and Republicans, and she apologized.

Links between organized white supremacists and radical Islamic terrorism are well-known to the FBI, the CIA, the Joint Terrorism Task Force, and U.S. law enforcement on state, federal, and even municipal levels in some major cities. For decades, psychologists, researchers, and academicians believed that most violent racists were mentally defective, which may well be true. But their thinking was that sane people couldn't engage in bloodthirsty violence, cause destruction, and be so evil. Such thought was largely discredited even before the 9/11 attacks.

Terrorism experts, political scientists, and other professionals revised their thinking, based in part on information obtained by confidential informants. They recognized that ideology is a motivating factor and that most violent terrorists tend to have an operational view of activism. To such people, terroristic acts are how they express their views. But the warped thinking and acts which follow are usually committed by those whose sanity isn't in question. The perpetrators can be the Nazis next door.

Whether it's the Aryan Nations, ISIS, the KKK, al Qaeda, neo-Nazis, or the PLO, their methods of fomenting terrorism are strikingly similar. There's also substantial overlap in ideology: such groups are all anti-Christian and anti-Jewish. These aren't merely bad people with evil ideas; their agenda manifests itself in violence.

Counterterrorism professionals say the concept of radicalization relies on indoctrinating vulnerable people who often are a few sandwiches short of a picnic. To potential terrorists, violence makes sense in a broader sociopolitical context. Logic dictates that there can't be many mentally dysfunctional people who run under-the-radar, terroristic organizations. Could 9/11 have been successfully pulled off if crazy people had comprised, or compromised, al Qaeda? Being evil doesn't always mean crazy.

The FBI agents I worked with were under no illusions about this. But after the 9/11 attacks, the concept of mentally deficient, or semi-sane, radicalized people was back in vogue at the top levels of the bureau and the JTTF. This recycled practice of emphasizing the psychological theory that mentally defective activists with hatred in their hearts caused most terrorism is faulty and dangerous.

This view is reinforced by retired FBI agent Mike Herman, who spent years surveilling some of these same groups and individuals. Upon leaving the bureau, Mr. Herman wrote a book titled 'Thinking Like a Terrorist'. He claims governmental policies can't be overlooked, because of the impact such policies have on those inclined to affiliate with, support, or join terrorist organizations. Herman describes these two approaches to monitoring terrorists – domestic, or foreign – as the practical vs. the operational schools of thought. And white racists aren't the only anti-Semites who comprise this genre.

My first exposure to the connection between radical, anti-Semitic Muslims and organized, far right white racists came in 1995, when I met the black Holocaust denier Robert Brock. Mr. Brock was then on Carto's payroll for decades and was a mentor to Khalid Muhammad, a militant anti-Semite who was so named by Louis Farrakhan. Brock and Muhammad referenced Jews as honkies. In the late 1990s, while I worked at Liberty Lobby, Mr. Muhammad said, "I'm like a pit bull against the Jews. I'm going to bite the tail off of the honkies." Robert Brock once told me, "there's more in common between David Duke and Louis Farrakhan than meets the eye." Brock and David Irving shared stages in America and Europe at Holocaust deniers conferences, seminars and other gatherings of anti-Semites.

The actual basis for their common hatred of Jews, in my opinion, is that they know they're inferior to them. That's a strong statement, but from what I've seen, it's the truth.

The Jewish culture has always placed an extremely high emphasis on education and hard work. Rank and file racists – regardless of race – don't. For every intelligent, workaholic, professional bigot like William L. Pierce, Willis Carto, Ed Fields, Don Black, Richard Butler, and others, there are thousands who are stupid, ignorant, lazy, and uneducated. Many of them are alcoholics or drug addicts, and/or have criminal records. Such losers resent those who are successful, particularly if such winners are different from them in ways they either misunderstand, or detest for whatever reasons.

The honchos of organizations within the Hate Movement know that their rank and file members fit this description. But such activists comprise their power base, and are crucial to their revenue stream. This explains the hate-based publications, websites, radio programs, email blasts, direct mail, DVDs and CDs, private events, and other forms of outreach they use to indoctrinate, influence, motivate, and activate their supporters. When white supremacists work with black Nationalists, it's because their shared hatred of Jews overrides even their hatred of each other.

In the summer of 2000, I attended a fundraising dinner at a restaurant in Arlington, Virginia, to support the neo-Nazi Pastor Richard Butler's legal fight. A trial was scheduled for September, and if Butler lost, it could mean that his Aryan Nations compound in Hayden Lakes, Idaho, would be surrendered to the plaintiffs. Beginning in the 1980s, Butler hosted conferences at his compound, each and every year, until 2000. These gatherings were called the Aryan Youth Conference, and the Aryan Nations World Congress. I never learned the specific amount which was raised for Butler's legal defense that night in northern Virginia, but two of the event's organizers told me that it exceeded $50,000. 100 or more Butler supporters ate in two dining areas on the restaurant's ground level.

Anyone who would've seen these well-dressed, nicely mannered people at their tables would've never guessed that they were neo-Nazis. Afterwards, most of them went upstairs to the second floor, for the 90-minute meeting.

Over about five years, several racist gatherings were hosted at this establishment, as referenced in an earlier chapter.

In July, maybe August of 2001, the FBI sent me to Midpines, a small central California town in Mariposa county. My purpose was to meet with anti-Semitic publisher Paul Hall, Jr. I also met with a representative of Pastor Butler, whom I'll refer to as Ray. After losing the compound, the Aryan Nations held some of their gatherings in public parks. Other times, they met on private property owned by multimillionaire, neo-Nazi benefactors. They were allied with a virulent white supremacist named Vinnie Bertollini, and another, even wealthier Holocaust denier whose name I've forgotten. After spending two days with Paul Hall, Jr., and his wife, I met with a prominent attorney named Edgar Steele.

Steele, a native Californian, was a graduate of the UCLA Law School, and had an MBA from the Berkeley campus. He'd been Richard Butler's lawyer in his Idaho trial, and often represented racists and anti-Semites in criminal and civil cases.

We met at his hotel, where we ate dinner, before driving to the property where the event was held. The owner allowed unlimited usage of his property by various White Supremacy organizations on a regular basis, and well over 200 attendees were present that night. The people I met that evening represented a cross-section of the Hate movement. There were tattooed ex-cons and KKK members – including many females – sitting with lawyers, doctors, bankers, realtors, CPSs, and other professionals. A mother and daughter who co-owned a beauty salon were at my table, along with Edgar Steele and a young lady who said she worked as an assistant in a public defender's office.

"Nobody with a brain and a clear conscience can work for a public defender and not find all minorities reprehensible," she said, to the agreement of all. Via mailings and email notifications, a contest was announced, to come up with the funniest alternative acronym for NAACP. Midway through, while we were still in what was called the clubhouse, contestants submitted their entries. About half of those present participated in this contest, for which there were three prizes. Among the submissions were:

Now, Apes are called People

Niggers aggressively attacking Caucasian Persons

Niggers are always causing Problems

A three-judge panel met during the first half hour of the meeting at a picnic table outside, where they determined the top three entries. Toward the meeting's conclusion, before we all went outside for the cross burnings, the results were announced. A stockbroker who was also a U.S. Marines reservist, won the contest with this:

Niggers are actually colored Parasites.

Grand prize was a weekend trip to a ritzy California resort, for two people, with all expenses paid. Second place was a $300 gift certificate at a California restaurant. Third prize was a gift card from a movie theatre chain, worth $150. Did the owners of these businesses donate the prizes, knowing the winners would be Holocaust deniers? Or were they bought by Butler's supporters? I never found out.

In 2010, Edgar Steele was arrested and charged with soliciting the murder of his wife and her mother. He offered his gardener $25,000 for the murders, with another $100,000 from his wife's life insurance policy, after the killings took place. A pipe bomb was found under Mrs. Steele's car when she took it in for an oil change. Between July, 2010, and February, 2011, over $120,000 was raised online by white supremacists for his defense! The hit man was sentenced to 27 months and Steele got 50 years. He died in 2014, while incarcerated in federal prison. Cyndi Steele, who shared her husband's neo-Nazi beliefs, believed him to be innocent after his conviction. "My husband is an honorable, loving man," she told reporters. "I'll follow in his footsteps," to expose how he was framed by the Jews. This isn't only hatred on display, mixed with ignorance; it's insanity.

After four nights in California hotels, I flew home to Annandale. I flew from Fresno to LAX, and boarded a flight to DC's Dulles airport. On the five and a half hour flight from Los Angeles to D.C., I thought long and hard about how I'd neglected my marriage since becoming both a crackhead - and, now, working for the FBI. Something had to give, and it did.

Linda was home when I arrived at our house, out on the backyard deck, which was connected to our kitchen via a sliding glass door. When I walked over to her, she didn't get up; there was no hug, or kiss, or even a hello. "Are you okay?", I asked her. "No," she said, "and I haven't been for quite awhile. Which you've not seemed to notice." It was going to be a long night, and not of a good kind. Knowing I was at fault, I acknowledged all her concerns. At this point, she didn't know about my drug addiction, but was feeling increasingly isolated. That night, we slept in our bed, but when I reached over and tried to embrace her under the sheets, she wasn't receptive.

We spent a fitful night with our backs to each other, and when I awakened, she'd already left for work. In retrospect, the best thing to have done was come clean about my addiction. I also should've resigned from my FBI gig after about 90 days instead of logging in 32 months for the bureau. But at the time, my addictive personality ruled my thoughts, desires and actions. And no junkie ever makes sound decisions or good choices while using cocaine, or other mind-altering drugs.

Throughout my life, I've always been determined, self-confident and persistent, in nearly everything. But in the case of my drug addiction, which as of mid-2002, still had four years to run, my determination and self-confidence to shake it plummeted. Yeah, I knew, in the back of my mind, that I could defeat it. But first, I had to WANT to get clean. So how, and when would that occur? Certainly not then.

Countless times, I'd tell myself I'd smoked my last hit of crack. Never again would I touch the stuff. It was wrecking my life, destroying my marriage, and undermining my friendships and relationships with my parents, siblings, and family members. It was weakening my resolve, and with it, the confidence I needed to take it on, and win. If I was to prevail, it wasn't going to happen soon.

The adage about politics making strange bedfellows is nowhere more true that in the world of white supremacy and illicit drugs. Just as white Supremacists worked with black Nationalists over their shared hatred of everything Jewish, racist, violent Skinheads work with Mexican drug gangs and with members of Native American tribes, to supply and distribute cocaine, crystal meth, and marijuana. Traffickers facilitate plenty of illegal activity through Indian Reservations in the USA. I was acquainted with some neo-Nazis who, prior to going to prison, were in contact with leaders, and rank-and-file members, of the Aryan Brotherhood, via their outside contacts. These contacts, in turn, have connections within the Mexican Mafia and on U.S. Indian Reservations. These individuals facilitate drug smuggling and ensure that coke, crystal methamphetamine, and heroin find their way into Americans prisons.

In 2019, California lawyer Kevin MacNamara was charged with attempting to sneak crystal meth, cell phones and tobacco into a high-security federal prison. Guards concealed the contraband in the seat cushion of the attorney's wheelchair. Also in 2019, an Iowa man was sentenced to 26 years in prison for smuggling crystal meth into a correctional facility, by using methamphetamine-laced pages of coloring books, greeting cards, letters and envelopes. He soaked them in meth and other controlled substances before providing the narcotics-laced paper to jail inmates.

U.S. Treasury Department agents, the DEA (Drug Enforcement Administration), the U.S. Secret Service, Customs officers, the JTTF, the IRS, and the United States Marshalls and the FBI, are aware of much of this activity, including that which transpires on native American land. But they're wary of undertaking police action on ANY native land. In some situations, they fear being shot and killed, because that's happened, as well. Indian Reservations in the U.S., particularly those located in states bordering Mexico, reap big profits by accommodating organized crime, Mexican drug cartels, illegal aliens who work as drug mules, and US-based money-laundering operations. Heroin, crystal meth, cocaine, 'black' diamonds and other precious – often stolen – gems, and counterfeit U.S. currency, all change hands on Native Americans land.

Some regional cocaine wholesalers in DC, Baltimore, and Philadelphia I knew all contracted with a drug supplier whose distributor got his product from dealers that made extensive use of Indian Reservations as way stations between its source and them. It's been 20 years since I last set foot on an Indian Reservation, but my contacts are certain that these crimes are still transpiring on these lands. However, politicians fear being tarred as anti-Native American. Several attempts by law enforcement officers and agencies have backfired, with claims of alleged abuse of Native American rights. The Canadian government has also mostly shied away from asserting itself, despite knowing what's been going on.

Turning a blind eye to this only plays into the hands of the drug traffickers, manufacturers, wholesalers, money launderers, and regional suppliers, while jeopardizing U.S. security. While working for the FBI, I became aware of bizarre phenomenon surrounding illicit drug activity, which is how thousands of tons of cocaine makes its way to the United States. Privately-owned drug re-hab facilities and clinics in Mexico effectuate the smuggling, transport, and distribution of cocaine. This has been going on since at least 2002 and it's now, in 2019, in full swing. Multi-billion-dollar drug cartels actually control and operate drug rehabilitation and recovery centers, where drug lords turn recovering junkies into drug smugglers. In some cases, addicts who desperately seek recovery are given the choice between working for the cartels or being killed. As of 2017, nearly 100 such people have been confirmed as being murdered in massacres at rehab facilities in Ciudad Juarez, which is just across the border from El Paso, Texas. "Rehabilitation centers are an extension of the battlefield," said Edgardo Buscalia, a renowned

Mexican drug expert. "There are no refugees anymore." The Sinola cartel has this down to a science:

Sinola members being sought by police or by their chief rival, the Juarez gang, check into rehab clinics posing as patients. There, the phony addicts lure real junkies trying to get clean into working for the Sinola cartel – or be killed. Such establishments have direct ties to American Indian Reservations, as is known to U.S. law enforcement.

In August, 2008, in Ciudad, Juarez, a clinic's priest was preaching a sermon to recovering addicts in the clinic's chapel. Suddenly, gunmen from the Sinola cartel converged on the rehab center. They began calling out the names of various patients before shooting 13 of them, eight of whom died. In June, 2009, gunmen killed five patients at another rehab center in Ciudad Juarez, as over 50 others madly scrambled over a back fence, attempting to escape. In September, 2009, 18 drug addicts were lined up against a wall in yet another rehab, and all were shot and killed. 15 days after this attack, a woman and nine men were blown away by Sinola gunfire, at a recovery center in an impoverished neighborhood.

When it was reported in April of 2019 that nearly 8,500 homicides had taken place in the first three months of that year – which represented a 9.6 percent increase over the same 90 days of 2018 – it didn't surprise me. 33,341 people were murdered in Mexico in 2018, and at the current rate of increase, the 2019 annual number of homicides in Mexico will exceed 36,000 deaths.

While I was smoking crack, I met some junkies from the Mexico City area. My friend Maria Elena is from the Yucatan Peninsula. In 2019, she described this brutality and similar attacks on drug clinics, saying she fears the worst is yet to come, including to America. The La Familia cartel owns its own rehab centers in eight different Mexican communities, according to Genaro Garcia Luna, who served as Mexico's Secretary of Public Safety.

As patients regress in their treatment, Mr. Luna told Julie Watson of the Associated Press, staffers – who work for the cartel – target these vulnerable addicts for what amounted to brainwashing seminars. "They'd tell them that, in the name of God, you have to kill." It was easy for the La Familia cartel to convince junkies that if it wasn't for the gang, they'd already be dead. Such recruitment tactics, and the targeting of insecure, vulnerable individuals, is eerily similar to how white supremacist gangs operate. In November, 2016, reformed racist Skinhead Christian Picciolini was asked about white supremacists, Holocaust deniers, and racist skinheads employed in law enforcement and public service.

Picciolini said, "there were a lot of people in our group who went on to become cops, fire fighters, and correctional officers." Mr. Picciolini also acknowledged that many "more polished" professionals now sympathize with 'Hate Groups', including doctors, lawyers and dentists, "who are tied to militia and sovereign citizen groups", and "white supremacy organizations", which sponsor "training in paramilitary camps." Police officers, Sheriff's Deputies, active duty military personnel and reservists, and National Guardsmen all employ members of such organizations.

Some members of my Narcotics Anonymous group in Texas bought drugs from a cop who sold cocaine and crystal meth in Alamo Heights, Texas. I began writing 'Republican Crackhead' in San Antonio, Texas, where I lived until 2015. On May 4, 2014, a police officer who lived and worked in the San Antonio suburb of Balcones Heights was shot and killed – execution style – by a hit man who employed by the Mexican mafia. Officer Julian Pessina was crooked; he sold drugs for the San Antonio branch of the Mexican mafia, and his body was inked-up with drug gang tattoos. Although Pessina may not have known it, he was under investigation by federal authorities for purported ties to crime at the time of his murder. However, when gang members learned, from Pessina's FaceBook page, that he was a cop, the mafia sentenced him to death. A sergeant with a drug cartel (yes, cartels assign officer rankings, just as the military does) enlisted two aspiring gang members to assist him.

Unknown to the killers, FBI agents had installed a pole-mounted, partially hidden camera to surveil Pessina and build their case. His murder was captured on video and implicated the killers. To be considered for membership, aspirants had to kill an enemy of the organization, or anyone a high-ranking leader wanted dead. The Mexican mafia's Constitution (yes, it actually has a Constitution, according to The San Antonio News-Express) states that cooperating with law enforcement is punishable by death. According to an article by reporter Cleve Wootsen, Jr., of The Washington Post, "it is not uncommon to find civil servants among the gang's ranks." Such government workers include police officers, corrections officers, and social workers. These people are Americans, who live and work in the U.S. Some smugglers impersonate professionals in positions of authority to move drugs.

On March 27, 2017, U.S. Customs & Border Protection officers arrested a cocaine smuggler who disguised himself as a Delta Airlines pilot. The passenger – a Jamaican – had flown from Kingston to New York city, where he was apprehended. His luggage contained five pounds of high-purity powder cocaine worth $85,000.

Sometimes, amateur drug smugglers gamble large, and lose to dumb luck. In April of 2017, three ladies from Quebec, Canada were caught in Australia with over 200 pounds of powder coke in their baggage. That stash was valued at $23 million. The gals made it across the ocean, but their unusually heavy luggage roused the curiosity of the authorities in Sydney. So when their cruise ship docked, officers from the Australian Border Force stopped them, and made the bust.

It's hard for lower-level smugglers to extricate themselves from drug-smuggling operations, and for some who try, it can be fatal.

At a Narcotics Anonymous meeting in San Antonio, I became acquainted with a young single mom who desperately wanted to break off her relationship with a man who was a 'made' member of the San Antonio chapter of the Texas branch of the Mexican mafia. I sympathized with her, but didn't know how to help. The problem resolved itself when the man got on the wrong side of a Mexican mob General.

My acquaintance said her ex was drugged and then transported in the trunk of a car to a remote Texas Ranch, where he was shot. His remains were fed to livestock and the bones were dumped in an abandoned well. Such travesties will continue as long as Mexican voters continue to elect crooks to public office. As former New York Times reporter wrote in his 1984 book, 'Distant Neighbors; a portrait of the Mexicans': "Public life could be defined as the abuse of power to achieve wealth and the abuse of wealth to attain power." The Mexican mafia has more thoroughly infiltrated the police than the FBI has been able to infiltrate White Supremacist organizations.

But as vicious as the Mexican mafia is, certain neo-Nazis are even worse.

It's now standard procedure for white supremacists to join the U.S. Army and other branches of the military. A banker friend of mine in Iowa often hires employees who received their training at rival institutions. He gets first-rate workers without having to pay the up-front costs of acclimating them to the job. When they start working for him, they're ready on day one. Neo-Nazis and white supremacists have effectively implemented this same idea, by encouraging young recruits to sign up for military service. According to reporters Daniel Trotta and John Hudson, "white supremacists, neo-Nazis, and Skinhead groups encourage followers to enlist in the U. S. Army and Marine Corps to acquire the skills to overthrow what some call the ZOG – the Zionist Occupied Government. Get in, get trained, and get out, to brace for the coming Race War."

Their articles appeared in The Huffington Post, The Atlantic, and newspapers across the US, once Reuters News Services began investigating this practice in 2012. These active duty enlistees and officers are convinced that RAHOWA is on the way, and they want to be prepared. RAHOWA – Racial Holy War – is, as referenced earlier, an oft-spoken term in anti-Semitic and white supremacist circles. Then there's the related problem of thefts of weapons and other expensive military equipment stolen by these recruits. I came across some of these guys, whose crimes went undetected and unreported. Some of these thefts were discovered, and the guilty parties charged and sentenced. In July of 2019, a U.S. Marine veteran, Angel Dominguez Ramirez, Jr., was charged with building and operating a cocaine pipeline – while functioning as a Mexican drug Kingpin – by prosecutors in San Diego, California. Mr. Ramirez, who holds dual citizenship with Mexico, used boats, airplanes, and land vehicles, to transport cocaine from Peru, Venezuela, and Ecuador, into Chiapas, Mexico. From there, his network delivered it to California and Texas, for distribution in the United States. 41 people were charged in this case, which yielded 5,000 kilos of seized coke and over $9 Million in drug profits.

U.S. Army bases, off-site ordnance storage facilities, and military installations are presumed to be secure, but that's not always the case. Repentant former Skinhead T.J. Leyden joined the U.S. Marines in 1988, while openly promoting white supremacy and Holocaust Denial. He joined to "learn how to shoot. I also learned how to use C-4 explosives, and blow things up. I took all my military skills … to train other people," Leyden told Reuters. Wade Michael Page also enlisted, to become skilled in basic and advanced weaponry. He turned those skills, full force, on the mosque full of Sikhs he gunned down in Milwaukee in 2012.

Matt Kennard's book, 'IRREGULAR ARMY: How the U.S. Military recruited neo-Nazis, Gang members, and criminals to fight the War on Terror', describes this phenomenon in great detail. Kennard is a Leftist whose liberal views are reflected in his book. But the problem is real, and ongoing. Racists who are veterans or reservists, or on active duty are accorded hallowed status by their fellow haters. They're seen as winners among losers. As T. J. Leyden said, "Treat someone normal like a winner and he'll fight for you. But treat a loser like a winner, and he'll kill for you." This is particularly true with haters who receive training as snipers, and in hand-to-hand combat, and explosives, who are urged by the leaders of Hate Organizations to join the United States military.

During my visits with Dr. Weiner, I expressed fear of being stalked by white supremacists and killed. Were this to happen, I told him, it wouldn't be the first time an FBI informant was murdered by people he was assigned to surveil. "You can quit whenever you want," he replied. "But we both know that as long as the Liberty Lobby exists, and William Pierce is in business, you enjoy getting back at them."

"Hell, yes."

"Then there's your need for an adrenaline rush, and pushing toward the edge. Your informant work fills that void, doesn't it?" I acknowledged that. Around this time, TV's Tony Soprano regularly saw a therapist on the hit show, 'The Sopranos'. My visits to Dr. Weiner, I realized, weren't unlike those sessions between Tony Soprano and his doc. Dr. Weiner's style worked well for my needs; he was always straight-up, and never sugar-coated anything. He forced me to recognize that I, and only I, could resolve to get my act together and live right. It's my hope that everyone who sees a psychologist or psychiatrist is lucky enough to have a therapist like him.

"Well, Todd," he told me, "it's pretty damn amazing that the agents you're working with haven't caught on to your addiction." Then he said, "I want you to keep thinking about what you're doing to your wife and your parents. I know this bothers you, as it should. You're good-hearted, Todd, and your conscience is bothering you. It's only a matter of time before you'll see the light, and you'll stop."

"Think so?

"Yeah. Trust me. You're making progress, and I'm proud of you."

I made another appointment, and left that one feeling hopeful. Weiner helped me to realize that it truly was within my power and ability to change. But first, I had to resolve to take the steps that would pave the way.

CHAPTER FOURTEEN

By the Spring of 2002, I had the cell phone numbers of 27 crack dealers on speed dial on my cell phone. It wasn't unusual for me to buy crack from six or seven drug pushers every two weeks. It was during this time I nearly got arrested by the DC Metropolitan Police.

In terms of an adrenaline rush, running from the cops and getting away ranks right up there with being shot at without being hit. Having experienced both, I'd give the edge to being able to elude the cops. I pulled it off because others I was with were slower than me, and they got caught as I escaped. My experience taught me it's better to fool the police than be chased by them.

More than three years before I was finally busted by the DC police, I experienced a near-miss on 16th Street, N.W. It began in a drug pusher's apartment. I drove there to buy some rocks from this dealer, whom I'd met only a few months earlier. Because some junkies I knew vouched for the guy, and he sold great stuff, I accepted his offer to smoke a few hits with him. His chick and another crackhead were with him at his apartment when I arrived. He lived at the Woodner, which is an old, 1950s style building on upper 16th Street. It had substantially declined since the likes of Bob Hope, John F. Kennedy, and Jayne Mansfield walked its halls.

After I'd smoked two or three hits, I had to take a leak. Now, normally, when in a dealer's crib, clients needn't fear having their crack ripped off. It's bad for business. But when I returned from his bathroom, five of the 15 double bags I had purchased were no longer on the table. At first, I was casual about it. "Hey, whoever took my stuff needs to put it back on the table right now." No one said a word, and no one replaced my rocks. I tried another approach. "Even if there's only one thief involved, there are two witnesses. Fix this problem before it gets worse."

Again, no takers. I reached over to the other side of the table and scooped up three unsold double bags. I was still down forty bucks, and was about to take two more when the dealer's pal – still sitting on the couch - slammed the palm of his hand, hard, upside my head.

That set me off in a way that I think could've constituted temporary insanity. I went bat shit crazy, stood up, and raised my fists. As my hands went up, the junkie produced a switchblade, seemingly out of thin air. He flicked and clicked the blade. This wasn't the first time he'd brandished this shank, but it also wasn't the first time one was pulled on me. One second later, it was pointed straight up. With a menacing grin, he warned, "we gots ways a-dealin' wiff 'dis kinda shit."

"Same, here," I replied, pulling my .380. I chambered a round and aimed the gun straight at him. "Drop it", I said, and he did. The chick gasped, and I said, "shut up, honey." She and the pusher stayed put, saying nothing. But the dude who had struck me didn't seem scared. He packed his pipe with a big rock, and said, "ain't no cracka be shootin' some niggas in they crib. Not in 'dis here nigga hood."

I said, "if you try to keep what's mine, it'll be painful. Don't make me have to take it from you."

He put the pipe to his lips and inhaled. The look in the pusher's eyes indicated he was fearful, and hoped I'd exit his place without further incident. That wasn't going to happen. His pal finished his hit and sat back to enjoy its effect. He appeared to not have seen a barber in years. His afro was egregiously top-heavy, towering seven, maybe eight inches above the top of his forehead. Whenever he moved, the entire thing shook like a willow tree in a tornado. "One more chance, asshole," I warned.

"Fuck you", he replied. I aimed at the tip of his gargantuan afro and squeezed off a round.

The bullet tore through his fro like a weed whacker, lodging in the wall, two feet from the ceiling. A thin mist of powdery, dry plaster filtered out, sifting to the floor. The junkies were horrified. I then pointed my .380 at the dealer, and said, "Got it, now?"

He replied, "Y'all a crazy white movva fuckuh!" The chick was shaking, but still quiet. "I won't waste another round, shit head." As he reached, slowly, for his pocket, I said, "Keep your hands at your sides, or I'll blast 'em off." I told the chick to remove from the thief's shirt pocket whatever was in it and do the same for with pants pockets. She fished out my the three C notes I'd paid, and the five missing $20 bags. I held out my left hand while my gun was in my right; she placed the bags and money in my open palm. I stuffed them into my jacket pocket, along with the dubs I still had.

"Hand me that switch blade and give me your cell phones," I said. The place had no land line. All three cell phones went into the inside pocket of my top coat, which was on a chair next to the sofa. "Okay, everybody, take your turn blazing a rock."

As each took a hit, I photographed them with my cell phone. They were so scared at that point, they'd have done anything I told them. They knew I was creating evidence so they'd not rat me out for carrying a gun. "The cops would love these photos, wouldn't they?," I said. "Do as you're told, or they go online tonight." As they cowered together, I put on my topcoat and walked, backwards, to the door to their unit. The door to the stairwell was directly across the hallway from the door to their apartment. I rushed down four flights of stairs, then exited to the lobby. It had been approximately five minutes since firing the shot, and I had to get out of there. My car was parked on the east side of 16th Street, N.W., about a half block from the Woodner's front entrance.

30 seconds after I left the building, a police cruiser pulled up and two of DC's Finest got out. This was no coincidence; there was a police station just up 16th street, and probably someone at the Woodner had called 911 upon hearing gunfire. I was wearing a sport coat, necktie, grey windowpane trou-

sers, and cordovan alligator boots. My top coat covered my pants pockets which contained my Walther .380 and the bags of crack. The dude's switchblade was in my left back pocket, covered by my blazer and top coat. My black leather gloves completed my professional appearance. To these cops, I looked more like a lawyer visiting a court- appointed client than a crackhead who'd just fired a gun.

"Excuse me, sir," the policeman said, "but have you heard any shots coming from inside this building?"

Feigning disbelief, I said, "SHOTS, officer? As in, GUN shots?" He nodded.

"In THIS building, where my cleaning lady lives?"

The cop's partner nodded her head as she said, "umm-hmmm. That's right. THIS building."

"That's scary," I replied. "Heck, no. Oh, my God. Hey, can you give me a lift to where I can catch a cab? I don't feel safe, even being anywhere near – "

Shaking her head, the cop interrupted. "Sorry, sir. We're here to investigate."

As they walked past me, the policeman pointed to the METRO Bus Stop in front of the Woodner. "You'll be okay. Just take a bus, sir. They come about every ten minutes. Have a good day." I never heard from anyone about that situation. Those officers had no idea that the white man wearing business attire who was carrying a gun, crack cocaine and a switchblade was their suspect.

Yet, some people still don't understand why DC has so much violent crime.

The memorable 1991 movie called 'Never Forget' (previously referenced herein) chronicles the legal dispute between Willis Carto's Institute for Historical Review and a Holocaust survivor named Mel Mermelstein. Much of the dialogue in this film is based on actual transcripts, public statements, and documented court proceedings. In an especially riveting scene that actually took place, Mr. Mermelstein – who is played by Leonard Nimoy – is shown speaking to some high school students at an assembly. A teenager says, "my father says there never was a Holocaust. That it's all a bunch of lies. There were never any Jews gassed at Auschwitz."

Mermelstein replies, "I suppose that this is the kind of thing that Hitler, himself, would say if he were alive. The question is: Would you believe it?"

Another actual event which is recreated in the movie features Nimoy's Mermelstein in a meeting with lawyers from the Anti-Defamation League (ADL), and staffers of the Simon Weisenthal Center. A lawyer says, "The Institute for Historical Review is part of an ongoing germ; it's a network of professional liars and haters who get pleasure out of telling their horrible lies, that there was no Holocaust." I know precisely how true this statement is, having worked for – and monitored, for the FBI - the very people who did this. Knowing the actual individuals portrayed in this movie was a weird feeling.

Another moving film is the classic 1995 HBO movie, 'The Infiltrator', which in a Variety magazine review is called "standout TV". Variety's stellar review of this classic film states that, "The Infiltrator is powerful TV, all the more unsettling for reminding us that right-wing extremism didn't die with Hitler." In these enlightening, full-length feature films, Willis Carto, his top associates, and his publishing empire, are all mentioned by name. A documentary titled, 'Dr. No', now available on YouTube, is about the life and career of William L. Pierce. In the hour-long film, a professional singer belts out a hymn written by Pierce. To the tune of 'Rock of Ages' Pierce changed the lyrics to what he titled, 'Race of Beauty'.

Among the stanzas:

"Race of beauty, race of light; We shall strive to build our might – Dreams of white humanity; Oh, for

all Eternity … Race of Beauty, race of light … the world we'll build, will be all white… "

Pierce also wrote hymns which castigated the practice he called "race-mixing". Another hymn he wrote endorsed activists – whom he called "race-conscious citizens" - manufacturing homemade bombs.

These pseudo-religious songs were, and still are, sung by racist church choirs and the parishioners. Shortly after the 9/11 attacks, William Pierce and I talked in his office about music, for recruiting and indoctrinating people into hatred. He had no idea I was working for the FBI, and had been for the previous 18 months. Had Pierce and his armed staff at his compound known, I'd not have made it off his mountain alive.

Two original editions of Mein Kampf were behind Pierce's desk in his office, on the built-in bookshelf on the back wall. Pierce reached up and showed one to me. Both were autographed by Adolf Hitler. "This book is my inspiration," William Pierce told me, as he tapped the cover. Willis Carto also owned lots of Hitler memorabilia, including personal possessions that had belonged to the Fuehrer.

Pierce then raised an issue Carto had raised with me, years earlier: his mortality. Neither of us knew that in less than 10 months he'd be dead, but he was already thinking about his successor. "You seem unhappy," he said, and asked about the state of my marriage. But is someone who had been divorced five times qualified to advise anyone on how to stay married?

"If you and Linda split the dishes," he said, "you should consider moving down here, and work full-time for the cause. Show your love for your race." But I wasn't any more interested in replacing Pierce after he died than I had been in becoming the next Willis Carto. Pierce asked me to meet with some of his staffers. On the second floor of his main building, I spent hours the next day with twelve, maybe fifteen, of his full-time employees. Most of these workers were very smart, and some were brilliant. All hated minorities, especially Jews. Pierce's business manager, Bob DeMarais, was a CPA and a former Professor of accounting. About a dozen workers, mostly men, packaged books, magazines, CDs, DVDs, and promotional products like coffee mugs, bumper stickers, and T-shirts, for shipping. They all wore holsters, with handguns and pistols – even six-shooters – strapped to their hip.

Most of them had a gun on each hip, and their firearms were loaded. Just after lunch, I joined them outside, where there was a shooting range. They shot at 40-inch by 40-inch targets, with red bullseyes overlapping the faces of noted Liberals – just as Pierce's wealthy, anti-Semitic skeet shooters had done. The images of Bill and Hillary Clinton, Jesse Jackson, Bibi Netanyahu, Al Sharpton, actor Rob Reiner, Oprah Winfrey, Elie Wiesel, and U.S. Senators Chuck Schumer and Diane Feinstein were enthusiastically obliterated by Pierce's staffers and volunteers.

My primary focus was on the white collar employees. Without exception, they were as skilled with computers as any software engineers and almost as adept as most sixth graders. It was also obvious that they were disturbed, and their jobs like an addiction for them. Absent those positions, where they were paid to foment, promote and spread hatred, they'd probably go out and shoot innocent people. That's exactly what some of them later did.

The following day, at the National Building Museum, I reported to the FBI agents about Pierce and some other professional haters I was monitoring. Later, Linda dropped me off at Reagan National airport, where I took a flight to Atlanta. Among my scheduled commitments was a picnic lunch in the south Georgia countryside.

Over 100 people sat at about 20 large picnic tables, each covered with a plastic, red-white-and-blue, checkered cloth. The youngest was a baby in a carriage whose first name was Duke – named in honor of David Duke. The oldest had to have been at least 85, and she used a walker. The bright sun beautifully adorned the clear, blue, late September sky. Surrounding the clearing were oak, peach, persimmon, magnolia, and lemon trees. Three propane gas grills were fired up. Chicken, pork ribs, ribeye steaks, hot dogs, venison, quail, hamburgers, and turkey were barbequed by Southerners, proud of their culinary skills.

A six-man band played a mixture of blue grass and rockabilly tunes, all featuring vitriolic, racist lyrics. They belted out their tunes from a makeshift stage, which consisted of wooden crates, plywood planks and cinder blocks. Among their songs were 'Coon Town', 'Nigger hatin' me' and 'Lookin' for a Hand-out'. Stomping their feet, the attendees clapped to each tune. Many either sang along or silently mouthed the lyrics. It was as though fans of The Beach Boys, Lawrence Welk, Doris Day and Johnny Cash were into the same music as fans of bands like Bad Wolves, Breaking Benjamin, Twenty-one Pilots, Bad Flower, and Mumford and Sons. When HATE is the common thread, this music covered all the bases. 'Nigger hatin' me' went like this:

'The N-double-A-C-P would sure LOVE to get ahold … of nigger-hatin' me Mirror, mirror, on the wall, who's the blackest of 'em all? A coon named Sharpton, who's a Commie red; let's put a bullet in that gorilla's head I ain't black, as y'all can see, so Uncle Sam won't help poor nigger-hatin' me Hey, Mister President, whaddya say - when are we whites gonna have OUR day? Niggers have had theirs for such a long, long time; well, I'm white; it's time for mine'

'Coon Town' went like this:

'If ya walk down the street and somethin' smells bad, you're in Coon Town

If ya look and see garbage about every ten feet – you're in Coon Town

Up and down in the hood there ain't nothin' but trash

But Nigger girl's tryin' to get a nigger boy's cash

And after they jump ya, it's off that they'll dash – here in Coon Town

On the corner there's a nigger with a beer in his hand, well, that's Coon Town

He's tryin' to bum a dollar from whoever he can, that's just Coon Town'

'Don't be surprised, you can make a bet, if ya go there tomorrow, he'll be there, yet

He's tryin' to get drunk, and drunk he's gonna get, down in Coon Town

Niggers never bother with a-goin' to work, in Coon Town

They seem to think that work is only for jerks, out in Coon Town

It amazes me to see the way that they live in Coon Town;

They do all the takin' while we have to give, to Coon Town

White folks worry, but niggers don't care; '

cause at the end of the month, their check'll be there 'Cause niggers get their livin from off of welfare, in Coon Town;

Yeah, niggers gets their livin' all off of welfare, in COON TOWN'

Even teenagers and children who were of elementary school age knew the words, and sang along with these horrible songs. The bandleader thanked the audience after getting a standing ovation. He then winked at the aging, exquisitely-coiffed lady who paid them fifteen grand to perform and chartered the private jet to transport the musicians from their homes in Mississippi, and back.

Tupperware bowls contained homemade potato salad, fried chicken, baked beans, and Jell-O with marshmallows and mandarin oranges. Ladies set out corn on the cob, black-eyed peas, hominy grits, fried okra, and tossed salad. An entire table was loaded with homemade pies, brownies, angel food cakes, puddings, fresh strawberries, chocolate chip cookies, homemade vanilla ice cream, and Hostess Twinkies. Three kegs of beer and three tubs of soft drinks were encased in ice. Near where the vehicles were parked, people played Frisbee, while younger kids played tag. Some folks were fishing the pond, which was about three acres in circumference. An elderly pastor would bless the food, having been chauffeured to the property by an Emory University student.

A young soldier stationed at Fort Benning was there with his parents and fiancée. It looked like a real-life version of a Norman Rockwell painting, or a modern version of 'The Waltons', or a scene from The Andy Griffith Show. On the surface, these people would've fit right in on Walton's Mountain, or in Mayberry. Some rural folks were seated at the table nearest the two banjo players and the guy with a violin. By comparison, they made the hillbillies from 'Deliverance' look like the stodgy aristocrats from 'Downton Abby'. I joined them at their table. "This lamb is really tasty," I told the lady who brought it, who sat across from me. Her daughter then informed me that the meat wasn't lamb: it was grilled raccoon. "We'll be eatin' on them raccoons fer another week, yet," her mom said.

"Them was all road kill, so y'all ain't gotta worry none about chippin' no teeth on no buck shot." The lady's teenaged son, perhaps sensing my discomfort, assured me that "when we picked up them six coons, they was all still warm. We done picked 'em up night 'fore last, and skinned 'em right quick." I somehow managed to keep my food down while considering what I was eating. "Coon meat keeps real good, 'specially if it's grilled," the lady's husband told me. He invited me to take some home with me, if I was "of a mind to." His wife added that, "that's what's great about grilled raccoon. It's just as good on the second day, or even the third." Of that, I had no doubt.

Why hadn't I stopped after getting the venison sausage? As I tried to eat, a middle-aged man with a John Deere cap dished up what looked like some kind of stew from a covered dish onto my paper plate. "Yore gonna love this here," he said. "It's my woman's stewed possum." The opossum was mixed with collard greens, red onions, celery, and beans, in a chili-like broth. I realized that since these healthy folks had probably been eating such fare for generations, I could stomach it, as well.

Barely.

And then only with Wonder Bread and Dr. Pepper. At least that stuff came from a grocery store. For the entire hour I sat there, an all-American-looking young family was seated at the next table. The well-dressed parents and their obedient blond daughters and little tow-headed boy could have been models for a Ralph Lauren ad. They were eating steaks, fried chicken, green beans, and grits. But looks can be deceiving, even when articulate people are wearing crisply pressed khakis and drive Escalades.

The man was a lawyer who had attended law school with William Pierce's personal lawyer. I had met Pierce's attorney, who was a partner in the Baltimore office of the law firm of Piper and Marbury. I asked this attorney what type of law he practiced. "I specialize probate and Trusts," he replied, "mostly estate." At that moment, a hillbilly from another table shouted my name, beckoning me over to him. "C'mere, Todd", he said, "I want y'all to meet my wife, and my sister."

I resisted the urge to him if the same lady filled both roles.

As I left their table, the elderly Holocaust denier Jamie Van Brunn sat at a picnic table with three large boxes. The boxes contained paperback copies of The White Man's Bible, which was published by the World Church of the Creator. As everyone finished their ice cream, the preacher rose to deliver the benediction. Pastor Richard Butler was known to, and admired by all who were present. The lady who introduced him said he had traveled "all the way from Idaho." The Emory University student handed Butler a cordless microphone.

"In the name of our Lord, please join me in prayer," Butler said. "Our heavenly father," he said, as all heads were bowed and eyes closed, "we thank you for this wonderful day. We, your righteous children, are grateful for this opportunity to gather as white people. Please guide us as we face the daily tribulations set upon us by the Jews. We know that you, along with our Savior, Adolf Hitler, want only good to come of our earthly existence. With you watching over us, we have faith in our destiny to prevail over the pervasive evil eternally perpetrated by the Jews. As your true, chosen people, we know you're on our side in the struggle against the Jews, and their pawns - the mud people, queers, and subversives – who've under-mined America. We ask in heaven's name for your blessed guidance in our daily lives, as we try to do what's right for our race. Until the time when those who killed your only son no longer inhabit the earth, we know you're with us in our desire, and our efforts to expedite the arrival of that preordained, glorious day. In the name of your boy, Jesus, and our Fuhrer, amen."

"AMEN", echoed the crowd. Several attendees continued to pray, in silence and with closed eyes and clasped hands. An elderly lady pushed her hands skyward, and repeatedly shouted, "Hallelujah! Praise God! Praise Juh-eee-zuss! Praise the Fuhrer! Hallelujah!" Pastor Butler posed for photos with his flock, including several small children. He signed autographs, and was hugged by numerous fans. As they left, Von Brunn gave each person a copy of The White Man's Bible. Standing next to him was the Emory student who'd driven Butler from Atlanta's Hartsfield airport to the picnic site.

On a table was a wicker basket into which cash, checks, and business cards, were deposited. As I drove back to my hotel in downtown Atlanta's Peach Tree plaza, I realized how surreal this had been. The folks at that picnic who comprise this little-known realm made 'The Twilight Zone' seem normal. Voltaire warned that "those who can make you believe absurdities can make you commit atrocities." That warning was played out at that picnic and would for years.

A decade later, the absurdity-believing, 89-year-old James W. Von Brunn, in his final atrocity, made the world take notice of his hatred. 'Aryan Jesus', by author Susannah Heschel, explains how and why people who consider themselves to be Christians became staunch supporters of the Nazis and Adolf Hitler. In Christianity's history, few, if any, chapters are as horrifying as the successful efforts by the Third Reich to craft a Nazi-friendly version of this faith. Not only did Christians legitimize the Holocaust, but they were active in placing overt anti-Semitism at the theological center of their efforts to promote Hitler's efforts. Throughout the reign of the Third Reich, these efforts by such 'Christians' continued.

While I was dealing with hatred in my job, I was killing love at home. On my 42nd birthday in 2002, Linda and I had dinner with my parents. In October, we all did the same thing for her birthday. On both occasions, I was just going through the motions. My work with the FBI was slowing down. William Pierce had died three months earlier, and Willis Carto was nearly bankrupt, as was Liberty Lobby. The SPOTLIGHT had been shut down; David Duke would soon be going to prison. Mark Cotterill had been ordered back to Great Britain, banned from the USA for the next 10 years.

Several times, I prayed about my situation, particularly asking for God's help in ending my addiction. However, I wasn't doing my part: I didn't want to quit using. As correctly observed by Sophocles, Benjamin Franklin, and others, "The Lord helps those who help themselves." But as I wasn't willing to do my part, I remained an addict.

A week later Linda and I attended a dinner party hosted by the partners in the oncology practice with whom she worked. It was not an enjoyable occasion. Some of the M.D's were Jewish, and aware of the controversy at the University club. "Your wife says you've been traveling, as part of your job, Todd," a doctor's wife told me. She sat directly across from me at a table with about a dozen others, including Linda. She asked, "what type of work do you do, since you no longer represent Liberty Lobby?" I told her I represented about 25 publications as their advertising consultant. This was technically true; the FBI paid for this service, and allowed me to earn commissions on ads I placed in far right, racist newspapers, magazines, newsletters, and websites.

"Do these publications," an oncologist asked, "tend to appeal to the same audience who read the SPOTLIGHT?" Linda side-glanced at me before I answered.

"Well, sir," I replied, "there's some overlap among those subscribers, and other reader, yes."

"I see," came the reply. "What impact is William Pierce's death having on the record company you and Dr. Pierce own?", he asked. This doctor said he was a subscriber to the Southern Poverty Law Center's publications, 'Hate Watch', and the 'INTELLIGENCE Report'; that's where he had read about me and my work. As Linda and I drove home, neither of us spoke a word.

Sometimes, when a marriage is coming apart what's not spoken means more than what's said. Not long after this encounter, a neo-Nazi investment advisor named Chris Temple was being heavily promoted in the mainstream media. I had worked with Temple when we were affiliated with Liberty Lobby and again while partnered with William Pierce. Temple, who once stayed overnight at our house in northern Virginia, would often conduct business at the University club when I was a member. Forbes magazine was among the mainstream publications enamored of Temple's economic expertise.

The Southern Poverty Law Center reported that Temple "found himself regularly sought out for his prognostications by some of the leading organs of the U. S. financial press. Temple's views on gold and other markets were prominently featured in Forbes ... and in Forbes' online publications. He was quoted in Barron's Online, CBS MarketWatch, Gold News Weekly" and elsewhere. Temple's bi-monthly newsletter, The National Investor, was lauded by the highly respected Hulbert Financial Digest (the HFD), which was then the top-ranked rater of U.S. stock market-oriented periodicals.

Concomitantly, Temple was embraced by the Aryan Nations, KKK chapters, Holocaust deniers, Skinhead organizations and nearly every leading white supremacist in America. Temple once joked to me and several others that he wanted "to establish a retail business that involved Jews." He said it would be called, "Lampshades-R-Us" – a spoof of the Toys R-Us retail chain. Temple was disgustingly referencing Nazi-manufactured lamp shades which were made with the skin of Concentration camp victims.

As a follower of the Christian Identity religion, Chris Temple believed that Jews are descended from the devil. Another core belief of Christian is that black and brown people are subhuman. Temple was David Duke's ballot access coordinator in the Klan leader's 1988 presidential campaign and often cited Adolf Hitler in his speeches, published articles, and private conversations. Before and during my years with the FBI, I accompanied Temple – often with Willis Carto, on business trips – on business trips to gatherings of wealthy Holocaust deniers and virulent racists, in numerous states. Oddly, even while Temple's whirlwind, mainstream activities were reported on websites which could be seen by scores of millions of readers, he wasn't busted until he began embezzling from his investors.

But as Edmund Burke wrote, "the only thing necessary for the triumph of evil is that good men do nothing." Doing nothing includes not keeping abreast of relevant, important news.

Around 1999, Chris Temple had asked me to invest money with him. At the time, I still had around $375,000 in various accounts, including in Grand Cayman, and a with a DC brokerage firm. Temple promised me annual returns of 15 to 20 percent, which I knew he couldn't deliver. I invested nothing. He and I lost track of each other once I stopped monitoring his militant milieu in late November of 2002. But in 2004 he was sentenced to 72 months in federal prison for embezzling $1.6 million of his investors' money. He also pled guilty to charges of mail fraud and money laundering. Upon his 2009 release, Chris Temple rejuvenated The National Investor. He violated the terms of his probation and in 2012 was re-sentenced to nine additional months in prison, with probation upon his release. As of 2017, his online newsletter is again doing a brisk business, and he's got a YouTube channel. Some people never learn.

Unpleasant encounters like the one which happened at the dinner party with my wife kept cropping up. At the Caucus Room restaurant in downtown DC, a party of four were seated at a table next to mine.

One of the ladies recognized me, and said, "Oh. My. God. I refuse to sit next to this Nazi." She called the maitre' d over, and insisted she be moved as far away as possible from me. This was especially embarrassing because a co-owner of the Caucus Room is my old friend and fellow White House staff member Haley Barbour, who later served as chairman of the Republican National Committee, and was twice elected as the Governor of Mississippi. Such occurrences became common.

Arriving home one night in 2003, I opened our mailbox, which was at the end of the driveway. Inside was a notebook-sized sheet of paper, on which was scrawled, 'MOVE AWAY, BLODGETT'. Linda hadn't yet returned from work, and I never showed it to her or told her about it. A few weeks later, Linda had a long talk on our back yard deck. She asked for a trial separation.

"You've changed, Todd," she said. "You don't seem to be the man I fell in love with and married seven years ago." She was right. My addiction had rendered me powerless to change.

Soon after this, I met with two of the FBI agents I'd worked with since March of 2000. "Todd, you look tired, and burned out," one said. When they told me details of an operation in the works, my disinterest was evident. As my marriage was cooling, and my work slowing down and becoming boring, my desire to get high rose. The following weekend, my mother called both agents, voicing her concerns. I had been home all day, and Linda called from her office. She asked if I wanted to meet for dinner with some nurses and their husbands. I declined. I wanted to get high, and called a dealer named 'Skeet', who had texted me earlier, about some great stuff that had just arrived. We arranged to meet near the Clifton

Terrace apartments, on Clifton avenue, near 11th Street, N. W. This led to an all-night crack smoking session, in a dangerous neighborhood, with a crack whore who tried, unsuccessfully, to get me into bed. I ignored her and left in a hurry. Linda called repeatedly to my cell phone; I ignored it, and finally, turned it off. Addiction truly meant more to me than anything else. When I'd become depressed about this reality, I got more coke. It was a vicious cycle.

In late November of 2002, I ended my professional association with the FBI. It was clear to me, and to the agents, that my heart simply wasn't in the work. While I didn't enjoy every day on the job, or every aspect of my work during those 33 months as a professional FBI informant, I'm pleased with the results of my assignments. In September, 2003, Linda and I began our trial separation. I rented an apartment at a building called the Saratoga, on upper Connecticut avenue, N.W. In January, 2004, I began a part-time job with a direct marketing firm also on Connecticut avenue, in the Kalorama neighborhood, working 30 hours a week.

The owners of the company were staunch Republicans, one of whom had been a consultant to my father's 1992 and 1998 political campaigns, in the Primary and General elections. My responsibilities included researching financial reports that candidates for public office are required to file. It's illegal to use records from federal campaign reports for commercial purposes, so I focused on reports filed in states - where utilizing such information is allowed. Each week, I submitted memos outlining campaign reports to obtain. A co-worker whose father had been a White House speechwriter for President Ford would either download the records or contact candidates directly and offer to buy their contributor lists.

It wasn't exciting, but it was a paycheck. By this time, my dad had taken nearly complete control of what little remained of my funds, which were being steadily depleted by my drug habit and exorbitant costs of the druggy lifestyle.

At the Lansburgh, I'd meet my parents three or four times a week. I continued to see Dr. Weiner each week, sometimes twice. We discussed how I was coping without Linda, and if reconciliation was possible. Linda and I met every week for dinner at Martin's Tavern in Georgetown. We hired a realtor who sold our house. I turned over my share of the proceeds to my mother, because my addiction had destroyed my ability to manage money. Out of those funds, she paid my rent, utility bills and other expenses for the next three years.

About six months after Linda and I began our trial separation, she told me she wanted a divorce. We were in a booth at Billy Martin's Tavern in Georgetown when she expressed her intentions. A few weeks later, in early 2004, I was served papers, and proceedings began. I didn't contest it, as it was my fault. No one should have to put up with a spouse who is an addict. She continued to live and practice in northern Virginia, and later moved to Las Vegas. She now works in another city in another state, which I won't mention, out of respect for her privacy. I've always loved her, and still do.

For weeks, I was bummed out over my failed marriage. Sitting alone in my apartment one evening, I listened to a Dean Martin CD. I played a song

401

over and over called 'Ain't Gonna Try Anymore'. The lyrics haunted me as I sat alone in my dimly lit den:

"Ain't gonna try anymore, to forget about you; ain't gonna try anymore – what good would it do? Some day, I'd like to forget this loneliness in my heart; now, you're only a memory, and I don't know where to start; Ain't gonna try anymore, to forget about you; ain't gonna try anymore - what good would it do?"

For 28 days in June-July, 2004, I lived at a renowned addiction re-hab facility called Father Martin's Ashley. Despite having very comprehensive health insurance, my out-of-pocket fees were nearly $25,000. This was my introduction to the 12-step approach to recovery from addiction. The facility is located on a beautiful campus, a beautiful old estate which had been home to two U.S. Senators from Maryland, named Tydings. The faculty was first-rate, and even the food was superb. Trained specialists were available for one-on-one counseling, and groups of five met for group therapy for two hours each morning and afternoon. I met the famous Father Joseph Martin, the founder, and made some lasting friendships from my 28 days in treatment.

Family members were allowed to visit on weekends. My parents joined the spouses, parents, and other family members of other patients for two of our weekend sessions. On my second day there, a familiar face sat at my table in the large dining room. It was Drew Lewis, who had served as Ronald Reagan's Secretary of Transportation. This was a return engagement for Drew, as he told me to call him. We became fast friends, despite our 30-year age difference, and remained friends for years. Drew was an alcoholic, and was one of the finest, most honest men I've ever known. He was the first President of MTV, and later was the CEO of the Union Pacific Railroad.

Another friend I made at Ashley was John Post, Jr. John is nearly 20 years younger than I, but our friendship continues to this day. His problem was cocaine and alcohol. John has been drug-free and sober since 2008 and is the director of Clinical Resources at Caron Centers, a leading addiction facility with campuses in Pennsylvania and Florida.

While I learned much of the dangers of drug addiction while at Ashley, I wasn't ready to quit. About two weeks after graduating, I relapsed. Ironically, the relapse took place at an Ashley-sponsored event in D.C. John Post and I were sharing a room at the Holiday Inn in Georgetown. But a fellow Ashley alum, whom I'll call J.P., was hosting some other recent Ashley graduates in his hotel room. He invited me over, and when I arrived, J.P. said, "Todd, you live here in D.C. We wanna get high, and I'll pay for everything. Will you call a dealer?"

I was speechless. But also tempted. Before I could say a word, the cutest chick in the room, a recent graduate of an Ivy League university, got out of her chair and rubbed my back. This beauty, whom I'll call Kristen, said, "Todd, please help us get some crack." She then whispered in my ear, and tickled my ear with her lips as she spoke.

"PleasePleasePleaseOhPleasePleaseToddPleaseOhPleasePleaseToddPleaseOhPleasePleasePLEASE ... " Then she whispered to me what I was excited to hear: her room number. I glanced sideways at her as she nodded her head up and down, and slid her tongue between her lips. No problem, honey. I'm glad to help.

The cheers in that room went up like everyone's favorite team had scored the Super Bowl's winning touchdown with no time left on the clock. "How much do you want?" J.P. pulled six hundred-dollar bills from his wallet and handed them to me. "Let's start with this. That'll get us four 8-balls, right?"

Everyone was quiet as I called a dealer. No answer. On the next call, a recording indicated that the number was out of service. On my third attempt, a lady answered. "Hi, is this Greg's phone number?"

"Yeah," answered a female voice. "Well," I replied, "may I please speak with him?"

"Who dis be?"

"My name's Todd. Greg and I are friends. It's urgent."

"Can't."

"Why not?"

"Nigga locked up fo' a minute. Whassup?" On my fourth attempt, a pusher named Kenny answered. When I identified myself, he was aghast that I'd relapsed. "Ah heard y'all done took the cure, Lightskin."

"It didn't take."

"Ah see dat. How much y'all wants?"

"Five 8-balls, for six hundred."

"Nice try, white boy. But five 8-balls be seven hundid fifty. Six hundid gets ya fo'. Where you is?"

"Holiday Inn, Georgetown. Twenty-one hundred block of Wisconsin avenue." I walked toward the door to J.P.'s room and, lowering my voice, I said, "I'll be in room number … "

Kristen and I went to her room for an enjoyable, 45-minute reunion before Kenny called back. Upon arriving, the dealer was smitten with Kristen. As Kenny left, he turned around, and winked at me as he gave a thumbs-up and grinned. "Later," I told him. "Ah'm quite sure of dat," he replied. "Ah be keepin' mah phone on fo' a minute," he said. "Dat be 'cause Ah knows y'all goin' call me again."

Sure enough, I called him again. And again. This relapse involved three other Ashley alums besides me and J.P. The following day, John Post hopped a taxicab to my apartment on Connecticut avenue to check on me. I was alone, coming down from my high. When I apologized for having relapsed, John said, "be sorry for yourself, Todd", as he opened the door to the hallway and exited my apartment.

After John took a taxicab back to the hotel in Georgetown, I sat alone, angry and humiliated. My dad was making arrangements to hire a private investigator to keep tabs on me. He knew that being divorced meant my harmful lifestyle would worsen, and it did. Later that summer, I returned to Clear Lake for about three weeks. My parents didn't want me at their main house, so I stayed at our family cottage at the Outing Club. This worked well, as breakfast, lunch and dinner were served in the members' Dining Room and a caretaker maintained the property.

With my parents in D.C., I took advantage of the opportunity to continue getting high. It didn't take me long to make an indirect connection to a drug dealer in Northwood, Iowa. My connection picked me up just after midnight in the parking lot at the Outing club, where the tennis court is located. West of the Northwood city limits in Worth county, we drove onto a gravel road. A few miles up this road, my connection said, "get your money ready. He's parked behind this abandoned farm house." As I handed him $400, he told me to stay quiet as the transaction went down. Seconds after he turned off the motor and lights, a bearded man wearing a flat black hat got out of a covered black wagon, like those seen in western movies, or on TV's 'Little House on the Prairie'. This crack dealer was a member of the Amish community. He appeared to be about 30 years old.

He walked up to the driver's window, where the drug deal silently went down. 45 seconds later, we were back on the gravel road. "What the Hell", I said, hardly believing what had just happened. "That Amish guy grows the best organic pot I've ever smoked," the driver told me, as he handed me $200 worth of crack. Our deal was that this source would get $200 for making this happen, with which he bought pot and meth. "That old-fashioned dude sells crystal meth, too. He trades his pot for coke and meth, and cooks the cocaine into some of the best crack you'll ever smoke."

The Amish drug pusher's stuff was awesome. The following night, I walked over to a bar called Players and met a brunette who said she loved to party. Back at the cottage, we smoked crack all night, which led to exactly what I had hoped it would. A few hours later, as dawn was breaking, I told her I'd walk her back to the bar, where her car was in the parking lot. "Wait a minute," she said, still naked beneath the bed sheets. "I want breakfast." Okay, I told her, and gave her $20. "That'll get you a good breakfast downtown. The best place is called the Town Pump." After taking my twenty, she said she wanted to eat breakfast in the members Dining Room. I told her it wouldn't open until 7:30, and I hadn't made a reservation for her. "Not this time, honey."

Oh, I get it," she replied, "I'm just not good enough to eat in the Outing club Dining Room."

"No, sweetie, that's not it. It's just that - "

Before I could finish my sentence, she slapped me, hard, right across my face. She tried for a second hit, which I dodged. She knew I couldn't call the local cops on her, because we'd been partying. She also knew I had to keep things quiet, or the neighbors on both sides of my cottage would become suspicious.

Referencing local print and electronic media, she threatened me. "I'll betcha reporters at the Globe-Gazette, or KIMT-TV, and the Mirror-Reporter would just love to know about your drug habit, Mr. Blodgett. I know who your Daddy is. If you don't want me to go to the newspapers and the TV and radio stations, pay me five hundred dollars right now."

This was no negotiation, and I had no choice but to comply with her demand. "You'll get your money once I walk you off of this property. Get dressed and let's go. Now." She silently followed me out of the cottage's street side door. I opened the gate directly in front of my street side patio and she followed me to the sidewalk. She kept her word to stay quiet until we walked past the entrance to the south parking lot. Once we were past that point, she said, "pay me", as she held out her hand. I stuffed five Benjamins into the conniving chick's hand and stopped walking. She asked if I wanted her cell phone number, and I said I don't like being extorted.

I turned around and walked back toward the gate to my cottage. It was bad enough getting slapped, but being extorted made it even worse. As I walked past the Outing Club's fenced-in, south parking lot, a longtime member, Dr. Bill Barnett, saw me. This retired MD walked toward the fence and asked, "Todd, are you all right?" I nodded my head, without speaking, and walked the final forty feet to my gate.

That night, I began attending Narcotics Anonymous meetings in Mason City. A week later, I flew back to D.C. My divorce finalized, I played the field and met many new girls. These gals included crack whores who, in some cases, were half my age. Crack whores charge money for hook-ups, but they'll discount their prices if crack is provided. Sometimes, I'd bring them to my apartment; other liaisons took place elsewhere. I spent an amorous evening with a gorgeous, light skinned black 21-year-old at a place she led me to believe she was renting. I verified her age before things got underway. As the effects of the cocaine wore off, our time beneath the covers was done. Then I found out the hard way that the house wasn't hers. The next morning, as we laid in bed together, still asleep, a loud crash seemed to shake the entire second floor.

In burst an elderly black lady wearing a light purple dress and pink shoes. She was spry, looked about 75 years old, with her grey hair rolled up in a bun. She wore a green and yellow hat, with an orange ribbon. The chick screamed as she pulled the covers and bedspread to her neck. "Nana! What's going on?" It turned out that this lady was her great-grandmother and owned the place. In this old gal's hands was a wooden baseball bat. "Ahh know what's goin' on, honey," the old lady replied, "and I'm stoppin' it, right here, and now. Mmm-hmmm. Yes, I surely am."

This geriatric invader was an Equal Opportunity human wrecking ball. Glaring at me, she said, "Ahh'm old enough to be your grandmother. And Ahh'm HER great-grandmother!", she hissed, while swinging her bat. "Y'all be layin' in sin. Dis da Lord's house; 'dat ain't happ'nin' here. No way, no how," she said, as her bat nailed my foot. "Hey, that hurt," I yelled, jumping out of bed. As I dodged another swing, she said, "Good. And 'dat ain't all's gonna hurt, you heathen. Ahh'm just getting' warmed up. Dis here be just da beginnin'." She wasn't joking. Her next at-bat missed, but it obliterated a cheap ceramic lamp.

"Just lookit what y'all done made me do," she said. "You payin' for dat."

My attempt to block the next swing slammed the back of my hand against the crack whore's ribs. My hand stung like a bitch, and I feared she'd broken my little finger. "Nana, Nana! Listen, please!", her great-granddaughter said. "Ahh prefer swattin' to listenin', honey child," came her reply.

The old gal's eyes were ablaze with righteous anger, and she had the energy of a team of six freshly-awakened mules. "Y'all be breakin' da Lord's laws," she warned, "ain't nobody gets away with dat."

I was stark naked, had to get dressed, and scrambled across to the other side of the freezing bedroom where my clothing was piled. Nanna paused for a moment to catch her breath as I grabbed my boxer shorts. I fumbled with them and leaned against the dresser to stay balanced as I tried slipping them on. It was imperative to get dressed before the next round began. Shaking her head from side to side, Granny's eyes focused on my groin. "Lord, almighty," she said. "Dat's pitiful", as I pulled on my boxers.

"And I do mean, powerful pitiful. Now, Ahh done seen it for mah self. What 'dem says about white boys is right true, umm-hmmm. Ahh seen me bigger cigarettes den what he got down dere. Mah goodness, child," she said, looking at the young lady. "Y'all can do better den dat." Shaking her head again, she admonished her great-granddaughter. "What in da whirl was you thinkin'? What self-respectin' colored girl would pass up a big, strong, strappin' black man for - for … dat?"

Now, that hurt.

CHAPTER FIFTEEN

In late November of 2002, following William Pierce's death, Willis Carto's bankruptcy, Mark Cotterill's deportation, David Duke's impending criminal indictment, and Liberty Lobby's demise, my FBI gig ended. After nearly three years as a spy, I was a spent force. This left me with more time than ever to get high. As a severely addicted crackhead who routinely carried a loaded gun in Washington, DC, I risked my freedom, and life, every time I ventured into the hoods to meet drug pushers and buy and use crack. By then, I was on a first-name basis with some very high-end cocaine dealers. To me, life as a sort of game, fraught with danger, where the goals were to maintain my addiction and not get in trouble for so doing.

Through a connection, I met a Baltimore-based supplier of cocaine, crystal meth, and heroin. I'll call this man Dino Cassini. His late father had been a high-level mobster in the 1960s and '70s, chiefly in New Jersey, who ordered up death like others order pizza. Cassini said his dad knew the men who had killed the late Teamsters Union President Jimmy Hoffa in 1975, in Detroit. He was about 60 when I met him, but looked much younger. He was unaffiliated, but still well connected to high-end, professional hoodlums in Baltimore, New York city, Philadelphia, DC, Boston, and other major cities. This distributor, who also owned several chop shops, supplied drugs to wholesalers, who then sold them to dealers who furnished them to street pushers. Inadvertently, he gave me hope that I could get clean.

This was because I had to stay off the crack pipe while I was on the job, for at least 24 hours before running cocaine, meth, and heroin for him. All of my deliveries transpired at night. I would drive to Baltimore, or Philadelphia, to pick up the stuff, and then deliver it to Cassini's clients. I always drove my 1999 Range Rover 4.6, which substantially lowered the likelihood of being stopped by cops, regardless of where I was driving. Cassini, who carried a .38 at all times, knew I was armed and could use a gun, if needed. This helped me land this gig. These transactions often took place in nice hotels – not cheap motels, where anyone in the parking lot or across the street could see who goes in and out of the rooms. We conducted our business from hotels where the doors to the rooms opened into hallways, not a parking lot, or onto a shared, outside balcony. Suppliers are at the top end of any drug enterprise, and they leave nothing to chance.

Transactions in New York city, Philadelphia, and Richmond were always conducted on private property, usually owned by those who accepted delivery. Once I was within a couple of blocks of the destination, I would call the client. Garage doors would open upon my arrival, just like that garage door in New York city, when I drove Willis Carto there to pick up his nearly three million bucks in gold coins. My Philly deliveries were made to either warehouses or spacious row houses in Frank Rizzo-style neighborhoods.

After making several deliveries to the City of Brotherly Love, a gregarious client of Dino's there invited me to stay to dinner. We sat down to eat at 2:30 a.m. His trophy wife, who was younger than his youngest daughter, served us Italian food. On another occasion, this guy got very drunk. To impress me, he asked me to drive him to one of his warehouses, which was in a decrepit section of Camden, New Jersey. He was bombed on his pricey wine, and after about a 15 minute drive, we arrived at his storage facility. The nondescript building, he told me, was of about 40,000 square feet. Upon entering an enormous storage area in the basement, he pointed to the only wall that wasn't either brick or oak paneled. "See all that drywall?," the wino asked. Four stacks were slanted against the back wall, each with six or eight sections of the stuff. "Yeah, what about it?"

Each of the 35 or 40 sections of sheet rock measured about eight feet tall, three feet wide, and three-quarters of an inch thick. "Pure coke. Every fuckin' one of 'em. Just got 'em in from Mexico." The fake drywall in front of me was easily worth twelve, perhaps fifteen million dollars - and this was in 2005. It was mixed with baking soda, from which the cocaine would be easily separated when boiled in hot water. Each kilo (1,000 grams) of this coke, which was refined in Colombia and the Dominican Republic, had cost the supplier $1,500. However, it was worth approximately twenty grand to this distributor, when he would sell it to his wholesalers at that jacked-up price. By the time they sold it to their dealers, who in turn sold it to street pushers, that kilo would be worth $25,000 to $30,000. Each section of this fake sheet rock contained approximately fifteen kilograms.

Incidentally, this guy wasn't even close to being a major player. But when some people are blitzed out of their right mind, they sometimes like to show off, and impress others. That's what this guy did. The next morning, he called me, and asked if we were at one of his warehouses the previous evening. I said, "what warehouse?" He then asked if he'd shown me any drywall. I replied, "Drywall? What drywall?"

He said, "you're a smart guy, Todd. Make sure you stay that way," and hung up.

From wealthy Holocaust deniers to flashy drug wholesalers, some of them impressed people with such displays, especially when they were drunk. In 2016, authorities in Dade county, Florida found $24 million in hundred-dollar bills stashed in buckets, hidden behind and within sections of drywall in a secret, attic room in the home of Luis Hernandez-Gonzalez. Another five million dollars of cocaine was discovered in this raid. Mr. Gonzalez came to law enforcement's attention by selling customers equipment for growing indoor marijuana and providing instructions to build indoors lab to process it.

While delivering cocaine and crystal meth to New York's Bayside section of Queens, a customer there told me that the city's police lab employed rogue analysts – chemists - who, for a price, rigged test results to make innocent defendants appear guilty. The same man said crooked chemists were working in Boston, and in upstate New York state. His claim was true. Annie Dookhan had worked for nearly ten years as a respected chemist for the state of Massachusetts. She analyzed samples for evidence of illegal drug use, and tens of thousands of defendants counted on her to be ethical, honest, and professional. But she wasn't. After Ms. Dookhan was caught forging the initials of another analyst, an internal investigation revealed she had deliberately sabotaged approximately 24,000 of the 40,000 cases she handled between 2003 and 2012. Convictions were summarily dismissed, prisoners freed and lawsuits were filed. Dookhan said she wanted to help prosecutors get drug dealers and addicts "off the streets." It wasn't established that Ms. Dookhan was paid for her crimes.

In 2014, another chemist employed by the state of Massachusetts, Sonja Farak, pleaded guilty to stealing and altering drug samples while analyzing them. The damages caused by that analyst are still, in 2019, being determined. Could Annie Dookhan have been one of the chemists working for the state of

Massachusetts that this Boston cocaine distributor mentioned? When I read about her crimes, that possibility crossed my mind. Shenanigans like Dookan's undermines the willingness of people to believe that their government is on their side and reinforces the perception that government is out to get them.

While writing 'REPUBLICAN CRACKHEAD', my 81-year-old father's advanced dementia morphed into Alzheimers disease, and he was diagnosed with Parkinsons. But his long-term memory, including the years of my addiction, is largely intact. Scores of billions of dollars have been spent on Alzheimers research and to care for those suffering from it. Lost revenue resulting from its sufferers being sidelined also amounts to tens of billions of dollars, even without taking interest into account. If monies lost to drug addiction and its consequences could be used to develop a vaccine, or a cure, for Alzheimers disease, our world would be a much happier, healthier, far more productive place.

For recover these funds, Americans must become serious about their priorities and implement policies which will save money and lives and foster constructive change. But until such changes transpire, crooks like Dino Cassini will keep raking in, collectively, hundreds of billions of dollars per year. Mr. Cassini paid me well, and like many addicts and white supremacists, he believed that laws were there to constrain lesser beings than himself. At our first meeting, he told me I'd make an ideal drug transporter. "You drive an expensive car to which you hold the title," he said. "You're clean-cut, you dress well, and are well-spoken. You've got the nerves of a cat burglar and you don't scare. You're tough; you carry a gun and you know how, and are willing, to use it."

He then said, "just don't kill anybody while you're working for me," he said. "I hate lawyers, and it costs money to have 'em knocked off." But I never even squeezed off a round at anyone while employed by him. After about three months on the job, I dealt with a Cassini underling whose job involved taking delivery of cocaine smuggled into the USA by drug mules. As earlier referenced, not all 'mules' are of the type personified by Clint Eastwood, in his 2019 film, 'The Mule'. This dude, who was about my age, took me to dinner at the Jefferson hotel on 16th Street, N.W., in downtown D.C. He told me that while working for a previous employer, he drove to Washington's Dulles International airport to pick up two sisters, one of whom brought three children. The members of this Latino family all had smuggled high-grade, pure powder cocaine - which they swallowed, using rubber pellets, covered with latex gloves.

He accompanied the mules to a nice hotel near Dulles airport. On the drive there, a twelve-year-old boy from Peru began twitching, sweating, screaming, and, finally, hallucinating. The cocaine had breached a pellet, or pellets, in his gut. This internal rupture led directly to the painful death of this pre-teenager. That's because within minutes, the rapidly-absorbed, acidic powder began circulating throughout his bloodstream, causing severe chest pain and rapid heart palpitations. This, in turn, constricted blood flow to his brain, causing stroke-like symptoms. Minutes after they surfaced, the gastric acid caused this 12-year-old's brain to lose its cognitive ability.

The kid – who wasn't related to the rest of his travel party - was unconscious when they arrived at the hotel. Once they were checked in, this man said, his employer separated the boy from the two adults and the two youngsters. The man then removed a large knife with a serrated blade from his luggage. After stripping the clothes off the unconscious boy, he placed him in the bathtub in the hotel room's bathroom. He then carved a gaping hole in the lower abdomen and removed the rubber pellets, including the two which had ruptured. The kid bled to death.

His drained body was double-bagged with industrial plastic, taped up, and then placed inside a fiberglass container designed to carry a golf bag and clubs. Another crony of the cocaine supplier wheeled this container down the hall to an elevator. Once in the hotel's underground parking garage, he loaded it into his SUV, and drove to a construction site in southern Virginia. The boy's remains were disposed of on that site, the man said. The $5,000 cash that the boy was to have been paid was sent back with the two sisters, who promised to deliver it to his grandmother, with whom this young drug smuggler had lived. The surviving members of that drug-smuggling team knew better than to ever even attempt to implicate the DC-based drug smuggler in the tragic, horrific death of that poor kid.

As he knocked back his third Jameson, the guy told me that he "resigned from that crazy gig about a week later." He the assured me that "Mister Cassini would never stoop to that low level." It turned out that the head honcho of this cocaine smuggling ring lived in a 20,000 square foot mansion in Greenwich, Connecticut. He was a major investor in several hedge funds, which were run by his neighbors and golf partners. This drug kingpin, who was a WASP, belonged to the Greenwich Country club, whose membership included several celebrities, Fortune 500 CEOs and former U.S. President Gerald Ford. He also owned high-end art galleries in Austria, Singapore, Lichtenstein, and Germany, according to his former employee.

In July of 2019, Australian authorities discovered that 384 kilos of powder cocaine – with a street value of nearly $145 million - had been smuggled into Australia, hidden inside of a second-hand excavator on a cargo ship that docked in Bungendore. But fifteen years before this crime was reported, Dino Cassini and his partners in crime were utilizing precisely that method of moving illegal drugs into the United States. These guys were way, WAY ahead of American law enforcement, and still are.

My employment with Dino Cassini ended abruptly about four months later, after I drove a shipment of powder coke to Boston. I made the drop-off, then delivered the cash to him at his office, in Baltimore. Later that evening, I met a pretty brunette in a Baltimore bar. We spent the night together at her place. While I was asleep, she researched me on Google. She shook me awake and asked about Resistance Records, and my nefarious connections. I was exhausted, drunk, and my mind was foggy from the crack I'd smoked. I explained the situation to her, truthfully, and fully. My mistake was in telling her about my nearly three years as a full-time, paid FBI informant. Word of this got back to Cassini.

He called the next day and asked me to meet him at his office the following day, which was a Sunday. Cassini was in his car when I arrived. We went inside, and in his private office, he was livid. "You never told me you worked for the goddamned FBI, you fuckin' shit," he said. "You were an undercover cop." No, I said, I wasn't. "I wasn't a bureau employee, sir, and was told to not discuss my work for them."

"Well, you're done workin' for me," he replied. Rising from from his leather chair, he reached out his hand. "I'm sorry, Todd. I like you. But this is how it's gotta be. Goodbye and good luck."

"Thanks." He walked me out, lighting a Merit Ultra Lite as we walked to my car. "I know you know to never implicate me in anything, or mention my name or business to anyone." He handed me his lighter as I fired up a smoke. "You've got nothing to worry about, Dino."

"Good. 'Cause that way, you won't have to worry about nothin', either."
Turning away, he walked back inside. I've not seen or spoken to him since,
but as of 2019, he's still alive, and retired in Florida.

59 years before the 9/11 attacks on America, Nazi terrorists, including
two U.S. citizens, attempted - and nearly succeeded - in unleashing a devas-
tatingly destructive, planned attack on the U.S. mainland. This attack was
foiled when one of the saboteurs had second thoughts and alerted the FBI.
But unknown to most Americans, an engraved, granite monument memo-
rialized these eight Nazis who, in June of 1942, tried to mount this violent
attack. For decades, this art deco-style monument was located on land owned
by the U.S. government. Pre-manufactured bombs, high-test fuses, four enormous crates of TNT, and other materiel, were among the weaponry these
Nazis had planned to detonate.

Two well-equipped, German U boats loaded with what was then the
latest in state-of-the-art explosive devices landed on America's shores; one
in Jacksonville, Florida, and the other on Long Island, New York. Had one
of the terrorists not tipped off the FBI, the scheme's perpetrators – two of
whom were Americans who were secret Nazis – they may well never have
been caught. This was despite the fact that at least twelve witnesses saw the
submarine anchored off of Long Island. American George Dasch was paid
$82,000 by the Third Reich for his role in the plot, which was called Opera-
tion Pastorius. That's approximately $1.2 million in 2019 money. But then he
got cold feet. Thinking he'd soon become a hero, Dasch contacted a top aide
to J. Edgar Hoover and spilled the beans. Dasch then agreed to meet some
FBI agents in Washington, DC three days later.

Things didn't turn out as Mr. Dasch had expected; upon arrival at DC's
Union Station, he was arrested and taken into custody. A secret, military
tribunal was convened, and all eight perps were found guilty. Only Dasch and
one other conspirator were spared the electric chair. After the war they were
deported. Years later, American Nazis Francis Parker Yockey and George
Lincoln Rockwell and several other members of the American Nazi party

commissioned a solid, rectangular slab of high quality granite to be engraved with the names of the eight terrorists to commemorate what they considered to be heroism.

Yockey, a World War II veteran and a lawyer, later worked for the old U.S. Department of War. The Departments of Defense and State now facilitate the functions of the old War Department.Following Yockey's 1960 suicide – which was made possible by a cyanide capsule, smuggled in to the San Francisco jail by Willis Carto, who slipped it to him – Yockey's supporters, including neo Nazis Carto and William Pierce, raised funds to complete the project. The granite slab measures nearly three feet across, more than 30 inches vertically, and is almost nine inches thick. It weighs over 200 pounds, and stuck two inches from the ground in a wooded, little-known section of southwest DC called Blue Plains.

Located there is an advanced, secondary waste management treatment plant which daily processes 300 million gallons of water. In August of 1942, when the six German Nazis were executed on FDR's orders, the water treatment plant had been there since 1938. After George Lincoln Rockwell, the-then leader of the American Nazi Party, was murdered in 1967, the granite slab ended up with Willis Carto. For years, it was stored it in a locked room in the basement of Liberty Lobby's Capitol hill headquarters. Carto wanted it displayed near where he believed the perps were buried.

However, not wanting to have it connected to any of his enterprises, he hired a stonemason to re-engrave a disclaimer stating it was paid for by the National Socialist White People's Party. Carto and Curtis Dall, whose DC connections proved useful, clandestinely arranged to have it placed in the thickets of grass and brush, basically hidden, in Blue Plains. This was done under the cover of darkness, in 1969. For decades, the only people aware of the significance of this monument, apparently, were Holocaust deniers, members of the Aryan Nations, Liberty Lobby employees and donors, and members of William Pierce's National Alliance. I never made the pilgrimage to Blue Plains to pay homage to the executed Nazis. I was invited, however, by Carto, Mike Piper, Dallas Naylor, Jamie Von Brunn, and – years later – by Dr. William Pierce and several National Alliance employees and a Resistance Records distributor.

Periodically, private ceremonies were held there. These small events included celebrations of Adolf Hitler's birthday, where candles were lit and floral arrangements left atop the slab, which resembled a tombstone. Naylor, the Liberty Lobby custodian, regularly drove over to Blue Plains with a weed whacker and small broom, to maintain the ground and trim the growth around the slab. He'd then light candles and leave flowers atop the thing.

Occasionally, Carto admonished him to better maintain it. "Damnit, Dallas, get your fat ass over there and show some respect to our heroes," Willis would yell at his lackey. The memorial in 2006 was discovered by some power company employees. They alerted James Rosenstock, a manager with the National Park Service. Years later, in 2010, the U.S. Park Service removed it. It's now in a government warehouse in Maryland. Federal archivists tagged it as item OXCO-575 at this storage facility. It's fitting that this monument was located on the grounds of a sewage treatment plant. But why, for decades, was it on land owned by the United States government? And why did it take over four years after its discovery to remove it?

The famed, late Nazi hunter Simon Wiesenthal claimed he had evidence of a clandestine network called Operation ODESSA, which was allegedly set up in late 1944 to help facilitate the undetectable, safe escape of high-ranking SS and Nazi party officials from Germany after the fall of the Third Reich.

According Dr. Wiesenthal and historians who support his claims, between April, 1945 and mid-1946, ODESSA operatives helped several hundred powerful Nazis and SS members leave Germany without a trace. With assistance from ODESSA, well connected Third Reich survivors were provided safe passage to Argentina, Paraguay, Uruguay, and other South American countries. Once there, they lived out the rest of their lives, or, tried to, and essentially escaped justice.

Frederick Forsyth's 1972 bestseller, 'The Odessa File', became a major motion picture in 1974. This book and film brought worldwide attention to Odessa and its mission. While most historians doubt Odessa's existence, no one has ever conclusively proven it didn't exist, and verifiable evidence suggests that it did. From being associated with more neo-Nazi honchos than anyone else on this planet, my view is that Odessa did, in fact, exist. Willis Carto, William Pierce, and others acquainted with Nazis who knew Hitler, said that the Odessa was real. In June of 2017, government investigators and officers with the international police agency INTERPOL discovered a large cache of valuable Nazi artifacts in a home in Buenos Aries, Argentina. A Judge-issued order to raid the home of a relics collector resulted in this mind-boggling discovery.

The entrance to this treasure trove was hidden behind a bookcase which led to a secret passageway. The narrow hall led to the room where were found the greatest collection of Nazi mementos from the 1930s and '40s in Argentine history. Historians said high-ranking Nazis who escaped to Argentina brought the items, many of which were attached to photos of Adolf Hitler holding them. The Fuehrer, himself, had actually used some of these things. This discovery was made in the wealthy Buenos Aries suburb of Beccar, which had been home to Nazis like Josef Mengele, Adolf Eichmann, and other notorious, close Hitler associates. Nearly 80 extremely rare, highly collectible relics from the Third Reich were found in the secret room behind that bookcase.

The collection was ordered impounded by Theresa Bullrich, Argentina's Minster of Security. There's tremendous demand for priceless collectibles like these by museums, private collectors, and historians. In 2011, Dr. Mengele's handwritten diaries sold were sold for $245,000. As earlier described in this book, I, too, was allowed inside some secret, hidden rooms where valuable Nazi memorabilia was stored. I've seen documents and books which were signed by Adolf Hitler, and held in my hands a Swastika paperweight and other items which belonged to him. Upon so doing, I felt like washing my hands. But his fans – and they're numerous, now – would love to get their hands on such mementos.

Around 1996, or '97, Willis Carto spent over $2.5 million on Hitler artifacts. What's one person's gold is like another's trash. During this period, the impact of America's lax immigration policies became apparent to me. Illegal immigration depresses the wages of low-skilled U.S. citizens, and drives many of the most vulnerable Americans out of the work force, as President Trump says. Effectively, the least-advantaged U.S. citizens are shut of the chance to achieve the American Dream. Our politicians should support the interests of those who are rightfully here, and not criminals who break our laws. Many such Americans turn to off-the-books, illicit work to survive. Many do so while receiving benefits from various Welfare programs.

Such policies induce many Americans into addiction, drug dealing, and organized bigotry. Young adults who lack skills and education become discouraged and give up hope – and many turn to illegal drugs. The same applies even more so to white supremacy. The bravado and machismo exhibited by members of Hate groups is merely a cover for the insecurity, deep down, that these people live with and feel, 24/7. Many anti-Semites became this way over liberal policies like open borders, affirmative action, racial quotas, soft-on-crime policies, and our Welfare-based Economy. It's not wrong to blame pro-Open Borders politicians, illegal aliens, and clueless Leftists, for many troubles confronting lower-skilled, lesser-educated, impoverished Americans.

"Formulate and stamp indelibly in your mind a mental picture of yourself as succeeding. Never permit it to fade," said Reverend Norman Vincent Peale. Thinking optimistically DOES, indeed, help to foster positive outcomes. Having known and worked for Ronald Reagan – who was history's ultimate optimist

– and growing up in a conservative, midwestern, Protestant household where positive thinking was second nature, Dr. Peale's words reinforced those beliefs. Being imbued with possibility thinking from an early age, and becoming convinced that a positive mental attitude helps, meant that throughout my seven plus years as a drug addict, I always knew I could stop using.

Since 2006, I've helped hundreds of junkies get off of, and stay off of, illicit drugs. The greatest challenges are always users whose lives haven't been very fulfilling. But as Abe Lincoln said, "most folks are usually about as happy as they make up their minds to be." This belief, which I share, also represents Ronald Reagan's belief regarding happiness, faith in God, and the value of being optimistic.

Many addicts are from financially, culturally, and educationally disadvantaged homes. Dysfunctionality is common in their families. Citizens must demand their elected representatives and judges step up, and stop enabling junkies to continue their harmful ways. In mid-2016, a young addict asked me to sponsor him as a Narcotics Anonymous member. He's now 30 years old and has been clean for over 30 months. His successful parents are divorced and both are respected professionals. He's been in jail and prison.

As a felon, he can't vote and his employment options are limited. For awhile, he was barred from driving and attended court-ordered, mandatory classes at an outpatient re-hab facility as a condition of probation. This young man had hit rock bottom, but was given what his judge called "one last chance", via a Drug Court, to avoid reincarceration in either a state or federal prison. He attends N.A. meetings several times each month, and has learned to divert his addictive tendencies by channeling them into work, fishing, working out, and reestablishing his relationships with his parents, sister, and friends. He decided to be happy and then worked toward attaining it. As he nails down his recovery, he's more pleased with himself. He works for a well-respected north Iowa drug rehabilitation facility, and hopes for even greater success. But successes like this intelligent, resourceful, fortunate young man's aren't common among addicts who have never truly known a good life.

A young lady in San Antonio, Texas whom I met in N.A., is the same age as the young man referenced above. She was raised by a single mother on welfare, and her father died in prison. Her four step- siblings all have differ-ent dads. Her mother is an alcoholic who has never held a job. This gal never learned much in school and dropped out at age 16. She has no concept of a work ethic, or being responsible with time, money, or her health. She isn't evil, and while she's not bright, she's not dumb. If she wants a job she could get one, and if she decides to beat drugs, she will. But with no positive role models in her life, it's unlikely this will happen. In a revenue-neutral manner, which would actually save tax dollars in the long run, this gal could become productive, happy, and self-supporting.

The costs of welfare and the irresponsible behavior it facilitates, and incarceration, and the damage that such wards of the state often cause to property and to other people, and wages and benefits paid to bureaucrats on all levels who administer such programs, amounts to billions of dollars every year. This doesn't include the lost interest on such funds.

It's sensible to divert tax dollars to effective programs which would save lives and stop facilitating life-styles that destroy them. Mandatory, random testing for drugs, work-for-welfare requirements, and effective, professional counseling with adequate follow-up, would accomplish for these impover-ished junkies what my costly re-hab efforts achieved for me and countless other recovering addicts. It isn't only a morally righteous policy; it will also save tax dollars and improve society.

President Lyndon Johnson's so-called Great Society and his infamous War on Poverty worsened matters for America's poor. Ronald Reagan said that "poverty won LBJ's War on Poverty", and he was correct. The Reverend Cecil Blye, a black pastor from the inner city of Louisville, Kentucky, makes the valid claim that these programs have "incentivized co-habitation" with-out marriage, "single motherhood, and unemployment." As the president of STAND (Stay True to America's National Destiny), Reverend Blye has seen the seamy, tragic effects of these nation-wrecking policies. "President Johnson gave us the Great Society," Dr. Blye said, at the National Press club. But "there can be no great society without great morality." LBJ's grandiose schemes not only destroyed black families, but also the family structure of poor white families. The Great Society was an equal-opportunity destroyer of American stability, and in 2019, we're still paying for it. It's time to take culture-preserving action.

Within weeks of living alone, with no wife to come home to, my life spiraled out of control. My mother and father lived just four miles away, but they were extremely busy. Mom was volunteering at the White House, in the office of first lady Laura Bush. Her good friend Nancy Theis - the director of the White House office of Presidential Correspondence, who died in 2019 - kept my mother busy, four days a week. My father always brought home a briefcase full of papers to read, for current and upcoming legal cases he was adjudicating. Addiction turned me inward, and I was ignoring longtime, close friends.

I didn't work, and didn't want to. My weekly visits to Dr. Weiner continued, and those hour-long sessions kept me somewhat sane. But I still was copping fixes and getting high. This meant stepping up my affiliation with crack pushers, junkies, and the sordid culture that goes with it. What I didn't know was that someone was watching me, and gathering evidence. My dad met the P.I. at a restaurant called Rosa Mexicana in DC, which was a block from the Lansburgh. The PI was waiting for my dad as he arrived. "Judge Blodgett?", he said, with an outstretched hand, "Let's go inside." For two hours, my dad told the man – a retired U.S. Secret Service agent – of my situation, and how he wanted his help.

Private investigators aren't cheap, especially if they're ex-Secret Service agents with prior experience as police detectives in big cities, as this guy was. Dad paid a $10,000 retainer fee, and, about three months later, paid him another ten grand. Without knowing it, I was being watched, photographed, and videotaped. A former spy was being spied on by another spy.

I've never been homeless, but for about two months in late 2005, I lived that way. It began when my Dad arranged for me to be denied access to my apartment. Knowing I'd not file a complaint against him for taking such action, he succeeded in having my access card invalidated, and the locks changed to my unit. For months, the rent and utilities were paid out of my own funds, to which he later restricted my access. My parents wanted me to stay at their place, in Penn Quarter. But I rarely did.

As I stuffed some clothes and a toothbrush into a backpack, I realized that normal people don't turn their backs on a good life in a nice home, with a warm bed, good food and loving, caring parents. But millions of junkies have turned down opportunities, preferring to retain their drug addiction. Before leaving my parents' apartment, a framed photograph of my parents caught my eye.

This photo was taken on our boat, years earlier on Clear Lake. My dad is steering the craft, with my mother sitting to his left. They're smiling. It had been awhile since I'd seen my parents smile, and it was my fault. It was stupid to abandon my best shot at getting clean, but the desire to remain was overtaken by the powerful urge to keep smoking crack. I left a note for my dad, who'd be home in a few hours. My mom was to arrive back in DC the following afternoon. A few hours later, I called a dealer known as Jamaican Mike, who worked the area between 12th and 17th Streets, N.W., and about 'N' and 'W' Streets. We agreed to meet at the Braxton hotel, where a client of his – a crack whore named Drucilla – rented a room by the week. Drucilla allowed drug deals to go down in her room at the Braxton in return for crack. This benefitted junkies and dealers who bought crack during daylight hours, as it's easier for undercover cops, informants, and narcotics officers to spot drug deals than at night.

The Braxton was on Rhode Island avenue, N. W., between 14th and 15th Streets, and was then an addict's paradise. Drucilla wore lots of eye liner, bright red lipstick, and more cheap, shiny trinkets than could be found on a pushcart in Tijuana. I bought 20 dime bags of crack, and five 'dubs' – $20 bags - and gave a dub to Drucilla. At a British Petroleum station on 13th Street I bought three glass tubes, called roses, some Chore-Boy copper wire and two lighters. Behind me in line was an attractive blonde of about 30 years old. She knew exactly what I was doing, and it was obvious she was a crack head.

She not only liked rock, but she was wearing a big one on her wedding band finger. Damn, there goes that – or, so I thought. When I completed my purchase, she initiated a conversation. Twenty minutes later, we were getting high in the penthouse apartment she and her husband shared in a nicely renovated building on 13th Street. Her husband, a stockbroker, was from an old-line Florida family. Christina was a successful architect. We became fast friends. When we'd smoked all of my crack, they ordered more. They also brought drugs from Jamaican Mike. My parents repeatedly called my cell phone over the next few days. Not once did I pick up, although I listened to their messages imploring me to return. It was almost like the prodigal son in the Bible's book of Luke.

I spent the night in their guest room, and ended up staying with them for ten days. Every day for the next ten days, I withdrew $300 from my checking account, using my ATM card. During the day, I often ate breakfast, lunch and dinner at one of the several soup kitchens in the district. The one I liked best was called Martha's Table, which was in the 2100 block of 14th Street. I knew some regular patrons of Martha's, and even a cook who worked there. I often wondered if the Private Investigator my dad had retained was back on the job, following me.

I also ate at various churches that served low-priced meals, and bought lots of processed food from the 7-Elevens that were all over the District of Columbia. This continued until my father arranged with PNC bank to block my account a week later. I had signed over power of attorney to him when I attended Father Martin's Ashley in 2004, which empowered him to take this drastic action. During this time, I wasn't always able to find a place to spend the night, or to stay during the day, so I stayed at some homeless shelters. The government of Washington, DC spends $80,000 per day on housing homeless people for whom there's no room in the city's shelters, according to Mayor Muriel Bowser's Director of Human Services, Laura Zeilinger.

But I wasn't going to live that way, regardless of the circumstances.

It's one thing to stay overnight at a nonprofit shelter, but I wouldn't accept what amounted to Welfare. My parents kept calling and text-messaging me. But I was zoned out. One night during this bender, my mother managed to get ahold of me, via J. Ralph. My parents wanted me to join them for dinner, at the DC Chop House, where they were going to host a young man from Iowa. This guy, Casey Callanan, had been an intern in my dad's office at the Iowa Capitol when my father served in the Iowa House of Representatives. He was now in DC, interning in the U.S. Congress. I didn't show up. Throughout the meal, my mother desperately tried to reach me, via her cell phone. She kept calling and texting, to no avail. The previous week, I was a no-show when my parents hosted Kevin Martin, the chairman of the Federal Communications Commission (FCC), and his wife, Catherine.

My addiction was my priority, not meeting up with Bush administration appointees, or anyone else but drug pushers and fellow junkies. Around this time, my father had really let me have it, over my addition. He told me, "if you're unwilling to accept our help, and you won't help yourself, then just keep on using drugs. But stay the hell away from me, and get out, right now." That's what I did, which really upset my mother.

On the evening that my parents were hosting Callanan for dinner, my mom excused herself from the table five times. My Dad told his guest, "our son is gone. Maybe for good. It's tearing us both apart, because we're fearful, and don't know what to do." When they returned to their apartment at the Lansburgh, it was after nine p.m. As my Dad got ready for bed, my mother decided to go out and look for me. She called Diamond Taxi, and minutes later, a cab driver met her in the lobby of the Lansburgh. From the P.I. that my Dad had hired, my mother had several pages of addresses and contacts, and this taxi driver took her to nearly all of them. More than once, the kindly, black cabbie cautioned my mother about the innate danger of traipsing around some of the District's worst neighborhoods after dark. But from about 10 p.m. until just after Midnight, my mother, who then was nearly 70 years old, did just that.

During this time, I was in a high-crime area called Naylor Court, in northwest D.C. It was well after 12 midnight and it appeared to be just another dark, dreary night in a desolate corner of America's capital city. Having absent-mindedly left my .380 under the front seat of my Range Rover, it wasn't in my pocket when, after I copped some crack, a crazed junkie slugged me, unprovoked, in the jaw. Before I could react, he slammed his fist into my mouth, straight-on, breaking my central incisors – my two front teeth. The pain was excruciating, but his cowardly, sneak attack really fired me up. He earned himself a swift, hard kick, straight to his balls. That's exactly what he got, but as he was big, he didn't fall forward. He fell back against a brick wall, hitting his head. He was dazed, but still standing.

I then administered an even faster, much harder kick to the same target. He tried to speak, but couldn't make a sound. As he fell to his right, I kneed him in his face. He hit the ground and was silent for about thirty seconds, then began moaning. Bending down to my knee, I grabbed his afro and saw that his face was a mess. Blood trickled from his nostrils and he, too, now had some broken teeth. His lower lip was split and his eyes weren't focusing.

"YOU COWARDLY MOTHER FUCKER", I shouted, not knowing if he heard me. As I spoke, I spat out blood and pieces of my teeth. I wanted to kill this worthless piece of shit, but I had made my point. I got back into my vehicle and drove to the apartment of Kitty, a pretty crack head. She was a beautiful black lady, about 35 years old, and she was always ready to get high. After she cleaned me up, we smoked the crack that my attacker had probably seen me buy, and tried to steal.

The next morning, I called my dentist and said I had to see him, immediately. He accommodated me. When I arrived at his office, he was horrified at my condition. "Good god, Todd – what happened?"

I told him I didn't want to discuss it, and we didn't. My incisors were so damaged that capping what remained of them wasn't an option. Ten days later, Dr. Breslerman fitted me with two dental implants. To this day, they're still in my mouth.

For about two weeks during this time, I stayed at the home of a drug dealer in Brentwood, which is a dangerous neighborhood in D.C. The dude, who was black, owed me a big favor: a few years earlier, he had phoned me, in desperation, asking me to meet him in Blagden alley. As I was only about two miles away, I agreed. He asked me to drive, immediately, as close as possible to a large dumpster that was next to a burned-out clothes dryer. Upon my arrival, he flipped up the dumpster's lid, climbed out, jumped into the back seat of my car and hunkered down. He was on the run from the DC police, who had warrants out on him. As I drove down 9th Street, and onto Florida avenue, N.W., I encountered six or seven cop cruisers while transporting this fugitive. My loyalty was now being repaid.

When I got to his crib in Brentwood, he high-fived me and promised me all the crack I could smoke. "What up, white boy?" We talked for hours that first night, and while I crashed there, I sometimes accompanied him on his deliveries. He knew that being in a vehicle with a white guy lessens the chance of being pulled over by the cops. My host's lady friend was a gorgeous black prostitute whom I'd gotten to know when I first became addicted. This gal, whom I'll call 'Madame X', also sold high quality crack, which she furnished to me, free of charge. She had always liked me and appreciated how I treated her and other women in a respectful manner. She also liked that I often carried a gun. My dealer buddy slept during the day, as did his girl. That week, I watched TV, ate soul food, drank cheap wine and smoked crack.

While this gal and my pusher buddy didn't use drugs, they had no problem with me getting high in their basement. Nearly every night, I would drive her to see clients while her boyfriend delivered crack. I waited nearby as she and her Johns did their thing. On my last night at their place, Marion Barry, the former DC Mayor, called her. Madame X hung up on him, after reminding Barry that he still owed her six hundred dollars. I never found out if the ex-Mayor's debt was for sex, crack, or a combination thereof. In 2019,

I tried to get back in touch with this good, loyal friend, but my remaining contacts in DC, including J. Ralph and Willie Mack, said he was "gone." By this, I presumed they meant he was dead.

In 2016, violent crime rate of DC's Brentwood neighborhood was 179 percent higher than the U.S. average, according to NeighborhoodScout. com, which rates America's neighborhoods. In 2005-06, When I was briefly a Brentwood resident, its violence was even worse.

My dad emailed me, and my lawyers, Jack Fornaciari and B. Jay Fetner, also tried to contact me. But I wasn't ready to come up for air. Shootings during daylight hours aren't unusual in Brentwood, but, somehow, I felt impervious to any potential violence. The most dangerous areas of any major city tend to also be where illegal drugs are most plentiful, and this hood was no exception. Back in those days, junkies knew that searching for crack in Brentwood was like being a probate attorney in a West Palm Beach retirement community, or an ivory hunter in an elephant graveyard in South Africa.

When drug addiction causes homelessness, several factors are often at play. It can be due to the homes of junkies being foreclosed on, or addicts being evicted from rental properties. But in some cases, homelessness results because junkies chose to live on the streets. This occurs when drug usage is their top priority. My descent into living on the streets, which began in mid-November, 2005, stressed out my parents like crazy. My dad finally asked me to meet him at his office in Baltimore. I'd only been there once, in early 2001. While this office wasn't as ornate as his office in Iowa's state capitol in Des Moines, Iowa, it was still impressive.

My mother was in Iowa, meeting with a farmer in Pleasantville who wanted to rent her land. She'd be there for several more days. My father, never one to waste time, came straight to the point. "O-D-ing on drugs isn't the only way addiction can kill you. You're lucky you survived your injuries." He added, "Todd, even before you were mugged, you were being watched by a private investigator I retained. Had he been surveilling you when those punks attacked you, he'd have protected you. But he was working for another client that evening." My dad handed me two large envelopes. On each were the words, "Todd Blodgett: Photos/interviews w/ drug pushers & addicts who are acquainted w/ subject" The subject of this investigation was me.

I must've stared at those envelopes for at least ten seconds, without saying a word.

"Go ahead," my dad told me. "Open 'em. Have a look. See how you look while you're engaged in this sordid, high-risk, nasty world of junkies, drug dealers, crack whores, pimps, and other losers." My dad then said, "I'd love to get those creeps to join me on a hunting trip." He was serious; if he could've arranged to being those misery peddlers out in an Iowa corn field, pheasants, quail, geese and ducks wouldn't be the only things that would find their way in his line of fire.

There were dozens of time-stamped photos in the two packets, along with typed notes describing the circumstances of each. "Subject buying crack cocaine from dealer in Anacostia", or "notes from interview with drug runner who has delivered crack cocaine to subject", and other details, and background information, were among the P.I's reports. The names of those whom my dad called my "associates" were redacted in the report I was provided. But in the investigator's original reports, The names of some people were included. My old man had me dead to rights, nailed.

As I read, my dad took a phone call. As I looked at the photos, one of his assistants brought him several folders containing documents relating to a case involving the merger of two health care corporations. Looking at his watch, my dad said, "my time is valuable, son. But I'll take whatever time's needed, and spare no expense, to get you back on track." It wasn't until years later, following my recovery, that I realized how relatively few drug addicts are so fortunate. Having such loving, smart, involved parents, who were so dedicated to my well-being, was indispensable to my recovery.

"You attended several re-hab facilities, without success," my father pointed out. "Your mother and I want you to vacate your apartment and move in with us. We'll monitor your progress and work with you, and some

430

qualified professionals, to help get you clean." My dad had already contacted the Kolmac clinic, a well-regarded Outpatient Recovery center in downtown DC. "You'll meet with a Kolmac counselor early next week," he told me. My father did what good, smart parents do: taking charge, and taking steps toward resolution. I was 45 years old, but still his son. He was nearly seventy, and wanted to make sure I reached that age.

"You won't stay at your apartment anymore," he said. "I've contacted some professional movers; we'll put your things in storage. You can live in the guest bedroom of our apartment." As it happened, the live-in manager of the Lansburgh – where my parents lived - was married to the lady who managed the Saratoga – the apartment building where I then lived. This made it easy for my father to facilitate what he wanted. The saying, "if the drugs don't kill you, then the lifestyle will", truly applied to my situation.

Days later, Dr. Gary B. Blodgett and J. Ralph Whitehead made an unannounced visit to one of my drug Dealers, at his crib in the hood. After J. Ralph tricked the pusher's lady friend into letting him into their townhouse, he told the dude – who trusted and respected JR – that "a federal Judge is outside. He's gonna talk to you, and if you're smart, you'll listen." JR then called my dad and said, "I'm at the door, Judge. Come on in."

Minutes later, my father, JR and the pusher and his chick were seated in front of a flat screen TV set. Taking the remote away from the gal, JR clicked it off. "Y'all be havin' me arrested, yo' honuh?," the dealer – whose street name was 'Sinbad' – asked. "Not today, unless you do something stupid," my dad replied. The crack pusher then said, "well, Judge, ahh ain't know nothin' about nothin.'"

"Lyin' to 'dis here dude be somethin' stupid," JR warned Sinbad. "If you know even a little about a little", my Dad warned the dealer, "then you'd know to not deal drugs, young man."

Handing him a large envelope containing the same photos I'd seen, my Dad said, "think of me as the parent of an addict who buys your drugs." J. Ralph and my father glanced at each other as Sinbad and his chick examined the evidence which implicated both of them. Upon seeing each photo, their eyes met, and their expressions became increasingly worrisome.

The young black lady said, "it ain't in my heart do do nothin' bad to Mistuh Todd, Judge. We not … "

Interrupting, JR replied, "shut up about yo' heart." She said, "nigga, y'all ain't know nothin' about my heart." Reaching into his boot, J. Ralph said, "I know if y'all don't shut da fuck up, in about ten seconds, yo' heart gonna stop beatin'."

"Hold it, JR," my dad said. "Let's hear from Sinbad. He's the drug dealer."

"Ah be protectin' m'self," Sinbad said. My father told him that "the best way to protect" himself was "to come clean, be honest, and stop dealing drugs."

"Actually, yo' honuh," the dealer said. "I provides high-quality, affordable, pharmaceutical alternatives. I'm sayin'." He added, "Ahh ain't be snitchin'. Dat' mean signin' my death certificate. Dazz how it work in 'dis hood." My Dad then offered Sinbad a deal. "You're not being asked to snitch, son. These photos, and I have more, and cell phone records, and other incriminating evidence against you, won't find their way to the authorities - provided you cease, forthwith, all contact with my son."

"Fo' real?"

"Your heard me. Furthermore, you'll notify every pusher, drug runner, crack supplier, and junkie you know, that I've got a private investigator scouring this hood, and others, for additional proof of what's going on. That's my offer. Your call." Without hesitation, Sinbad replied, "y'all gots a deal."

"Good," my father said, as he got up to leave. "Double-cross me, and our agreement is null and void. I'll see to it that the DEA, the Justice Department, and the United States Marshalls, will be on your drug-dealing butt like a fat kid on a sack of cupcakes. Got it?"

"Okay, okay. Ahh – ahh means, WE – we gots it. Yessir."

"Good", my father said, as he shook hands with Sinbad and his lady friend. "Mistuh Gary," Sinbad told my Dad, "when Ahh tells peoples about 'dis, well, 'dem niggas gonna stay away from Todd like him be a hooker wiff AIDS." JR and my Dad then drove to Ben's Chili Bowl, on DC's 'U' Street, N.W., for a dinner of half-smokes, ribs and french fries.

In the realm of junkiedom, overdosing is but one way for addicts to bite the dust. In this sense, it's very similar to the realm of organized hatred. This is because life-destroying, hateful beliefs wreck the souls of the believers. Worse, yet, the self-destructive ways of haters, the innate violence, and the entire culture of the Hate movement and those who populate it, can also lead to death. As with drug addicts, haters also wreak havoc on innocent people, who become unwilling victims of the unwise choices of others. Everything my dad told me was correct, and he was totally sincere.

I felt terrible about the harm my addiction was causing my parents, just as I had earlier about what I'd put my ex-wife through, for the last four years of our marriage. My father's assessment of my situation and the solutions he proposed were sound. If I took his advice and worked the plans he was putting together, I'd get off of drugs and stay clean. My life would return to normal and I'd be happy, and productive again. There was only one problem: I wasn't ready to quit.

On a late September evening in 2005, I nearly lost my life after I was stabbed and viciously assaulted. A cute crack whore named 'Blondie' had invited to her apartment. Blondie was black, and had earned the nickname because she dyed her hair blonde. She turned tricks, sold crack, and picked up some extra bucks by fencing stolen property. By this stage in my addiction, I was getting high on a regular basis with friends of friends, and even with girls who were, basically, mere casual acquaintances.

This was a major mistake.

Blondie lived in a one-bedroom, walk-up unit in a three-story building around 11th and 'R' street, N.W. I had to buzz my way in to the building. As I walked to the third floor, she sent me a text message: 'Can't Wait!!!' Before I knocked on her door, Blondie – who'd been watching through the peep hole – opened it. But where was she? She whispered, "I'm behind the door, honey." After walking in far enough for her to shut the door, she appeared. Stark naked.

"I can't wait, either" I told her. She embraced me, and we got down to business. About 40 minutes later, she rose from the bed and opened a dresser drawer. We smoked fourteen dime bags of crack. I was ready to go at it again, but that's when the crack whore in Blondie kicked in. "That's all I've got," she said. "Why don't you go buy more? We've got all night, right, sweetie?" Indeed we did. Two pushers I called didn't answer, and a call to another went straight to voice mail. As Blondie sat up naked in bed, she reached for a pack of Virginia Slims menthols and lit up. "Hey, I know a dude who always has great stuff. And he lives only about four blocks from here," she said.

I told her to call him. As she waited for him to answer, she asked, "how about an eight-ball? It'll cost a hundred fifty." Before I could reply, the guy picked up. Once she sealed the deal, she said, "okay, he'll meet you behind the Black Cat." She then gave the guy my cell phone number. She said his name was Marquis, whom I was to meet him in 20 minutes. Real-time minutes, not drug dealer minutes. I got dressed and left her building. As I was at 13th and 'R', my cell phone rang. "Da blonde bitch done give me yo' number, dude. Where y'all is?" Within minutes, we met on 13th Street, and ducked into an alley. Behind a dumpster, we made the exchange. "Later, dude," Marquis said. "Call if y'all want mo'. I be around fo' a minute." Blondie phoned me as I walked back to her place. "See you in ten minutes," I told her. It was nearly 11:45 p.m., mid-week, and the streets were strangely quiet.

Somewhere near 12th and 'R' Streets, I was attacked by three young black men. They ran out of an alley, and hit me from behind, knocking me down. Rising quickly to my feet, I tried to stay calm as they circled me like piranhas surrounding a pond frog. Suddenly, from out of nowhere, a fourth punk joined them. Instinctively, I reached for my gun – which was locked away in my dad's safe at the Lansburgh. The best I could hope for was to defend myself, find an opening, and run like Hell. Luck was with me, at first. I ducked and dodged several punches, and landed blows on two of them. I kicked another straight in the balls, which sent him howling in pain to the ground. The streetlight enabled us to see each other's faces; their expressions were as mean as any neo-Nazi I'd ever encountered. With their backs toward the street lights, I looked past them and yelled, "Help me!" Sure enough, all four geniuses took the bait, turned around, and saw nothing. I bolted, taking off down the sidewalk. But I was 45, high on cocaine, and tired from my previous activities with Blondie. As I was about a block from Blondie's apartment, one of the young punks dove at my lower legs and tackled me to the ground.

Adrenaline coursed through my system, and I was back on my feet. One of the thugs sucker punched me as another kicked me in the shin. Somehow, I was able to get back up, again. I was still stunned, staggering, when I noticed a shiny object in the hands of one of my attackers. The others moved aside for him. He then charged into me, hard and fast. At that moment, I was shoved from behind, just as I collided with the dude in front of me. A burning sensation suddenly permeated my lower left abdomen, but it wasn't all that painful. "Damn, nigga," one of them said, "y'all done kilt 'dis honkey!"

Another voice said, "he ain't livin' now… " I wondered whom the guy thought wouldn't survive. They were referring to me. The sharp blade of a knife had just been plunged into my lower abdomen, piercing my spleen. Until I looked down, I didn't even know I'd been cut. Beads of sweat instantly broke out on the forehead of the kid who sliced me. Our eyes locked. I decided that even if I died, he wasn't going to get away with my murder. I was then hit from behind. Falling forward, I broke my fall, pivoting to avoid falling on the knife. One of the degenerates yanked the blade out, turned around, and ran off into the night.

One perpetrator remained, and this one wanted me dead. Before I could say a word or even breathe, he kicked me hard, breaking three ribs. He was about to kick again, when a voice said, "Let him be!" An elderly black man, probably in his mid-80s, saved my life. "I'm a-callin' me nine-one-one right 'dis minute, boy," he told the punk who'd just knifed me. Instantly, the perp ran down the block like a Klansman escaping from an NAACP convention.

The old man helped me up, and steadied me, as I tried to catch my breath and not pass out. I felt faint, and nauseous. "I done seen 'dat shank slicin' into you. Y'all gotta see a doctor 'fo you bleeds out, son."

"Are you on hold with nine-one-one?," I asked. "Hell, no. It takes 'em fo' ever to get to 'dis hood. It'd be an hour or mo' befo' dem gets here, even if you is white." When I laughed at his observation, my entire inside hurt. "Son, you be hurt bad; worser din you knows. Where y'all stayin'? Grab hold of me. Ima help ya git dere."

"Thanks. It's about a block." As we slowly walked toward Blondie's place, she called again. With one hand on the shoulder of the good Samaritan, I removed my phone from my pocket and answered.

"Where are you?", Blondie asked. "Did something bad happen?"

"Yeah," I replied, "you might say that."

As I spoke to Blondie, with the old black man at my side, she was frantic. But she wasn't worried about my serious injury. Her concern was for the crack cocaine I had gone to buy. "They didn't get the crack, did they?" The fear she expressed was a typical reaction from a junkie: all addicts care about is getting a fix. "Please, Todd, please tell me that you still have the crack." I ended the phone call and asked the senior citizen to help me over the 17th Street, where my buddy Myles lived.

Walking the three or four blocks to the Rutland – the co-op where Myles owned a unit – was more painful with each block. The old man wry observed what he'd seen. "I ain't sayin' y'all wasn't punchin' above yo' weight class, 'cause you was. Y'done pretty good, and y'all was quick." But, he said, "dey was fo' on one and dem was young'uns. Ya'll never stood no chance, boy." When we arrived at the front door of the Rutland, the old man kept warning I could bleed out. I didn't know, then, that my spleen had been nicked by the blade, and damaged by the vicious kicks. The pain from the kick was horrendous. As X-ray images later showed, my spleen was split in two. I dialed the number for Myles's unit, and we were buzzed inside the building.

22

The old man walked me down two long halls on the first floor of the Rutland to Myles's' unit. A junkie friend of Myles named Cheryl answered the door. I thanked the old man for his kindness, and we shook hands. I never saw him again, and don't recall his name – or if I ever even knew it. I remember him as my guardian angel. Once inside, Myles asked what happened. He brought me two, high-dosage morphine pills, which did no good. As I writhed in pain on the floor of his book-lined den, Max told Cheryl to call 9-11. "An ambulance is on the way", she said. I had the presence of mind to empty my pockets of the fifteen dime bags of crack that Marquis had sold me. At least a junkie who was my friend and his lady friend would enjoy them. I also knew that the last thing I wanted the hospital personnel to find in my pocket was crack cocaine.

About ten minutes later the EMTs – Emergency Medical Technicians – arrived, with a wheeled stetcher. Twelve minutes later, I was at the George Washington University Medical Center's Emergency Room. This was the same ER at the same hospital where Ronald Reagan was taken in 1981, after he was shot. The pain was so extreme that it hurt to breathe, especially when I inhaled. My trousers, socks and boxer shirts were removed by ER nurses. My jacket, shirt, and sweater, were cut away with medical scissors.

A few minutes after being examined, I was wheeled into surgery. Meanwhile, my parents were sound asleep in their apartment at the Lansburgh. At approximately three a.m., Myles called them. Shortly thereafter, a hospital staffer also called my parents. Within minutes, they drove to the hospital. But when they arrived, I was in surgery. Upon awakening, my surgeon told me that my spleen had been removed. He also said that had I arrived at the ER 20 minutes after I had, I'd have died of internal bleeding. My parents were present as I was taken, under anesthesia, to the Intensive Care Unit. They left before I awakened. By the time I was conscious, it was 11 p.m. It had been nearly 24 hours since I was attacked.

Awakening in a strange environment is always confusing, but that's particularly true when one awakens in a hospital's intensive care unit. There were IV's in both arms, and an oxygen tank was connected to me via a tube in each nostril. I was fitted with a catheter, and clear bags of liquids were hanging near my bed. My parents had arranged for me to have a private room, a nurse informed me when she noticed I was conscious. A morphine drip was also hooked up, which I could access about every 15 minutes. The ICU staff didn't know of my addiction, I thought. The nurse gave me a sedative.

When I awakened, it was nearly lunch time. When my mother arrived, she looked like she hadn't slept in days. I later learned that she had been there earlier, and sat by my side for four hours while I slept. A close family friend, the late Doda de Wolf, had also sat with me as I fought for my life.

"Your dad and I want to know what happened, Todd", Mom said, gently. "But we'll talk about it later.

The doctor says you'll be here in the ICU for at least a week, and for just as long in another section of the hospital." Then she told me that the nurses had found a small bag of crack in my pants pocket. "We'll discuss that later, as well." My loving, compassionate mother is one tough lady, who wasn't going to allow her son's drug addiction to cost him his life. 12 days later, I was released from the GW Medical Center, with 26 staples fastened to my lower abdomen. The scars are still there, and always will be. I spent the next two weeks recuperating at my parents' apartment before moving back into my place at the Saratoga. Twice daily, my mother walked to the Maggie Moo's ice cream parlor in Penn Quarter, and brought back to me a large malt. She cooked all my favorite foods, and we began taking short walks between Penn Quarter and Chinatown.

The doctor examined me each week. Five weeks later, the staples that hadn't worked their way out of my torso were removed, and I no longer needed pain killing medications. By the time I returned to my apartment, I'd lost 25 pounds. But I hadn't lost my craving for crack cocaine. During this time, I was very stupid, and haphazard. My fellow junkie Tray Mitchell introduced me to a drug dealer who had previously been a lawyer. The guy had lost his law license and told me he needed a place to stay for a few days, while he awaited a wire transfer. He had been staying at Tray's co-op in downtown D.C. But Tray was to host a friend of his from his law school class, and the guy's wife, so the pusher needed to crash elsewhere for about three nights.

I agreed to let him stay in the guest bedroom of my apartment at the Saratoga for those few nights. Big mistake. On what was to have been his second night there, I returned from dinner with my parents to find he had stolen items, valuable, irreplaceable things, from my place. Gone were several photos of me and Ronald Reagan, taken in Iowa before he became President and while he was in office. Reagan had signed some of those photos. Three personal notes from Reagan to me were also missing, along with an auto-graphed, pre-presidential photo of Reagan. Signed photo of me with Gerald Ford, George H.W. Bush, and George W. Bush, had also been taken. The thief also made off with about $45,000 worth of coins, some of them gold. Among those coins were three Morgan silver dollars minted in 1893 by the San Fran-cisco mint, each of which was worth between $1,500 and $2,500 at the time.

Those coins were given to me by my late Grandmother, who had owned them for over sixty years. They also stole my laptop computer and a set of eight, heavy crystal tumblers that had been given to me and Linda as a wedding present. Using a spare set of keys to my car, they removed my jumper cables, a radar speed detector, and two high power flashlights, and a loaded, blued steel, Smith & Wesson .38 snub-nosed revolver. I called Tray, who checked around his condo. He learned that approximately five grand in 100 dollar bills was missing. The dealer also stole two gold wristwatches and valuable cufflinks from a drawer in Tray's desk. As those watches and cufflinks had belonged to his late father, for whom Tray was named, he was inconsolable for weeks.

As Dad warned me: If addiction doesn't get me, the druggy lifestyle will. My mother made me promise I'd not seek any revenge against those thieves. Reluctantly, I agreed. Not long after, I let a drug pusher borrow my Range Rover for what was to been an hour, in exchange, for two 8-balls of crack. She then disappeared for two days. Worse, she drove it to New York and back.

In the process, she clocked the vehicle about 35 miles over the 50,000 limit covered by my warranty. The following week, repairs exceeding $3,000 were needed, which would've otherwise been covered. My father insisted I sell my car. We sold it via CarMaxx, in Marland, for $16,500, which I turned over to my parents, because I no longer could trust myself with money.

CHAPTER SIXTEEN

The night I finally got busted was in early February, 2006. The black chick I was with was stunning, and she enjoyed smoking crack cocaine as much as I. Arriving at her place, I paid her $500, which was good for three hours, as long as I supplied the drugs. "Hookers have it better than drug pushers," she told me. I asked her why, and she replied, "because us hookers can wash our crack and sell it again." Ghetto perspectives reflect a unique view of economics and culture. While racing down the stairs of her apartment building, my dealer's girlfriend, who was making rounds with him that evening, called my cell phone. She told me to meet them in 15 minutes near Malcolm X Park. It's official name is Meridian Hill Park, but many DC residents call it Malcom X Park. Some junkies refer to it as 'racist park', because a statue of President James Buchanan, a white supremacist, has graced the property since 1930.

The pusher's Muslim name was Khwaab, which means "dream". Khwaab's dream was to be a famous rapper. Every few weeks, he would rent, at $375 an hour, for three hours at a time, a soundproof, state of the art recording studio. This studio was owned by Baltimore dude who primarily used the facility to launder drug money. As far as the IRS knew, the studio's five soundproof rooms were each booked for 10 hours a day, seven days a week. The reality was, as Khwaab told me, that he and his girl often were the only people there when he recorded his hip-hop tunes, which he wrote.

Khwaab was on time, driving a black, early 1980s, fully restored Cadillac coup DeVille. His girl, Raven, was in the front seat. He slowed to a stop, turned right off of upper 16th Street, N.W., and on to Euclid Street. As I got in the back seat, Khwaab asked, "how much?" I told him I wanted two 8-balls, which would cost $300. The windows were down, despite the cold weather, and Khwaab's CD player was cranked up to full volume. It was a Friday night in an area known to cops as a drug market. Khwaab was highly intelligent, but even smart dudes make bad choices when they're simultaneously smoking a blunt, driving, singing along with their own CD, and dealing drugs. "Hey, Khwaab," I yelled. "Yeah, whassup?"

"The fucking volume on your stereo, THAT's what's up. How about turning it down about 50 notches, while I'm in your car making this buy?" He lowered the volume a bit, and nodded to his chick. My instincts told me that making a drug buy in this car, in this hood, and with the blaring noise, wasn't a good idea. "Everything's cool, Khwaab?" Looking into his rear-view mirror, he assured me it was.

"Don't worry, Todd – I gotcha. We're fine." Raven unzipped her belt-pack and pulled out two bags, each containing an 8-ball. Khwaab reached his right hand back toward me. This De Ville lacked bucket seats, which, basically, led to our getting busted. The vehicle's bench seat made it easy for the cops in the unmarked police car directly behind us to see what went down. I stuffed three Benjamins into his hand and then grabbed the two bags from Raven.

Because the cops saw this, we never stood a chance. By this time, we were near 14th and 'W' Streets. Feeling uneasy, I looked back at the sedan directly behind us. The first two letters of its DC license plate were 'GT'. That meant only one thing: this car was an unmarked government vehicle. How could we have been so careless? Khwaab had assured me he was on the lookout, and all was cool. Any doubt that the cops hadn't seen what had just transpired vanished when, about two seconds later, the blue and red lights inside the grill went on, and the alternating lights appeared within its motor grill.

I knew instantly that the chick I was buying this crack for would never get to smoke it, nor would I. I also knew that the three of us were spending the night, and maybe the next, in jail. "You dumb fuck!," I yelled at Khwaab, "we're gettin' busted." He pulled over, and said, "I'm sorry, Todd. It's my fault." No kidding. With Khwaab pulled over, three of DC's Finest jumped out of the car. One of them was wearing a black military-like face mask, and black gloves. He looked less like a cop than an ex-Army sniper anxious to return to Iraq. With an officer at each front car door, and one outside the door closest to me, the masked one said, "Outta the car! Keep your hands where we can see 'em." Khwaab got out first, and was led over to the curb.

Khwaab was about 6'2" and weighed over 300 pounds, so he was largely immune to being roughed up. Raven got out next, and her bag of marijuana – which weighed a half pound – was confiscated. As I stepped out, two cops grabbed me, ripping my coat. One of them pushed me towards the top of the trunk. Minutes later, the three of us were sitting on the curb, handcuffed from behind. We were told that we had the right to remain silent, and that anything we say, "can and will be used against" us "in a court of law." The third officer radioed for back-up, which was unnecessary. I heard him say he wanted assistance with a distribution collar, a possession with intent to distribute collar, and a possession charge. A little black boy with a lady who was likely his mother walked past us on the sidewalk on the opposite side of the street. The kid, who looked to be about five, stared at us with a knowing, wise-beyond-his-years look on his tiny face. He pointed at us with his little hands and began singing:

"Bad boys, Bad boys" – the lyrics from the theme song to TV's 'Cops'. "Whatcha gonna do; whatcha gonna do", he sang, "whatcha gonna do, when they come fo' you? Bad boys, bad boys... "

His mother knew a teaching moment when she saw one. "You is right, child. Them's bad boys, they is. They be gettin' locked up, fo' real. Mmm-hmm."

An hour later, our mug shots were taken. We were fingerprinted, booked, and locked up. For real.

The jail cells beneath the DC courthouse are even worse than most people can imagine. Drunks, rapists, home burglars, violent perps charged with assault, and murder, and pickpockets, drug dealers, muggers, and junkies, are among those in lock-up. My handcuffs were removed by a uniformed guard who led me to a private cell, one of probably 100, in the sub-basement.

It was cold and the air was damp. The man in the cell to my right was dozing, and never stirred. The dude to my left was another matter. Unlike the DC Detention center, those in the courthouse facility are allowed to wear their street clothes. My shoelaces, belt, necktie, and watch, were confiscated, along with my jacket, pen, and ring. But I still had on my seersucker pants, wingtip shoes, and monogrammed white dress shirt. My new neighbor took immediate notice of all this, and became loud and vocal.

"Hey, what up, fancy pants? Do 'dis place be up to y'all standards?" I ignored him, but he kept it up.

"Y'know, 'dis here ain't no Waldo Hysteria," he said, apparently referencing New York's Waldorf Astoria hotel. "No kidding," I replied. "Why don't you pipe down, and try to sleep? Because that's what I'm going to do. Goodnight."

Suddenly, he began singing. To the tune of the song, 'Hot child in the City', he belted out: "White Boy in da Lock-up; White Boy in da Lock-up … "

It would be a long night. The dude kept up this refrain until the guy in the cell to his left warned him.

"Nigga, y'all either goin' shut da fuck up, or when you gets out, I'm a-break my foot off in yo' ass. And 'den, me and my homeys, we gonna rape yo' mama, and yo' bitch, and any kids you has. Hear? And 'den, we takin' yo' ass fo' a ride, out to da Anacostia river. Motha fucka, y'all gonna be carp food. Filet of big-mouth jigaboo. Only thing be leff of you gonna be yo 'fro and y'all sneakers. Ya feel me?"

The jailhouse crooner instantly went silent. His interrogator said, "Nigga, Ah'se talkin' to y'all. Ah knows you hearin' me. It's cool if ya ain't wanna say nothin'. 'Cause if you makes anothuh motha-fuckin' PEEP, y'all is gonna be quiet fo' EVER, once yo' black ass outta 'dis here shit hole. Ah ain't playin', homey. And 'dat be fo' real. Just sayin.'" My mouthy neighbor said nothing more.

We were awakened at around 6 a.m., and were provided water from a cooler. We then were led, in groups numbering about 12 each, to holding cells that each held about 35 defendants. There, we awaited our chance to appear before the Judge. "Whatchu be in fo'?", a young black man asked me. "DWI? Public intox?" I looked away, and he said, "I know y'all ain't in here fo' resistin' no arrest, or fighting wiff a PO-leece. What it is, lightskin"

"Possession of narcotics," I replied. "Heroin? Meth? Love Boat?", he asked. "No, crack cocaine."

"No shit?", he said. "I'd think you was into powder, not rock."

"You're profiling me," I told him. "Don't stereotype." Once we were in the courtroom, I sat next to Khwaab and Raven as our names were called by the bailiff. The Judge released us on our own recognizance. We were all assigned a court date for our preliminary hearing. Our cases were to be treated as one, insofar as prosecution. We were also told to report, on Monday morning, to the DC Probation office. Khwaab and Raven were assigned court-appointed legal counsel; I knew I'd have to contact my lawyer, Jack Fornaciari. My suit jacket and other items were returned, but not the three hundred dollars I'd given to Khwaab for the drugs. Between my billfold and money clip, there was seven hundred dollars cash when I was locked up. Four hundred was returned to me.

Khwaab shook his head back and forth, from side to side, and briefly closed his eyes. "Let's talk outside, dawg," he told me. As a Muslim, Khwaab didn't smoke. As I lit up, he said, "This is your first time being locked up in DC, Todd. What you just experienced is standard procedure. Let it go." When I objected, he said, "it's your word against theirs, man. You can't prove they took some of your dough. They're the law, and you're a crackhead who just got arrested for possession. Leave it alone. You can't win." He was right, but he shouldn't have been. "That's the DC government for you, Todd," Khwaab said.

As the DC Courthouse was only about four blocks from my parents' apartment, I walked over there. My parents were in Iowa, to meet with the farmer who rented land from them. They had left Thursday and wouldn't return until Tuesday night. Inside their apartment, I felt safe, but lonely.

Linda had been out of my life now for just over a year, and my parents were out of town. What would it be like when my parents were no longer

445

alive? Would they ever live to see me kick this disgusting, life-wrecking habit? But first, I needed to call a drug dealer for some crack cocaine.

I knew I'd test positive for cocaine when I visited the Probation office on Monday morning, so I figured I might as well get high. But if being busted by the cops, arrested, thrown in jail, and made to stand before a judge didn't stop my desire for drugs, was there anything that would?

The dealer I called went by the name of 'Q' – short for Quentin. He delivered an eight ball to the Lansburgh. Q and I talked for awhile after I bought the eight ball. "Hey, Mister Todd," he asked, "you want me to line y'all up with some brown sugar?" By that he meant a black hooker. "This bitch, she real fine, mmm-mmmm … I'm sayin'." The idea intrigued me, but I finally said, "maybe another time."

On Monday morning, at the Probation office, I submitted a urine sample and calmly walked over to Judge Iscoe's chambers. While appearing before the Judge, my Probation Officer appeared, and disclosed the results of the drug test I had taken 90 minutes earlier. The Judge said, "I think you need some time to think about the consequences of your actions, sir." He then sentenced me to two nights in the DC Jail – the so-called Big House. The bailiff and a deputy United States Marshall removed me from the courtroom, and I surrendered my suit, wristwatch, cell phone, wallet, shoes, belt, and everything else. Shortly thereafter, I was a passenger on the bus that was mentioned at the beginning of this book.

Being a white dude locked up in the DC Detention Center educated me on what's like to be a minority. After showering, all of us jail birds lined up for breakfast. Just as food was about to be heaped onto my paper plate, a big black guy tapped my shoulder. "Light skin," he said, "I'm a-thank y'all fo' dem eggs and bacon." I asked him what eggs and bacon he was talking about. He said, "Da eggs and bacon 'dat y'all be givin' me." The man directly behind him was absolutely gigantic. He assured me I would get to drink my orange juice. I reached out my hand, looked up at the guy, and replied, "Thank you.

My name is Todd. Who are you?" He said, "Ahh be da dude dat's takin' yo' toast and jelly."

Based on my experience, the DC Detention Center is probably more effective than Weight Watchers, or Jenny Craig. That night, the very able DC defense attorney Lorenzo Fitzgerald visited me in lock-up, and told me he'd do all he could to spring me the following day. Mr. Fitzgerald, who is black, is a former DC Police Officer. He took a genuine interest in me and my case for which I'm forever grateful. He's smart, dedicated, and was assisted by a very able staff. Lorenzo guided me toward the path to staying clean, and out of trouble. He was true to his word; a day later, I was placed on pre-trial status.

Among other requirements, I wasn't allowed to leave the District of Columbia without probation officer's permission, and I had to be drug-tested three times a week: every Monday, Wednesday, and Friday. If my results were negative following the upcoming Wednesday test by the date of my preliminary hearing, I would only have to be tested twice a week.

When my parents returned to DC, I couldn't pick them up at the Ronald Reagan national airport. They took a cab to the Lansburgh, and I told them what had happened. They were both extremely upset. My dad left the apartment, and took a long walk. My mother wept, almost uncontrollably. The knowledge that their despair was of my making nearly made me cry. But as upset as I was, I also wanted to get high. Such is the pervasive power of addiction.

About a week after my arrest, word got out on the streets that I'd been busted. Dealers avoided me like an STD. In the realm of drugs, pushers fear newly-arrested addicts will rat them out to the cops. To say my mother was distraught is putting it mildly. She was upset when Linda and I divorced two years earlier, and terribly sad when her elderly parents died, in 2001 and 2003. But upon my release from the D.C. Correctional Center, she was an emotional wreck. "Todd, your dad and I don't know what to do," she told me, between sobs. Indeed, they didn't. I had attended three re-hab facilities, and relapsed after each stint. Now, in less than three months, I had been jailed twice; first, for possession of narcotics, and then for failing a court-mandated drug test while on pre-trial status.

I suppose that any boy, or man, would say that their mother is beautiful, in one or more ways. But my mom truly is a beautiful, lovely lady – inside, and out. As an Iowa farm girl who attended a one-room school in the 1940s, she was raised to attend church every week, and respect her parents. As a young bride and, later, a loving, dedicated parent, she was the mom that all my buddies loved. But now, my drug addiction and resultant problems made her feel like a failure. "I've prayed", she told me, "prayed harder than I've ever prayed for anything." Maybe now, it was time for me to pray again – and this time, reinforce my prayers with an unwavering commitment to quit the drug life, forever.

As my mom spoke, the events of that afternoon replayed themselves in my mind. My dad had driven us to their apartment in downtown DC after my release. Judge Iscoe agreed, at my lawyer's request, to spring me from lock-up and remand me to the custody of my parents. My dad took a photo with his cell phone of me wearing the jail-issued orange jump suit, and the blue jump suit that I wore home. "If you screw up again, your brother, sister, and nephews and nieces will see these pictures," my father warned. We took the Lansburgh elevator from the parking garage to their apartment. A front desk employee, a black lady with whom my mother had become friends, was already on the elevator when we entered.

She was aware of my drug issues, and my clothing and my mother's sad expression told her all she needed to know. As the elevator doors opened, she said, "I'll pray for you folks." That was nice, we all thought. I thanked her, as did my parents. Because despite my determination to never use illegal drugs again, I needed all the prayers I could get. My dad took a long walk, from Penn Quarter to Chinatown, alone. While he was out, my mom and I talked, and prayed together. She was so exhausted she went to bed at 5:45 p.m.

Before she went to her bedroom, we embraced. I promised her that I would never use any illegal drugs again, or abuse any substance. I sat up and awaited my dad's return. When he got back, he suddenly seemed old to me. Until my father was 65 years old, he always looked much younger than his years. Now, at 68, he looked his age, and then some. My parents felt powerless over my problem. They may have been, but I wasn't. The power was within me, with God's help, to turn my life around. At that moment, I decided to never again use drugs. I owed it to my parents, even more than to myself. My days as a drug addict were done, I decided, and would never return.

"I want to believe you," my dad told me. "And I don't doubt your sincerity, or your desire to stop using. But the proof of the pudding is in the eating." That's been a favorite phrase of his for his entire life. His parents also used it, so it goes way back in our family. My dad had to be up the next morning at 4:30, so he went to bed. But as we said goodnight, he said, "I have faith in you, son. So please, please, don't let me down."

"I won't, dad," I replied. "Promise?"

"I promise."

That night, I realized just how much I had let myself down. I was raised to have good character, morals, and ethics. To this day, I find hypocrisy and dishonesty appalling. But the life I had been living for the better part of a decade wasn't a good, or Godly, existence. How many of the Ten Commandments had I broken? I certainly hadn't honored my parents. I had placed my loyalty to cocaine before honoring my maker. But with repentance comes forgiveness. I asked God to forgive me, and I know that He did.

But could I ever forgive myself?

There were people to whom I needed to make amends. I began writing that list that evening. Yet, it was of paramount importance, as I made plans to turn my life around, to forgive myself. Was such forgiveness warranted? Perhaps not. But to move forward, I had to free myself from the negativity associated with how I'd been living, and the damage I'd done. Fortunately, I wasn't a thief, and hadn't killed anyone, or even tried to. But I had done wrong, and harmed my loved ones. My mind, while still in druggy mode, was functioning better than it had in years. From that moment on, my attitude reverted to the positive, where it has remained since. That night, I resolved to move forward and to learn from, instead of dwelling, on the past. All recovering addicts must do this in order to have any hope. Because absent hope, recovery efforts are worthless.

After I'd been drug-free for about four months, my parents wanted me to attend a residential treatment program, to nail my efforts down. So, in the early fall of 2006, my Dad and I took an early AMTRAK train to Boston, Massachusetts. He's always loved trains, as his dad was a 40-year railroad man for the Rock Island Lines. That afternoon, we toured the Harvard campus, where is located the Blodgett pool, which is named for a deceased, distant relative of ours, who was from Michigan. At dinner at Mr. Bartley's, on the campus in Cambridge, we discussed the re-hab program I would enter two days later. Harvard university's McLean hospital then operated a substance abuse program in the upstate Massachusetts city of Ashburnham. My 21 days there were successful, because I'd quit using drugs in May, and was determined to remain clean. Of the five recovery programs I attended, McLean of Harvard's was the one that made the difference; I've been drug-free ever since.

The program is now called McLean Naukeag at Prescott and is located in Petersham, Massachusetts. I highly recommend it, based on my personal experience. When I returned to DC, my parents insisted I live with them, at their apartment at the Lansburgh in the Penn Quarter. It wasn't easy being 46 and living with my parents, but I wanted to please them, so I spent the next six months at their place, before moving into an apartment of my own, at the corner of Van Ness street, N.W., and Connecticut Avenue.

A lucky break fell my way as I tried to comply with my dad's directive that I get a job that entailed lots of exercise. I was waiting to meet a friend for lunch at the Zoo Bar on Connecticut avenue, across the street from Washington's National Zoo. While at the bar, a patron asked me if a lady named Debbie Lehan used to work for me. Deborah Lehan had been my first office manager from 1994 to 1996, at the Kennedy-Warren. "Yes, she was," I replied. It turned out that this man was the manager of the Daumit Dance studio in

Cleveland Park, and he and Deb were friends. He also owned a landscaping business, and was hiring. He introduced himself as Mark Gustafson, offered me a job on the spot, which I accepted. "Great," he said. "Be at work tomorrow at 8 a.m." He then pulled out a business card, and wrote the address of the location where his crew was working on the back.

It wasn't until he left that I realized that the next day was a Sunday. I showed up, worked for 10 hours, and impressed Gustafson with my work ethic. From then, until I left D.C., I worked as a professional landscaper. On a few jobs, clients recognized me as I placed sod, planted saplings, hauled dirt, and shoveled gravel. It was humbling, because these people knew of my past professional success. On the terrace of a luxurious DC penthouse apartment, the screen door was open on one such occasion. The husband, who had his back to me, told his wife, "I've heard he was on drugs, and his wife left him. Also heard he did prison time." I never let on what I had heard them discussing, and didn't try to correct him. Whether it's jail or prison, incarcerated means being locked up. And I'd been there, and done that.

My dad, an accomplished tennis player, downhill skier, and golfer, has been an athlete since he played high school basketball and football, and ran varsity track for the University of Iowa in the 1950s. His insistence that I work out with weights, swim, run on a treadmill, take long walks, and do calisthenics, was critical to my recovery. He also told me to sit for 15-20 minutes every day in a Sauna, and in a steam room. Doing so, on a daily basis, for well over a year cleansed my body of the drug toxins what had permeated it for so many years. An M.D. he played golf with told him of Niacin's efficacy in treating depression, aiding sleep, and easing the pain of withdrawl experienced by addicts who stop using drugs.

Long-term drug usage severely lowers the body's Niacin levels. Niacin depletion can cause depression and anxiety, and lower energy levels. It can also impede production of Serotonin and Dopamine. This can trigger the desire for addicts to use drugs.

My dad bought me some over-the-counter Niacin caplets, and later prescribed higher doses for me. He and my mother also randomly tested me for drugs, with a testing kit he purchased online. I passed each time. The value of spending 30 to 40 minutes each day in a sauna and steam room can't be emphasized enough. But it must be done in conjunction with walking, or jogging, and vigorous workouts. Taken together, this forces the toxic substances out of the body. During the first few months of this regimen, I experienced 'cocaine highs' while in the sauna and steam room. This occurred because the cocaine residue embedded in my cells, glands, and other tissues, were being forced out of my system. This felt weird, but with God's help, I dealt with it. Those who believe that addiction is a disease should ask themselves: Can cancer patients force their disease from their bodies by using this procedure?

I avoided alcohol and significantly curtailed my sugar intake. This meant shunning foods comprised of carbohydrates. White bread, most cereal, dairy products, rice, beans, potatoes, corn, and most processed foods were off the menu for the next 18 months. I abstained from alcohol until January of 2009. When I resumed drinking that month, it had been nearly 31 months since I'd had alcohol. The sugar cravings often associated with recovery from addiction disappeared within 90 days and never returned. I drank only iced water for years. Occasionally, when I felt sluggish, I drank iced tea or coffee, but never more than about 16 ounces of either per day.

Every morning, I took a multiple vitamin consisting of vitamins B1, B5, B6, C and E. Coupled with the Niacin I ingested daily, my immune system improved, and the cocaine cravings vanished. Each day, my father and I spent 15 minutes in the sauna, followed by 20 minutes in the steam room. Between steam blasts, he said, "using drugs was your choice, son, and it led to addiction. You've now decided to cleanse yourself of the residual cocaine in your system." This boosted my confidence, just knowing I'd made a sound decision. Attending Narcotics Anonymous meetings was also essential to my recovery. Despite rejecting the 'disease' theory of addiction, it helped to hear the stories of fellow junkies of how using drugs had wrecked their lives and those of others.

Conditions which lead to drug addiction can also set the stage for creating vulnerability to hate others. People who are unhappy, or profoundly upset with what's happening in their lives (or, not happening) will often turn to drugs. Over time, this leads to addiction. The same is true for those who become resentful, and then hateful, toward others. This can lead to becoming obsessed, which can cause, and has, for many people, caused hatred to manifest itself by joining Hate Organizations. Even those who aren't formally affiliated with such groups can self-indoctrinate by visiting websites, reading racist publications, and associating with haters. But cocaine, crystal meth, heroin, and other drugs provide only temporary relief from the pain that users wish to escape, mask, or submerge within themselves.

Becoming part of the Hate Movement offers similar relief, with equally destructive consequences. Just as addiction to drugs destroys souls, addiction to hatred does, as well. Drug addiction causes dependency, whether it's mental, physical, or emotional – or a combination thereof. That's why people have such difficulty getting out of, and leaving behind, such addictions. The relief or pleasure junkies find in getting fixes, whether of drugs, or attending Hate Metal concerts, or shouting, 'Heil, Hitler' as they burn crosses while wearing a Klan uniform, or Swastika earrings, is only temporary. But it leaves the addict wanting more of the same.

The chief impediments to sustained recovery are the withdrawl pains and ineffective de-toxification. Junkies who can't get past the cravings for their drug of choice, be it crack, crystal meth, or watching videos of David Duke and other haters on YouTube, won't end their addiction. Walking briskly is as helpful, if not more beneficial, for unhappy people than drugs, whether they're legal or not. Walking evens out one's perspectives, by allowing time to contemplate. A long walk will also tone down a short temper. Friedrich Nietzsche said that great thoughts are conceived while walking. Soren Kierkegaard wrote that, "every day, I walk myself into a state of well-being and walk away from every illness. I have walked myself into my best thoughts, and I know of no thought so burdensome that one cannot walk away from it." A recovering addict I once knew said he had two doctors: his left leg and his right.

Learning about, and becoming exposed to, other cultures and people of other races, enables those who are inclined to hatred to see others as human beings, and not objects of vilification. A belief in a higher power is as helpful to recovering drug addicts as it is in curing hatred. Nearly every junkie I've known who had conquered a drug addiction has believed in a higher power. Likewise, nearly every former hater who jettisoned hatred from their lives has believed in God. The exceptions are so few that it's clearly best for addicts to believe in a power greater, and higher, than themselves if they wish to seriously attack their malady and put it away for good.

As covered in this book, I wasn't a hater when I was working in the realm of hate. While monitoring haters for the FBI, what I saw reinforced my view that hate is the most negative, counterproductive emotion known to man. However, after my years of surveilling haters had ended in November, 2002, I found myself starting to detest the people who had pushed for my expulsion from the University club. While most of them weren't Jewish, my negative thoughts centered on the Jewish members, who had pressured members of the club's Board of Governors to oust me. They were organized, determined, and effective. But why was my focus on them, and not so much my foes who were of different faiths?

Why was I overlooking my Jewish friends who supported me throughout the entire ordeal? How was it that while I knew it was wrong, and evil, to become hateful, I still found myself thinking about how it would be appropriate, and justifiable, to take revenge on them? At one point, I even thought about the two hit men – professional killers – who proposed taking out my enemies whose campaign resulted in my being expelled. Was it wrong to have rejected their offer? I was even blaming some of the club's Jewish members for prolonging my drug addiction – which had begun over a year before the club booted me. Such unfair thoughts made no sense, but it they were real. But this can occur when people are upset, angry, or frustrated with what's going on in their lives, and sets the stage for hatred.

I can still recall my thoughts regarding the Jewish members who had pushed for my ouster. It was audacious, I remember thinking, of them, because they only were admitted as members because the law, and court decisions, required that they be. Why didn't they stick to their own, damn clubs, and their own kind? How can anyone who crashed our gates, as they had, be so damn pushy? How were they any different from whores who join churches and then want to lead the choir and serve as head deaconess on their first Sunday? Luckily, I came to my senses shortly thereafter.

But can America's and Europe's future be free of drug abuse and hatred?

Adolf Hitler was born in 2006 and he lives in New Jersey. His parents are avid Nazis, and their last name was originally Campbell. His younger sisters are named Aryan Nation Hitler, and Honszlynn Hitler. His little brother's name is Heinrich Hitler, in honor of Heinrich Himmler. Young Adolf came to worldwide notice at age three, in 2009, when a New Jersey Shop-Rite bakery manager refused to decorate his birthday cake. Adolf's parents wanted 'Happy Birthday, Adolf Hitler' inscribed atop the white cake, in red frosting. The father of these kids, Heath Campbell, has a Swastika tattooed on his neck and is a dedicated Holocaust denier.

The family is the subject of a 2016 documentary called, 'Meet the Hitlers'. Heath Campbell has another tattoo on his arm which features the Nazi-inspired names of his children. He says, "this is my circle of love." In 2013, Mr. Campbell walked into a child custody hearing with a New Jersey Judge wearing a Nazi military uniform. His children's mother – who has since left him – was wearing her Nazi uniform. Mr. Campbell's children had been removed from his home, and he wanted them back. The Judge denied his request. In 2016, Campbell was arrested on assault charges, after beating his then-fiancee'. Adolf's dad has nine kids with five different women, and one of little Adolf's half sisters is named Eva Braun. The infamous Eva Braun of the 1940s was the original Mrs. Adolf Hitler.

Court records showed that the parents of these little Hitlers were abused as children, and that young Adolf frequently threatens to kill people. Can a name can determine fate? Meanwhile, Adolf's dad keeps busy with his organization, which is called 'Hitler's Order'. Its members are not nice people. Dysfunctional families like the aforementioned one are breeding grounds for young people becoming susceptible to racial hatred and drug addiction. Many neo-Nazis and drug addicts are from ostensibly stable families, with nice homes in the suburbs, and even in bucolic, rural areas – as shown here in 'Republican Crackhead'. But appearances can be deceiving.

The story's headline in the March 29, 2017 edition of USA Today, 'Suburban Drug Overdoses fuel Spike in premature Death rate' caught my eye. Throughout the U.S., deaths from O.D's is increasing at almost an exponential rate. This alarming acceleration of drug-related fatalities, especially among those aged 25 to 44. Drug deaths are also accelerating among people aged 15 to 24 years old, according to a report by the Robert Wood Johnson foundation. A common thread in this trend is what is called "Youth Disconnection". It refers to 16 to 24-year-olds who aren't working or in school. This category represents an "untapped social and economic opportunity", said scientist Marjory Givens, who is the RWJF's county health program. Dr. Givens said it's "easier to prevent" such young people from being disconnected than to "try to re-engage" them, after they've "dropped out of school or gone without work for some time." But America's suburbs aren't the only areas where drug addiction is on the rise.

In April, 2017, CBS News reported that drug use among U. S. Navy SEALs has increased at an alarming rate since 2012. Addiction to methamphetamine, cocaine, heroin, ecstasy, and other illegal hard drugs is common among the SEALs, according to an active SEAL, and retired SEALs who were interviewed.

Captain Jamie Sands, who commands 900 SEALs on the east coast, said, "I feel like I'm watching our foundation, our culture, erode before our eyes." Five Navy SEALs had been dishonorably discharged just three months after Sands began at his command post. His chief of staff reported a "staggering" number of drug cases pending. Required urine testing only takes place when the SEALs aren't out on missions, in violation of official Navy policy. But's while on such maneuvers that most drug usage takes place.

In March, 2017, former United States Border Patrol agent Juan Ramon Pimentel was sentenced to 13 years in prison. Agent Pimentel pleaded guilty to possession with intent to distribute 50 kilos of cocaine and accepting bribes as a public official. Pimentel was driving to Chicago with the drugs in his vehicle, and was to be paid $50,000 to deliver the 50 kilos. He'd been a Border Patrol agent in Arizona for nearly 15 years when caught. He'll be on probation for five years upon release. These cases aren't unlike those involving crooked cops I encountered in Washington, D.C., and Baltimore.

More than a few times, I was ripped off by some drug dealers in DC, and two in Baltimore. In one instance, instances, I got my money back, and some sweet revenge, courtesy of some robbers who played cops. Not all robbers who play cops are weirdos with fantasies of being a law enforcement officer. The police impersonators I knew did it for profit. They jacked two thieves who stole from me, after I provided them information as to their whereabouts. This enabled me to partially recover my losses.

Websites and dealers sell police uniforms and customized, realistic-looking IDs stamped with any name and law enforcement agency. Also for sale are police scanners, police-style radios, official-looking shields, and cop caps, department jackets and overcoats, and all of the specialized equipment needed to enable purchasers to look like cops. Anyone who watches 'Blue Bloods', 'Law and Order', or 'COPS' can learn how to read rights to suspects and slap handcuffs on them.

I knew some black dudes whose customized, silicone masks made them look like they were white. Their mask supplier also manufactured masks which made men appear to be Asian, regardless of their actual ethnicity. Robing drug dealers is about as close to what career criminals call a 'freebie' as it gets. After all, what victim of such thefts reports such crimes, when they're perps, themselves? Such thieves nearly always work in teams of three, or four. Real cops call them 'Drug Rip Crews', and they're more common than most Americans would believe – as are the crooked cops I've described.

Regrets, regrets; addicts do have regrets. No one knows this better than junkies.

"I saw men become insane in prison, due to regret." Those words were spoken by neo-Nazi Jamie Von Brunn. Other former inmates have told me the same thing. The role that regret plays in addiction and hatred not only can't be ignored; understanding it is critical to eradicating these scourges. It's second nature for people to dwell on past mistakes, when they should take productive action with an eye to the future. This is where those who wish to help stop, and prevent, addiction and hatred can play a positive, meaningful, positive role. By changing their heart, they'll change their world – and improve their life.

Drug addiction and Hatred can be cured and prevented by living a meaningful Life. As Ronald Reagan told me: "young people can get high on their accomplishments." Happy people whose lives hold meaning for them and others aren't likely to become drug addicts, or haters. Having purpose in life is, in and of itself, highly rewarding. It's also conducive to not using drugs, or becoming hateful.

Anyone wishing to overcome regret and move forward must ask themselves three questions:

1. What can I learn from this?
2. How could it have been even worse?
3. How can I make sure it won't recur?

Based on my experiences with thousands of addicts and just as many hateful bigots since the 1990s, I've learned that answering those questions will set the stage for improvement. Once the two questions are answered, then three steps must be taken:

1. Forgive yourself.
2. Move forward by taking constructive action.
3. Be kind and respectful to others.

That's all there is to turning regret around, and successfully applying its lessons to our life. Many people suffer from impediments which aren't of their making. Wrongful government policies can and do cause, exacerbate, and prolong drug addiction, AND racial and religious hatred. Federal and state policies in recent decades have rewarded bad decisions and penalized those who make sound choices. This can't be overlooked as causal to addiction, and hatred. One cause of racial hatred is affirmative action and race-based quotas. Ending them would, in my view, prevent many people from becoming haters. Mandatory, random drug-testing of welfare recipients will also mean fewer drug addicts.

Scores of millions of American workers are subjected to such routine testing; why exempt those who get their tax dollars? As I've stated earlier, I witnessed Medicaid recipients squander money on high-end cell phones, fancy cars, flat screen TV sets, and top-of-the-line tennis shoes which cost $350 per pair. While not all such recipients are irresponsible, many are. The truth is that there's a large subset of the U.S. population comprised of those who simply won't take care of themselves. This problem also must be addressed.

America's drug problem is largely due to cocaine and heroin from Mexico, and from opioids made in China and brought to the USA via Mexico, with the collusion of Mexican authorities. The Mexican government encourages its people to leave Mexico because their own economy won't support them. They then have the audacity to use aid given them by Americans on lawyers who represent Illegal aliens. This is disgraceful, and it cannot be permitted. Allowing it to continue will only fuel more racial hatred. Liberals who falsely accuse Americans of being racist for wanting their government to enforce its laws do society a horrid disservice. A nation's desire to protect its borders doesn't constitute hatred.

Former Vice President Joe Biden, after watching a Trump-Pence rally in Wilkes-Barre, Pennsylvania, realized that Mr. Trump could well be elected weeks later. "They're all the people I grew up with," Mr. Biden told reporters. "They're their kids. And they're not racists. They're not sexists." When Barack Obama's Vice President stated that the Americans who elected Donald Trump and Mike Pence aren't sexist or racist, that obliterated arguments advanced by liberals who say otherwise. Just because David Duke and other white supremacists endorsed President Trump's candidacy and support his presidency doesn't mean most Trump voters are racists or sexists. They're not, but falsely labeling them as such will also, in my opinion, foment more – and worse - violence.

Even the liberal journalist Fareed Zakaria acknowledged in July of 2019 that President Donald Trump is correct in wanting to alter the U.S. asylum laws.

In June, 2007, I attended my last meeting with my probation officer, Carla Reeder. As I got up to leave, she shook my hand. She said, "You made it, Todd! I'm so proud of you, because you really, really tried. Congratulations." Our handshake turned into a hug, and I thanked my higher power – God - for bringing this professional, kind, smart, dedicated young lady into my life.

I thanked her, and the Probation Office receptionist for working so well with me over the last 12 months. Outside the DC police substation it was about 70 degrees. The sun was shining, the sky was clear, and it was a gorgeous day. While walking two blocks to 14th Street, N. W., I noticed several black teenagers – girls and boys. Statistically, those kids were far more likely than I was to become addicted, get arrested, land in jail, be on probation, and someday be sent to prison. The chances were likely ZERO that any had successful, happily-married, supportive parents like mine, who provided them with good homes and fine educations, and who could and would take the costly steps my parents had to kick-start my recovery and maintain it. Would illegal drugs do to these minority teenagers what organized hatred has done to the white, working-class young adults I had encountered at KKK cross burnings, Resistance Records concerts, and Aryan Nations conclaves and Holocaust Denial conferences?

While walking south on 14th Street to the Shaw/Petworth METRO station, I stopped at a small café owned by a kind-hearted, elderly black lady I'd gotten to know over the previous year. Every visit to Ms. Reeder included a stop at this quaint establishment, where she and another black woman cooked what they called comfort food. I had grown fond of these sweet ladies, whose names I've forgotten. After a few months of my regular visits, they were comfortable enough with me to ask what was bringing me to their neighborhood on such a regular basis. When I told them I was on probation for narcotics possession, they weren't judgmental; they offered encouragement. They weren't busy on this day, which would be one of the last times I'd see them. The three of us chatted as one prepared fried eggs, bacon, and toast. The other poured me some decaf coffee in a Styrofoam cup. As I finished eating, they and I were still the only ones inside the café. "Everything okay today, honey?", the older lady asked.

"Yeah," I replied. "I've just completed my probation." Her face instantly brightened into the kind of beautiful smile that made me feel like a million bucks. Taking both of my hands into hers, she looked over at the counter that separated the dining area from the stoves, grill, counter space and a small sink. Her colleague busied herself as she spoke. "I'm so glad y'all made it, Todd. Not everybody does." She then turned to me and asked if my mother was alive. I told her she was. After hesitating for a few seconds, she said, "I had me a son who had your same problem. For a lotta years, he did. He was busted, locked up. Got probation, after his second offense. Went to meetin' after meetin'. For awhile, he stayed clean," she told me, looking toward the window. Then, almost in a whisper, she said, "but that wicked stuff, it was just too powerful. He went back on it and got himself shot. Been gone now near seven years."

She collected her thoughts for a moment, then resumed speaking. "Y'know, they's not a day I don't think about that boy." Her eyes were misty; her expression wistful. "Oh, was he a handful; he surely was. But he was a good boy. Now, they's this hole in his mama's heart that ain't never gonna heal." The other lady nodded, as she looked into my eyes before averting hers to the floor. "I'm so sorry," was all I could say. "Me, too," she replied, gently touching my shoulder. "Now, you take care. And y'all stay off that wicked stuff, hear?" As I reached for the check, the other lady – the owner – took it, tore it up, and said, "no charge for you today. Today's a special day." They refused to take my money, even a tip.

As I walked toward the door which opened out to 14th Street, the woman who had lost her son walked back behind the counter. The owner remained seated at the table where I'd eaten. "Remember," the owner told me, "Don't open up no cans of whoop ass." She winked at me, knowing I understood. In the hoods, when someone warns another to not open up a can of whoop ass, they're saying to not mess with them, or anything that won't go well. Opening a can of whoop ass risks a violent beat down, if not worse. Until that morning, when I had heard that phrase, it usually was spoken by tough ghetto dudes fully capable of cleaning the clocks of those they warned away. Sometimes, that warning was issued by equally tough females. But this was the first time I'd heard it spoken by a gentle, kind, 70-ish, churchgoing lady who radiated wisdom and goodness.

"I'll remember that, and don't worry; I won't. Thanks, again." A few minutes later, as I approached the METRO station, a twenty-something black man was smoking a cigarette on a bench about 15 yards from me. As I passed by, he asked, "hey, is you all right?" That's the universal question that drug dealers ask strangers whom they sense might be prospective customers. It implies that the person asking has drugs. "Yes, sir," I answered. "I'm fine, thanks." And I was. As the underground subway glided over the three-rail track to the Gallery Place METRO station, I made myself a silent vow, which I have kept ever since.

I've yet to open a can of whoop ass.

My final session with Dr. Weiner was pleasant, and reinforced my desire to stay clean, and try to help addicts avoid what I had gone through, and put my parents, family, and friends through for so many years. It's impossible for me to over-emphasize the value of a competent, caring therapist, especially for recovering addicts. Before leaving Washington, I stopped in to see my old buddy, fellow Iowan Chuck Manatt, at his office on DC's 'K' Street, N. W.

As I entered his office, his desk was stacked with papers, and an ever-present Salem cigarette burned away in a fancy ashtray. Mr. Manatt was a special friend, whom I first met in Des Moines, Iowa, in 1983. Since arriving in DC in 1984, I had met him many times for breakfast at the University club, in the Taft dining room. He was appalled over my expulsion, and made his views known. Chuck didn't hesitate to express his views on anything, which I always admired as much as I admired him.

"You're heading back to our home state, right?"

"Yeah, it's time. I need to nail down my recovery, and rebuild my life."

"Are you on decent terms with your ex?:

"Getting there. I put her through a lot of - well, a lot of … "

"Hell. You put her though a lot of hell. You put yourself through hell. But that's in the past. What's important now is to keep making progress. I think you will, and I'm betting on you, Todd." I thanked him, and then he said, "But always remember, Todd: very few people have had your advantages. And it never hurts to try looking at things with that in mind."

"Yes, sir."

"You stay in touch. We'll never agree on most things, but let me know if I can ever help you in any way." I thanked Mr. Manatt as we shook hands and said goodbye. The 40 minutes we spent in his office easily represented thousands of dollars that he chose to forgo. As I left, I couldn't help but think of how much more could be accomplished in government if more people were like Chuck Manatt. This is particularly true today, with the polarization in Washington, D. C. I never saw him again. Charles T. Manatt died less than three years later, at age 75. He's buried in the Maple Grove cemetery in Audubon, Iowa.

Upon leaving Manatt's office, I stopped in at a dry cleaners in the 4000 block of Connecticut avenue, N.W., to pick up some shirts. In line ahead of me was Craig Iscoe, the Judge who, in 2006, had sentenced me to jail and probation. He couldn't have been nicer. "You know," he said, "you actually looked better AFTER you were locked up than before you went in." He then said I looked well, and asked about my life. Upon hearing I was getting my act back together, he was genuinely pleased. As he left the dry cleaners, the Judge wished me continued success. He will be sent a copy of this memoir, as I want him to know that had he NOT sentenced me to jail, and then to probation, I'd either be still using drugs, in prison, or dead. Seeing him that day, shortly before I left D.C., reminded me of what President Reagan told me in the oval office, back in the early 1980s. Things happen for a reason, and sometimes, we don't know what the reason is as things occur. I truly believe that God arranged me seeing this good man before leaving Washington. The encounter left me feeling good.

Days after, I ran into a colleague from the 1988 Bush campaign, Mike Connell. We met in 1984 when he was attending the University of Iowa and volunteering for the Reagan-Bush campaign. He later became a respected GOP elections operative, and was highly instrumental to the Bush-Cheney re-election. I'm glad we had such a pleasant chat, because the following year, Mike died in a plane crash. None of us are promised tomorrow – as all recovering addicts know.

On my last morning in DC, I spoke with the respected DC attorney Bob Levin. Bob, who was Jewish, had been a good friend over many years, and felt I'd been dealt with unjustly by the University club's Board of Governors. He also knew of my surveillance work, and said he was proud of what I had done, working for the bureau. "History should remember you kindly, Todd," he said. I said it depends on who writes it.

AFTERWARD

My paternal grandfather died when I was three years old, in 1963. Weeks later, my parents and I, and my younger brother, watched Burl Ives sing 'The Blue Tail Fly' on TV. 'Blue Tail Fly' is an anti-slavery folk song, written by a slave during the antebellum days. This catchy tune's haunting, melancholy lyrics describe the death of the slave's master, after he's thrown by a horse that was bitten by a blue tail fly. After he's buried, the slaves break out some cheap whiskey known as "crack corn". The narrator – a slave named Jimmy – refers to himself in the third person, as he drinks the rotgut liquor. He now takes a devil-may-care attitude toward life, having been demoted to field hand following his master's demise.

He no longer cares about much, and becomes insufferably cynical. The song's memorable stanza is:

"Jimmy, crack corn, and I don't care; Jimmy, crack corn, and I don't care; Jimmy, crack corn, and I don't care – my master's gone away"

Perhaps because my grandfather's first name was also Burl, this tune has stayed with me. Whenever I hear it, which isn't often, I think of my grandfather, and how his early death must have affected my dad. As a kid, I thought of it in terms of how I might deal with my own father's death, when that day arrives. After all, aren't our fathers our masters? Many friends of mine no longer have their dads, some having died decades ago. I've been lucky. But since 2009, when my father was diagnosed with early-onset dementia, it's been a downhill slide for him. As of October of 2019, he's still with us.

Had I still been addicted to cocaine, I'd be useless to him, and to my mother. My very existence would, indeed, be counterproductive. Being able to spend time with my parents now is a major reason I'm a grateful, recovering addict. As a crackhead, I did whatever I had to do to get my fix. Now, in recovery, staying clean is my priority. As a junkie, I cared only about myself, and I personified selfishness.

In recovery, I'm once again a caring person who wants to help others. Having gotten a second chance to live a righteous life and be of use to others, I'll maintain my drug-free status. Having won back my freedom from addiction and exited the Hate Movement, I won't put himself back into such servitude. If forced to choose between being shot at, and reverting to addiction, I'll take my chances with a bullet. After all, God helped me to dodge some real bullets, back in the day, and he'll be there for me again.

Just as cocaine, crystal meth, and heroin rob addicts of their emotional connection to others, recovery restores it. In many instances, junkies who beat addiction are able to establish even better relationships than they had before they became addicted. But in order for that to occur, the loved ones must still be alive and well. I'm constantly mindful of recovering addicts who never got that blessed opportunity.

On a warm day in May, 2017, my father and I visited the Outing club. As we walked around the grounds, Spring was in full bloom, with life returning to what was dormant, while my dad was in the autumn of his life. Since September of 2017, he has lived in a private room in the Memory Care unit of an assisted-care facility in Mason City, Iowa. He still lives there, and still knows his family and friends.

There's something about enjoying a beautiful spring day with a senior citizen suffering from a terminal disease that makes one reflect on life's cycles; there's truly a time for everything. The day is drawing nearer to when he won't know anyplace anymore, or me, or anyone. My mother, who is still vibrant, beautiful and healthy, won't be around forever, either. I've been fortunate to have such caring, strong, intelligent, kind, wise, and wonderful parents. Without them, I'd either be dead, in prison, or still using drugs and destroying my life, and the lives of others. It saddens me to know that so many people who are caught up in drugs, and/or the realm of hatred, lack the kind of loving, wise parents with whom I've been blessed. Knowing this has made me less judgmental. I'm also lucky to have some good friends who supported my efforts.

Thanks are due to wonderful Iowans like the late Harold 'Hal' Winston and Carol Winston, and to O. Jay and Pat Tomson, and John and Carolyn Hanson. Casey Callanan, who is an elected County Supervisor in north Iowa, also was instrumental in this book taking shape. I'm forever grateful to Dr. Ron Weiner, my psychologist, and Dr. F. Rodney Drake, a superb DC psychiatrist. Of course, J. Ralph Whitehead deserves much credit for my sustained recovery from addiction. Mrs. Lora Holding, a voracious reader, did a wonderful job of editing and proofreading the manuscript. She also advised me on continuity.

The late Nathan 'Nate' Brooks was a U.S. Army veteran from Mason City, Iowa. Nate was sympathetic to my recovery efforts and never judged me as others did. His joking references to me as a "Republican Crackhead", inspired me to use that moniker as this book's title.

Jim Burgess and Jack Campbell had, for years, urged me to write my story, as did Mark L. McManigal. John Duffy, a very able lawyer who practices in Mason City, provided superb legal advice, especially as we dealt with a New York City-based literary agent with whom I parted ways. Thanks, John, for your valuable assistance. My very perceptive sister-in-law, Brenda Blodgett, encouraged me to write this when no one else did, earning my eternal gratitude. Mrs. Connie Patridge, an outstanding educator, was my third grade teacher, in 1969-70, in Mason City, Iowa. Had she not instilled in me a genuine love of reading, this book would likely have never been written.

Another former teacher, Ann Sewell, also encouraged me to "share" my story.

Of course, my parents were fully supportive of my time-consuming efforts to make this memoir a reality. The past cannot be changed, but it can be useful. It's a lesson, as I was taught – and not a life sentence. I'm at peace knowing that in 2006, I kicked the drug habit and began rebuilding my life. I have heard many recovering addicts express, often very emotionally, of their profound regret that their parents and other loved ones didn't live to see them get clean, and put their lives back together. Their "masters" have "gone away" and now reside in Heaven. That's also true of ex-Skinheads and others who left the vile realm of organized hatred. I've attended thousands of Narcotics Anonymous meetings since 2005.

In these meetings, I've heard such regrets expressed hundreds of times by recovering drug addicts in these fourteen years. Members, especially women, but also men, have broken down and cried while expressing such profound regret. It's heartbreaking.

I've also heard similar stories, and seen similar reactions from former racists, violent skinheads, anti-Semites, other ex-haters who saw the light and left their former lives. With God's loving help, they repented, made amends, and now live righteously.

When I hear such remorse, I remind them that a merciful God presides over Heaven and Earth. To me, this means that their loved ones whose souls are at rest know what has transpired here on earth. I assure them that their loved ones know about their successful recovery, whether from drug addiction, racial hatred, or, sometimes, both.

I believe that God, in His eminent mercy, has informed these departed souls of such wonderful news. Their loved ones - who now exist in the afterlife – know, I assure them.

Yes, they know. How could they not? Upon hearing this, they usually agree.

Sometimes, they even smile, though it's often through tears.